D0209564

MI6

MI6

**British Secret Intelligence
Service Operations
1909-45**

Nigel West

Random House
New York

Library of Congress Cataloging in Publication Data

West, Nigel.
MI6: British Secret Intelligence Service
Operations, 1909–45.

Bibliography: p.
Includes index.
1. Great Britain. Secret Intelligence Service.
MI6—History. I. Title. II. Title: M.I.6.
III. Title: MIsix.
UB271.G7W47 1984   327.1′2′0941   84-42532
ISBN 0-394-53940-0

Manufactured in the United States of America
2 4 6 8 9 7 5 3

First American Edition

Contents

Illustrations

Acknowledgements

I owe a debt of gratitude to the following:

The numerous retired Secret Intelligence Service officers who were kind enough to assist in my reconstruction of the overseas Stations, but would prefer not to be thanked individually.

My researcher, Camilla van Gerbig, and my secretary, Joy Whyte.

David Mure for his guidance on the various wartime Allied intelligence organizations in the Middle East; Roman Garby-Czerniawski for his help in charting his INTERALLIE network; Madame Marie-Madeleine Fourcade for lending me her wartime intelligence questionnaires; and Erik Hazelhoff for allowing me to publish two of his photographs.

The staff of the Public Record Office in Kew, the British Museum, and the Hoover Institute at Stanford University.

Abbreviations

ACSO	Assistant Chief Staff Officer
ACSS	Assistant Chief of MI6
BCRA	Bureau Central de Renseignements et d'Action
BEF	British Expeditionary Force
BSC	British Security Co-ordination
C	Chief of MI6
CID	Committee of Imperial Defence
CIFE	Combined Intelligence Far East
CIS	Combined Intelligence Service
COI	Co-ordinator of Information
CPO	Chief Passport Officer
CSO	Chief Staff Officer
CSS	Chief of MI6
DCSS	Deputy Chief of MI6
DMI	Director of Military Intelligence
DNI	Director of Naval Intelligence
DSO	Defence Security Officer
FBI	Federal Bureau of Investigation
GC&CS	Government Code and Cipher School
GCHQ	Government Communications Headquarters
GS(R)	General Staff (Research)
IIC	Industrial Intelligence Centre
ISIC	Inter-Service Intelligence Committee
ISLD	Inter-Services Liaison Department
JIC	Joint Intelligence Committee
MEIC	Middle East Intelligence Centre
MI5	British Security Service
MI6	British Secret Intelligence Service
MI9	Escape and Evasion Service
MI(R)	Military Intelligence (Reasearch)

MO5	British Imperial Security Intelligence Service
NID	Naval Intelligence Division
OGPU	Soviet Political Intelligence Service
OSS	Office of Strategic Services
PCO	Passport Control Officer
RIC	Royal Irish Constabulary
RSS	Radio Security Service
SD	Sicherheitsdienst, Nazi Security Service
SIM	Italian Military Intelligence Service
SIME	Security Intelligence Middle East
SIS	Secret Intelligence Service (MI6)
SLU	Special Liasion Unit
SOE	Special Operations Executive
UVOD	Czech Resistance
VCSS	Vice-Chief of MI6

Introduction

The British Secret Intelligence Service, known variously as SIS and its military intelligence cover designation, MI6, maintains a strong tradition of secrecy. None of its staff are allowed to write books or give interviews, and the much misunderstood 'thirty-year rule' does not apply to the organization. Yet, in spite of these apparent barriers, 'the firm', as it is referred to by insiders, enjoys a unique reputation for stealth, devious efficiency, ruthlessness and, it must be said, treachery. It has often been considered all-powerful, wielding enormous secret influence. It was once said in America in the 1920s that 'six institutions rule the world: Buckingham Palace, the White House, the Bank of England, the Federal Reserve Bank, the Vatican and the British Secret Service'.

Is this reputation justified? Although much has been written on the subject of intelligence, especially about operations during the last war, most books have tended to raise rather more questions than they have answered. This book does not pretend to clear up all the mysteries or to answer all the questions; it just hopes to leave the reader better informed.

That so little is known about SIS is hardly surprising, given the restrictions on those who have had first-hand experience. Only one book published since the war has been written by a former SIS officer, Leslie Arthur Nicholson. He adopted the pseudonym John Whitwell and wrote *British Agent*, which was published in America in 1966. Nicholson had joined SIS in 1930 and almost immediately had been posted as Head of Station in Prague. He remained with 'the firm' until after the war, but when his wife fell ill he asked his Chief for a loan. Major-General Sir Stewart Menzies responded by offering to commute Nicholson's pension, and reluctantly the officer agreed. Subsequently Nicholson resigned; as he had no pension left to protect, he felt free to write his autobiography. Menzies and his successors made dire threats to prevent him, but a heavily censored edition of *British Agent* was published by William Kimber in 1967 in England. In the face of such opposition Nicholson's second volume of memoirs was not published. The author, incensed by his treatment, offered to help the American historian Ladislas Farago on a book about Nazi intelligence operations, and gave him much of the information that appeared in *The Game of the Foxes* published in London by Hodder and Stoughton in 1972.

Farago's book, which also drew on previously unpublished German archives, prompted a number of other researchers to fish in the same murky waters. Some that followed proved less than reliable and a team of Cambridge historians, led by Professor Harry Hinsley, was commissioned to write an official history of the influence of British intelligence on wartime strategy and operations. Those who believe that this official account, *British Intelligence in the Second World War* (HMSO, 1979, 1981), is a comprehensive version of what took place should be referred to Volume I's qualified statement made in connection with MI6's relations with the Abwehr: '... insofar as the British records are any guide A-54 was the sole Abwehr officer who collaborated directly with the Allied intelligence organizations.'

As the reader will discover, this statement is a clear illustration of the problems facing the modern historian who relies entirely on official documents. In fact, there were a number of Abwehr officers who collaborated directly, not the least of whom was the Abwehr chief himself, Admiral Canaris. His Polish confidante, Madame Szymanska, was an MI6 agent who reported direct to the SIS Head of Station in Berne, Major Vanden Heuvel. Canaris was perfectly aware that he was giving secrets directly to the Allies, as was Stewart Menzies, the MI6 Chief. Evidently this information was either too valuable to be entrusted to the SIS Registry or was deleted for other reasons.

The dangers of placing faith in documentary records was pointed out by one particular retired Head of Station who told me that much of the information in his Station's Registry was pure fiction. Unfortunately SIS's secret history, which was written for internal consumption by a senior SIS officer, Neil Blair, is still considered too sensitive to be released. A number of individual reports, including that of the important Dutch Country Section, written by Colonel John Cordeaux RM, are also apparently regarded as too controversial to be circulated outside SIS headquarters.

SIS secrecy has rarely been penetrated. Neither the name of Stewart Menzies, nor that of his predecessor, Hugh Sinclair, both heads of the Service, appear in the official history. Indeed, only a handful of people are identified by name. More often than not the posts held by officers are mentioned but this is clearly unsatisfactory, especially when one considers some of the remarkable adventures experienced by these extraordinary individuals. Some of these officers later became well known in other roles. Graham Greene, for example, was an SIS Head of Station in West Africa. He is now better known as a novelist, but inside the Secret Intelligence Service he is remembered for one of his famous telegrams in which he endeavoured to include the word 'eunuch'. When Greene was first sent to

Freetown, he discovered that the standard SIS cipher book contained five-figure groups for words frequently encoded. Among them was eunuch and Greene was intrigued. Eventually, in 1942, Greene found an opportunity to send a message including the word. He had been invited to spend Christmas with a Secret Service colleague in Bathurst but, as Greene telegraphed, 'Like the eunuch, I cannot come'.

Official reluctance to name individual officers is nothing new, but by adding names to the published posts one can make discoveries of considerable historical importance. For example, Stewart Menzies's younger brother, Ian, was married to an Austrian subject named Lisel Gaertner. Her glamorous sister, Friedle Gaertner, was extremely close to both Ian and Stewart Menzies. Incredibly, she was also an Abwehr spy and a double agent for MI5. Code-named GELATINE (because her Security Service case officer thought she was a 'jolly little thing'), she supplied her German contacts with high-grade political intelligence from the Anschluss in 1938 to the end of the war in May 1945.

Instinctively the professional intelligence officer will comment that there are good reasons for official discretion. With the passing of some forty years and the admitted penetration of MI6 by the Soviets, it is difficult to justify these 'good reasons'. The structure and methods of the Secret Intelligence Service described in the following pages have little relevance to the organization's current operations. The few hundred SIS officers and agents identified here have, to a man, retired. Furthermore, several of the most experienced and distinguished former members of SIS have given me their assistance and are satisfied that this account will not pose a threat to anyone except those who have their own reasons for perpetuating myths. I have also given the Ministry of Defence the opportunity to ask for alterations, and where these requests have been justified I have agreed to them.

Those who are expecting a standard 'debunking' work will, I am afraid, be disappointed. Many will find the truth much stranger than fiction and, I hope, much more enlightening.

Briefly, a word concerning the structure of the book. It is intended primarily as a detailed description of the Secret Intelligence Service and its operations during the last war. However, to do justice to the subject I have covered the events which led to the organization's creation in 1909. It would also have been impossible to explain the MI6 of 1939 without describing the inter-war preoccupations of the Service, which led to the recruitment of so many of the important personalities who influenced its conduct in the war.

There have been several accounts of the code-breakers at Bletchley, Special Operations Executive, and the contribution made by the American Office of Strategic Services, so I have concentrated on the nuts-and-bolts of MI6's operations: the Stations overseas, their agents and staff, and the SIS organization at home. I do describe, in passing, the development of the Government Code and Cipher School, but other, better qualified historians have analysed its contribution to the Allied victory. My aim is to give the reader an understanding of how MI6 as a whole played its wartime role, but to do so without the frustrating coyness of previous commentators.

Finally, a word on sources. Much of the information that appears in the following pages has been volunteered by former MI6 officers and their agents. I was particularly fortunate in tracing former members of the staff from each of the overseas Stations, and I am grateful to them all for their patient help. To my surprise I discovered that the Public Record Office at Kew holds a large quantity of SIS documents which have somehow escaped the weeders. Those who wish to pursue the trail further will be rewarded in FO 369-72.

The Wartime Organization of the Secret Intelligence Service

SIS Organization, September 1939

Chief (CCS): Admiral Sir Hugh Sinclair
Assistant Chief (ACSS): Lieutenant-Colonel Claude Dansey
Chief Staff Officer (CSO): Captain Rex Howard R N

Administration

Assistant Chief Staff Officers (ACSO): Commander Cuthbert Bowlby R N
Commander Frank Slocum R N

I	II	III	IV	V
POLITICAL	MILITARY	NAVAL	AIR	COUNTER-ESPIONAGE
Malcolm Woollcombe, David Footman	Colonel Stewart Menzies, Major Hatton-Hall	Captain Russell R N, C. H. Arnold-Forster R N	Wing-Commander F. Winterbotham, Squadron-Leader J.S.B. Perkins	Colonel Valentine Vivian, Major Felix Cowgill

THE EUROPEAN STATIONS PRIOR TO 1940

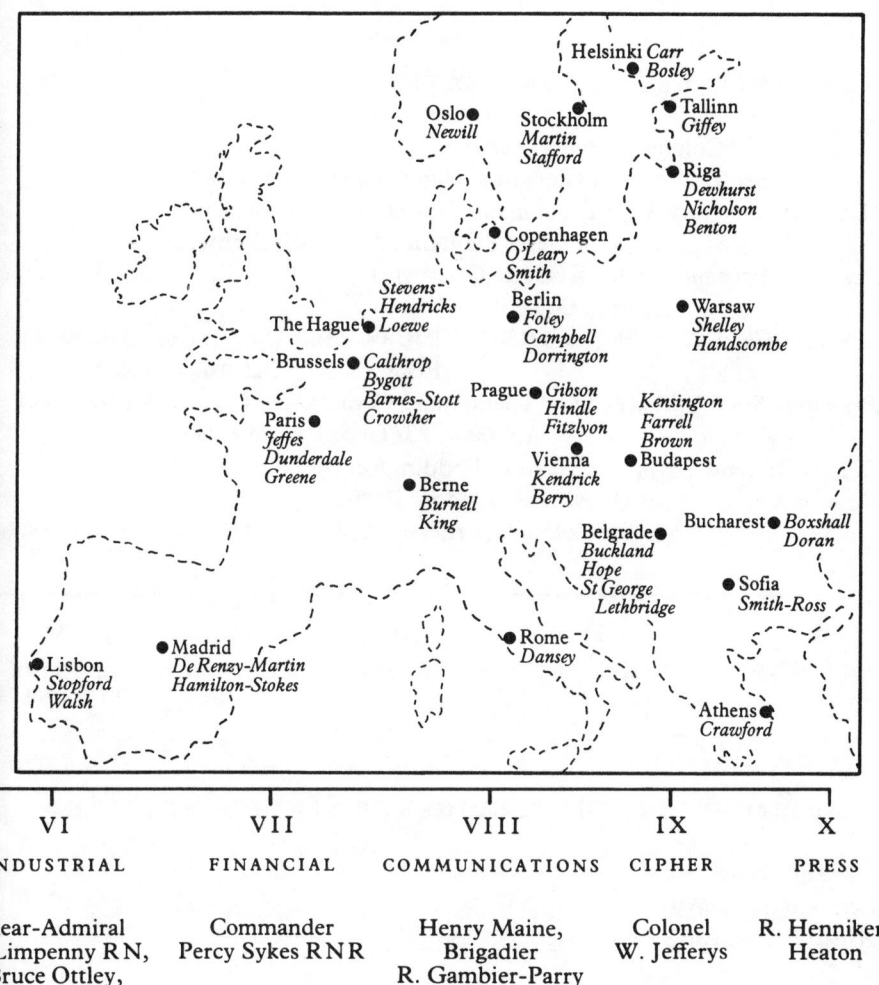

VI	VII	VIII	IX	X
INDUSTRIAL	FINANCIAL	COMMUNICATIONS	CIPHER	PRESS
Rear-Admiral Limpenny R N, Bruce Ottley, Robert Smith	Commander Percy Sykes R N R	Henry Maine, Brigadier R. Gambier-Parry	Colonel W. Jefferys	R. Henniker-Heaton

SIS WARTIME REORGANIZATION

Chief (CCS): Colonel Stewart Menzies
Deputy Chief (DCSS): Lieutenant-Colonel Valentine Vivian
Assistant Chief (ACSS): Lieutenant-Colonel Claude Dansey
General Sir James Marshall-Cornwall
Personal Assistants: Peter Koch de Gooreynd
David Boyle
Assistant Chief Staff Officers (ACSO): Patrick Reilly (Sept. 1940–Oct. 1943)
Robert Cecil (Oct. 1943–Apr. 1945)
Principal Staff Officer (PSO): Lieutenant-Commander C.H. Arnold-Forster
(Admin) Air Commodore Peake
Deputy Director (Army): Brigadier Beddington
(Air): Air Commodore Payne
(Navy): Colonel Cordeaux R M

I	II	III	IV	V
POLITICAL	MILITARY	NAVAL	AIR	COUNTER-ESPIONAGE

WARTIME SECRET INTELLIGENCE SERVICE STATION

Head of Station
Personal Secretary
Assistant Head of Station

AGENTS (with access to SIS Station)	AGENTS (with no access to SIS Station)	COMMERCIAL SECTION	KING'S MESSENGERS	SECRETARIAL STAFF

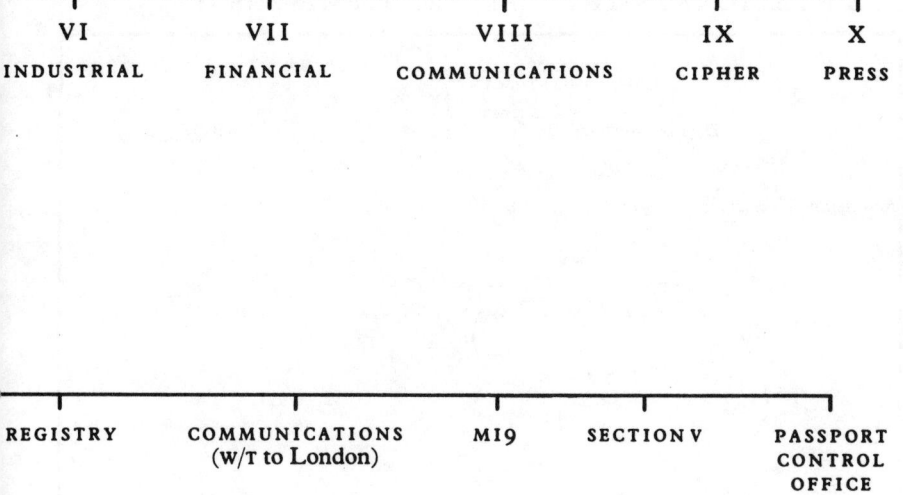

	VI		VII		VIII		IX		X
	INDUSTRIAL		FINANCIAL		COMMUNICATIONS		CIPHER		PRESS

REGISTRY	COMMUNICATIONS (w/t to London)	MI9	SECTION V	PASSPORT CONTROL OFFICE

Security Intelligence Middle East
Inter-Services Liaison Department

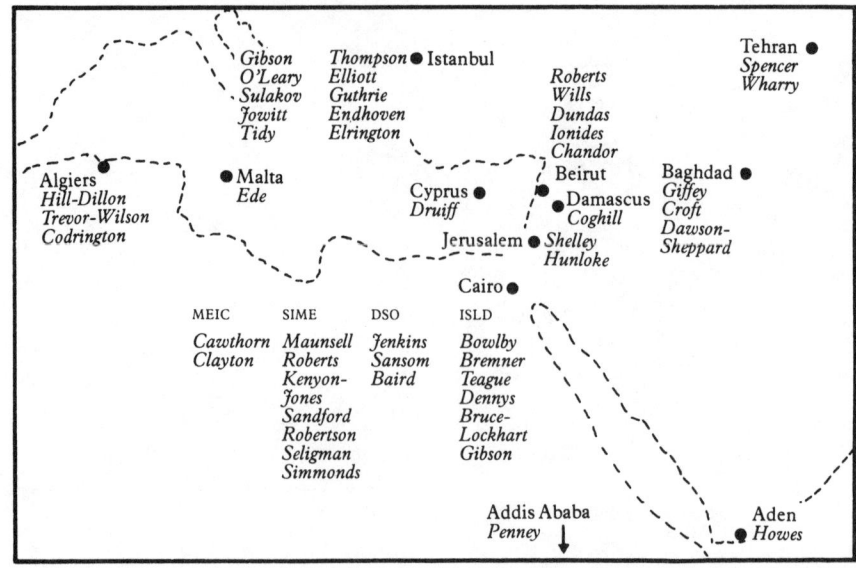

SIS Stations in the Western Hemisphere

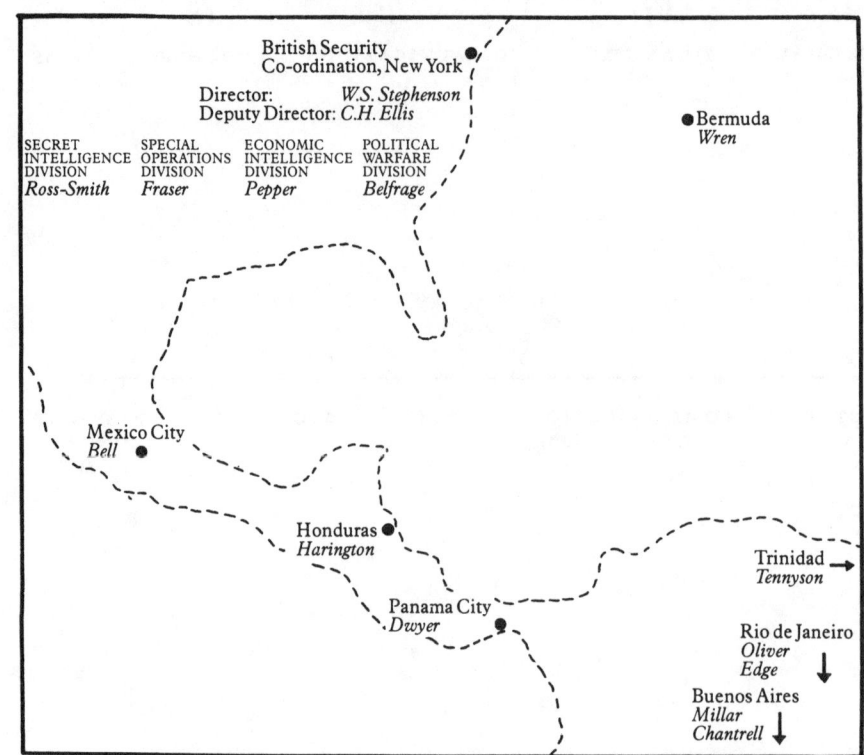

Part One

1909-40

The whole point of a Secret Service is that it should be secret.

COMPTON MACKENZIE, *Water on the Brain*

1

Early Days
1909–14

Intelligence gathering is the business of acquiring information from both overt and covert sources. From time immemorial, nations have sought to protect their interests by collecting intelligence. Sometimes this has been done openly through diplomatic channels and by reading published material. However, there has always been a demand for information from clandestine sources, varying from businessmen and travellers returning from abroad to sophisticated networks of undercover agents.

This book is principally concerned with the latter, but such networks cannot be developed overnight. Indeed, it often takes years to establish a group of reliable informants in positions of trust where they can gain access to really useful intelligence. Once an agent has achieved such a position, his (or her) influence can be of critical importance.

Creating well-placed networks is no easy task and once a flow of information is initiated, a second equally important responsibility falls on the professional intelligence officer, which is the correct assessment and distribution of agents' reports. There is little use in manœuvring an agent into a position of advantage, if his product is to be ignored or, perhaps worse, channelled to the wrong recipient.

During the years of Queen Victoria's reign, Britain grew lax. She presumed that the supremacy of her navy would maintain the Pax Britannica and left it to her diplomats cavorting themselves in the capitals of the world and her consuls and representatives in lonely outposts of empire, like George Macartney at Kashgar in Central Asia, to report on untoward events. The only places it was thought necessary to have professional agents in were Ireland and India. The only foreign power watched fairly closely was Russia, for fear of her possible designs on the route to India. As a result Britain was caught napping by the Boer War. As Thomas Pakenham says in his volume on the subject, *The Boer War* (1979), the central problem which was to dominate the war was lack of intelligence of the enemy's strength, his movements and his intentions; it proved to be a major handicap.

Fierce criticism ensued. The Committee of Imperial Defence (CID), which included the Chiefs of Staff under the chairmanship of the Prime Minister, recognized the need for change. In 1907 the secretary of this committee was Rear-Admiral Sir Charles Ottley, and his assistant was a young Royal Marines officer called Maurice Hankey. They now set about reviewing the country's intelligence organizations. During the course of this investigation, Hankey learned to his amazement that there was not one single British agent in the whole of mainland Europe. This astonishing state of affairs was a well-kept secret, so well kept in fact that most countries believed that Britain possessed the most extensive and sophisticated espionage service in the world.

Before 1909, the principal intelligence gathering organization had been the Naval Intelligence Division (NID), which distributed lengthy questionnaires to all Royal Naval captains requesting each to appoint an officer to complete the forms. When ships returned to their home ports, these forms were collected and sent to the Admiralty in London. This information was augmented by similar reports from naval attachés, Lloyds' agents and British consuls.

In May 1909 Reginald 'Blinker' Hall, captain of the cadet training ship HMS *Cornwall*, went further than his usual brief and obtained permission from the Director of Naval Intelligence (DNI), Admiral Sir Edmond Slade, to undertake a clandestine photographic survey of Kiel Harbour. Hall successfully completed the mission in the company of Captain Trench RN and a Royal Marines officer, Lieutenant Brandon. The second such operation took place in May the following year and was less of a success. This time the targets were the German naval forts on the Frisian island of Borkum, at the mouth of the River Ems, and the operation was planned by the Assistant Director of Naval Intelligence, Captain Cyril Regnart RN. Brandon and Trench, who had volunteered again, were arrested by the German police, tried and sentenced to four years' imprisonment for espionage.

When the Committee of Imperial Defence learnt of these somewhat amateur espionage experiments and studied the depressing summary of Britain's intelligence written by Colonel Fraser J. Davies, former Military Commissioner of Police in Johannesburg during the Boer War, it decided that a national intelligence service should be created. The date was 24 July 1909.

Ottley's recommendation to the Cabinet was that a Secret Service Bureau be set up to co-ordinate and restructure existing arrangements which had proved so inadequate. The proposal, actively supported by the War Minister, Lord Haldane, was for the formation of a single body divided into two completely separate sections: home and abroad. The Cabinet duly approved the plan and Ottley set about recruiting men to run the two sections. He accepted the suggestion of Colonel Edmonds that Captain Vernon Kell, late of the South Staffordshire Regiment, should head the home section, which was initially known as MO5. To head the foreign section, Ottley turned for help to the current senior British intelligence officer, the Director of Naval Intelligence, Admiral the Honourable Alexander Bethell. Bethell's candidate was Commander Mansfield Smith-Cumming, a fifty-year-old Royal Navy officer engaged, since November 1898, on special duties at Southampton.

Smith-Cumming had been born plain Mansfield George Smith on April Fool's Day 1859. The youngest son of a Royal Engineers colonel, he had become a cadet at the Royal Naval College, Osborne, when he was thirteen years old and had joined his first ship, HMS *Bellerophon*, in June 1878, as acting sub-lieutenant. During the next seventeen months, he also served on HMS *Ruby* and HMS *Daring*, chiefly on patrol in the East Indies. He took an active role in the Malayan Campaign in 1876 whilst his ship patrolled the Straits of Malacca and, in February of that year, he was gazetted as aide-de-camp to Captain Buller who commanded the Navy's operations against the Malay pirates. In the summer of 1882 he took part in the Egyptian Campaign and was given a mention in dispatches by Sir William Hewett. His naval file records that he 'speaks French, draws well'. In addition he was later described as 'a clever officer with great taste for electricity. Has a knowledge of photography.'

In spite of these apparent attributes, Smith-Cumming could not have expected a long naval career because he was afflicted with terrible seasickness. By August 1883 his health was causing concern and he was sent home for a long period of leave before returning to HMS *Sultan* in September 1883. In March 1885 he transferred to HMS *Raleigh* as flag lieutenant to Rear-Admiral Sir Walter Hunt-Grubbe, Commander-in-Chief of the Cape of Good Hope. Six months later he was appointed Transport Officer aboard the *Pembroke Castle*, an Indian troopship, but once again Smith-Cumming was stricken with seasickness. His condition deteriorated further in December 1885 when he joined another troopship, the *Malabar*. Within a week he was reported unfit for further service. His pay was cut to £109 10s a year and his name was added to the Retired List with the rank of lieutenant-commander.

Smith-Cumming's first wife was Dora Cloete, the daughter of a wealthy South African barrister who had been the British Crown Agent in Pretoria. His second wife, whom he married in 1889, was Leslie Valiant, the daughter of Captain Lockhart Valiant of the Bombay Lancers. Her maternal grandfather was a certain Mr A. Cumming, a wealthy Scottish landowner, and it was to preserve his name that Mansfield Smith began to call himself Smith-Cumming. His service record shows that on 7 July 1889 the Admiralty warned him that if he had changed his name he should report it 'at once'. On 15 July he duly reported that he wished to be known as Mansfield George Smith-Cumming, although he did not formally assume the name Cumming until 1917.

Little is known of Smith-Cumming's occupation during the early years of the 1890s, but in April 1898 he joined a torpedo course for retired officers run by the Admiralty at HMS *Vernon*. Two months later he withdrew from the course citing 'private affairs' as his reason, but by August of that year he was back studying Southampton's boom defences. For the next five years he was based on HMS *Australia* and HMS *Venus*, both shore bases on Southampton Water.

Smith-Cumming's work on boom defences was evidently much appreciated by the Admiralty, for in January 1906 he was granted the rank of a retired commander and his services were described officially as 'valuable'. When Commander-in-Chief Portsmouth, Admiral of the Fleet Sir Arthur Fanshawe, retired, he recommended that Smith-Cumming be decorated.

Smith-Cumming accepted the post of head of the foreign section of the Secret Service Bureau on 1 October 1909 and moved into the War Office, which initially at least had taken responsibility for both sides of the Bureau. The post of Director of Military Intelligence (DMI) had been abolished in 1904, so responsibility for special intelligence duties had been given to the Military Operations director, Lieutenant-General Sir Spencer Ewart, and his assistant, Major-General Charles Callwell. Smith-Cumming moved up from his home in the Hampshire village of Bursledon, overlooking the River Hamble, to a flat in Whitehall Court, a large mansion block close to the War Office.

Within a year of its formation, the Bureau had divided. Kell's home section was made responsible for investigating and countering espionage in the United Kingdom and the Empire and, until a 1916 reshuffle, it remained under the aegis of the War Office, where it was housed; whereas, by agreement between Smith-Cumming and Bethell, the foreign section found new premises in Northumberland Avenue and came under the jurisdiction of the Admiralty, on the grounds that the Admiralty was the principal Service requiring intelligence from overseas. However, the navy already had its own lively intelligence department headed by a vice-admiral, so that Smith-Cumming was outranked from the beginning.

Smith-Cumming combined his new career with several other interests. One of his ideas was to organize a special committee to monitor the growing private ownership of motor boats. The Admiralty adopted his scheme and, with his help, developed it further by enrolling the boat owners into a Motor Boat Section of the RNVR. The new sport of flying was another of Smith-Cumming's enthusiasms. He was taught to fly in France in 1913 and, in December of that year, obtained a French Aviator's Certificate when he was fifty-four years of age. He also passed a similar flying test set by the Royal Aero Club.

At the outbreak of war Smith-Cumming was still a relatively junior officer. He was not granted the rank of acting captain until January 1915, and his organization was still virtually non-existent in terms of agents. His office acted as a clearing house for strategic information about Germany, but the Foreign Office continued to pay the occasional volunteer for political intelligence. Smith-Cumming was later to gain a reputation for toughness and mystery, but at the time he had little to be mysterious about. He invariably initialled papers that passed over his desk in green ink, a tradition continued by his successors, and as his title was Chief of the Secret Service (CSS) he was soon referred to simply as 'C', another tradition that was to outlast him. However, it was a tragic event that took place in France on 3 October 1914 that established Smith-Cumming as a living legend.

On that date Smith-Cumming was in France and was on his way to an appointment in a car driven by his son, Alexander Smith-Cumming, a subaltern in the Seaforth Highlanders ('detached for Staff Duties'). According to an account later given by (Sir) Compton Mackenzie in the third volume of his war memoirs, *Greek Memories**:

The car, going at full speed, crashed into a tree and overturned, pinning C by the leg and flinging his son out on his head. The boy was fatally injured and his father, hearing him moan something about the cold, tried to extricate himself from the wreck of the car to put a coat over him; but struggle as he might, he could not free his smashed leg. Thereupon he had taken out a penknife and hacked away at his smashed leg until he had cut it off, after which he had crawled over to his son and spread a coat over him, being found later lying unconscious by the dead body.

This extraordinary story is indeed true. Lieutenant Smith-Cumming was listed as 'killed' on 3 October (as opposed to the more usual entry in the Army List of 'killed in action'), and records show that his father broke both his legs in the accident. His left foot was surgically amputated the following day and for most of the following week his condition was reported to his headquarters as 'serious'. A telegram on 8 October 1914 described his progress as 'satisfactory'. For the rest of his life he was to disconcert people by absent-mindedly tapping his wooden leg as he talked to them.

Establishing a world-wide secret intelligence organization takes time, it cannot be hurried. Before the newly fledged SIS was five years old, before it had had time to establish a useful network of agents of its own, Britain was at war; before it had managed to establish itself under the mantle of the War Office, it had been moved to the Admiralty, where it was juxtaposed to a rapidly expanding naval intelligent organization. Possibly senior naval officers breathed heavily down Smith-Cumming's neck, maybe they just ignored him; whichever it was, SIS got off to a shaky start whilst NID soared.

* Chatto & Windus, 1932

2
The Great War
1914-18

The enterprising young naval captain who had photographed Kiel Harbour in 1909, Reginald 'Blinker' Hall, was appointed to the post of Director of Naval Intelligence in November 1914, in succession to Vice-Admiral Sir Henry Oliver who had become Chief of Staff at the Admiralty. Although he was Chief of the Secret Service, Commander Smith-Cumming RN must have been acutely aware that Hall was considerably his senior in rank, if not in age. The precise relationship between SIS and the Naval Intelligence Division is never easy to discern, but with SIS the responsibility of the Admiralty and with the head of NID senior in rank, it cannot have been easy for Smith-Cumming. Up to now the SIS had operated in parallel with naval intelligence: both established local representatives in the major European capitals, both received military assessments prepared by military attachés based on British Legations and Embassies overseas, and both liaised closely with the French Deuxième Bureau, headed by General Dupont. But Smith-Cumming had not yet been able to train many officers or agents whereas Naval Intelligence already had a sophisticated network of overseas coast-watchers established in position. Power and political muscle therefore passed increasingly to the naval side of intelligence, whilst responsibility for gathering intelligence about Germany fell on the General Staff of the British Expeditionary Force (BEF). In December 1915, the Commander-in-Chief, Field Marshal Sir John French, was replaced by one of the two British Corps commanders in France, Sir Douglas Haig, and he in turn appointed a young engineer officer, Major John Charteris, as his Director of Intelligence.

By the outbreak of war the Naval Intelligence Division had placed volunteers in strategic positions overseas to observe and record shipping movements. The system acted like a human radar chain and was greatly reinforced during the summer of 1914. For example, the port of Göteborg in Sweden usually merited one British consul-general. By August 1914 his staff had increased to seven. Similarly in Norway, there had previously been just one consul. By the end of 1914, there were thirty-three, with a further twenty-five vice-consuls. Between 1910 and 1914 107 persons were convicted of espionage in Germany, of whom fifteen were alleged to have been working for Britain.

At the end of 1915 Lord Kitchener reorganized the War Office. Colonel (Sir) George Macdonogh was appointed Director of Military Intelligence (the first since the position had been abolished in 1904) and George Cockerill was appointed as his deputy with control of special intelligence. Under this reshuffle, the embryonic Secret Intelligence Service returned to the control of the War Office and was henceforth known as MI 1(c). MO5 now became known as MI5. Under this new regime, which came into force early in 1916, there was Macdonogh and under him Cockerill, then came four separate units: MI 1(x), organization and administration; MI 1(a), operational intelligence; MI 1(b), censorship and propaganda; and MI 1(c), secret service and security.

At the time of the 1916 reorganization, both the Security Service and the Secret Intelligence Service routinely attached individual officers to the British Expeditionary Forces' headquarters. It was these officers' responsibility to conduct counter-espionage operations in the rear echelons, to interrogate prisoners and to gather intelligence from behind enemy lines. SIS also retained responsibility for running agents from neutral Switzerland and Holland. The Brussels Station at 7 rue Garchard had been headed by the 1910 Assistant Director of Naval Intelligence himself, Captain Regnart RN, and Herbert Long, but had been evacuated in the face of the German advance.

The business of running agents in enemy-occupied France and Belgium fell mainly on a Secret Service network directed by an artillery major, Cecil Aylmer Cameron (code-named EVELYN), from an out-station in Folkestone on the south coast of England. With the help of a Belgian-born deputy, Georges Gabain, Cameron supervised two further Stations, one on the Boompjes near Rotterdam, the other at Montreuil on the French coast. The Dutch organization was headed by Commander Richard Bolton Tinsley RNR, a former director of the Uranium Steamship Company. Subordinate to him were a military section, headed by Captain Henry Landau, a naval section headed by Commander Power RN, and a counter-espionage section headed by an officer named de Mestre. Others in the Station included the son of the Russian Consul-General at The Hague, de Peterson, who was in charge of administration, and a locally employed book-keeper named Meulkens. Ewart's local representative was the British Commercial Attaché, Sir Francis Oppenheimer.

At Field Marshal Sir Douglas Haig's headquarters at Montreuil, responsibility for intelligence was in the hands of Colonel Walter Kirke, who was assisted by Captain Reginald Drake, on secondment from the Security Service. Also based at the counter-espionage division at Montreuil was Captain James Torrie, whose place was to be taken in December 1915 by the Adjutant of the 2nd Life Guards, Captain Stewart Menzies DSO, MC. Further counter-intelligence operations were conducted from St Omer by a Combined Intelligence Bureau, led by George Macdonogh. His staff included Captain Bell and a team of ten Scotland Yard detectives on secondment from the Special Branch, and headed by Inspector Martin Clancy.

Operations in southern Europe were directed by the one-legged Major (Sir) John Wallinger, with Lieutenant-Colonel Frederick Browning taking responsibility for censorship and propaganda. In 1917 the latter was taken over by the Ministry of Information with John Buchan its Director of Intelligence, assisted by Harold Baker (then Liberal MP for Accrington) and Hugh Macmillan (later Lord Macmillan).

British intelligence operations on the Continent obtained considerable benefit from close co-operation from the local authorities, and this was especially true in Belgium and Holland where the French Deuxième Bureau, now under Colonel Wallner, was particularly active. However, the Belgian Intelligence Service, led by Major Mage, was initially somewhat wary of British intentions.

By the end of 1916 the combined Allied intelligence organizations had achieved complete penetration of the Western Front and had a well-established network of train watchers. Virtually every German troop movement was recorded and the information passed back over the lines by carrier pigeon. This was by no means the only method of communicating with agents behind enemy lines. From 1915 onwards No. 70 Squadron of the Royal Flying Corps (under the command of Captain G.L. Cruickshank) flew individual agents into occupied territory. It was also possible to infiltrate agents through the German frontier from neutral Holland until late in 1916 when the Germans constructed a sophisticated fence running the length of the border. Wireless telegraphy was, of course, in its infancy during the early stages of the Great War, but considerable use was made of unsolicited military questionnaires which were floated into enemy territory by balloon. Civilians who found the balloons were asked to complete the enclosed forms and then release them back over the lines when the wind was in the right direction. Surprisingly, this method was quite successful.

As well as intelligence gathering, it fell on the Allied intelligence services to operate the escape lines for evading prisoners of war. By 1916 these lines were well established and smuggled back large numbers of military personnel to the British lines. Invariably the escapees brought with them valuable intelligence, and it was for this reason that the Germans concentrated much of their effort on tracking down the organizers of the lines.

The first major inter-Allied network was that known as FRANKIGNOUL, after one of its chief organizers, and was based on some twenty train-watching posts spread throughout Belgium and northern France. The network was eliminated by the Germans in the autumn of 1916 after they discovered the ring's principal means of communication, a tram which ran between Lanaeken and Maastricht in neutral Holland. The Germans intercepted the train-watchers' reports until they could identify most of the agents involved, and then arrested them. On 16 December 1916 ten members of the ring were executed at Hasselt and thereafter the tram was prevented from crossing the frontier. Instead, the passengers underwent a thorough personal search and were then obliged to walk across the border to transport awaiting them on Dutch territory.

The collapse of FRANKIGNOUL was followed by the successful German penetration of BISCOPS, a Belgian network run by Catholics who had obeyed Cardinal Mercier's instructions actively to resist the German invaders. There were so many nuns and priests involved that the organization was sometimes known as the SACRE CŒUR ring. It was eventually compromised by an oculist who was under investigation for quite a separate matter. The police found an appointment with a certain 'W' mentioned in his diary, and their suspicions were aroused when the oculist refused to answer any questions concerning the mysterious 'W'. Early in September 1917 a stool-pigeon elicited the information that the 'W' stood for Marguerite Walraevens, whose home in the rue Medori, Brussels, acted as a central receiving station for the BISCOPS train-watching reports. The Germans kept the house under observation and then rounded up the members. Virtually the only person to escape was an engineer named Léon Leboucq, who headed the ring from his home in Charleroi. It so happened that Leboucq was away attending Mass when the Germans came to arrest him, so he was able to take refuge in Brussels and rebuild what remained of the organization.

Most of the early networks were plagued by poor security and intermittent communication with the SIS branch Stations in Holland and France. The Germans were adept at planting informers and stool-pigeons, and on occasion substituted their own agents for escaping prisoners of war. In this way they plugged some of the numerous escape lines which played such an important role in repatriating escapees. One such line was run by Edith Cavell, who engineered the successful escape of several dozen wounded Allied troops who had found themselves cut off after the retreat from Mons. Miss Cavell was executed with one of her confederates, Philippe Baucq, on 10 October 1915. Although she herself was not a British Secret Service agent, many of those who used her escape line were, and it was regarded as a useful conduit for couriers. Miss Cavell was posthumously decorated with the award of a Civil Division OBE, thus emphasizing her non-military role. The world-wide publicity given to her execution proved a propaganda disaster for the Germans, who were, of course, perfectly entitled to execute spies and those aiding evaders, whether they were male or female.

Quite the largest of the Allied networks in enemy-occupied territory was the one code-named WHITE LADY, which was based on Liège and was still operational at the time of the Armistice in November 1918. At its peak the ring boasted a total of fifty-one train-watching posts which reported to twelve secretariats, where the individual reports were collated, typed and then enciphered for transmission over the front lines. More than a thousand civilians were recruited into the organization, of whom only forty-five were arrested by the Germans. Of that number, only one was executed. It has been estimated that during the last eighteen months of the war WHITE LADY was responsible for seventy-five per cent of the intelligence coming from the occupied areas.

The early German intelligence successes had led to a virtual collapse of the Allied networks in 1915 and 1916, but the lessons learnt from those bitter experiences left Britain well equipped for the latter part of the war. The military intelligence units of the British Expeditionary Force fared less well, and Charteris was replaced as Haig's Director of Intelligence by Sir Herbert Lawrence soon after the first battle of Cambrai in November 1917. At Cambrai British troops, supported by the newly introduced tanks, had encountered unexpectedly large numbers of fresh German troops. Military intelligence had failed to inform GHQ that the Germans had recently reinforced that sector of the front and Charteris was sent home to England.

By the end of the war a total of 235 Allied agents had been convicted of espionage by the German authorities. Of this number, some fifty-five are believed to have been working for SIS, although only three were British nationals.

The activities of the Secret Intelligence Service were by no means limited to the Western Front. MI 1(c) had Directors of Intelligence in all the major theatres of war. Smith-Cumming's largest overseas outpost was located in Cairo, where General Gilbert Clayton was the local Director of Intelligence, with a Special Intelligence Bureau based in Alexandria also under his command. This distant cousin of MI 1(c) was responsible for both security and intelligence in the eastern Mediterranean theatre and consisted of two sub-divisions: A Branch (concentrating on the acquisition of enemy intelligence) and B Branch (counter-espionage). The head of the Alexandria Bureau was Major (Sir) Philip Vickery, an officer from the Indian police service who was later to head the Indian Political Intelligence Bureau in Delhi.

One member of Vickery's staff in Alexandria was (Sir) Compton Mackenzie, who subsequently recounted his experiences in a series of auto-biographies. To this day Mackenzie remains the source of a number of interesting stories about SIS and, in particular, Smith-Cumming. On one occasion Mackenzie recalled asking a British naval attaché if C was a naval man. 'Yes,' replied the attaché, 'but apparently attached to the War Office, though he gets his money from the Foreign Office.'

Amazingly enough, neither knew for sure. Unbeknownst to either of them, the statement was correct, for a further transfer of responsibility had taken place during the latter part of the war: MI 1(c) had been removed from the War Office to the overall control of the Foreign Office.

At the same time as this change took place, in 1917, it was decided to amalgamate the Admiralty cryptanalysts formally into the Naval Intelligence Division, whereupon they became known as 'NID 25'. That same year naval intelligence took much of the credit for the successful interception and deciphering of the famous telegram which helped propel America into the Great War. Dated 16 January 1917, the telegram was addressed to the German Ambassador in Washington, Count von Bernstorff, from the Kaiser's Foreign Minister in Berlin, Arthur Zimmermann. From Washington the message was relayed on to its ultimate destination, the German Ambassador in Mexico City. The text was decrypted by two of Ewing's recruits who specialized in the German diplomatic traffic, the Reverend William Montgomery and Nigel de Grey, and sent to President Wilson.

The contents of the telegram were political dynamite, as Zimmermann proposed to the Mexican President that he join the war on their side. In return for his support, Zimmermann promised, Mexico would receive substantial territories in the southern United States. The text also said that the German navy was about to begin 'unrestricted warfare', which suggested that neutral vessels would now become vulnerable.

President Wilson was suitably outraged. Once Wilson had confirmed the authenticity of the German proposal, he denounced the Germans' intentions to Congress and, on 21 March 1917, recalled Congress to hear an announcement of 'grave matters of national policy'. It was to be a declaration of war.

Five days earlier, on 16 March 1917, Nicholas II, Czar of all the Russias, had abdicated and handed over power to a provisional government headed by Prince Lvov. Three months later an abortive revolution in Petrograd failed, but caused the formation of a new Socialist regime under the leadership of Alexander Kerensky, Lvov's Minister of War.

Kerensky himself was totally committed to the war against Germany, but he was quite incapable of holding the balance between the Bolsheviks and the other Socialist revolutionaries. Lloyd George's administration in London was extremely anxious to support the Kerensky Government, mainly because of its desire to keep Russia in the war. Somewhat belatedly, SIS tried to shore up Kerensky by dispatching a well-funded agent to Moscow to offer financial support.

The cash was channelled to Kerensky via New York, where SIS had opened an office headed by Sir William Wiseman and Colonel Norman Thwaites. Wiseman, a Cambridge-educated baronet, was a partner in the New York broking house of Kuhn, Loeb. On the outbreak of war he had been commissioned into the Duke of Cornwall's Light Infantry and badly gassed in Flanders. After a brief recuperation, Wiseman was sent back to America to liaise with Colonel Edward House, President Wilson's special adviser. He was joined in 1917 by Colonel Thwaites, and together they worked to bring America into the war while at the same time running the British Purchasing Commission. It was Wiseman's job to send the funds to Moscow and, fortuitously, there was on hand an experienced SIS agent in New York available to undertake the mission.

The agent selected for the mission was W. Somerset Maugham, one of John Wallinger's agents who had successfully completed two tours of duty in Switzerland, one late in 1915, when he had been based in Geneva, and a second the following year in Berne. In June 1917 Maugham agreed to take Wiseman's cash to Moscow and embarked on a long journey via Japan and Vladivostok. He was equipped with an elaborate code which identified Lenin as DAVIS, Kerensky as LANE and Trotsky as COLE. Maugham himself was to sign his cables SOMERVILLE and the British Government was disguised as EYRE & CO.

On 24 September Wiseman cabled the following message to London:

I am receiving interesting cables from Maugham, Petrograd:

(A) He is sending agent to Stockholm for promised information, and also to Finland. He has reports of secret understanding for Sweden and Finland to join Germany on capture of Petrograd.

(B) Government change their mind daily about moving to Moscow to avoid Maximalists. He hopes to get agent into Maximalist meeting.

(C) KERENSKY is losing popularity, and it is doubtful if he can last.

(D) Murder of officers continues freely. Cossacks are planning a revolt.

(E) There will be no separate peace, but chaos and passive resistance on Russian front.

(F) Maugham asks if he can work with British intelligence officer at Petrograd, thereby benefiting both and avoiding confusion. I see no objection providing he does not disclose his connection with officials at Washington. If DMI agrees, I suggest he be put in touch with KNOX, but positively not under him.

(G) I think Maugham ought to keep his ciphers and papers at Embassy for security. He is very discreet and would not compromise them, and may be useful as I believe he will soon have good organization there. Anyway I will cable you anything interesting he sends me.

The following month Kerensky called for Maugham and entrusted him with a personal message for Lloyd George. Kerensky described his own position as precarious and asked for substantial material support. He also demanded that Sir George Buchanan, the British Ambassador, be replaced. Kerensky insisted that this message was so secret that it be delivered verbally to the Prime Minister and never committed to paper. Accordingly, Maugham rendezvoused with a British destroyer in Oslo and then called on Lloyd George at Downing Street. In spite of his instructions, Maugham prepared a brief note detailing Kerensky's plea for help; he was worried that his stutter would hinder the delivery of such an important message. The

Prime Minister read the note and then asked Maugham to return to Moscow to explain that he would be unable to comply with the demands.

On 8 November 1917, before Maugham could retrace his steps, Alexander Kerensky's Government in Moscow collapsed and Lenin's underground Military Revolutionary Committee seized power. Chaos gripped Russia and the Allies concluded that the German General Staff, which had expedited Lenin's secret return to Petrograd from Switzerland, had helped to engineer the entire affair. Certainly, from the military viewpoint, the Germans stood to gain a strategic advantage from manœuvring Lenin into power. Lenin's declared policy was the immediate initiation of peace talks with Berlin.

Not surprisingly, the events in Russia were viewed with alarm in London and Paris, and the situation was made all the more serious by the lack of information from within the Bolshevik headquarters which had moved from Petrograd to Moscow. Such western diplomatic missions as had not been withdrawn were located in Vologda, a small railway town to the north-east of Moscow on the main line to the White Sea port of Archangel.

The British Embassy, headed by Sir George Buchanan, was evacuated on 28 February 1918 and thereafter British diplomatic representation was left in the hands of Robert Bruce Lockhart, the former Consul-General, who remained at his post in Russia to lead an unofficial mission to the Bolsheviks with the aim of keeping them in the war. The rest of the Embassy staff travelled to Archangel for a rendezvous with Royal Naval vessels, which had been instructed to carry them to England. Among those in the party were the two senior British intelligence officers in Russia, Colonel (Sir) Terence Keyes and Major Stephen Alley. The British Military Attaché, General (Sir) Alfred Knox, being the Director of Military Intelligence's local representative, was also evacuated, although he returned the following year as Chief of the British Military Mission to Siberia.

Among those who remained with Bruce Lockhart was the Director of Naval Intelligence's representative in Russia, Captain Francis Cromie. His new task was to prevent the immobilized Russian Baltic Fleet from falling into German hands, and to this end he began recruiting a network of saboteurs who would take whatever action was necessary to prevent such a catastrophe. He was soon joined in April by Major Alley's replacement, Commander Ernest Boyce, who was sent out from London by Smith-Cumming. Boyce's task was to collect intelligence about Bolshevik intentions and to try to remove Lenin.

The response to the revolution in London was disorganized. Alley, who was Russian born and Russian educated, had been thoroughly compromised and would not have been tolerated by the new regime. The British Government was ill-informed on developments in Russia, and the Foreign Office and the War Office launched a belated campaign to recruit suitable Russian linguists for missions to help keep Russia in the war.

The first such recruit, from the War Office, was Captain George Hill. Hill had been wounded at Ypres and had subsequently been commissioned and posted to intelligence duties with MI5. His knowledge of Russian had resulted in him being infiltrated into the Alexandra Palace internment camp ... disguised as a Bulgarian. When SIS began searching for Russian linguists, (Sir) Edward Ross, himself an expert on Russia and the Middle East who was then on MI5's staff, recommended that Hill be transferred to the Foreign Office. By mid-1917 Hill had been taught to fly by the Royal Flying Corps and was busy flying agents behind enemy lines in the Balkans.

Hill was brought back to London for a briefing by the Director of Military Intelligence, Brigadier George Cockerill, and then sent to Petrograd to liaise with the Soviet forces. He was to report back to the War Office using the code-prefix identification of IK8. However, soon after arriving in Russia late in 1917 Hill undertook a mission, on his own initiative, to rescue the foreign reserves of the Romanian Government, which were then stored in Moscow, and return them to Bucharest. Hill completed this mission successfully, but only after many extraordinary adventures in Bolshevik-held territory. His remarkable exploits earned the thanks of the Romanian royal family, who were particularly grateful to have their crown jewels returned safely, but it did little to improve Smith-Cumming's knowledge of what was happening in the apparent chaos of Russia. Accordingly, in April 1918, SIS recruited a second Russian-speaking adventurer in the Hill mould.

This second volunteer, a captain in the Royal Canadian Flying Corps (RCFC), answered to the name of Sidney Reilly. In fact, he was the bastard son of a Jewish doctor named Rosenblum, who had a practice in a small town near Odessa. Sigmund Rosenblum later emigrated to Brazil, and from there moved to London where, in 1899, he had married an English widow, Margaret Reilly Callaghan, and changed his name to Sidney Reilly. By the time war had broken out, Reilly had established himself in New York and had bigamously married a second wife, Nadine. He had also got himself appointed as a munitions purchasing agent for the Russian government and had come into contact, albeit briefly, with Smith-Cumming's two principal representatives in New York, Colonel Norman Thwaites and Sir William Wiseman, who headed the British Purchasing Commission.

At the end of March 1918 Reilly was transferred from the RCFC to SIS and was assigned the task of travelling to Bolshevik-held Russia and making contact with Ernest Boyce. Reilly arrived in Murmansk in April 1918 and was promptly arrested by the Royal Navy who controlled the dock area. Apparently Reilly had been issued with travel documents by the Soviet representative in London, Maxim Litvinov, but his surname had been misspelt 'Reilli'. After the intervention of Rear-Admiral Kemp, the senior

British naval officer in the White Sea, Reilly was able to continue his mission and report to Boyce.

Reilly turned out to be a natural secret agent and, as a result of his harrowing adventures during the following five months, developed a life-long hatred for the Soviet regime. He was supposed to report to Boyce using the code-prefix ST 1, but he quickly disappeared from view and began organizing a counter-revolution.

Reilly's plot was complicated, like everything he did, but it was designed to unify the many different opposition groups, including a powerful collection of Czarist officers financed by the local French secret service representative, Colonel de Vertement. On 6 July 1918 the German Ambassador, Count Wilhelm von Mirbach, was assassinated in Moscow to provoke the reopening of hostilities between Germany and Russia. The attack was co-ordinated with an attempt on Lenin's life at a meeting of the All-Russia Congress at the Moscow Opera House, but the Soviet leader had been forewarned. The coup failed, and early the following month 17,500 Allied troops under General Frederick Poole disembarked at Archangel to suppress the revolution. The campaign was badly organized and was doomed to failure from the start.

The Soviet heirarchy responded to the Opera House attempt with undisguised ferocity. Thousands of suspect dissidents were liquidated and Reilly was obliged to go underground with his group. Bruce Lockhart was taken into 'protective custody', but released soon afterwards. The reign of terror continued, but on 31 August a second assassination attempt was mounted; once again Lenin survived, although he was hit by two bullets at close range. This prompted a second wave of arrests, and the following day Captain Cromie was killed defending his office in the old British Embassy in Petrograd. Bruce Lockhart was rearrested and threatened with execution, along with other British personnel, including Ernest Boyce. It was later estimated that some 8,000 counter-revolutionaries were summarily shot during the next few days. Reilly and Hill made their escape across the Baltic to Sweden, and the lives of Lockhart and Boyce were saved by the arrest of Litvinov in London. They were released on 2 October and they subsequently reached Aberdeen by ship on 18 October 1918. Reilly was rewarded with a Military Cross, Hill with the DSO.

The failure of the counter-coup once again resulted in an end to the flow of reports from Moscow to London, and SIS cast around to find someone to reconstruct its shattered networks. Its chosen candidate was a young Englishman named Paul Dukes, who was then undertaking relief work with an American mission in Samara. Before the war, Dukes had been studying music at the Moscow Conservatoire, where he had hoped to become a conductor. Instead he was summoned to the Foreign Office in London; upon arrival in August 1918, he was briefed by Smith-Cumming, given the code-prefix ST 25 and sent back to Russia via Archangel aboard a troopship. His task was to re-establish contact with Cromie's networks and report on the situation in the Russian capital.

Dukes eventually entered Russia from Helsinki in late November 1918 and stayed there for nearly ten months, gathering intelligence under a number of different disguises. Among his forged papers were documents identifying him as Joseph Ilytch Firenko, a member of the Cheka, the dreaded Soviet secret police. His information was passed to a newly formed resistance movement, the Natsionalnyi Tsentr, which co-ordinated political opposition to the Soviet regime. Dukes also channelled military information to the White Russian Army and, on occasion, to the Royal Navy, which was engaged in semi-official actions against the Soviet Baltic Fleet.

In one incident in June 1919 Dukes was scheduled to rendezvous with a Royal Naval fast patrol vessel just off the Baltic coast, but failed when his dinghy sank. The patrol boat returned without him, torpedoing the cruiser *Oleg* on the way. For this exploit, and another involving the sinking of two Soviet battleships on 17 August, Lieutenant Augustus Agar RN, the patrol vessel's commander, was decorated with the Victoria Cross.

Dukes remained in Russia until September 1919, when he was obliged to escape to Finland after several of his contacts had been arrested by the Cheka and charged with plotting to overthrow the Communist state. According to the evidence heard by the Revolutionary Tribunal, four of the defendants, all leading dissidents, had been receiving financial support from Dukes to the tune of half a million roubles a month. Leontev, Shchepkin, Trubetskoi and Melgunov were given death sentences, which were subsequently commuted to ten years' imprisonment.

On his return to London, Dukes was awarded a knighthood in recognition of his anti-Bolshevik efforts. He was also congratulated by Sidney Reilly, who was now attached to the Foreign Office from the Royal Air Force and engaged in advising Smith-Cumming on further measures that might be taken to destabilize the Soviet regime.

Smith-Cumming ended the war with a glittering array of decorations. In July 1916 the Czar had awarded him with the Order of St Stanislaus (Class II) and the following year the Belgians made him an Officer of the Order of Leopold. On 11 November 1918 his rank of acting captain was confirmed captain (retired) and in June 1919 he was knighted 'for valuable services in the prosecution of the war', calling himself Sir Mansfield Cumming. He was invested by the King at Buckingham Palace on 26 July. In December the same year the Italian Government appointed him a Commander of the Crown of Italy. His war work was evidently much appreciated.

By far the most comprehensive wartime intelligence organization had been that of the NID, which had incorporated the famous cryptographers of Room 40. Much of the credit for the Division's operations should have gone to Rear-Admiral Sir Reginald 'Blinker' Hall, who had been knighted in 1918, but he was not a popular figure, either inside or outside the Admiralty, although few could criticize his proven ability. He retired in January 1919, before the Paris Peace Conference, and was then elected as the Tory MP for the West Derby Division of Liverpool. He was replaced as Director of Naval Intelligence by his deputy, Captain Hugh Sinclair, who was promoted to rear-admiral on the appointment.

Naval intelligence had already been well established by 1913: it had used this in-built advantage to the full. However, SIS had also performed most creditably.

When the Great War began, SIS had been in its infancy, led by a Chief still recuperating from a major operation. Moreover, between 1909 and 1918 SIS was shunted between the War Office, the Admiralty and the Foreign Office. Despite these handicaps, it managed to establish branch Stations in Holland, France and Egypt, to put a large number of agents into the field, to liaise effectively with other Services, to conduct counter-espionage activities, to interrogate prisoners, to gather information from behind the enemy lines and to help organize escape routes for evaders and prisoners of war. SIS also opened up a New York office and maintained a series of agents in Russia before, during and after the revolution.

3

Sir Mansfield Cumming
1918-23

After the Armistice, various changes were suggested in London's intelligence bureaucracy: some feared that one or other branch was becoming too powerful; others were more alarmed at the thought of the power a united MI5-SIS might wield, although it clearly made economic sense to combine them under one roof, now that Hall had retired. In September 1918, General William Thwaites became Director of Military Intelligence and urged Kell to merge with Smith-Cumming. He felt that SIS was still officially a department of the War Office, for it still retained its military designation MI 1(c) even though the Foreign Office had had *de facto* control during the latter part of the war. The move failed, Kell being particularly against it.

The following year the Cabinet, at Lloyd George's instigation, approved the formation of a Secret Service Committee to advise on a new peacetime structure for both Britain's intelligence organizations. This Committee gave MI5 responsibility for counter-espionage, counter-sabotage and counter-subversion both in the United Kingdom and in her overseas interests in the Colonies and in the Dominions under Colonel Vernon Kell, whose title would be Director-General of the Imperial Security Intelligence Service. MI5's powers would be primarily investigative, based on the card index, for the right to search, arrest, cross-examine, interrogate and prosecute suspects lay with the Special Branch at Scotland Yard. A small separate department was also set up, entitled the Directorate of Intelligence, under Assistant Commissioner of the Metropolitan Police, Sir Basil Thomson, to deal with countering Bolshevik-inspired subversion. The Secret Intelligence Service would deal with all the other areas of the world outside the empire and would remain under the leadership of Smith-Cumming, or Sir Mansfield Cumming as he had now become. Its peacetime budget would be £125,000 a year, a cut of £115,000 from its wartime allowances. SIS would be placed under the overall control of the Foreign Office and was expected to build up a world-wide network of Stations headed in each case by the Chief's local representative. The cryptographers of Room 40 were to continue under the leadership of Captain James RN during peacetime; they would remain under Admiralty administration, but would be retitled the Government Code and Cipher School (GC & CS).

The Foreign Office was cautious about its new charge. While the war had lasted, Cumming's information had been welcome, but now the Foreign Office feared SIS's potential for creating embarrassing incidents. Although the Foreign Office felt that it was better qualified than the War Office to exercise control, it was anxious to distance itself from any activity that might jeopardize its relations and treaty obligations with foreign powers. Its attitude was fraught with ambiguity.

It has always been accepted that general information in the public domain can be collected by diplomats and sent back to their own countries: indeed their communications, both postal and radio, are sacrosanct for this reason. But it is not acceptable for them to go out of their way to prise secret information out of their host country. For behaviour incompatible with their diplomatic duties, they can be considered *persona non grata* by the host country and asked to leave. Such an occurrence would be frowned upon by the diplomat's own government, because his duty is to improve relations between countries, not to create ill-feeling. But, above all, it would displease his sovereign. For ambassadors are the officially accredited personal representatives of the sovereign of their country to the sovereign of another; as such, their personal immunity from interference while on foreign soil, based on internationally recognized agreements, is extended to their entourage – provided their behaviour is beyond reproach. However, if one of the entourage offends, he compromises the ambassador's status and so indirectly the sovereign whom he represents.

If SIS officials abroad held diplomatic rank, they compromised the Foreign Office; if they were not Foreign Office employees, how could they be restrained? The line between what information was collected in what way by whom became grey. The ingenious solution was to create a Passport Control department of the Foreign Office, whose officials would be employed by the Foreign Office but would not enjoy diplomatic status.

Cumming's nominee, Major Herbert Spencer, was appointed the first Director of Passport Control early in 1919. His office was situated on the ground floor of 21 Queen Anne's Gate, which also doubled as the new London headquarters of the Secret Intelligence Service, an arrangement which was eventually to cause problems and result in some unusual Foreign Office correspondence. There was also some confusion: for example, in October 1919, Cumming appointed Captain W.R.C. Hutchison as Head of Station for the SIS in Berne. The Foreign Office then explained to the British Minister in Switzerland that Hutchinson would be 'attached to the Legation ... but will not form part of the diplomatic personnel'.

However, despite early misunderstandings, the Passport Control system, once it had got under way, initially at any rate, was able to satisfy the Foreign Office's bureaucratic requirements and enabled the Secret Intelligence Service to conduct its operations behind a reasonably plausible cover. It also provided a career structure for its staff, who were ranked Chief Passport Officer (CPO), Passport Control Officer (PCO), Assistant PCO, Examiner and, at the end of the scale, interpreters, clerks, secretaries and messengers. The Chief's authorized overseas establishment consisted of twenty-five PCOs (each paid £800 per annum), two Assistant CPOs (£500 per annum), twenty Examiners (£350 per annum) and a total budget of £20,000 to pay the clerks and other support staff.

Although the new Passport Control arrangement appeared to be a convenient compromise for both SIS and the Foreign Office, there were some unforeseen consequences. Cumming may have believed that the transfer of departmental responsibility for SIS would be quite straightforward, but the Foreign Office turned out to have strong views on the matter. Indeed, its new interest went further than mere concern for diplomatic niceties. SIS's finances suddenly came under scrutiny and the Chief found himself in the embarrassing position of having to discard several long-serving officers. Certainly the change-over, which took place in the usual conditions of secrecy, came as a surprise to some of the Stations. The Athens Station, for example, had been headed by Lieutenant Crowe, the Military Control Officer. He was aided by the Assistant Military Attaché at the British Legation, an officer named Welch. When Crowe was demobilized, he recommended that Welch take over his post and be appointed Passport Control Officer, but on 24 September 1919 a telegram from MI 1(c) pointed out that 'Welch could not remain with the Military Attaché as the passport control work had been transferred to the Foreign Office'. The obvious solution was to recruit Welch into the Consular Service, but this involved a long-term financial burden on the Foreign Office so they declined. Instead, they appointed him 'vice-consul to undertake passport duties', a post that could be terminated without notice and any pension rights. For a senior SIS officer, who had already spent four years in the Station (without leave), this attitude resembled ingratitude.

Welch was not the only SIS officer to be treated shabbily by the Foreign Office. The case of Henry Gann was another example. Gann had been recruited (reluctantly) into SIS by Colonel Louis Samson late in 1917. At the time, Gann had been invalided out of the Royal Navy and was about to take up a post of temporary vice-consul in Milan. Samson persuaded him to go to Switzerland for MI 1(c), and he was duly attached to the Berne Station, then headed by Major Hans Vischer. The Berne Station's geographic proximity to Germany and its neutral status lent it a strategic importance during the last twelve months of the war and Gann executed his duties faultlessly. Vischer, who had been born in Basle and was educated in

Switzerland before going up to Emmanuel College, Cambridge, later wrote Gann a letter in which he commented (in his poor English):

You are the man on my Consular staff on whom I absolutely rely. I don't say this to send you sweet words but I know you have had good experience with Consular work and you won't compromise myself and the whole Service by rushing about with a blue beard meeting nasty people round the corner.

When the Foreign Office took over SIS, Gann was instructed to continue his work at the Station and apply for a permanent post in the Consular Service. MI 1(c) implied that this was a mere formality, but the Consular Service rejected his application.

In another similar case, the Foreign Office tried to close down the Tokyo Station. Its Far East Department found that it had acquired the services of Smith-Cumming's local representative, Colonel D.D. Gunn, who had been working under 'Military Control Officer' cover. The British Ambassador in Japan commented that:

... as Colonel Gunn is unacquainted with the people or language he will be dependent upon the Embassy and Consulate and serve only as 'a fifth wheel to the coach', whereas the funds might have been used for providing a competent staff for Consul Davidson.

In other words, if the Station was closed down, the Foreign Office would have more money to spend on its own interests.

It was such bureaucratic irritations, like those experienced by Welch and Gann, which later paralysed SIS's overseas Stations. Although the Passport Control system did at first appear to satisfy everyone's interests, to Cumming and the Foreign Office alike, it was to prove a recipe for disaster.

These changes in Whitehall did nothing to diminish SIS offensives against the Soviet regime in Moscow. As will be remembered, a young Englishman Paul Dukes had originally been sent to establish a Moscow network in November 1918 and had remained there until September 1919 when he had been forced to make a hasty departure. Sidney Reilly had also tried to build up contacts in Soviet Russia, but had finished the war attached to the Foreign Office as adviser to Cumming at SIS.

After Dukes's speedy return from Russia, SIS concluded, on advice from Reilly, that further adventures on Red territory were to be avoided, and that the key to success lay in the funding of 'democratic anti-Bolshevik' movements. Principal among these was the organization headed by Boris Savinkov, a former Minister for War under Kerensky. Savinkov had worked closely with Reilly and Dukes and had played an active part in the south Russia campaign with George Hill, who had been appointed to Sir Halford Mackinder's staff after his first Russian mission which had ended in the Romanian capital. Savinkov was a rallying point for some 250,000 displaced

White Russians, and he made his headquarters in Paris where he was largely financed by SIS in the persons of Ernest Boyce, who had been appointed Head of Station in Paris, and his deputy, Major W. Field-Robinson. Savinkov divided his time between supervising guerrilla operations from Warsaw (where Andrew Maclaren, the local SIS representative, was based) and Finland, from where most of the illicit border-crossings were organized.

During the following three years, Reilly worked unceasingly to muster support for Savinkov's movement. He bombarded the Foreign Office with highly optimistic assessments of the gains achieved by the counter-revolutionaries. In an assessment dated August 1921 Reilly reported that:

The anti-Bolshevik movement all over Russia is proceeding with unprecedented vigour and is rapidly reaching a culminating point. The sporadic peasant risings from which no district in Russia is now free, owing to the actions of various leaders, of whom the most important is Boris Savinkov, are rapidly moving into a General Rising which according to the best information appears inevitable by the middle of September.

Reilly's hopes were never fulfilled and his relationship with SIS became more and more tenuous. In the same year that Reilly submitted his Minute about Savinkov's prospects, his principal supporter, Ernest Boyce, was transferred from Paris to Helsinki. There he headed a small Station consisting of Harry Carr, a young intelligence officer who had served on General Poole's staff, H.A. Bowe, and two secretaries, Miss Galbally and Miss Cooper. In financial terms the Station was on a par with Rotterdam and Brussels.

The sudden change in Reilly's fortunes is not simply explained by a political change of heart in London, although this was undeniably a factor. Also to be taken into account were the very limited results achieved by SIS's heavy expenditure on Savinkov's organization, and the increasingly suspect motives of Reilly himself. He had been placed under surveillance by the Security Service on the occasions that he had visited London, and there was a certain uneasiness about his contacts with the Soviets in official circles. He had either come too much under the influence of those in the White Russian community who would stop at nothing to discredit the Soviet regime, or, alternatively, he had thrown in his lot with the OGPU, the successor to the Cheka. Either way, Reilly was becoming a liability to SIS and his intelligence reports were frequently contradicted by the Soviet diplomatic telegrams intercepted and decrypted by the Government Code and Cipher School.

Back in 1913, Rear-Admiral Henry Oliver, the Director of Naval Intelligence before Reginald 'Blinker' Hall, had been passed a number of unidentified signals which had been received by the Royal Navy's coastal radio stations. He had suspected that they might well be German naval messages and had presented the problem to a remarkable Scot who had been Director of Naval Education since 1903, Sir Alfred Ewing. Could Ewing decipher the German texts and then translate them? Ewing apparently grasped the possibilities immediately and recruited a number of German-speaking academics from Osborne and Dartmouth into his tiny office, located in Room 40, Old Admiralty Building, and known within the Service simply as 40 OB. His colleagues included Alistair Denniston, Captain G.L.N. Hope RN (the DNI's personal representative), E.J.C. Green and W.H.H. Anstie.

Initially Ewing's cryptanalysis team made slow progress, but in September 1914 the Imperial Russian Navy confided that they had recovered a code book from the body of a German officer who had been lost in the Baltic in the light cruiser *Magdeburg*. A copy of the code book was delivered to London and enabled the expanding NID to begin its work in earnest. There was no shortage of raw material to work on because the five German transatlantic telegraph cables (which happened to be British-owned) had been deliberately severed by a British cable-layer, the *Telconia*, in the first days of the war. The Germans were therefore obliged to rely on their transmitters for long-distance communications, and accordingly the navy placed interception stations along the east coast at Lowestoft, York, Murcar and at Lerwick in the Shetlands. The Naval Intelligence Division's success in locating German vessels and, in particular, German submarines, established the interception of enemy transmissions as a valuable intelligence weapon and certainly enhanced the reputation of Oliver's successor, Reginald 'Blinker' Hall.

In peacetime, the decrypters, now headed by Commander Alistair Denniston, a Scottish professor of German from Osborne, who had been educated at Bonn and the Sorbonne and had always been fascinated by mathematical teasers, were nominally presumed to be studying captured German code books and working out secure codes for use by Britain. In fact, they were still listening in to foreign wireless traffic, in particular that gleaned from their discreet radio station at Grove Park in Camberwell, South London. In March 1922 the Secret Service Committee proposed switching control of codes and ciphers to the Foreign Office, so at the beginning of the next financial year, Denniston and his twenty-four officers moved from their Admiralty home into Broadway Buildings which backed directly on to 21 Queen Anne's Gate. The following year, the Secret Service Committee completed its review of British intelligence services by placing the newly appointed Chief of SIS, Admiral Sinclair, at the head of the Government Code and Cipher School with the title of Director.

The post-war reorganization of Britain's decrypters coincided with the change in objectives which had been prompted by the 1917 revolution in Russia and the German Armistice the following year. One consequence of the revolution was the flight to England of a number of Russian cryptographers, principal among whom was an émigré named Felix Feterlain who was able to reconstruct many of the Czarist codes inherited by the new Communist administration in Moscow. Taking advantage of this inside knowledge, the decoders in London began intercepting a substantial part of the Soviet diplomatic traffic and built receiving stations in India and the Middle East to relay the transmissions that were out of the range of the receivers based in England.

The Soviet messages were distributed by the Government Code and Cipher School in the form of intelligence summaries and were the basis of a number of significant reports on Russian intentions. Each was marked MOST SECRET and was headed:

NOTE: The information in this Summary has been obtained from *SIS sources only*, and should, of course, be considered in conjunction with reports from official sources.

The primary customers for this GC & CS material were Colonel Alexander's military subversion section in MI5, and Basil Thomson's short-lived Directorate of Intelligence which, between 1919 and 1921, bridged the activities of Scotland Yard's Special Branch and MI5.

As well as these intelligence summaries, GC & CS provided certain members of the Cabinet and selected senior officials with 'original' flimsies; it was Lloyd George's decision to publish details from these in August 1920 which first alerted Moscow to the fact that the British Government had not abandoned her wartime deciphering capability. The Soviet Trade Delegation was secretly funding the *Daily Herald* and direct evidence of its covert financial arrangements became public knowledge on 15 September 1920 when the *Morning Post* and the *Daily Mail* actually published extracts from the intercepted signals.

In spite of the source for this intelligence being obvious to the Soviets, they neglected to alter their ciphers for a further three months, when they introduced a courier service between the Trade Delegation and Moscow. This new system defeated GC & CS, who inevitably (but incorrectly) blamed the politicians for compromising a valuable source of intelligence, but the respite proved to be brief. Within a matter of weeks the Russians produced new ciphers and reverted to a heavy dependence on wireless traffic to and from London. However, the new ciphers proved rather more difficult to decrypt, and SIS was obliged to try alternative methods to obtain access to the Soviet codes. Fortuitously, SIS was in a position to supply the key information required by GC & CS.

In February 1921 the SIS Head of Station in Estonia was Lieutenant-Colonel Ronald Meiklejohn, a former Royal Warwickshire Regiment officer who had served in the North Russia Campaign in 1919 and, the following year, had commanded the British Military Mission to East Finland.

Meiklejohn's main target was Maxim Litvinov's headquarters, which were located in the Estonian capital. Deputy Foreign Commissar Litvinov was suspected of financing Sinn Fein, the revolutionary Irish republican movement, as well as providing funds for some notorious Indian nationalists. Sir Basil Thomson's Directorate of Intelligence had discovered several indications of Soviet subversion, and Colonel (Sir) Cecil Kaye, of the Central Intelligence Bureau in New Delhi, had traced various Bank of England notes found on Indian extremists to a Russian Trade Delegation account in London. The Foreign Office required absolute proof of the Soviets' duplicity, so Meiklejohn and his two assistants, L.G. Goodlet and H.T. Hall, concentrated their efforts on Litvinov's headquarters. With surprising speed they succeeded in recruiting an agent with access to Litvinov's code room. The agent was a Volga German named Gregory and, in accordance with the system of numbering agents with a code-prefix to identify the controlling Station, Gregory was dubbed BP 11. He subsequently supplied some 200 'paraphrases' of Soviet telegrams, and comparison between these and the intercepted signals in their original form might have provided valuable clues for the GC & CS decrypters. BP 11 was, however, unable to provide the vital originals and in April was discredited as a reliable source when the GC & CS achieved a breakthrough and found the 'paraphrases' to be somewhat inaccurate.

On 16 March 1921 the British Government had signed a trade agreement with the new regime in Moscow, thus effectively giving the Communists recognition for the first time. Of particular interest to SIS and MI5 was the paragraph in the agreement in which both the British and the Soviet Governments undertook not to engage in subversive activities against each other. Evidently the Russians did not intend to pay even lip service to the anti-subversion clause because BP 11's intelligence suggested that the Trade Delegation in London was indeed secretly financing Sinn Fein in Ireland.

This proved to be particularly disturbing news in Whitehall. Ireland had been in a state of virtual civil war since the Easter Rising in 1916 and the prospect of a Bolshevik element in the already volatile situation was treated with alarm. Before 1920 responsibility for internal security and intelligence had remained with the Royal Irish Constabulary (RIC), the civil police force headed by Brigadier-General (Sir) Joseph Byrne. In the spring of 1920 the Ulster-born Byrne was transferred to the Governorship of the Seychelles in the Indian Ocean and was succeeded by Major-General (Sir) Hugh Tudor. At the same time, General Sir Nevil Macready, the Metropolitan Police Commissioner, was appointed Commander-in-Chief of the British forces in Ireland. Tudor and Macready recognized the woeful lack of any effective intelligence gathering organization in Ireland, and Tudor chose Colonel Ormonde de l'Epée Winter to be his deputy and, at the same time, head a new Combined Intelligence Service (CIS) which would take on the existing responsibilities of MI5 and draw on the manpower resources of the SIS. It quickly became known as Dublin Castle, after the location of its headquarters, but its officers and agents were spread widely throughout Dublin and the provincial towns.

Winter's first success was the shooting of a notorious IRA leader, Sean Treacy, in a Dublin street on 14 October 1920. However, this act sparked off further violence and led to an attack on some CIS safe-houses in Dublin early in the morning of 21 November. During this first 'Bloody Sunday', Michael Collins's IRA execution team killed fourteen of Winter's men and two RIC police officers. The Dublin Castle organization never recovered from this massacre, and it was against this background that SIS reported the following year that Sinn Fein was being channelled vast sums by the Soviet Government.

The growing suspicion within the SIS and elsewhere that its Estonian source, BP11, was rather less than reliable was increased by Sir Basil Thomson's failure to link the Soviet Trade Commissioner in London, Krassin, with any financial transactions, and the apparent impoverished nature of the IRA as confirmed by Winter in Dublin. BP11's reliability was therefore down-graded, thus placing a greater urgency on the need for Russian decrypts.

In April 1920 GC & CS again succeeded in cracking the Soviet diplomatic cipher and began monitoring messages passing between Moscow, London and the Middle East. Although the subsequent GC & CS intercepts in no way matched the previous paraphrases from Tallinn, they did provide damning evidence of the continuing efforts of the regime in Moscow to subvert the British Empire. This was particularly true of India, but Cumming was reluctant to have GC & CS compromised for the second time in as many years. He warned the Government in the strongest possible terms of the likely consequences if such a valuable source should be denied to GC & CS. Instead, he offered an alternative which would satisfy the Foreign Office's demand for indisputable proof of Moscow's breaches of the 1921 trade agreement. The substitute source provided by Cumming turned out to be a diplomatic catastrophe.

During the summer of 1921 the SIS Station in Berlin, headed by Major Timothy Breen, reported the discovery of a number of copy-documents apparently originating from the Soviet representative's office. The stolen papers served Cumming's purpose ideally and gave chapter and verse of Soviet policies and intentions. This 'evidence' was approved by an inter-departmental committee specially created to monitor Bolshevik activity and was used as the basis of a formal Note on 7 September from the Foreign Secretary, Lord Curzon, to Georgi Chicherin, the Foreign Affairs Commissar in Moscow. The Note was delivered by the British Agent in the

Soviet Union, (Sir) Robert Macleod Hodgson, but the Communists lost no time in denouncing its contents as forgeries. Worse, the Soviets actually compared the Note with *Ostinformation*, a propaganda sheet distributed by White Russians based in Germany. Reluctantly the SIS Station in Berlin admitted that it had indeed bought the allegedly 'secret' papers from a White Russian. Apparently, his informant had claimed possession of a source within Victor Kopp's Berlin office.

Unfortunately for the Secret Intelligence Service, Curzon demanded a review of the documents used in his Note; the majority, it was believed, had indeed come from the Berlin Station's tainted source. Curzon was furious and prepared a suitably ambiguous reply for Hodgson. In his second Note, Curzon implied that the evidence quoted by him was indeed genuine and that it must have been published in *Ostinformation* after it had come into his possession. This unconvincing effort served at least to inform the Soviet leadership that their professed intentions had been disbelieved by the British Cabinet.

This first protest by Curzon failed completely. MI5 reported that the Communist Party of Great Britain's subsidy from Moscow was uninterrupted and the Central Intelligence Bureau in India noted no appreciable change in Soviet-inspired subversion. Furthermore, GC & CS decrypted further diplomatic telegrams from Moscow, destined in particular for the Middle and Far East, in which the Communist leadership endorsed further measures designed to support local nationalist movements and thus undermine the Empire.

In early 1923 GC & CS became aware that the Russians had somehow learned of the insecurity of their diplomatic codes; nevertheless, they continued to use them and GC & CS continued to intercept them. Curzon, however, now saw the opportunity to redress the balance and duly reported to Stanley Baldwin's Cabinet that he wished to present the Russians with an ultimatum. Either they ceased the hostile acts as revealed by their secret communications, or the 1921 trade agreement would be cancelled. On 25 April 1923 the Cabinet approved the plan and a second protest was delivered to Moscow on 3 May. On this occasion the Note simply quoted Russian diplomatic messages and made no attempt to disguise the source of the material. The Russians responded by claiming that their communications had been distorted, but this in itself was sufficient admissions of the validity of the Foreign Secretary's charges. In the months following the protest, and no doubt to Curzon's intense satisfaction, GC & CS circulated a number of Soviet decrypts indicating that the ultimatum had been successful. One such intercept from the Soviet representative in Tehran, dated 16 May 1923, advised his consular officials to cease political activities and suspend temporarily all work with secret agents.

Although other similar telegrams were monitored by GC & CS late into the autumn of 1923, the Soviets had no illusions concerning Britain's code-breakers, and this was demonstrated by their gradual replacement of the compromised cipher series. This new (and not unexpected) development effectively prevented GC & CS from compiling summaries of Soviet telegrams until the following year. In the meantime, Ramsay MacDonald was replaced by Baldwin as Prime Minister, and Sir Mansfield Cumming had died. Cumming was replaced by the former Director of Naval Intelligence, Admiral Hugh Sinclair, and Admiral (Sir) Alan Hotham was appointed the new DNI. Sinclair, as the new director of GC & CS, approved a system whereby its decrypts would not be circulated to the incoming Cabinet or, for that matter, to the new Prime Minister.

The event that ultimately isolated the SIS anti-Bolsheviks was, ironically, the very thing that helped bring the Conservative Stanley Baldwin back to power in the 1924 general election. Sinclair had only been confirmed as the new Chief of the Secret Service for a few months when the intelligence community in London began to buzz with news of an intercepted communication between Gregori Zinoviev, Lenin's President of the Third Communist International (the Comintern), and the Communist Party of Great Britain. The rumour spread that the 'Zinoviev Letter' was political dynamite in that it spelt out the Soviets' true subversive intentions to undermine the United Kingdom. In short, it was a flat contradiction of the terms of the 1921 trade agreement and was a significant embarrassment to the Prime Minister and the Labour Party, who had been enthusiastic about the trade agreement with their new Soviet allies. According to the popular story, the Labour administration had therefore decided to suppress it. This news was leaked to the former DNI, Sir Reginald 'Blinker' Hall, who had become a Tory MP, a few days before the general election and he was understandably outraged.

The remarkable point about the story was the very limited number of people who had actually seen the controversial document. Certainly it had not been obtained from Communist Party of Great Britain sources; neither Sir Vernon Kell nor Scotland Yard's Special Branch had ever heard of it, although its reported contents went along with what they knew to be the Comintern's true line on Soviet policy. Neither the Assistant Commissioner (Crime), Sir Wyndham Childs, nor the DNI, Admiral Hotham, nor the DMI claimed to have seen the original of the letter, but all had been informed of the text. Within the Foreign Office few appeared to have any doubts about the letter. The Permanent Under-Secretary, Sir Eyre Crowe, vouchsafed his belief in it, as did the Head of the Northern Department, J. Don Gregory.

The text of the letter, dated 15 September 1924, was passed to Fleet Street by Sinclair's Vice-Chief, Colonel Frederick Browning, thus forcing the Foreign Office to acknowledge its existence. It was duly published on

25 October 1924 and it is universally agreed that the effect of the letter on the electorate was dramatic, suggesting as it did that the Labour Party and the Soviet Union were not to be trusted. But what was its provenance?

The actual authors remain unknown, but it was Sidney Reilly who passed it to MI5 and SIS, via an intermediary, a former MI5 officer named Donald im Thurn. It was Reilly's friend Colonel Alexander who received it on behalf of the Security Service, and it was Browning himself who took delivery of SIS's copy. Neither saw an original, although Guy Liddell, Scotland Yard's expert on the Comintern, confirmed the authentic nature of its contents.

The incoming Prime Minister urged Sinclair to investigate the Zinoviev affair and, to his intense embarrassment, found that Reilly had been Colonel Alexander's original source. By this date Reilly's fortunes were on the wane. His bigamous marriage had given SIS some awkward moments, especially when his first wife turned up unexpectedly on the doorsteps of several of Reilly's SIS colleagues demanding to know his whereabouts. His fanatical support for Boris Savinkov's White Russians and his self-confessed ruthlessness had undermined his standing with Cumming, so it was not surprising that Sinclair decided to wash his hands of him. To associate with him was altogether too dangerous and unpredictable.

Reilly himself probably had little idea of the political consequences of his forgery, that a Conservative government would be elected with a large majority, for it seems unlikely that he would have chosen this moment to endanger his valuable (and profitable) links with SIS. He was himself at a particularly low ebb, having failed to dissuade Savinkov from making a dangerous visit to Russia. Savinkov had heard of a powerful anti-Bolshevik movement which called itself the Moscow Municipal Credit Association, but was known more widely as The Trust. The Trust was apparently well organized and well funded. It had a reputation for being able to move agents across frontiers with comparative ease, and its leaders had guaranteed Savinkov safe passage to Moscow so that he could re-establish contact with some of his old networks. Reilly advised Savinkov against making such a journey, but Savinkov ignored Reilly's pleas and set off for Moscow from Berlin on 10 August 1924. Reilly never saw him again, but a fortnight later the Russian press announced Savinkov's arrest, trial, death sentence and pardon. Savinkov, the bulwark against communism, had defected to the Bolsheviks.

Reilly was stunned by the news and infuriated, especially when he heard that it had been The Trust's influence that had saved Savinkov from execution. Reilly never discovered his mentor's full story because Savinkov committed suicide in May the following year.

The loss of Savinkov convinced Reilly that it was now his responsibility to carry on the struggle, and he began a desperate money-raising campaign to finance further armed resistance within the Soviet Union. By the end of 1924 Sinclair had distanced SIS from Reilly's activities, but this did not stop Reilly corresponding with Winston Churchill and other senior politicians to gain support for his schemes. Virtually his only remaining link with SIS was Ernest Boyce, still Head of Station in Helsinki where he was secretly financing The Trust in exchange for information. Boyce confirmed to Reilly that he had considerable faith in The Trust and introduced him to The Trust's local representative, Alexander Yakushev, one of Boyce's most successful agents who also happened to be an OGPU official.

Yakushev told Reilly exactly what he wanted to hear: The Trust was an enormous organization with influence in every level of the Soviet structure. It enjoyed the protection of certain high Party officials which virtually guaranteed that its agents could enter and leave the country at will. The Trust was so powerful that even if someone was arrested his release could be arranged with only the minimum of delay. Reilly was intrigued and asked to meet The Trust's leaders. He was told that they occupied such important posts in Moscow that they were unable to leave the capital ... but they would be willing to attend a rendezvous with him if he came to Moscow. Incredibly, Reilly swallowed the bait, and on 25 September 1925, when Boyce was in London, Reilly was led across the Finnish border into Russia near Allekul by two Trust couriers. Two days later Boyce received a postcard from Reilly, postmarked Moscow, but the following week *Izvestia* reported that a group of smugglers had been intercepted by the police close to the Finnish border. Three people had been killed and a fourth, a Finnish soldier, was reported a prisoner.

A notice of Reilly's death was included in *The Times* on 15 December 1925, and this prompted further inquiries about his fate. Nobody, however, was ever able to establish what had happened, although The Trust was later exposed as an elaborate OGPU front. The OGPU Chief, Feliks Dzerzhinsky, decided it had been too badly compromised to continue with in 1927 and began liquidating his principal agents. Among them was Alexander Yakushev, who escaped to Finland and admitted his duplicity.

Sinclair had no idea what had happened to Reilly and was not particularly interested. Reilly's file was passed to MI5 and all future snippets of information (gleaned mainly from references to 'Britain's master spy' in Soviet newspapers) were forwarded by SIS to Scotland Yard and marked for the attention of Guy Liddell. Boyce, who had been completely duped by The Trust, took early retirement from SIS and found a job with a commodity firm in Paris run by Stephen Alley. Reilly's disappearance marked the end of SIS's 'Russian adventures'. Most of Reilly's supporters, like Sir Paul Dukes and George Hill, had already left SIS. Nevertheless, Reilly's memory was to linger among Sinclair's younger staff for many years.

★　　★　　★

Although I have run on into Admiral Sinclair's time at SIS in order to tie up all the strands about Reilly, before going any further I would like first to sum up the fourteen years in office of Mansfield George Smith-Cumming, who was appointed first Chief of the Secret Service in 1909 at the age of fifty and who died in harness on 14 June 1923 at his London home, 1 Melbury Road, aged sixty-four. In his will, which was witnessed by Commander Percy Sykes and Ethel Cory, he left most of his property to his widow, Dame Leslie Cumming, with four bequests of £100 to his three secretaries, Margaret Churcher, Bridget Battye and Nina Vertier, and his chauffeur Ernest Bailey; he was a kind and thoughtful employer.

Seasickness marred Cumming's naval career and a leg amputation at the beginning of the Great War must have been a hindrance. Nor did he find it easy to build up an embryo department in such close proximity to the Naval Intelligence Division led by Reginald 'Blinker' Hall. After the Great War, when overall control passed to the Foreign Office, Cumming had to fight hard to retain his relative independence, to obtain a decent budget and to keep overseas Stations open. He also worked most successfully to gain control over the Government Code and Cipher School, which he rightly saw as extremely important to his department.

Despite inauspicious beginnings, he gradually built up a small viable overseas intelligence network. In the twelve months before his death, he had defended his department from outside interference with some success, but he had been forced to meet in full all the economies demanded of him. Some had been achieved simply by relaxing visa requirements for French and Belgian subjects, which had enabled Cumming to close almost all the Passport Control sub-offices in both countries, leaving offices only in Paris, Brussels and Antwerp. These three Stations were instructed to reduce their running costs by fifty per cent, saving £7,000 per annum. This was the kind of sum the politicians were anxious to save, but Cumming was particularly skilful in seeking support for his cause in the most unlikely quarters. On one occasion, in May 1922, Cumming attended a Whitehall committee to tell it about the consequences of enforcing cuts in his operations; he warned that the partial relaxation of the visa system might be 'the thin end of the wedge' and result in large numbers of undesirable aliens gaining entry to Britain. His statement had the desired effect. Sir Basil Thomson announced that such an event would 'render necessary an extension of the police powers so as to allow the summary ejectment of undesirable aliens'. In addition, Mr Lascelles from the Ministry of Labour said that his department would not tolerate any step 'which made it easier for the alien workman to come to this country at a time of unexampled unemployment'.

Through the intervention of such allies as the Ministry of Labour, Cumming was able to limit the demands of the politicians. Nevertheless, he did lose some important Stations in the cuts: Madrid, Lisbon and Zurich were

Secret Intelligence Service Administrative Accounts 1920-21

STATION (HEAD)	SALARIES AND WAGES	RENT	EXPENSES
General Headquarters	3,914 17 0	254 13 6	129 16 5
Headquarters Salaries a/c	16,963 15 2	– – –	– – –
Vienna *Forbes Dennis*	835 6 0	54 10 0	241 10 8
Tallinn *Meiklejohn*	463 15 9	33 14 3	67 16 10
Riga *Meiklejohn*	1,033 17 4	67 18 0	91 1 7
Brussels *Westmacott*	2,684 12 10	15 7 0	340 14 2
Sofia *Elder*	6 0 0	9 10 6	7 18 6
Prague *Norman*	205 18 2	– – –	73 8 11
Copenhagen *Hudson*	2,304 8 4	130 8 10	329 1 10
Helsinki *Boyce*	2,066 14 8	202 0 3	278 4 7
Paris *Langton*	6,319 6 4	1,050 3 8	736 19 0
Berlin *Breen*	5,102 8 10	284 7 3	970 0 9
Athens *Welch*	852 5 6	153 13 7	94 1 0
Rome *McKenzie*	2,160 6 6	114 17 0	251 12 6
Japan *Gunn*	1,662 2 3	– – –	127 12 2
Rotterdam *Wood*	2,191 17 11	293 13 2	192 7 11
Oslo *Lawrence*	1,542 4 3	212 9 11	214 3 10
Warsaw *Marshall*	335 9 2	68 19 4	72 19 4
Lisbon *Chancellor*	855 8 0	– – –	57 4 2
Bucharest *Boxshall*	343 19 3	45 7 0	46 18 4
Madrid *Hollocombe*	1,567 10 4	169 11 10	333 13 7
Stockholm *Hitching*	1,453 5 4	511 5 6	395 19 10
Berne *Langley*	3,684 7 10	255 1 4	702 7 11
Vladivostok *Kirby*	334 5 9	– – –	– – –
Beirut *Thomson*	93 12 0	12 10 0	62 15 7
New York *Jeffes*	11,065 2 8	2,771 14 6	437 0 3
Buenos Aires *Thomson*	1,739 15 5	56 17 0	323 5 0
Liepaja	266 13 4	5 6 8	21 9 6
TOTAL	£71,779 5s. 11d.	£6,784 0s. 1d.	£6,600 4s. 2d.

POSTAGES			TELEGRAMS			TRAVELLING EXPENSES			TOTAL		
	2	4	–	–	–	819	13	10	5,119	3	1
–	–	–	–	–	–	–	–	–	16,963	15	2
–	–	–	49	12	9	53	12	6	1,234	11	11
–	–	–	162	14	9	15	11	9	743	13	4
2	5	6	2	19	10	22	9	6	1,220	11	9
–	–	–	36	5	10	53	16	0	3,130	15	10
–	–	–	9	17	3	–	–	–	33	6	3
	9	4	17	13	4	7	18	0	305	7	9
13	0	6	2	6	6	50	3	3	2,559	9	3
6	3	7	5	8	10	23	19	9	2,582	11	8
26	12	6	21	4	10	298	18	6	8,463	4	10
3	15	0	–	–	–	119	17	9	6,480	9	7
3	16	3	7	11	0	–	–	–	1,111	7	4
30	16	0	79	19	9	76	6	3	2,713	18	0
	17	0	607	0	11	–	–	–	2,397	12	4
65	11	9	43	11	10	11	5	6	2,798	8	1
14	19	0	16	16	6	128	6	0	2,128	19	6
	10	10	37	0	2	44	16	8	559	15	6
–	–	–	–	–	–	16	9	2	929	1	4
–	–	–		10	1	8	1	0	444	15	8
28	3	6	5	14	9	131	15	4	2,236	9	4
52	14	3	28	5	0	64	16	0	2,506	5	11
40	0	2	52	2	10	297	7	4	5,301	7	5
–	–	–	500	3	2	–	–	–	834	8	11
–	–	–	–	–	–	–	–	–	168	17	7
87	13	6	200	14	9	–	–	–	14,562	5	8
–	–	–	139	0	0	–	–	–	2,258	17	5
–	–	–	3	8	0	5	7	0	302	4	6
£377 11s. 0d.			£2,030 2s. 8d.			£2,250 11s. 1d.			£89,821 14s. 11d.		

abolished, as well as the relatively insignificant Station in Luxembourg. Rome (Mr McKenzie) and The Hague (Mr Wood) suffered a staff reduction, but escaped a threatened closure. The Head of Station in Lisbon, Mr W.G. Chancellor, fought hard to retain his job and, unusually, enlisted the help of the British Minister, (Sir) Lancelot Carnegie. The entire Station was given one month's notice in April 1923, but Carnegie protested that Chancellor 'constantly supplies me with useful information' and pointed out that his Consul would be unable to cope with the extra work. The plea was ignored.

The closure of the Swiss Station caused more complicated problems. In October 1922 the Head of Station, Major Hutchison, asked SIS headquarters for advice about what he should do with the Station registry. He explained that 'a great deal of what may be termed "explosive" war information is contained in these files'. The secret and confidential archives consisted of 'at least twenty-five thousand dossiers'. Eventually the files were put into secure storage in the Consulate-General until SIS could afford to reopen the Station.

It was in this atmosphere of financial economy that Cumming prepared his last estimate for future expenditure during the year 1923-24. The total number of Passport Control Officers had been reduced from twenty-eight to twenty-five. Their combined salaries totalled £20,600. Cumming calculated that his entire PCO network would cost £53,800 to maintain. This was the organization inherited by Admiral Sinclair.

4

Hugh Sinclair
1924-38

Hugh Sinclair had joined the Royal Navy in 1886 and three years later was serving aboard the battleship HMS *Magnificent* with special responsibility for torpedoes. This duty led to a lifelong interest in torpedoes, and he was later posted to Portsmouth as an assistant to the Director of Naval Ordnance. In 1912 he commanded the battleship HMS *Hibernia*, but the following year he was recalled to supervise target practice in the Solent. He spent the first two years of the war in the Admiralty's mobilization division and the Naval Intelligence Division, and then he commanded HMS *Renown*. In 1917 he was appointed Chief of Staff to the battle-cruiser force before succeeding Reginald 'Blinker' Hall as Director of Naval Intelligence in February 1919. In 1921, he was appointed head of the submarine service. It was Cumming's unexpected death in 1923 that caused Sinclair to sell his modest home in Fishery Road, Maidenhead, and take up residence in the first-floor flat of 21 Queen Anne's Gate, his home above the shop. Sinclair, known to his friends as Quex, C to the Establishment and Chief to those who worked for him, was soon to be made a widower. After the death of his wife, he leant increasingly on his unmarried sister Evelyn, whom he brought into SIS.

Frederick Winterbotham was interviewed by Sinclair in 1929 and he describes the Admiral as 'a short stocky figure with the welcoming smile of a benign uncle. His handshake was as gentle as his voice, and only the very alert dark eyes gave a hint of the tough personality that lay beneath the mild exterior.'* When the interview was over, Sinclair went off to see the Prime Minister wearing a bowler hat which was rather too small for him, perched precariously on the top of his head.

The Secret Intelligence Service which Admiral Sinclair had inherited in June 1923 was largely staffed by officers who had fought in the Great War and were 'attached special duties' to the Foreign Office. Many were in receipt of retired pay, which was an extremely convenient arrangement for SIS as it saved it spending money on salaries. This was important as the Secret Service Committee had recommended in 1921 that SIS be funded

*F.W. Winterbotham, *The Nazi Connection* (Weidenfeld & Nicolson, 1978).

entirely from the Foreign Office Secret Vote. As mentioned at the end of the last chapter, Cumming had worked out, before he died, that salaries for the year 1923-4 would total £20,600 for the twenty-five Passport Control Officers and that the entire network would cost £53,800 a year to maintain, so all savings were much appreciated.

To maintain such economies, Sinclair had the choice of keeping Stations undermanned or closing some down. Surprisingly it seems that one of the sacrifices he decided to make was not to open a Station in Moscow, although the Zinoviev Letter fiasco had highlighted the need for a base there and Sinclair, like his predecessor Cumming, had identified Soviet Russia as his principal target. Perhaps Sinclair was mindful of Boyce's visit to the Lubyanka in 1918. Whatever it was that influenced him, he appears to have shelved the idea of a Moscow Station for a decade; instead a representative was infiltrated into the country under the cover of a building project.

Unfortunately, under Cumming a considerable amount of SIS energy and time had been devoted to Soviet Russia with no great success: this policy had two unhappy results. The first was an understandable reduction in the credibility placed on reports emanating from SIS, particularly by the Cabinet and the Foreign Office, and the second was that very little notice had been taken of Germany. This last was to have serious consequences. A review of the headquarters' organization of Passport Control Officers in the late 1920s illustrates this point well for it shows the overseas Stations seemingly ringing the Soviet Union; the rise to power of the Nazis in Germany was not being monitored nearly so closely.

Harold and Archie Gibson covered the western Soviet flank and Harry Carr was promoted in Helsinki to replace Boyce and reinforce the existing Stations at Tallinn (Major Giffey) and Riga (Captain Sillem). The other principal Stations were Stockholm (J.J. Hitching), Warsaw (Captain Marshall) and Vienna (A.E. Forbes Dennis), which was closed down temporarily in 1927 because of pressure from the Treasury. There were also important Stations at Prague (E.G.P. Norman), Sofia (Alex Elder), Bucharest (Edward Boxshall), Budapest (Captain E.C. Kensington), Berne (Major Langley) and Athens (F.B. Welch). The only extra-European Stations were New York (Captain H.B. Taylor), Buenos Aires (Captain Connon Thomson), Yokohama (Colonel Gunn), Beirut (E.G. Thomson), and Vladivostok (F.B. Kirby).

Since the Great War it had been the custom for individual Stations to concentrate on collecting information on their neighbours, rather than on the country they were stationed in, to avoid falling into disfavour with their hosts. In particular, those close to Russia were asked to find out everything possible about the Soviet Union.

In doing this, Sinclair was following a trend going back to Victorian times when Disraeli and Palmerston had always kept a wary eye on Czarist expansion policies. The rise of the Bolsheviks had not assuaged British fears, and proof of Communist interference in India and Ireland in the 1920s and the breaking of the 1921 trade agreement by the Soviets had made that country SIS's principal target.

MI5 and most of Whitehall agreed with this view: they too saw the Soviet Union as the empire's major source of instability and subversion. This can now be seen to have been something of a distraction, but it was the accepted view of the time so they were not alone in their misapprehension. Moreover, the SIS was in existence to provide other government departments with secret intelligence. There was little mileage in offering material that would remain 'unsold', so SIS inevitably concentrated on providing what was wanted, which was data about Russia.

To obtain military intelligence about the Red Army and political information concerning future Soviet intentions, SIS relied heavily on groups of exiled White Russians. Support for these groups was justified on the grounds that they enjoyed good covert channels of communication with sympathizers inside the Soviet regime. Unfortunately, however, these groups exaggerated their own importance and, indeed, the military strength of the Red Army. It was not until much later that it became widely accepted that Russia's largely agricultural peasant population was finding it hard to cope with overnight industrialization, because émigré groups based in Paris and Istanbul were providing an entirely different picture. In fact, it was France who first reported that Stalin had begun decimating the Red Army officer corps, but acceptance of these facts in Whitehall was slow.

SIS, therefore, was spending much time in the 1920s collecting misinformation about Russia; meanwhile, Germany was failing to keep the terms of the 1919 Treaty of Versailles.

SIS officers sent their intelligence to London either in the form of a periodic report written in longhand or in a coded telegram. In order to distinguish SIS information from the regular Foreign Office traffic a new system was introduced, for there was at that time no separate channel of communication for SIS. This new 'CX' system was introduced by Sinclair and Maurice Jeffes.

Jeffes, the son of the former British consul in Belgium, had been educated entirely on the Continent, first in Brussels and then at Heidelberg University. In 1916 he had joined up with the Royal West Surreys and had subsequently transferred to the newly created Intelligence Corps for work with the SIS networks in Belgium. In 1919 he had joined C's staff as Head of the Paris Station, and had later been appointed Head of Station in New York in succession to Norman Thwaites who wished to stand for Parliament. (In 1924 Thwaites unsuccessfully contested the Hillsborough Division of Sheffield for the Conservatives.) The 'CX' system, developed by

Jeffes and Sinclair, consisted of a two- or three-digit prefix on SIS telegrams which immediately identified their recipient to the Foreign Office clerks. 'CX' indicated a message personal to the Chief, while 'CXG' was the more general traffic which was handled by one of Sinclair's two 'G' officers.

The 'G' officers were the individual case officers who supervised the incoming intelligence from the Stations in their geographical region. A decade later there were to be four such 'G' officers, but in the late 1920s there was simply Bertie Maw to handle all the European traffic and Colonel Edward Peal to deal with the rest. Further, to identify the sending Stations each was given a five-figure code number, the first two digits of which related to the host country. Thus Denmark was always referred to as 19000, Romania 14000, France 27000, Holland 33000, etc. The system also included Station personnel and even the agents. The Head of Station in, say, Madrid (Captain Hollocombe) would be known as 23100, and his deputy as 23200. Agents recruited by an SIS officer based at an overseas Station would be registered as a further number. Thus the sixth agent recruited by the Assistant Passport Control Officer in Helsinki would be referred to as 21306 and a message from the Head of Station to his 'G' officer would be prefixed 'CXG/21100'. The code referred only to the Stations, so if the Head of Station in Oslo (26100) was appointed to Lisbon (24000) he would acquire a new code number (24100).

For their part the headquarters' staff in London were divided into sections identified by a system of Roman numerals designed to prevent confusion with the Stations. Because their principal role was to distribute the information gleaned from the Stations, they were known as 'Circulating Sections'. Initially there were only three: Section I dealt with political matters; Section II, the War Office section, liaised with all the military; and Section III liaised with the Admiralty. At the end of the Great War, and as a result of pressure from the Chief of the Air Staff, Air Chief Marshal (Lord) Trenchard, Section IV, the air section, was added and, later still, a security and counter-espionage unit, Section V, was introduced.

The head of each section was identified by the addition of an alphabetical suffix to the relevant Roman numeral. Thus the head of the military section, Stewart Menzies, was known as IIa and his assistant, Humphrey Plowden, as IIb; the head of the naval section, Captain 'Barmy' Russell RN, was known as IIIa, and so on. Stewart Menzies DSO, MC, it may be remembered, had been Adjutant of the 2nd Life Guards and had then joined Haig's counter-espionage division at Montreuil in 1915.

It was in part the Treasury's persuadion which led Sinclair to depend upon the cover of the Passport Control Office which had been developed by Cumming, because each Station enjoyed a regular income in the local currency from visa fees. Visitors to the UK and to certain other territories of the Empire were required to submit their travel documents so an official visa stamp could be issued for which they had to pay. The man selected in 1919 by Cumming to oversee the PCO organization had been Major Herbert Spencer, a Boer War veteran who had served in Belgium during the Great War before joining SIS in 1919. His headquarters in London consisted of himself, an assistant (H.E. Parkin), a secretarial staff of five, a codist (Miss Montgomery), a transport officer (C. O'Neill Crowley) and a porter. This was the sum total of people actually devoted to genuine visa work. The rest of the PCO staff in London were SIS officers, with the majority established in independent premises throughout Europe; officially they did not enjoy any diplomatic immunity. Their exact relationship with the Foreign Office, and indeed the particular British Embassy in the host country, very largely depended on the personality of the individual CPOs. Their exact status was the subject of much internal debate, and the Foreign Office reluctantly agreed that where it was absolutely essential a CPO might be given a diplomatic title, such as 'Honorary Vice-Consul', so as to discourage a hostile local police chief from asserting himself. The difficulties faced by the PCOs because of their ambiguous positions were legion. The official line in France, for example, was that it was 'open to objection to claim that Passport Control Officers were entitled to privilege as members of the embassy staff since they were not performing diplomatic functions under the direct orders of the Ambassador.' In February 1925 the Czechoslovak Ministry of Foreign Affairs inquired about the 'title, designation and nationality' of the Head of Station in Prague, Mr L.A. Hudson. The British Minister confirmed that Hudson 'should be regarded as a member of the staff of His Majesty's Legation', but when the Czech authorities challenged a large consignment of duty-free wines and spirits destined for Hudson the Foreign Office backed down, explaining that 'Mr Hudson's status was technically not such as to make his case at all a good one'. In 1928 Meiklejohn's successor in Riga, Norman Dewhurst, devoted much effort to obtaining an insurance policy for his motor-car. Apparently the insurance company needed to know his exact status, whilst the Foreign Office was hesitant even to acknowledge his existence. The Foreign Office invariably displayed considerable reluctance to get involved in what it regarded as the very dubious activities of the CPOs, and as a rule resisted including the name of a CPO in the Diplomatic List.

Dewhurst was subsequently replaced by Leslie Nicholson, who took the question of diplomatic status into his own hands. In August 1936 he simply persuaded the British Minister, Sir Hughe Knatchbull-Hugessen, to appoint him an honorary attaché. The Foreign Office felt that this was 'undesirable' and commented:

Such appointments can only be made by the Secretary of State and no one can properly be regarded as having been appointed to a Mission abroad until the appropriate minute of appointment has been initialled by the Secretary of State. This was never done in the case of Mr Nicholson and strictly speaking therefore, he is not honorary attaché in Riga, at all events from the point of view of the Foreign Office. There have, of course, been cases when persons specially attached to Missions abroad for short periods have been given the title of honorary attaché to get them on the foreign government's diplomatic list and give them some kind of official standing. The case of Captain de Gaury at Jedda and Lieutenant Cotton at Addis Ababa are recent examples, while the attached file shows that two years ago an army officer on language duty at Riga was made honorary attaché at the Legation there for a few months. It is, however, I think, obviously undesirable that this practice of camouflaging officials as honorary attachés should be extended, and this seems particularly so in the case of passport control officers.

Very occasionally Sinclair would intervene, as in the case of Frank Foley (who obtained his diplomatic status in 1927 after seven years as the CPO in Berlin), and Colonel Shelley in Warsaw in 1936. The Foreign Office also voiced strong objections to officers who had held Passport Control jobs being appointed military attachés. It was 'undesirable', as was the use of SIS officers in routine consular work. A senior Foreign Office official on a visit to Riga in October 1933 commented:

The practice of deputing a Passport Control Officer to take charge of a Consulate is one which I think personally should never be adopted, for it is incompatible with the sound principle that no member of the staff of a Consulate should be associated with the hidden ramifications of 'Passport Control'.

The official tactfully went on to add: 'My objection is purely one of principle, for Mr Berry has frequently taken charge of the Legation and Consulate in Kovno without untoward results.'

The amount of cash flowing into each Passport Control Office now began to cause problems. Scarcely a single Station was not without its own financial scandal, and each incident had to be investigated by the SIS paymaster, Commander Percy Sykes. Sykes had qualified as a chartered accountant in 1897 and had joined the Royal Navy as an assistant paymaster after five years in a City accountants' office. In 1915 he transferred to the newly formed Royal Naval Armoured Car Division, and at the end of the war joined SIS to look after its finances. It will be remembered that Cumming had chosen Sykes to be one of the witnesses to his will in 1920.

SIS's financial troubles began in Nicosia in 1929, when three locally recruited clerks were found to be running a private service to Jews unable to meet the financial qualifications required for migration to Palestine. (At that time Palestine was a Mandate administered by Britain for the League of Nations, and the British required all prospective immigrants to obtain a $10 visa and to show assets of $10,000 so that they would not be a financial burden on the taxpayer when they arrived in Palestine.) The three local clerks were prosecuted. During the same year, the reopened Vienna Station experienced financial embarrassments, as did Athens and Prague. So did the Warsaw Station in 1930 and 1932; both times for illegal trafficking in visas for Palestine. In 1935 Lieutenant-Commander John Martin RN, the Head of the Stockholm Station, reported a 'shortfall in fees', and the following year there was yet another case of fraud in Warsaw. In 1937 Brussels, The Hague, Rome and Rotterdam were unable to balance their books and account for all the visa stamps issued.

The experience in Warsaw was especially embarrassing because the Foreign Secretary became involved. Hamilton-Stokes had been the Head of Station in Warsaw until June 1936, when he was transferred to Madrid and replaced by Colonel Shelley. When Shelley arrived, he found a large but well-organized Passport Control Office staff and inevitably he left much of the day-to-day affairs of the PCO to his deputy Head of Station, Captain H. T. Handscombe. He, in turn, left much of the visa business to the locally employed personnel, and this led to trouble. In July 1936 the Polish police arrested three men on a charge of extortion. According to the evidence of seven prospective emigrants to Palestine, the British PCO staff were running a black market in visas. All three suspects were Polish clerks who had been taken on by Hamilton-Stokes to cope with the flood of Jewish applicants. Immigrants who could show the necessary assets were granted A1 immigrant status and speeded on their way; for the rest, the formalities were complicated and time-consuming. Evidently the three Poles had decided to speed up the system and make a fortune into the bargain. The racket relied on the intervention of three Jewish intermediaries, Jakob Dudler, Anszel Gurfinkel and Lejzor Finkielkraut, who would approach the desperate refugees and offer assistance ... at a price. A Zionist organization in Warsaw complained to the police and identified a PCO employee, Serafin Czernikow, saying that he was selling Palestine permits corruptly.

Understandably neither Shelley nor Handscombe were anxious to give evidence in a public court about the PCO, but the Zionists pressed the police to bring a prosecution. The British Ambassador was sufficiently concerned about the possible consequences of the affair to write to Lord Halifax, the Foreign Secretary, in August 1936:

In view of the special position of the Passport Control Office and of the fact that the name of the present Passport Control Officer has not been placed on the diplomatic list (please see in this connection your telegram No. 49 of June 11th), I am uncertain as to whether or not the Polish authorities are within their rights in requiring the attendance of Major Shelley or Captain Handscombe in court, and I shall be glad of your guidance as to the attitude which I should adopt in the event of summonses being served upon them. From a practical point of view it seems undesirable to allow these officers to appear in court, since they might well be asked questions about the internal affairs of the Passport Control Office which it would be inexpedient for them to answer.

Fortunately the Warsaw police conducted a very thorough investigation which concluded that there had indeed been a racket at the PCO, but Czernikow had been denounced because he had refused to participate in it.

The rise of the Nazis to power in Germany during the early 1930s increased the demand for emigration visas to Palestine, which led to some Passport Control Offices being inundated with requests for these travel documents, especially in Berlin, Vienna, Warsaw and The Hague. Inevitably a large number of those applying were unable to meet the financial qualifications; in desperation they resorted to offering bribes to PCO staff. This came to light when, on 4 September 1936, London received the news that Major Hugh Reginald Dalton at The Hague had committed suicide.

When the news of Dalton's death reached Sinclair, he ordered an immediate investigation and chose a trusted senior officer, Valentine Vivian, to conduct it. Vivian, the son of Comley Vivian, the Victorian portrait painter, had been recruited into SIS from the Indian police by Smith-Cumming in 1923. Vivian discovered several discrepancies in Dalton's accounts and called in the SIS paymaster, Percy Sykes. Together Vivian and Sykes concluded that Dalton had taken his own life, and that he was guilty of the misappropriation of Palestine funds.

Dalton had been posted to The Hague some years earlier and by 1936 had been the senior SIS officer in the Netherlands, an out-Station in Rotterdam having been closed in the late 1920s as an economy measure. Dalton, like many other European CPOs, had found himself besieged by Jewish visa applicants. The competition amongst the refugees to be included in the British quotas for Palestine had been intense, and Dalton apparently had been unable to resist the temptation presented by the large sums of cash paid by Jews for their vital travel documents. When Dalton had embezzled the currency equivalent of £2,896, he shot himself. When Vivian and Sykes eventually closed the Dalton file, they recommended to the CSS that a system of surprise Station inspections be instituted.

Passport Control Officers were, of course, meant to be collecting information to send back to London and providing reasoned assessments about what was going on in Germany and in neighbouring countries; they were not meant to be spending all their time in routine office work. As a result, the actual inspection of travel documents and the issuing of visas were usually left to an assistant, who probably employed two or three locally recruited clerks to do the day-to-day work. However, wherever the demand for visas was extremely heavy, it tended to lead to permanent disruption of intelligence gathering. It became so bad, for example, at the Warsaw Station that a special Palestine bureau had to be opened, which was staffed jointly with individuals from various Jewish charitable organizations. However, in some cases the local Jewish communities were hostile and such arrangements were impossible. In these circumstances the PCOs were overworked to the point of collapse. In December 1938 the Head of Station in Prague, Harold Gibson, decided to conduct an experiment and monitor the number of incoming requests for assistance from refugees. His Passport Control Office consisted of himself, two additional temporary Examiners (Hindle and Philips), two secretaries and a messenger. The astonishing daily average was sixty letters received, seventy-five letters sent, sixty telephone calls in and approximately 110 visitors: all to be dealt with in three cramped rooms in the British Legation. As well as coping with this volume of business, Gibson was expected to liaise with the Czech Deuxième Bureau, run agents into Germany and find time to make his twice annual reporting visits to London. The task was an impossible one, and the same thing was happening all over Eastern Europe in the most vital SIS outposts. At one point in Vienna, for example, the Head of Station, George Berry, received 2,500 visa applications a month. He calculated that each Examiner could interview a maximum of thirty people a day. In some places, therefore, Palestinian visa applications were swamping SIS, rendering the Passport Officers incapable of carrying out their proper duties.

Short of officers and staff, and with those who were there frequently inundated with visa requirements, the burden and responsibility for developing SIS networks within Nazi Germany fell upon those in the bordering neighbour Stations in Warsaw, Prague, Berne, Paris, Brussels, Copenhagen and The Hague: by 1936 these had become the front line. Dalton's suicide at The Hague was, therefore, a major blow.

As the 1930s progressed, London realized that it was receiving insufficient factual information from its hard-worked Section heads, all too much of it was merely a flow of political gossip; more technical data was required and greater detail on economic statistics and military installations.

One development which reflected this change in emphasis was the introduction in January 1930 of an air section at Broadway Buildings in Victoria, an SIS office directly behind, and linked to, 21 Queen Anne's Gate. The man chosen to head the new section was Wing-Commander Frederick W. Winterbotham, who had trained in the Royal Flying Corps, been a prisoner of war in Germany and had then been seconded to SIS on the recommendation of the Director of Air Intelligence, Charles Blount, and his deputy Air Commodore Archibald Boyle.

Winterbotham's initial task was to assess Soviet air strength, but he soon discovered from SIS's White Russian networks that little threat was posed by the ill-equipped and badly led Red Air Force. What technical assistance the Soviets were getting came from Germany, so he turned his attention there.

The Secret Intelligence Service inside Germany was certainly spread thinly on the ground: there were two senior officers in Berlin and four out-Stations at Frankfurt (Captain MacMichael), Cologne (J. Lennstrand),

Hamburg (G. La Touche) and Munich (A.G. Tyler), all of whom had a healthy respect for the efficiency of the Gestapo and Abwehr, so all messages to London were sent via King's Messengers. The two senior officers in Berlin were Captain Frank Foley and Major Timothy Breen. Foley, who had served as an intelligence officer during the Great War and was in danger of having his offices swamped by Jewish refugees, had succeeded Breen as Chief Passport Officer in 1921; he remained in Berlin until 1939. Breen had transferred in 1921 from CPO to the British Embassy with the rank of First Secretary and the nominal role of press secretary. He remained based in the Embassy itself until 1937. As Press Attaché, Breen was in a position to make valuable contacts among the foreign press community. Two important sources for him were Ian Colvin and Sefton Delmer, both distinguished British journalists who had developed close links with the regime and its opponents. The Berlin Station was thus able to provide Section I with detailed assessments of the political situation in Germany and keep Broadway abreast of changes inside the Nazi Party, but there was little opportunity to obtain accurate reports of Germany's military build-up. It is no exaggeration to say that military intelligence concerning the Luftwaffe and the Wehrmacht was limited to what the Military Attachés could pick up and such information that Fred Winterbotham could extract from his main agent, Baron William de Ropp.

William de Ropp was an émigré aristocrat in his forties, from one of the Baltic states annexed by the Soviet Union. He looked like 'a perfectly normal Englishman, about 5 foot 10, with fair hair, a slightly reddish moustache and blue eyes, dressed in a good English suit'. He lived with his English wife in Berlin and was thoroughly Anglophile, having been commissioned into the Wiltshire Regiment and then transferred to the Royal Flying Corps during the Great War. Winterbotham's first mission to Berlin took place in February 1934, the culmination of three years spent building up the local standing of de Ropp. As well as occasionally contributing to *The Times*, de Ropp, under an arrangement made by SIS, was appointed German representative of the Bristol Aircraft Company; this opened many doors for him in Berlin and he was able to cultivate a number of senior Nazi politicians, including Alfred Rosenberg. Indeed, de Ropp was sufficiently well placed by 1934 to introduce Winterbotham to Hitler. The visit was so successful that Winterbotham was invited to return for the 1935 Nuremberg rally and for further visits during the following three years. On all these trips he took care to avoid contacting the local SIS Stations.

Whilst in Germany, Winterbotham obtained information about the detailed build-up of the new Luftwaffe, the new aerodromes being built, types of aero engines being constructed at the Messerschmitt, Junker, Heinkel and Daimler-Benz factories, as well as any intelligence he could find on Hitler's intentions. He heard about the dangers and difficulties of training

Stukas to dive and recognized the part these planes were destined to play in Hitler's *Blitzkrieg* strategy, but he found the RAF extremely sceptical. There was just not enough similar information coming in from other sources for a pattern to be discernible. Too few agents and informants meant insufficient breadth and depth of comparable data. Although Winterbotham's depressing intelligence reports on German rearmament were believed by Sinclair and Archie Boyle, they failed to impress Whitehall, and his first mission to Germany resulted in a major row with the Foreign Office. It took the view that Winterbotham's German visits were having political consequences, so Sinclair was asked to limit his excursions.

Whitehall's dissatisfaction with the Secret Intelligence Service was increased by receiving little warning of Italy's African adventure into Abyssinia in 1935, and several departments in Whitehall demanded an explanation. Sinclair was quick to respond. He pointed out that the Defence Requirements Sub-Committee of the Committee of Imperial Defence had already reported on the inadequacy of SIS's finances, and he stressed that unless he received further substantial funds more SIS stations abroad would be closed down. As it was, SIS was pared to the bone and SIS's expenditure was currently no more than the normal cost of maintaining one Royal Navy destroyer in home waters. In February 1936 the Cabinet approved a modest increase, but this was not enough to reopen the lost Stations.

Later the same year, in the spring, Germany's occupation of the Rhineland highlighted the problem. If SIS could not afford to operate efficiently in Western Europe, a matter of a few hundred miles from London, how could the Service be expected to provide comprehensive reports from further afield? The Cabinet reluctantly approved a further, interim grant to SIS, but the sum involved was too small to make any difference. Throughout the crisis Sinclair relied almost entirely on the Paris Station, which in turn depended heavily on the two French intelligence organizations, the Deuxième Bureau (headed by General Gauche) and the Service de Renseignments (headed by Colonel Louis Rivet).

One significant result of the collaboration with SIS's French counterparts was a decision to fund a programme of covert aerial reconnaissance. The Paris Station learned that the French had succeeded in photographing almost all of the German frontier region. Encouraged by this development, Fred Winterbotham was authorized to set up a commercial front in Paris, the Aeronautical Research and Sales Corporation. By March 1939 the company, which was a joint SIS/French venture, had purchased a pair of twin-engined Lockheed 12A aircraft, and had hired a colourful Australian pilot, Sidney Cotton, to undertake a series of flights over German territory. The first aircraft was fitted with concealed Leica cameras and quickly proved itself. At the end of April Cotton and his Canadian co-pilot, Robert

Niven, moved their base to England and continued to fly over Germany for the rest of the summer from Heston. As additional cover SIS provided Cotton with travel documents identifying him as a film director seeking movie locations in Europe. Although Cotton's enterprise produced a wealth of information for interpretation, his unorthodox approach was not well received by the RAF. Indeed, it was not until the war had actually broken out that the RAF conceded that a specialist unit ought to be formed to co-ordinate the execution and analysis of aerial photo-reconnaissance flights.

Slowly and steadily Whitehall's belief in the SIS was being undermined and eroded. When information was needed, it was not forthcoming. When it was available, it did not seem credible. To add to this, the Foreign Office found SIS people created problems both political, economic and diplomatic. With the Foreign Office determined to place restrictions on SIS activities, the burden of acquiring technical and other information from Germany was falling on Passport Officers at Stations in neighbouring countries, and it was against this background that the Germans pulled off a major coup against one of SIS's most vital Stations, The Hague.

It will be remembered that SIS's man at The Hague, Major Hugh Dalton, had committed suicide in September 1936. Dalton had been succeeded by Monty Chidson, who had been a gunner in the Great War and had transferred to the Royal Flying Corps at its inception. Chidson had distinguished himself as a pilot and shot down the first enemy aircraft over England, a Zeppelin, in 1915. In 1915 he had been shot down and taken prisoner and, during his months in a prisoner-of-war camp, he had developed a method of communicating with England. He took up carving wood and secreted an intelligence message into each item mailed home. His family had been mystified by the arrival of the carvings, all labelled to fictitious relatives, and had consulted the War Office. In due course MI5 had examined the wood-work and had discovered the hidden messages. After the war, the head of MI5, Captain Vernon Kell, had offered Chidson a job, and arranged for him to investigate alleged German atrocities. He had then been posted to Gibraltar as Defence Security Officer (DSO), as MI5's regional representatives were called, and on his return to London in 1929 he had accepted an offer from Admiral Sinclair to represent the SIS in Vienna. After two years there, he had gone to Bucharest as Head of Station, and it was from there that he had been asked to clear up the mess left by Major Dalton at The Hague. Chidson was particularly well qualified for the post because his wife was Dutch and he spoke the language fluently.

However, like anyone arriving in a new job, Chidson relied on the staff he found at The Hague for guidance and on one person in particular, Adrianus Vrinten, a veteran SIS employee and former Dutch Ministry of Justice investigator who liaised with the local authorities. With SIS financial support, Vrinten had built up a small detective bureau specializing in credit inquiries. In fact, the agency was a cover for his activities for SIS and was run in his absence by his partner, a former SIS agent named Zaal.

One of Vrinten's responsibilities was the recruitment of local labour, and on the recommendation of Zaal, he introduced Chidson to a young candidate named Folkert van Koutrik. Even though van Koutrik was married to a German wife, he was taken on and given relatively unimportant work to do. One of his tasks was to follow and report on the movements of a retired German naval officer living in The Hague. The retired officer, Traugott Protze, was suspected by SIS of also being an agent of the Abwehr, and they were right. However, Protze was no mere novice and quickly spotted van Koutrik. Having identified van Koutrik as a British agent, Protze proceeded to recruit him as a double agent, paying substantially better wages than SIS. As we shall see, this penetration was to have disastrous consequences for SIS.

By recruiting Folkert van Koutrik, the Germans obtained a junior, but nevertheless well-placed, source within The Hague Station, and it was one they used to their advantage. One of van Koutrik's jobs was to observe and protect a certain German diplomat in The Hague, who was one of the Station's most prized agents. The agent kept a rendezvous with the Head of Station and van Koutrik was occasionally employed to observe the proceedings from a distance and ensure that no one else was keeping watch, but he never learnt the agent's real name which was, in fact, Wolfgang zu Putlitz. However, not knowing his name did not stop van Koutrik telling Protze of the Abwehr enough about the mysterious agent to thoroughly alarm Protze and for him to tell the German Minister, Count Zech-Bürckersroda, that one of his German Embassy staff was a British agent.

In fact, zu Putlitz had been supplying information to Valentine Vivian and MI5 since June 1934, when he had first been posted to the German Embassy in London. There he had met another ardent anti-Nazi, Iona von Ustinov, who had been the German Press Attaché. Ustinov, known to his friends as Klop, had been friendly with zu Putlitz in Germany and had introduced him to Sir Robert Vansittart, the Permanent Under-Secretary at the Foreign Office. When Ustinov (whose son Peter was to become the well-known actor) decided to defect, he had arranged for zu Putlitz to take over as MI5's principal source of information in the German Embassy. Furthermore Ustinov, who had adopted the cover-name 'Middleton-Pendleton', had persuaded his recruit, zu Putlitz, to increase his standing with the German diplomatic corps by joining the Nazi Party. Reluctantly zu Putlitz had agreed, and for four years had kept Ustinov (and his MI5 case officer, Dick White) and the Foreign Office (in the person of Vansittart) in touch with everything that took place within the German Embassy in London. In May 1938 zu Putlitz had been transferred to the German

Legation in The Hague and had continued to supply SIS with high-grade information for a further sixteen months.

The fact that zu Putlitz had been working for MI5 for some time remained a closely guarded secret (although some members of the SIS Station in The Hague were eventually to be informed). This led to an extraordinary incident early in August 1939. Two members of the British Embassy in The Hague decided to take a long tour through Eastern Europe during their vacation, which they were going to take in September. They were naturally anxious that they should not be trapped by a war, so they both decided to sound out their contacts on the likelihood of hostilities breaking out. The younger of the pair, an honorary attaché named Nicholas Elliott, was friendly with zu Putlitz. He asked him to dinner to inquire if Germany intended to interrupt their holiday. Zu Putlitz, believing that they both knew he was a British agent, said that as far as he knew the invasion of Poland would begin on 26 August although it might be delayed for a week. Elliott and his companion, the Press Attaché at the British Embassy, the Earl of Chichester, practically choked on their food and hastily ended the meal. They raced back to the Embassy and sent a long telegram to London warning the Foreign Office of the Germans' intentions. They also cancelled their holiday.

After the declaration of war on 3 September 1939, Zech-Bürckersroda, the German Minister, and Protze, the Abwehr officer, imparted the information to zu Putlitz that they knew that someone in the German Embassy was working as an agent for the British, for they had penetrated the SIS Passport Control Office at The Hague. Realizing that he might be betrayed at any moment, zu Putlitz decided to defect immediately to England. He got in touch with Ustinov in London, and Ustinov organized an escape plan through Chidson's replacement as CPO, Major Richard Stevens, involving a flight from Schiphol piloted by the famous Dutch long-distance airman Parmentier. The plan nearly failed at the last moment when the homosexual zu Putlitz refused to leave Holland without Willy, his valet. A car was sent to collect Willy and the party took off successfully. Once in London he again reported to SIS how close he had come to being discovered because of the SIS Station's insecurity. Efforts were made to trace the source of what was evidently an SIS leak, but nothing was discovered.

This last whole episode had sprung from changes brought about by Major Hugh Dalton's suicide in The Hague in 1936. Now Dalton's suicide was to have further consequences. During the course of their investigations into the reasons for Dalton's demise, the two SIS men sent from London, Vivian and Sykes, had learned that as well as selling certificates for travel to Palestine, Dalton had also been paying off a blackmailer. The blackmailer was one of his own staff, a naturalized British subject named John Hooper. Hooper, code-named KONRAD, was Dutch by birth and had discovered

Dalton's lucrative secret. When confronted by Vivian, Hooper made a confession and was taken off the payroll.

This was to prove a disastrous mistake, for Hooper had been approached by the Abwehr almost as soon as he had left SIS. At first he had become merely an occasional informant for his German contact, Traugott Protze, but by 1939 he had become an agent of considerable importance and had been passed on to an Abwehr counter-intelligence expert, Hermann J. Giskes.

Giskes served in Abwehr IIIF as deputy to the Section chief, Captain Adolf von Feldmann. Early in 1939 von Feldmann was posted to Portugal, and in his absence Giskes took over responsibility for supervising the penetration of the SIS Station in The Hague. During one of his first meetings with Hooper, Giskes learned the name of SIS's star agent in northern Germany. In all SIS correspondence the agent had been referred to as 33016, but inside the Station he was simply called 'Dr K'. He had been supplying SIS with top-grade intelligence since the end of the Great War, when he had set up a naval engineering consultancy business. His chief client had been the Reichsmarine and he was a regular visitor to most of the Baltic shipyards. Dr K's prospering business provided an ideal cover for his espionage activities, and SIS paid for his information by making dummy payments for non-existent manufacturing licences. The arrangement had worked well, and Dr K had been elected eventually to the board of the Federation of German Industries.

Hooper had learnt of Dr K's true identity when he had accompanied his SIS case officer and deputy Head of Station, Harry Hendricks, to a safe-house. The purpose of the visit had been a regular rendezvous, and through an accidental lapse in security Hooper had discovered that Dr K was a retired German naval officer named Otto Kreuger.

As soon as Giskes learnt Kreuger's name from Hooper, he arranged for Dr K's home in Godesberg to be placed under a twenty-four-hour watch. The surveillance operation continued for more than a month, but no evidence was found to support Hooper's claim. Kreuger was followed on his routine visits to the Blohm & Voss shipyards in Hamburg, and his trips to Holland were carefully monitored. Indeed his activities appeared so completely innocent that Giskes checked further with his contact within SIS, van Koutrik, whom he cross-examined about a certain Belgian named August de Fremery. Kreuger had once been seen to dine in the Dutch resort of Scheveningen with de Fremery and then both had visited a seaside villa together. Now van Koutrik revealed that 'August de Fremery' was, in fact, a cover-name used by the SIS deputy Head of Station at The Hague, Harry Hendricks.

Kreuger was arrested on 8 July 1939 and he promptly confessed to having supplied the British with German naval secrets. Two months later he committed suicide in his prison cell.

The loss of Dr K was a severe blow to SIS, but no one at The Hague Station guessed that Hooper had been responsible for his betrayal. In fact, shortly after this incident Hooper had returned to the Passport Control Office to improve his standing and had volunteered his services as a double agent. He explained that he had been approached by a German intelligence officer, who had proposed that Hooper should spy for him. The Head of Station at The Hague had relayed this offer to London and had received permission to take Hooper back on the strength. Giskes, however, was not fooled because his other source, van Koutrik, had reported Hooper's duplicity.

As well as torpedoing that particular scheme, van Koutrik had also been responsible for keeping the Abwehr informed of all SIS contacts with German opposition groups. These fledgling conspiracies were useful channels of information for SIS and The Hague Station had become the focus of a multitude of networks inside Germany. Most were based on Jewish refugee routes and underground political movements willing to trade with SIS in exchange for financial backing and the inducement of recognition in any post-Hitler government.

After the suicide of Major Dalton in 1936, the SIS Head of Station at The Hague had been Monty Chidson, but his time there had been short-lived, apparently because he had been unable to get on with his French opposite number from the Deuxième Bureau, Commandant Trutat. In any event, he was ordered back to London in 1937, which left a key post vacant. Under normal circumstances the job would have simply become another two-year tour of duty to an available senior SIS officer; instead a new recruit was assigned, Major Richard Stevens.

Stevens spoke fluent German, French and Russian and had been introduced to military intelligence whilst serving in an evaluation post in the North-West Frontier Province. His father had been British Minister in Athens. Although a novice by SIS standards, he was assured in London that he was being sent to a largely administrative post. The Hague Station was one of the largest in Europe (only Paris was bigger) and, since Dalton's suicide, was staffed by a greater than usual proportion of SIS regulars, backed by a smaller number of locally recruited Dutch personnel. In effect the Station ran itself, with such capable officers as Jan Hendricks, Lionel Loewe and Jack Hooper managing affairs. The Station was, with Berne and Brussels, the principal base of operations against Germany and, by the same token, had become an important target for the Nazis.

By the autumn of 1939 Stevens's Station had developed into the vital link between Broadway, London, and the dissident factions within Germany who were planning to eliminate Hitler. The participants ranged from Conservative monarchists to Social Democrats, but all pinned their faith in the British Government to lend their movements support and some definite terms with which they could sway the numerous waverers closer to the top of the Nazi regime.

Whenever approaches were made via SIS, which invariably originated with a member of the Berlin Embassy staff, Broadway passed on the message to Sir Robert Vansittart at the Foreign Office. If the subsequent exchanges implied an addition to the regular SIS sources, then neutral post office boxes in Holland were provided and serviced by Stevens's growing staff. These networks were run by such Germans as Baron Rudolf von Gerlach (code-named DICK), Count Felix von Spiegel-Diesenberg, and the youth leader, Theo Hespers. The organizations were already well planned and operated, as in the case of Gerhard Willems's WILLEM II, in which case only a minimum of SIS supervision was required, or else they required a degree of technical and financial support, as happened with BRIJNEN and PFAFFHAUSEN. In Austria SIS financed an ineffectual anti-Nazi group headed by the Archduke Otto of Habsburg.

The various anti-Nazi leaders who made contact with Downing Street during 1938 and 1939 included Ewald von Kleist-Schmenzin, who sent a peace proposal via the British Embassy's Counsellor, Sir George Ogilvie-Forbes. Kleist followed this up with a visit to London in August 1938, but received little official encouragement. Later in the same year Victor von Koerber arranged a similar visit with Mason Macfarlane, the British Military Attaché. The following year, in the middle of the deepening crisis, Dr Erich Kordt risked a trip to Sir Robert Vansittart, but again the trip proved futile.

Arguably the best connected of these emissaries was Kleist, who enjoyed close relations with the Abwehr chief, Admiral Canaris, and his deputy, Hans Oster. At the early stage in his negotiations Kleist grew exasperated with the attitude of the British Government and suggested to Canaris that the British Secret Service might collaborate with them to remove Hitler, even if this was not a policy endorsed by the Cabinet. Canaris warned against this idea, stating that SIS had been thoroughly penetrated and was therefore untrustworthy.

This, indeed, proved to be the case. Zu Putlitz had narrowly escaped to England, but many of the networks established from Stevens's SIS network in The Hague were not so lucky.

The loss of zu Putlitz as an agent was a blow for SIS, but he was by no means SIS's only senior German source. There was another important agent at work in Germany, run in tandem with the Czechs. The Chief Passport Officer in Prague since 1933 had been Harold Charles Lehrs Gibson, a Russian-speaking veteran SIS officer who had previously served in Constantinople (1919-21), Bucharest (1922-30) and Riga (1930-33). His Station, based in the British Legation, enjoyed a close relationship with the Czech Military Intelligence Service, headed by Colonel Dastich. In 1937

Secret Intelligence Service Administrative Accounts, 1935–6

STATION (HEAD)	PASSPORT CONTROL OFFICER	ASSISTANT PCO	PASSPORT EXAMINER	CLERKS MESSENGERS	RENT	GENERAL EXPEND.	TOTA
Vienna *Kendrick*	760		350	250 120	257	300	1,78
Budapest *Hindle*		550		300 120	143	145	1,14
Tallinn *Giffey*	870		350	250 50	160	120	1,64
Riga *Nicholson*	870	540	300	300 62	178	120	2,19
Brussels *Calthrop*	870		350	300 30	155	150	1,70
Sofia *Smith-Ross*		640	350	60	70	76	1,07
Prague *Gibson*	870			300 100	200	100	1,37
Copenhagen *O'Leary*	870	870		300 80	140	.155	1,40
Helsinki *Carr*	870		350	250 100 56	116	125	1,75
Paris *Dunderdale*	1,170	600	350 350 400	100 150 90 95 150	951	550	4,00
Berlin *Foley*	1,220		420 264 235	360 300 176 47	851	165	3,48
Athens *Crawford*		640	250	200 72	250	265	1,42
Rome *Dansey*	870			250 78	102	26	1,22
The Hague *Dalton*	870			250 60	240	250	1,43
Oslo *Newill*	870			300 100	167	175	1,44
Warsaw *Handscombe*	870		350 350	84	66	265	1,91
Stockholm *Martin*	870		500	300 100	110	118	1,88

STATION (HEAD)	PASSPORT CONTROL OFFICER	ASSISTANT PCO	PASSPORT EXAMINER	CLERKS MESSENGERS	RENT	GENERAL EXPEND.	TOTAL
New York Taylor	1,470	1,040	584 642 428	428 428 374	3,043	1,110	6,504
Istanbul Lefontaine	1,000		400	350 150 36	3	10	1,946
	15,190	4,010	7,523	8,356	4,225		39,304
					Postage		309
					Telegrams		863
					Travelling		688
					Exchange		9,373
					TOTAL		£50,536

Dastich was succeeded by Major Frantisek Moravec, who also proved to be favourably disposed towards the British.

The immediate advantage of the Gibson/Moravec relationship was access to the Czech networks in Germany and, in particular, to A–52. A–52 was one of Moravec's senior sources, who worked for purely pecuniary motives. He was, in fact, a Luftwaffe staff officer named Major Salm. Salm had been recruited by the Czechs in Zurich late in 1934 and had proved to have access to a mass of secret information concerning Goering's illegal German Air Force, which broke the terms of the 1919 Treaty of Versailles. Indeed, many of the SIS estimates of the Luftwaffe's strengths (which were suppressed by Baldwin and later Chamberlain) originated from him. Unfortunately, Salm's unjustifiably high personal wealth reached the ears of the Gestapo and he was arrested and executed in the summer of 1938.

However, all was not lost for Moravec had another agent in Germany, A–54, who had volunteered his services late in February 1937, in a letter sent direct to Moravec, postmarked Chomutov, a small town close to the Sudeten frontier. Moravec had provided a post office box number to reply to and had made it clear that he wanted to buy German secrets. At their very first meeting A–54 had established his credentials by producing some secret Czech plans and the name of the Abwehr agent who had betrayed them. He was Captain Emerich Kalman, a Czech staff officer. Once identified as an Abwehr agent, Kalman had been arrested, induced to confess and then been hanged.

After this somewhat dramatic introduction A–54 had settled into a pattern of regular meetings with Moravec, who eventually had succeeded in establishing his true identity. A-54 was Paul Thümmel, a senior Abwehr officer and long-time member of the Nazi Party. Thümmel enjoyed access to a goldmine of information concerning the organization and structure of both the Abwehr and the Sicherheitsdienst (SD), the Nazi Security Service. He had also produced a near-complete order of battle for the Wehrmacht and the Luftwaffe, and had given advance warnings of the German annexation of the Sudetenland and the invasions of Czechoslovakia and Poland, all of which were passed on to SIS's Head of Static in Prague, Gibson, and so to London.

A-54's detailed descriptions of Hitler's ans for the occupation of Czechoslovakia on 15 March 1939, which he delivered on 3 March, enabled the SIS Prague Station to make a number of contingency plans. Among them was the transfer of Moravec and his organization's financial resources to London. Gibson's strategy was to secure A-54's goodwill by arranging a plane for the escape of Moravec, his family and eleven of his key officers. Gibson also promised that the aircraft would have room for all of the Czech Intelligence Service's files.

When A-54's prediction that the Wehrmacht would take over Czechoslovakia on 15 March had been confirmed from other sources, Gibson carried Moravec's files to overnight storage at the British Embassy. The day before the German occupation a Dutch civil aircraft landed at Ruzyn, just outside Prague, and loaded Moravec and his party aboard. In the event Moravec left his wife and two daughters in Prague, preferring to secure the safety of an extra three Czech intelligence officers. The plane took a direct route to Amsterdam (overflying Germany on the way) and, after a brief refuelling stop, continued to Croydon Airport where a breach of security led to the entire group being photographed by the London newspapers. The following day the *Daily Mail* reported the arrival by air of a mysterious group of publicity-shy Czechs. Only a handful of senior SIS officers knew the truth: that Moravec was, in effect, delivering his best agent over to the British. Thümmel continued to supply SIS with high-grade information from inside the Abwehr until March 1942.

Admiral Hugh Sinclair's first sixteen years as Chief of SIS were made extremely difficult for him because he was starved of funds. This made him close much needed Stations and keep on too many rundown old pros from the Great War. Nor did he use what monies he had to great advantage: he spent too much on Russian intelligence from gullible émigré sources and too little elsewhere. As a result, he was caught napping by the rise of Nazism.

The Passport Control Office cover was also a mistake: it exacerbated relationships with the Foreign Office and laid the overworked, underpaid officers abroad open to bribes; financial peccadilloes took place which undermined morale. It led, too, to the suicide of Major Dalton. This led to the appointment of a new man who took too much upon trust from his subordinates and so gave the Abwehr a chance to obtain a toehold inside the SIS. Chidson's replacement by Stevens, a raw recruit trained in the North–West Frontier of India, in a most important post at a crucial time, was also to lead to grievous disaster.

During the inter-war period, SIS lacked clout in Whitehall. Cumming's Russian reports had lost the Service credibility, so that when officers like Winterbotham did field useful data, they were not believed. This lack of enthusiasm for SIS deepened in Whitehall when the Abyssinian and Rhineland *coups d'état* arrived unforeseen and unheralded by SIS. Sinclair's belated recognition of Germany as its principal target had meant that when Whitehall's demands for German intelligence began to increase, Sinclair was in no position to deliver. Good sources take years to develop and the hostile security climate in Nazi Germany made SIS's task an arduous one. In addition, SIS was fettered by frequent directives from the Foreign Office, who was anxious to prevent it from compromising its dealings with the Nazi regime. SIS was an important channel of communications for good intelligence information offered by the Germans themselves, but was not in itself a useful primary source.

However, there were some forward looking aspects to Sinclair's policies which came about as a result of his recognition of the meaning of the Anschluss: these I shall develop in the next chapter.

5

Anschluss
1938-9

In March 1938 the Wehrmacht marched over the Austrian frontier and proceeded to occupy the country. Five months later, on 17 August, the SIS Head of Station in Vienna, Captain Thomas Kendrick, was arrested near Freilassing, a town to the west of Salzburg. Kendrick, accompanied by his wife and chauffeur, had completed two-thirds of a journey to Munich, where he planned to stay the night before motoring on to London, when they were stopped by the Gestapo. Kendrick was driven back to Vienna, where he was lodged for the night in the Hotel Metropole, the Gestapo headquarters. His wife and chauffeur were released, but for the next two days Kendrick underwent a gruelling interrogation. In the meantime Kendrick's deputy, Kenneth Benton, alerted Broadway, and the two principal SIS secretaries in the Station, Margaret Holmes and Betty Hodgson, were evacuated. The arrest of such a senior SIS officer filled Sinclair with alarm, and Sir Nevile Henderson, the British Ambassador in Berlin, was requested to intervene. Kendrick was finally released at noon the following Saturday, 20 August, after having admitted various acts of espionage, and was allowed briefly to visit his apartment in Vienna before being expelled to Hungary. As soon as he arrived in Budapest, he signalled to Sinclair and then caught the first flight to London. He arrived at Croydon late on 22 August and described his ordeal to Sinclair the next morning. He was eventually given an administrative job at Broadway and later became an interrogator in a prisoner-of-war camp for Luftwaffe aircrews.

The arrest was an unfortunate one for all concerned. Kendrick himself had spent more than a dozen years in SIS and was now completely blown to the Germans. He denied having made any statement to the Gestapo, but subsequent reports in the German press made it clear that the Chief Passport Officer's dual role was well known in Vienna. The episode was to have repercussions all over Europe, for Sinclair felt that all the remaining British personnel should be evacuated from the Vienna Station as soon as possible. Thus Kendrick was followed back to England in 1938 by Misses Steedman, Wood, Birkett, Mapleston and Mrs Howe. It was then decided that as a precaution staff from the other two endangered Stations, Berlin and Prague, should also be withdrawn. Foley and his Assistant CPO, Mr Jacobsen, led a party of four secretaries home (Misses Lloyd, de Fossard, St Clair and Molesworth), while Gibson and Mr Mowbray accompanied Miss Williams to London. All were given a brief leave and, after a spell at Broadway, they volunteered to return to their Stations. This return to relative normality was the Chief's opportunity to make some important changes in personnel.

There was obviously no question of returning Kendrick to Station duties, so the Head of Station in Riga, George Berry, was appointed to Vienna in his place. Berry was swopped for Kendrick's deputy, Kenneth Benton. The Vienna Station, which was evidently something of a German target, was further reinforced by Victor Farrell, the Head of Station in neighbouring Budapest. Farrell was, in turn, replaced by Mr P.G. Brown. The SIS representation in the Eastern European theatre now consisted of Stations in Budapest (Captain Kensington), Prague (Gibson), Bucharest (Boxshall), Belgrade (Buckland) and Sofia (Smith-Ross). Throughout the Anschluss and the months following, the SIS networks based on these Stations had remained intact, but the temporary suspension of Berlin, Prague and Vienna had been a sobering experience for all concerned. At least Sinclair recognized it for what it was ... a warning of events to come.

The Anschluss served to convince Sinclair that war with Germany was inevitable and he became increasingly convinced that the Luftwaffe would mount a knock-out surprise attack on London. To counter this threat, Sinclair made preparations to transfer all his London-based sections to alternative headquarters in the country. Codes and ciphers were moved to Bletchley, communications and transmitters to Hanslope Park. He also made other determined efforts to get onto a war footing by creating a special unit which would take the war right into the enemy's camp.

Before explaining how this new unit, Section D, was set up, it is necessary to go back in time for a moment to 1935 when the Committee of Imperial Defence formed the Inter-Service Intelligence Committee (ISIC) in order to stop a log-jam developing in the co-ordination and distribution of SIS's information. The ISIC was designed to assess the performance of the various Service intelligence branches and to administer the end product, but it soon proved unworkable because the duplication of effort which had previously so hampered SIS, Naval Intelligence and, to a lesser extent, the European sections of the Directors of Military and Air Intelligence, continued. By June 1936 the shortcomings of the ISIC had become plain, and so the DMI proposed an alternative arrangement.

The suggested replacement of the ISIC was eagerly supported by the CID's Secretary, Maurice Hankey, and his newly appointed deputy (a post specially created, thus bringing the strength of the permanent CID Secretariat to eight), Colonel 'Pug' Ismay. The new body was to be named the

Joint Intelligence Sub-Committee (JIC) and, unlike its predecessor, would be provided with finance and a permanent staff. The Secretary of the Joint Planning Staff, Major Leslie Hollis RM, was appointed the JIC's first Secretary, a post he was to hold until June 1939. The membership of the JIC consisted of representatives of the three Service intelligence branches, chaired by a Foreign Office counsellor, Ralph Stevenson, who held this post until he went to Moscow in June 1939, when he was succeeded by William Cavendish-Bentinck (now the 9th Duke of Portland). One extra member was Desmond Morton from the Industrial Intelligence Centre (IIC), a semi-independent research unit created in 1930 (with the approval of Sinclair) to improve the flow of information about the German economy. It was not until May 1940 that MI5 and SIS were granted full membership status of the JIC.

The JIC proved to be lasting, and started its work by meeting fortnightly, an interval which was to reduce as the political and military situation in Europe deteriorated. News that the JIC had been formed was announced to the public by the Minister for the Co-ordination of Defence, Sir Thomas Inskip, on 19 February 1937, more than six months after its inception.

The apparent ease with which Hitler had managed to reassert himself in the Rhineland appalled many British politicians, and it served to underline Sinclair's growing fear of German militarism. In March 1938 Sinclair authorized the formation of a special unit, Section D, which would begin a detailed examination of alternative forms of warfare and operate under the cover title of the Statistical Research Department of the War Office. What Sinclair had in mind was, in plain language, sabotage, and the man chosen to look into this murky area was Major Laurence Grand, a thirty-seven-year-old Sapper and a Cambridge graduate. Grand was recommended for the post by Stewart Menzies, still Sinclair's Head of Section II, the military section. In only a matter of months Grand had succeeded in obtaining a large Victorian mansion, The Frythe, in Hertfordshire, not far from Welwyn, although Treasury limits restricted his activities to preparing lucid reports on the advantages of 'irregular warfare' conducted by well-organized and well-armed partisan units. His efforts were in part duplicated within the War Office by another Sapper, John Holland, who had served with Grand in Ireland during the Troubles. Shortly after Grand had been appointed to Section D Holland, who was in poor health, had been posted to GS(R), standing for General Staff (Research). GS(R) had no particular brief (and, indeed, consisted only of one officer plus a typist), but it gave Holland the freedom to concentrate on his special interest ... irregular tactics executed by regular forces.

The Director of Military Intelligence, General Henry Pownall, was not entirely pleased with the idea of Section D, although his deputy, Paddy Beaumont-Nesbitt, welcomed it. Opposition from such senior Whitehall Establishment figures as Pownall (who was to be knighted in 1940 and appointed Inspector-General of the Home Guard) meant that Grand was obliged to limit his activities to writing pamphlets expounding the advantages of guerrilla armies, in much the same way as did John Holland.

The whole concept of guerrilla warfare conducted in enemy territory (embracing espionage, counter-espionage, para-military and para-naval operations) was anathema to some for it was inevitably bound to involve varying degrees of illegal or unethical methods which would violate normal peacetime morality. Such an irregular force would also need to be endowed with special powers and privileges for communications, for transport, for cover from government departments or Embassies abroad, for equipment and weapons and for non-accountable funds, so it was bound to antagonize those who feared such privileges would be misused and monies misspent.

In March the following year, however, despite Pownall's misgivings, Grand and Holland, who by this date had established a common purpose and were sharing office premises, had set out their ideas for the expansion of Section D and submitted them to the Foreign Secretary, his Permanent Under-Secretary and the CIGS, Lord Gort. Halifax, Cadogan and Gort all approved of developing a resistance capability in territories threatened by Germany and gave the go-ahead to Grand and Holland. GS(R) was also authorized to hire extra help. Colin Gubbins, who had also been impressed by what he had seen in Ireland during the Troubles, joined. Later, in 1940, GS(R) and Section D were to merge to form Special Operations Executive (SOE).

Early in 1939 GS(R) was renamed Military Intelligence (Research), or MI(R), a label reflecting its new status in the military intelligence directorate, one that brought it, in theory at least, under the jurisdiction of the Director of Military Intelligence. Little else altered, however, and Grand and Holland combined their efforts informally to acquaint suitable candidates with the techniques of guerrilla operations. Such men were invited to attend short courses at The Frythe to gain an elementary grasp of high explosives; how to sabotage key industrial and military equipment, such as factories and power stations; how to murder; how to assist underground secret armies in enemy-occupied territory and how to create subversion.

During the summer of 1939 Gubbins was detached from MI(R) for two special missions: one down the Danube valley, the other to Poland, Latvia and Lithuania. On 25 August he travelled to Warsaw as the Chief of Staff to General Carton de Wiart, head of the British Military Mission to Poland. Accompanying him were two other MI(R) recruits, Harold Perkins (a former merchant navy officer and owner of a steel mill in Poland), (Sir) Peter Wilkinson from the Royal Fusiliers, Captain F.T. Davies (from Courtaulds), Captain Hazel (formerly of the Baltic Steamship Company), Major Hugh Curteis and Captain Routon. The mission was obliged to plan its escape from the advancing Wehrmacht almost as soon as it had arrived, and Gubbins took a route through Hungary and the Balkans, attended by Colonel J.P. Shelley, the SIS Head of Station in Warsaw, who was then in mourning for his Polish wife, and his two coding assistants. Wilkinson was later appointed head of the British Military Mission to the Czech and Polish forces in France and was responsible for helping General Sikorski extract the Polish General Staff from Biscarrosse, after the fall of France.

When Gubbins finally returned to England, General Carton de Wiart requested his attachment to the British Expeditionary Force to Norway, and Gubbins achieved a number of successes with his 'Striking Companies' (later to be termed 'commandos') before the evacuation.

Grand's deputy at Section D was Monty Chidson, who had been Head of Station at The Hague after Dalton's suicide. He was now given the task of forming a cadre of skilled saboteurs who could create chaos behind the German lines. Among their successes during 1940 were the rescue of Madame de Gaulle and the removal (by Monty Chidson) of Amsterdam's diamond reserves. Chidson was aided by Guy Burgess, who joined Section D in January 1939 from the BBC talks department. Chidson and Burgess established a training centre at Brickendonbury Hall, a large country house near Hertford (and the home of Lady Pearson, widow of Sir Edward Pearson), and placed a retired naval officer, Commander Frederic Peters RN, in command. Others drafted in to help put the Section D saboteurs through their paces were George Hill, who had been so active in Russia, and an explosives expert named Clark. They were joined by two former Shanghai police officers, Fairbairn and Sykes, who were appointed instructors in the art of silent killing and unarmed combat.

Peters continued to run Brickendonbury until July 1940, when he was returned to normal duties. He was later killed at Oran and was awarded a posthumous Victoria Cross.

Sinclair's determination to promote an 'irregular' operational capability was not the least of his watershed decisions. The Anschluss taught the senior hierarchy of SIS (if not the Treasury) some important lessons, and these were reflected in the importance he attached to counter-intelligence.

The SIS department charged with responsibility for counter-intelligence *per se* was Section V, a two-man unit headed by Valentine Vivian, the officer who had conducted the investigation into Dalton's suicide in 1936. Vivian was a close friend of the Head of Section II, Stewart Menzies, whom he had met whilst serving with the British Army of the Rhine in 1921. He was well suited to run Section V as he was highly experienced in all types of intelligence work. He had joined the Indian police in 1906 at the age of twenty and, during the Great War, he had seen action with the Indian army in Palestine and Turkey.

Vivian's department consisted of himself, his secretary, Miss Taylor, his assistant, a retired Indian police officer (and a chronic hypochondriac),

S.S.H. Mills, and his secretary, Miss Todd. Counter-intelligence has no geographical boundaries, so inevitably Vivian found that although his principal job was to compile up-to-date appreciations of hostile bodies, which in practice was chiefly the Comintern, he spent much of his time liaising with Brigadier Jasper Harker, the Director of MI5's 'B' Division, his deputy, Guy Liddell, and Colonel Alexander, the head of MI5's section dealing with Soviet-inspired subversion. Vivian's task was to create a semi-independent security service within SIS, and Sinclair instructed him to concentrate his efforts on the German intelligence organizations. Vivian's first move was to increase his obviously inadequate staff and he sent an offer of employment to Felix Cowgill, then Deputy Commissioner of the Special Branch in Calcutta. Cowgill had been in the Indian police since 1923, and, since March 1930, had served three Directors of the Central Intelligence Bureau in New Delhi as personal assistant: they were Sir David Petrie (who was Director during the period 1924-31), Sir Horace Williamson (1931-6) and Sir John Ewart (1936-9). He had become a leading authority on the activities of the Comintern and in 1933 had written an intelligence handbook on the subject of Communist subversion as it affected India. After consulting the Governor of Bengal, Lord Brabourne, Cowgill accepted Vivian's offer provided he increased the (tax-free) pay to £850 per annum. This was agreed by Sinclair and Cowgill began a long journey back to England, taking up his post in February 1939.

Cowgill found that although the overseas staff of SIS had been dramatically increased over the previous twelve months there was little centralized appreciation of the activities of the future enemy in the intelligence field. Reports from the Heads of Stations abroad were all channelled to their respective case officers, who compiled summaries for Malcolm Woollcombe and David Footman in the political section, Section I. They, in turn, distributed the intelligence to SIS's customers, the Services.

Cowgill regarded the system critically and saw a deep flaw in terms of counter-intelligence. All the overseas Stations were transmitting a steady flow of information, but none appeared to be devoting its efforts exclusively to the Germans. On the advice of Vivian, backed by Cowgill, the CSS was urged to expand Section V and appoint counter-intelligence officers at each of the overseas Stations. This idea was not well received by many of the more experienced CPOs, who resented the interference with their Stations. Paris Station, for example, complained that it did not need an extra officer who would report direct to London rather than via the Head of Station and the individual case officer in Broadway. Others resented the implication that they had perhaps not been executing a counter-intelligence role. In any event, Section V encountered stiff resistance to its plan to train and post specially briefed men.

Vivian and Cowgill did, however, score a success at The Hague, where

Major Richard Stevens was the Head of Station. Stevens had only discovered the details of Dalton's suicide and Chidson's removal on the
cocktail-party circuit in The Hague. Undaunted, he had moved into his
apartment over the shop in Nieuwe Parklaan and had begun to cement an
already well-established relationship with the Dutch and, in particular,
with General van Oorschot, their Director of Military Intelligence. Stevens
was a success in his new post, and also had the distinction of being the first
Head of Station to welcome a Section V officer. The Section V representative, Rodney Dennys, was the son of a British civil servant in Malaya. He
had been recruited by Vivian in 1937 after having left the London School
of Economics. Stevens and his staff accepted Dennys onto their strength
without difficulty, and the Brussels Station, headed by a veteran intelligence
officer, Colonel Calthrop, did the same, but they were certainly not the rule.
While Dennys was specifically attached to The Hague Station by Section
V, Colonel Calthrop agreed to second one of his existing officers, Keith
Liversidge, to counter-intelligence duties. The gradual expansion of Section V is given in chapter nine.

Sinclair had seen the writing on the wall just in time: in 1938 after the
Anschluss, he began to make positive commitments in preparation for war
by creating Section D for sabotage and guerrilla warfare and Section V for
counter-intelligence.

6

Stewart Menzies
1939

The opening of hostilities in September 1939 is an appropriate moment to make a formal review of the Secret Intelligence Service and Britain's other main intelligence gathering organizations.

Some thirty years earlier the Committee of Imperial Defence had authorized the creation of the Secret Service Bureau, which had divided itself into the home and foreign sections. This division of labour had survived the internal struggles in Whitehall and there still remained two dominant organizations: the Security Service (MI5) which had responsibility for all the territories of the Empire, and the Secret Intelligence Service (MI6) which undertook a less defensive role in the rest of the world. In September 1939 Kell was still Director-General of the Security Service, and had developed a sophisticated system of representatives abroad who were known as Defence Security Officers. In the cases of Canada and India, which both enjoyed semi-independent local security bureaus, Kell maintained an MI5 representative known as the Security Liaison Officer. In 1935 Combined Intelligence Far East (CIFE), a joint headquarters for the region, had been established in Hong Kong, and in 1939 it moved to Singapore. A similar organization, the Middle East Intelligence Centre (MEIC), was created somewhat belatedly in Cairo in 1939.

The Secret Intelligence Service was represented abroad initially by a chain of foreign Stations generally based on Passport Control Offices and staffed by regular SIS officers who maintained a fairly transparent cover as Chief Passport Officers. The PCOs were linked by wireless to the CSS's headquarters in London and the alternative centre of operations in Bletchley. The chief drawback to the PCOs were their concentration in Europe. The only Stations further afield were in New York (where Sir James Paget was the CPO), Buenos Aires and Istanbul. SIS was virtually unrepresented in the Middle East, although various British army garrisons had created local intelligence staffs.

There were two further problems associated with the PCOs. Firstly, as a result of economy measures imposed by the Treasury, most of the personnel based abroad were retired Royal Naval officers. Unfortunately, many of the CPOs were by no means wealthy and took the opportunity of being based abroad to avoid paying tax. This led to several cases where the local tax authorities decided to impose the local income tax; a row would ensue and the Foreign Office invariably failed to support the CSS's representative which, in turn, caused more dissension. Such cases occurred in New York to two successive CPOs, Captain George Taylor RN and Captain Sir James Paget RN, and in 1932 there was considerable acrimony when the Paris CPO, Maurice Jeffes, found he was being taxed twice, once by the Inland Revenue and again by the French! Jeffes protested to Broadway, but the Foreign Office declined to intervene. In February 1933 the British Ambassador in Paris, Lord Tyrell, was instructed that

the members of the Passport Control Office are full-time salaried officers engaged in no business activities beyond their official duties, but these are of a kind which are ordinarily entrusted to consular officers, and that it is hoped that in view of these considerations the French Govt may find it possible to exempt them from income tax on their official salaries, especially as the French officials similarly situated would be so exempt in the UK.

The second operational disadvantage to the Passport Control cover, as the Germans were not slow to realize, was that the British Secret Service representative in any particular capital could be identified by the simple expedient of visiting his office to apply for a visa.

Sinclair came to realize the danger of relying on such an overt system and took steps to rectify the situation by creating a second, continental Secret Service operating under commercial cover, which remained largely unknown to his own staff until the Venlo fiasco, which will be considered later in this chapter.

And what of Britain's other intelligence gathering organs? By far the largest was the Naval Intelligence Division, now under the leadership of Admiral John Godfrey. He maintained representatives, known as Naval Reporting Officers, in all the major Royal Naval bases abroad and his office in London received regular reports from volunteer observers aboard most British vessels. The NID was divided into more than a dozen separate departments, each with its own special responsibility. Their assessments of Germany's naval strength in 1939 were almost completely accurate in respect of surface ships, whose existence and performance could be verified with relative ease; but when it came to submarines, the NID and SIS did not agree.

According to the Anglo–German Naval Treaty of 1935, Germany was allowed to construct up to fifty-seven submarines. The NID was inclined to believe that this was indeed the German figure, but SIS's naval section, Section III, insisted that the Nazis had secretly built a further nine U-boats which were deployed in the Atlantic and thus difficult to trace. It was later established that the NID's assessment was correct, and that the SIS had been misled by inaccurate reports from unreliable agents.

Equally inaccurate were the assessments made by the Director of Military Intelligence. His principal informants were his military attachés posted to British Embassies abroad, and they in turn relied on their own observations and the acquisition of publicly available material. Whatever the reasons, the DMI's assessments were unjustifiably pessimistic. For example, in September 1939 the War Office estimated that the Wehrmacht possessed 5,000 tanks, of which 1,400 were judged to be medium tanks. The true figure was a total of 3,000, of which only 300 were medium tanks.

The relative newcomer to the intelligence establishment was the Air Intelligence Branch of the Air Ministry. Thanks to the combined efforts of Fred Winterbotham and the Air Attaché in Berlin, Group Captain John Vachell, who both undertook numerous risky aerial reconnaissance missions, the Air Intelligence Branch produced rather an accurate picture of the Luftwaffe's strength. Together these two officers provided the Chiefs of Staff with a comprehensive order of battle for the German Air Force, but their figures were later distorted by exaggerated projections of the German air industry's production capacity. In addition, the Air Intelligence Branch was handicapped by its ignorance of the technical specifications of individual German aircraft. It was only late in 1939 that the Air Ministry obtained the services of an artist whose job it was to sketch the dimensions of the various different Luftwaffe fighters and bombers. He was only employed on the understanding that he was officially listed as a cartographer!

It was the Government Code and Cipher School that was to hold the most promise for British Intelligence. In September 1939 it was firmly established at Bletchley Park under the cover title of Government Communications Headquarters (GCHQ), still under the leadership of that most remarkable cryptographer, Alistair Denniston. His deputy was (Sir) Edward Travis, who headed the naval section of GCHQ, an innovation made in 1924. Thereafter, an army section had been introduced (in 1930) and finally, in 1936, an air section.

GCHQ, which was still under the direct control of SIS, had been considerably helped in its search to decrypt German wireless traffic by French and Polish expertise. As we shall see, it was the Paris Station's liaison with the French Deuxième Bureau and the evacuated Polish cryptographic service that enabled GCHQ to acquire a treasured Enigma code machine. However, even with a specimen to tinker with, it was not until January 1940 that GCHQ experienced any significant success in breaking the elusive German Enigma keys.

This brief summary of the British Intelligence structure in September 1939 serves to illustrate the quality of the information reaching the three Services and the vulnerable position of the SIS Stations in Europe. It had been to improve this parlous situation, and shore up the Passport Control Offices, that Sinclair had authorized the development of an entirely separate ring of agents operating under commercial cover. The man at the centre of the network, which was known simply as Z, was a former MI5 officer named Claude Dansey.

The impetus behind Z came from Dansey, himself an extraordinarily 'larger than life' figure. His involvement in the world of Intelligence really pre-dated the Great War, and he had the widest possible range of friends, including such men as William Wiseman and Alexander Korda in America and Nubar Gulbenkian and Basil Zaharoff in the Middle East. All, at some time or another, undertook special missions for Dansey, who has in the past been variously described as 'ruthless' and 'bearlike'. However, to most of his colleagues he was affectionately known simply as 'Uncle Claude'. Many of the international companies connected with these financiers provided cover for SIS personnel. Edward Boxshall, the long-serving Head of Station in Bucharest, was also the official representative of Zaharoff's Vickers Company and ICI. (Boxshall, who was married to the daughter of Prince Stirbey, a powerful politial figure in pre-war Romania, was revealed in a parliamentary question in 1978 to be Britain's oldest serving civil servant. His unique knowledge of SIS operations in Eastern Europe had made him indispensable to Registry.)

Claude Edward Marjoribanks Dansey was twenty years old when he fought in the Matabele Campaign of 1896, and subsequently saw action in Borneo (to suppress the rebellion of Mohamed Salleh), the Boer War and Somaliland. He then travelled to Manhattan, where he made a number of highly influential friends and founded a country club in Sleepy Hollow in upstate New York. During the Great War he served in France and Belgium before being posted to MI5, where he worked in the overseas branch. He subsequently made himself indispensable to the Chief of MI6, although around 1934 a rumour began circulating that Sinclair had finally got rid of him because of some financial mismanagement. This may indeed have been true, or it may have been a convenient cover for Dansey's development of Z. In any case Dansey appeared to go into a self-imposed exile abroad, living first in Rome (where he had once been CPO) and then in Switzerland.

Dansey's return to London in 1936 came at the moment when SIS was attempting to expand its networks in Europe, such as they were. Dansey apparently pointed out the dangers of relying on the overt, fixed Station system and offered to build a more flexible parallel ring which would operate under commercial cover. Sinclair, according to some sources, grasped at the idea, but baulked at putting Dansey back on the payroll. Instead, a compromise was reached: Dansey would be paid his expenses and provided with premises in London; he would also be compensated for payments to individual agents and, in the event of an emergency, he would be brought back to

Broadway. This freelance arrangement became the basis of the Z-network. Premises were found in Bush House, and Commander Kenneth Cohen RN was formally appointed liaison officer in 1937. The office consisted of Cohen and his personal secretary, Doreen Bett; a former Coldstream Guards officer, John Codrington, as his assistant; three secretarial staff (Sheila Deane, Joanna Shuckburgh and Mrs Phillips); and a doorman, Norman Wells, a tough ex-RN petty officer who had served on the royal yacht.

With the Chief's secret financial backing, Dansey undertook a long tour of Europe looking up his old acquaintances and offering them part-time employment with 'the British Secret Service'. Most fell into two groups: expatriate Englishmen settled into foreign communities, and business executives who worked for British companies, some of which would now broadly be described as multi-national.

New recruits picked by Dansey were invited to attend an interview at a front organization, the Albany Trust, which had a one-room office in Abbey House, Victoria Street. This was presided over by Colonel Marcus Haywood from MI5 who, having approved Dansey's candidate, would pass his file to Vincent Auger, a retired detective, who would make background inquiries. Once enrolled, the agent was given a 'Z-number' to identify himself. According to the Z-system, Z-1 was Dansey, Z-2 was Cohen and Z-3 was John Codrington.

As well as running the Albany Trust office and the Bush House headquarters, Dansey operated through a number of other addresses in London. They included the Export Department of international fine art dealers Sir Geoffrey Duveen & Company, Menoline Limited, H. Sichel & Sons, the wine shippers, and a Highgate-based holiday firm, Lammin Tours. One useful source, which later became Z's naval section, was the General Steamship Navigation Company, headed by Ian Hooper. His special responsibility was the recruitment of ship's masters as agents, and this project was considered so successful that it was extended, with the help of the National Union of Seamen, to include other sharp-eyed seafarers who made regular visits to foreign ports. By far the most important of these commercial covers was London Films, the feature film production company headed by Alexander Korda. Dansey subsequently became a director of it, and Korda was rewarded for his war work with a knighthood.

By the Anschluss, Dansey's organization had established agents all over Europe. John Evans was Z–Prague, building up a network of German Social Democrats; Basil Fenwick, a representative of the Royal Dutch Shell Company, was Z–Zurich; Graham Maingot was Z–Rome; R.G. Pearson, a South African representing Unilever, was Z–Basle, along with Sir Frank Nelson and Tim Frenken; Richard Tinsley, of the Uranium Steamship Company, was Z–Rotterdam; Frederick Voight, the Central European correspondent of the *Manchester Guardian*, was Z–Vienna. All the Z-agents were well travelled and well connected with others who shared anti-Nazi feelings. In this latter category was Gottfried Treviranus, code-named SPEAKER, a former minister in Brüning's Government who was run personally by Dansey and regarded as one of the Z-network's best agents. (SPEAKER was eventually identified by the Gestapo and Dansey had to facilitate his escape to Canada.)

The Z organization was extremely sophisticated and, considering the short time it took Dansey to construct it, a truly remarkable achievement. It remains, none the less, a highly controversial subject. Some believe that Z was simply a mischievous influence which fabricated exotic intelligence reports when it failed to find any genuine material; others say it was discredited by Dansey using it as a power base within SIS. Either way, there can be no doubt that it was a major factor in the Dutch disaster of November 1939, now infamous as the Venlo incident.

The story began in earnest on Monday, 4 September 1939, the first day of the war, when the Head of Station at The Hague received what he regarded as a particularly bizarre *Eyes Only* telegram from Broadway. Major Richard Stevens was informed that a senior SIS operative would that very morning make himself known to the Station, and in the future all plans and operations should be executed jointly. The visitor who subsequently arrived at Stevens's office later the same morning needed no introduction. He was Captain Sigismund Payne Best, a somewhat larger than life English businessman resident in The Hague and a prominent member of the local expatriate community. He was not particularly well regarded, partly because of his 'more English than the English' postures (a not uncommon characteristic at that time of people who were of a mixed Anglo-Indian background), and partly because of his ostentatious manner. For example, he habitually wore spats, a source of some comment among the Dutch, and sported a monocle. Although Best himself, then aged fifty-five, was less than popular, his Dutch wife Maria Margareta was a renowned hostess and was well connected in Holland through her father, Admiral van Rees. Stevens was astonished to learn that such a well-known figure could possibly be connected with SIS, but Best proceeded to enlighten him.

According to Best, who had been decorated with the OBE as well as a French *Légion d'honneur* and a Belgian *Croix de Guerre*, he, Best, was The Hague's resident Z officer, and Z was a super-secret intelligence network run in parallel to the SIS Stations by Claude Dansey. All of this was news to Stevens, although some other Heads of Station had suspected members of their local English community of being mixed up in espionage.

Dansey's chief agent in Holland was indeed Captain Payne Best, whom he had first met during the Great War when Best was engaged on intelligence duties on the Western Front. After the war Best started the Continental Trading Company, an import–export firm based at his home at 15

Nieuwe Uitleg beside a picturesque canal. The enterprise gradually expanded, got a Dutch partner from a drug and pharmaceutical concern, Piet van der Willik, and was relatively successful. Among their more profitable acquisitions was the licence to import Humber bicycles from England. As well as running his business Best also did a thriving trade in information, passing virtually worthless items of intelligence to Dansey and claiming considerable expenses on behalf of his usually fictitious agents. Of the thirteen 'head agents' Best boasted of running, only four or five actually existed.

One of his nine imagined spy-rings, which seemed to incur unavoidably high running costs, was code-named HOUSE and consisted of sub-agents code-named TABLE and CHAIR. After the war, when Best had to account for this deception, he protested that he had been starved of funds and Stevens had declined to subsidize him because the Station was still trying to live down the Dalton scandal.

Best communicated with Z in London via a business cover, Menoline Limited, based at 24 Maple Street, London W1, where his case officer, Commander Cohen, was based, operating as 'Lieutenant-Commander Cowan' and, occasionally, 'Keith Crane'. Other messages were either taken by courier to Bush House or handed directly to Dansey, who held frequent meetings with Best at the Travellers' Club in Paris.

During the summer of 1939 Best received a directive from Dansey, who had set up a temporary headquarters in Brussels, announcing a contingency plan for use in the event of war with Germany: the whole of Z was to join forces with the local CPOs. The purpose of this amalgamation was to prevent the wasteful duplication of effort, a problem which was much in evidence according to Broadway. Best was, of course, perfectly aware of the dual role of the local Chief Passport Officer, as indeed was most of The Hague, and that is why he had duly presented himself at Stevens's office on the outskirts of the capital. There the two men exchanged confidences and prepared to merge their two organizations.

Similar meetings were being held throughout Europe, though in some instances the new arrangement was scorned. For example, the Head of Station in Riga, Leslie Nicholson, was approached by a colourful local English resident less than an hour after Chamberlain's speech. His cover was that of an author researching a book on Baltic politics, and Nicholson had long suspected that he was some sort of an agent. He never dreamed that the man could also have been working for SIS and declined to have any dealings with him.

During 1939 The Hague Station had acquired a special importance because of the worsening political climate in Europe. It was also becoming a major clearing station for information concerning Germany. Stevens's Station had, of course, enjoyed a long tradition of being at the centre of anti-German operations, in much the same way that Riga had become the chief Station for anti-Soviet operations during the 1920s. The Hague's position had been mildly enhanced by an embarrassing trial in Denmark the previous year, when one of Dansey's Z agents, a man named Kneuffen, had been tried for espionage and convicted. Much to the prosecution's astonishment, Kneuffen had confessed to working for the British, not the Germans. The Copenhagen Station was suitably miffed at this disclosure, since its Head, Major Bernard O'Leary, had known nothing about Z, but as a result of Kneuffen, he was obliged to reduce SIS activities.

Another contributor to The Hague's increase in stature was the closure of Frank Foley's Berlin Station on 24 August 1939, just a week before the outbreak of war. Foley had been the CPO Berlin since 1920 and ran a small office in the Consulate-General, a building overlooking the Tiergarten (and thus convenient for meeting agents) but uncomfortably close to Dr Goebbels's propaganda ministry, which was located next door. The Berlin Station had operated for a number of years with only a handful of staff. Foley employed two senior SIS secretaries, Ena Molesworth and Evelyn Sinclair (the Chief's sister), and could draw on the help of his assistant, Colonel Insall, but the Nazi persecution of the Jews made it extremely difficult for the Station to carry out its dual role. Each day the offices were besieged by Jews anxious to obtain the necessary travel documentation for emigration to Palestine. Foley did his best to accommodate as many as he could, and cut a number of corners in the issuing of the vital papers (and thus helped to save many thousands of Jewish lives), but the queue outside the Consulate-General appeared to be endless. In 1938 the Foreign Office authorized the recruitment of an extra six female clerks to cope with applications, but they were evacuated to England less than a year after their arrival in Berlin.

On his recall to Broadway, Foley was appointed CPO, Scandinavia, and sent with his coding clerk cum secretary, Margaret Reid, to reinforce Commander Newill's Station in Oslo.

Meanwhile, in The Hague, Best was following Dansey's instructions to amalgamate with Stevens. The order was a fortuitous one for Best, who had been cultivating a ring of anti-Nazis in Germany via several refugees who had managed to make their way to Holland. His link to the mainly Catholic refugees was his Dutch aide, Peter Vrooburgh, who in turn had a useful German source named Dr Franz Fischer. Before coming to Holland Fischer had been a major coal distributor in Württemberg, and both Best and Dansey rated him as an important sub-agent. He had many useful connections, especially in Munich where his brother was a well-known theatrical director. Best's dilemma, about which he consulted the CPO, concerned a request made by Fischer through Vrooburgh. Apparently, the refugee, Fischer, had claimed possession of some momentous intelligence and would only impart it if he was able to make direct contact with an official from the

British Secret Service. After some discussion, Stevens agreed to seek advice from both Dansey and Broadway. At the Z headquarters 'Cowan' reported that Dansey was abroad and, therefore, unavailable. In fact, both Broadway and Bush House were in turmoil. On 4 November 1939 Admiral Sinclair had died. Dansey was in Switzerland saying his last farewells to the Z staff in Lausanne, apparently confident that he was going to be the new Chief.

At Broadway, Stevens's telegram landed on the desk of the Head of Section II, Stewart Menzies, who ordered Stevens and Best to proceed with caution. As the Acting Chief since Sinclair's death, Menzies considered the matter so important that he dispatched an officer from his staff to deliver his instructions to the CPO by hand. It was thus agreed that Fischer should make direct contact with the desired 'British Secret Service officer'.

A preliminary meeting subsequently took place which led to Best being introduced to a Major Solms, a Luftwaffe officer who demanded confirmation that Best was indeed acting with the full authority of the SIS. Authenticity was established to the satisfaction of Solms when Best arranged for a particular item to be inserted into the BBC's German News Service, twice, on 11 October 1939.

This was to be just one of several meetings that Best unwittingly attended with representatives of the Nazi Security Service, the Sicherheitsdienst. They played a tantalizingly elaborate game, which resulted in both Best and Stevens arranging for a high-ranking anti-Nazi Wehrmacht general to be flown to London for secret talks. At stake, according to the SD double agents, was a military coup in Berlin and the arrest of Hitler. In fact, the entire episode was a brilliantly executed counter-intelligence operation, which led to the kidnapping in broad daylight of both Best and Stevens at the German–Dutch frontier near Venlo in eastern Holland on 9 November 1939.

News of the affair, which was to become known as the Venlo incident, did not reach The Hague for some hours. The contact with this alleged branch of the German underground was so secret that only one other member of the Station, Stevens's deputy, knew the full details: Major Lionel Loewe was the SIS liaison officer with the Netherlands military intelligence service, and he was actually in the office of Major-General van Oorschot when the Dutch DMI learned of the catastrophe. (Van Oorschot and his English wife were both closely connected with SIS. His ability to complete *The Times* crossword in half an hour made a lasting impression on his British colleagues.)

At first it seemed that the disaster might be limited to the loss of two senior SIS officers and Lieutenant Dirk Klop, the Dutch military intelligence observer provided by van Oorschot. However, it soon became clear that there were more serious issues at stake. Klop had been fatally wounded by a German bullet during the struggle at the frontier, and both Best and Stevens were apparently alive and under interrogation at Düsseldorf. To complicate the matter further, the so-called German resistance cell that they had been negotiating with continued to communicate with The Hague Station by the transmitter provided at the outset by Stevens.

Broadway was in turmoil over the incident. Conflicting reports poured into Menzies's office in Queen Anne's Gate, whilst the neutral Dutch Government tried to disassociate itself from any involvement in espionage.

The facts, which were established after the war by a Dutch parliamentary commission and an SIS inquiry, were relatively straightforward. Best and Stevens had been manhandled over the border into Germany by a Nazi Sicherheitsdienst team led by Walter Schellenberg and Alfred Naujocks. Throughout the same afternoon the two British officers underwent a preliminary questioning, and it was during this interrogation, according to Karl Ditges, the SS translator present, that Best mentioned the existence of the Z organization for the first time.

The immediate consequence of the affair in The Hague was the virtual closure of the Station. All the staff were instructed to suspend their work, and the Section V representative, Rodney Dennys, was transferred to the Brussels Station. Loewe became the Acting Head of Station in the absence of Stevens, and remained in that post until the evacuation of the Station in May the following year. The only intelligence activity taking place in what remained of The Hague Station was conducted during a twice-weekly visit from Belgium by Dennys.

By any standards the Dutch disaster was the equivalent of a supposedly healthy body experiencing a heart attack. It gave the entire system a severe shock and led to the organization reassessing its pre-war activity. It dramatically reduced the acquisition of intelligence and ensured that Anglo–Dutch relations would never be the same again.

At Broadway, Dansey's first reaction to the news of Venlo was to blame John Hooper, who had originally been dismissed from The Hague Station for blackmailing Dalton in 1936, after which he had been approached by Giskes of the Abwehr. When Hooper later confessed to this, Dansey had wanted to 'eliminate' him, but instead he had been reinstated. Now Dansey wanted to 'eliminate' him again. Once again Vivian intervened, pointing out that there was no direct evidence that Hooper had participated in the Venlo incident. As far as Vivian knew, Hooper was still operating for SIS in Rotterdam under the cover-name of Arthur Rumbelow. When Loewe and his staff were evacuated the following May, Hooper and his family were also given passages to England. His wife and three children were billeted with the Cowgills at Wavendon Manor, near Bletchley, whilst Vivian hatched a plan to send Hooper back to Holland as a double agent. Dansey vetoed this idea, and little is known of Hooper's wartime role. After the war it was reported that Giskes spotted his former agent exercising in the central compound at MI5's Camp 020, Latchmere House, Ham Common.

Both Best and Stevens provided their captors, under duress, with a mass of detail about the Secret Intelligence Service. The Nazis displayed considerable skill in handling their prisoners and never once gave them the opportunity to compare notes and thus minimize the impact of their answers. The two men were kept separate and each believed the other was responsible for providing their interrogators with the basis of their apparently extensive knowledge of 'der Britische Nachrichtendienst'. After the war Best and Stevens were repatriated and debriefed by both MI5 and MI6. They each admitted to having been quite candid with the SD, and it was decided not to take any further action against them. Stevens took up a translating job with NATO and eventually retired to Brighton, where he died in 1965. Best became a bankrupt, but won a campaign to receive compensation for his imprisonment from the post-war German Government. The British Government opposed the inclusion of his name on the list of those who had suffered at the hands of the Nazis, but Best did eventually receive an award of £2,400 in 1968. He died in 1978 aged ninety-three.

Best always believed that he had been badly treated by Stewart Menzies (who, he later claimed, had paid him off with an attaché case full of tax-free money after a long lunch in White's Club) and never ceased petitioning the Foreign Office for a proper pension. When he filed his bankruptcy in 1965, he described himself as 'a former Secret Service officer' so as to embarrass his former employers and perhaps extract further financial aid from them. In fact he failed, but he did become one of the few SIS officers ever to publish his memoirs. In 1950 he wrote *The Venlo Incident*, in which he described the kidnapping and his subsequent incarceration. It was largely based on a document he wrote in May 1945 for his MI5 debriefer, Colonel Green.

It was more than twenty years before the full story of the Stevens/Best saga came to be discovered. Then Allied intelligence officers, sifting through Nazi records after the war, came across a summary prepared by the Reich Security Agency early in 1940, made in preparation for the German invasion of England, which was based on information gained from Best and Stevens. It appears at the end of this book in the Appendix.

With hindsight, several baffling decisions seem to have been made. It seems surprising that Sinclair sent a new recruit, trained only in India's North-West Frontier, to head such an important post as The Hague when war was imminent; Hooper's reinstatement after twice confessing to serious breaches of security also seems bizarre; and the suggestion that the Z parallel intelligence networks should suddenly announce themselves to their regular SIS colleagues the moment war was declared seems to be asking a great deal of both networks at a crucial time. Were they supposed to integrate the two tiers as they prepared to manœuvre onto a wartime footing? However, had Sinclair been alive at the time, he might have suggested that the initial approach to Major Solms be handled with greater circumspection and so have averted tragedy.

The disaster in Holland spelt the end of the Z network because so many of its members had been compromised. Sinclair's death in the London Clinic on 4 November 1939, caused by a combination of a malignant tumour and sheer exhaustion, heralded further changes. Sinclair had been ill for some time; his will, in which he left everything to his sister Evelyn with two small bequests to his sons Maurice and Derek, was dated 4 November 1938.

Sinclair's name was largely unknown to the British public because the CSS went to considerable lengths to protect his identity. The Navy List described him as having had his name 'placed on the Retired List at his own request' on 1 May 1926. His brief entry in *Who's Who* made no mention of his SIS work and described him simply as 'RN Retired, 1926'. In fact, in the sixteen years he held the post there was only once a danger of the name of his post becoming known. In October 1932 Compton Mackenzie tried to publish the third volume of his war memoirs entitled *Greek Memories*. The book was promptly banned and Mackenzie was charged with offences under the Official Secrets Act. He later pleaded guilty at the Old Bailey and was fined £100. The book was eventually published by Chatto & Windus in 1939, by which time it was thought that his description of the author's work as an intelligence officer in the eastern Mediterranean in 1917 could not possibly jeopardize security.

In spite of Sinclair's desire for obscurity, his memorial service was held at St Martin-in-the-Fields and was attended by virtually every senior intelligence officer who had ever come into contact with him. Sir Vernon Kell, the Director-General of the Security Service, described the event as having been attended by a 'very full congregation'.

When Admiral Sir Hugh Sinclair took over SIS, it was fifteen years old. He was its Chief for a further fifteen years. After thirty years of existence, SIS was still felt to be somewhat too slender. Staffed in the main by Royal Naval officers, both active and retired, it appears to have provided rather inadequate information of doubtful quality, slightly belatedly, to a sceptical Whitehall. Its potential strength lay in the Government Code and Cipher School, the burgeoning communications network, and in the new sections devoted to subversion and counter-intelligence – GS(R), Section D and Section V. At Sinclair's death in 1939, SIS's peacetime record was poor: the first few months of war had shown SIS to be equally ineffective.

Shortly before his death, Sinclair had entrusted his secretary, Kathleen Pettigrew, with a letter addressed to the Foreign Secretary, Lord Halifax.

In it he recommended that the Head of Section II, Stewart Menzies, be appointed his successor. Instead, Halifax suggested that Menzies be considered the Acting Chief until the Cabinet could be consulted.

In theory, the post of Chief of the Secret Service is in the gift of the monarch, who takes the advice of the Prime Minister. In practice, there had only been two such appointments ever made: Smith-Cumming in 1909, who had been selected by the Committee of Imperial Defence, and Sinclair in 1923, whose name had been approved by the now defunct Secret Service Committee. The question of a successor for Sinclair was debated by the Prime Minister with the Defence Cabinet and, for the first time, some quite shameless lobbying took place. The favourite for the job was Stewart Menzies.

Menzies was then forty-nine years old and had been deputizing for the CSS for the past twelve months. He had been educated at Eton, where he had won the Consort's Prize for French and German. He had also been something of an athlete, having won the Eton Steeplechase and been Captain of the First XI. He had also been Master of the Eton Beagles and had been voted President of Pop, the Eton Society.

When he left Eton, Menzies had been commissioned into the Grenadier Guards, but when his mother was widowed she married Colonel Sir George Holford who was the Commanding Officer of the Life Guards. Menzies, therefore, transferred to his step-father's regiment. In October 1914 his regiment was sent to France and took up a position with the 7th Division in Houthem Gheluvelt-St Julien, a few miles to the east of Ypres. This part of the front was the focus of some of the bitterest fighting of the entire war. According to the description given when he was gazetted for the DSO, Menzies

showed the greatest coolness during the attack on German positions led by Major Stanley, 1st Life Guards, on 7 November 1914, in support of the right flank of the 4th Guards Brigade, and again on the evening of that day.

The King presented Menzies with his decoration on 2 December 1914. Of the 400 officers and 12,000 men sent to that part of the front, only forty-four officers and 2,336 men survived. Menzies later returned to the front and took part in the battle for Hill 60. This notorious pimple of a hill had taken on tremendous strategic importance because of the view it commanded across the British trenches. On the night of 17 April 1915 sappers exploded three huge mines under the German positions and the hill was captured. The Germans counter-attacked the following day and retook most of the hill. Undaunted, the West Ridings went onto the attack and beat off the Germans, in spite of appalling losses. Over the following weeks Hill 60 was the scene of some great displays of gallantry. On the night of 20/21 April Lieutenant Woolley won the Victoria Cross for continuing to lead his men in the desperate position on the hill. The battle raged until the Life Guards finally drove the Germans off the hill.

Menzies's citation for his Military Cross read:

Near Ypres, on 13 May 1915, after his Commanding Officer had been wounded, displayed conspicuous ability, coolness and resource in controlling the action of his regiment and rallying the men.

On 18 December 1915 Menzies was posted to Sir Douglas Haig's head-quarters in Montreuil as an intelligence officer under the command of Brigadier-General John Charteris. Menzies's unit was MI 1(b), which was headed by Colonel (Sir) Walter Kirke and had responsibility for 'secret service and security'. Menzies never returned to regimental duties.

In November 1918 Menzies married Lady Alice Sackville, the daughter of the 8th Earl de la Warr. Thirteen years later he divorced her so that she could marry Colonel Fitzroy Spicer of the 16th Lancers. The following year he married Pamela Beckett, one of the four daughters of the Hon. Rupert Beckett, an immensely wealthy Old Etonian who was Chairman of the Westminster Bank and proprietor of the *Yorkshire Post*. For many years Menzies and his brother Ian were also both intimately involved with Lady Portarlington, wife of the 6th Earl, and Valentine Vivian's sister-in-law.

In short, Menzies was extremely well qualified for the post of CSS and possessed the advantage of having friends at Court, for his father-in-law, who died in 1926, had been an intimate friend of the King's. Menzies also had a number of political friends, most of whom were members of his London club, White's, considered then (and now) the most exclusive club in England. Among those supporting Menzies for the top job in SIS were David Margesson, Chamberlain's influential Chief Whip, and Lord Hali-fax. However, there were other possible candidates for he job. The most likely was the Director of Naval Intelligence, Rear-Admiral John Godfrey, who had discussed the question of Sinclair's possible death and his likely successor with Maurice Hankey, the former Secretary of the Committee of Imperial Defence, the previous August. Whether he had himself in mind for the job is unknown, but certainly his name was canvassed. His wife later denied that Godfrey had any interest in the job for himself. Certainly both Cumming and Sinclair had come from the navy, but the Secret Service Committee had minuted, at the time of Sinclair's appointment in 1923, that the post should be rotated among the Services.

On 28 November 1939, the Prime Minister, Neville Chamberlain, Lord Halifax, Churchill and the War Minister, Hore-Belisha, decided that Menzies would be confirmed as Sinclair's successor. According to the account of Sir Alexander Cadogan, then Permanent Under-Secretary at the Foreign Office, Halifax 'played his hand well and won the trick' for Menzies.

Two vital tasks now confronted Menzies. The first was to deal with the growing volume of complaints from the Services about the quality of SIS intelligence. Many believed that the elimination of the Z-network would put matters straight, but that was hardly an explanation that could be offered to the Cabinet. However, in true bureaucratic style the Prime Minister agreed to a major investigation of all Britain's secret services; he would arrange for a special report on the subject to be made and would then submit his recommendations. The author chosen to undertake this was Maurice Hankey, who had joined the War Cabinet on 1 September as Minister without Portfolio. However, Hankey had still not completed his report when Churchill's administration took office in May the following year. It was rumoured that it was considered so secret that all copies were destroyed to prevent them falling into German hands after an invasion scare. Menzies's second task was to try and mitigate the damage done at Venlo and put SIS into fighting trim.

The SIS order of battle inherited by Menzies in November 1939 was, to put it mildly, ill equipped to cope with a second war with Germany.

The Secret Intelligence was divided into two separate divisions: 'Y', the headquarters posts, and 'YP', the overseas Stations. The 'YP' organization was further divided into four 'Production' or 'G' sections: G1, G2, G3 and G4. All communications to and from the Stations had to be read and approved by the individual 'G' officers, Messrs Bremner, Bowlby and Slocum, who held the title of Assistant Chief Staff Officers (ACSO). The fourth, additional 'G' officer was Captain George Taylor RN, the former Head of Station in New York, who handled the Mediterranean Stations, such as they were. These four 'G' officers each concentrated on a particular aspect of intelligence or liaison, and overseeing the entire organization was the Chief himself. In Menzies's case he sought the additional help of the former Z-1, Claude Dansey.

Sinclair's Chief Staff Officer (CSO) had been Captain Rex Howard RN, a retired naval officer who had been responsible for SIS's administration. His duties included recruitment, finance and appointments to the overseas Stations. He was little concerned with the aquisition or distribution of intelligence, which was in the main left to the two ACSOs, Commanders (later Captains) Cuthbert Bowlby and Frank Slocum. Bowlby had first gone to sea in 1912, aged seventeen, after graduating from Osborne and Dartmouth. During the Great War he served with the Battle Cruiser Squadron and the original coastal motor-boat flotilla, and was decorated with the Distinguished Service Cross and bar. He joined SIS shortly after Sinclair's appointment as Chief and was Menzies's choice to establish SIS in the Middle East in 1940. He was to spend three years in Egypt directing the Cairo Station before moving to similar posts in Algiers and Italy. He retired from SIS in 1955.

The Chief's other ACSO was Frank Slocum, Bowlby's junior by two years, who had been recruited into SIS from the Royal Naval Tactical School in 1937. In 1940 Menzies placed Slocum in command of the SIS 'private navy', a clandestine boat service which ferried agents to and from occupied territory. His wartime activities in Europe were later rewarded with a *Croix de Guerre* from the French, the Norwegian Liberty Cross from King Haakon, the Danish Freedom Medal from King Christian and the Legion of Merit from the Americans.

The ten 'Y' headquarters sections were: Section I, the political section, headed by Malcolm Woollcombe and David Footman. Woollcombe had been invited to join SIS by Cumming in 1921, having served as an intelligence officer during the Great War. Footman was an expert on Soviet affairs who had spent ten years in the Levant Consular Service before being recruited into SIS in 1935.

Section II, the military section, was headed by Stewart Menzies until his appointment as Chief, and he was succeeded by Major Hatton-Hall, his former deputy. This section maintained liaison with the DMI of the day, distributed intelligence to the War Office, and channelled War Office requests for information to the appropriate case officers who managed the geographical regions.

Section III, the naval section, was headed by Captain Russell and his assistant, Commander Christopher Arnold-Forster RN, a former assistant naval attaché during the Great War to Captain Sir Guy Gaunt in Washington. In 1942 he was to return to the NID as Assistant Director of Naval Intelligence to the newly appointed DNI, Rear-Admiral Edmund Rushbrooke.

Section IV, the air section, was in the hands of Wing-Commander Fred Winterbotham, a swashbuckling character who had spent the pre-war years concentrating on the Luftwaffe. In the first months of the war Winterbotham's principal role was that of liaison between the Air Ministry's current director of Air Intelligence, Air Commodore Charles Medhurst, and the air attachés on the Continent. His deputy was Squadron-Leader John S.B. Perkins. Later Menzies was to appoint him as his link with the GCHQ code-breakers at Bletchley.

Section V, the counter-espionage section, will be described in detail later in chapter nine, but in the first months of the war it was undergoing a belated, but rapid, expansion. It was eventually to become the largest of the departments with a staff numbering 120, inclusive of secretarial staff. Section V's objective was firstly to establish as comprehensively as possible the order of battle of the opposition's intelligence service, and having made at least this gain, the Section was to concentrate on the wholesale deception of the enemy. It was headed by Colonel Valentine Vivian, the former Indian police officer, with the man who was later to succeed him in January 1941,

Felix Cowgill. The catastrophic penetration of The Hague Station emphasized the importance of counter-intelligence, and the Section developed a parallel system in the 'YPs' of regional case officers. Recruitment to the Section was enhanced in early 1941 by the transfer of a number of MI5 officers and some public school masters. The entire Section had been evacuated from Broadway in August 1939 and re-established at Bletchley Park, where most of the Broadway sections were duplicated.

Section VI, the industrial section, was headed by Rear-Admiral Charles Limpenny DSO, RN, a former ADC to the King. His principal assistants were Robert Smith and Bruce Ottley, a wealthy merchant banker from the City who combined his war work in Broadway with running Wilton's oyster bar. Linked to Section VI was Desmond Morton's Industrial Intelligence Centre and the new Ministry of Economic Warfare.

Section VII, the financial section, was the province of Paymaster Commander Percy Sykes RNR, the chartered accountant who had been a long-standing friend of both Cumming and Sinclair.

Section VIII, the communications section, headed by Richard Gambier-Parry, operated from Hanslope Park and Whaddon Hall in Buckinghamshire. Initially the Section concentrated on developing its own communications, under Major Maltby, and co-existing with the Foreign Office, whose communications department had been headed since 1925 by Harold Eastwood. One of Eastwood's staff, Henry Maine, had been seconded to Bletchley to act as a liaison officer, with an SIS officer, Cecil Barclay, as his assistant. Later in the war, as we shall see, it was to wrest control of the Radio Security Service (RSS) from MI5.

Section IX, the cipher section, was the department responsible for the creation and distribution of one-time pads. Initially headed by Colonel Walter Jefferys, this post was latterly held by Brigadier E. F. J. Hill DSO, MC, another former Indian army officer.

Section X, the press section, was run by Raymond Henniker-Heaton, a well-known historian of primitive art and formerly the editor of *You*, 'the magazine of practical psychology'.

By the time war had broken out in September 1939 the Secret Intelligence Service was in serious organizational difficulty. These difficulties had been compounded, as we have seen, by the skilful long-term penetration of The Hague Station by the Germans which culminated in Venlo; the Kendrick fiasco at the Vienna Station; and the complete withdrawal of all personnel from Prague, Warsaw, Bucharest and Berlin. The Soviet invasion of Finland had forced Harry Carr's Station in Helsinki to seek refuge in Stockholm. Then the *Blitzkrieg* of May 1940 eliminated the Stations in Paris and Brussels and left the structure of the Passport Control Office system in shreds. Frank Foley suffered the double indignity of evacuating the Berlin Station and then, within months, evacuating the Oslo Station. Giffey in Tallinn and Nicholson in Riga were also obliged to withdraw. Sinclair's pre-war neglect of the Mediterranean left SIS almost completely unrepresented in that theatre.

The amalgamation with the Z-network did little to improve the overall picture, and Menzies was obliged to begin his term as Chief at a disadvantage. The collapse of France, Belgium, Denmark, Holland and Norway left him reliant on three major Stations in Europe: Stockholm, Lisbon and Berne. A review of his assets in these capitals on the Continent in 1940 shows how meagre they were.

In Stockholm the pre-war Passport Control Officer had been Lieutenant-Commander John Martin RN (code-numbered 36100), an SIS veteran who had previously served in Dakar. His intelligence gathering work at the Passport Control Office in the Birger Jarlsgatan was to continue until 1942 when he was replaced by Cyril Cheshire, a former timber merchant. Other PCO staff included his secretary, Peggy Weller, and two assistants, David McEwen and Victor Hampton.

McEwen, the homosexual son of Air Vice-Marshal N. D. C. McEwen, knew many German homosexuals. When von Kramm, the German youth leader, visited Sweden he always stayed with McEwen and he invariably delivered a mass of political information. Hampton's efforts focussed on Denmark and took responsibility for SIS operations in that country after the evacuation of the CPO Copenhagen, Sidney Smith.

Martin, as Head of the Stockholm Station, also employed two other intelligence officers, Whistondale and Appleby, whose duties included issuing visas, running agents and vetting the passengers of the twice-weekly courier plane to RAF Leuchars. Communication with Broadway depended on the transmitter in the British Legation, located in Stockholm's eastern suburb.

The Passport Control Officer's intelligence network was reinforced by the Naval Attaché, Captain Henry Denham RN, who had been appointed in December 1939. He eventually built a very successful friendship with Colonel Bjoernstierna, the Chief of the Swedish Combined Intelligence Bureau, largely based on a 'regrettable incident', in which a Swede was caught red-handed trying to plant a microphone in Denham's flat. Denham and the British Minister, Victor Mallet, agreed to keep the incident quiet if Bjoernstierna would be co-operative. Although Denham did valuable work, much of his value was in his rather obvious espionage activities which served to draw the fire of the Swedes and the Germans.

Also located in Stockholm were two other, smaller, SIS offices. One was the Helsinki Station, recently evacuated because of the Russian invasion of Finland, which consisted of Harry Carr and his deputy, Rex Bosley. The second was an economic section run by Ronald Turnbull, who operated under diplomatic cover at the Legation from 1941. The Section V representative, Peter Falk, did not arrive until March 1943.

By contrast the Lisbon Station was in a particularly bad way. The long-serving CPO, Commander Austin Walsh RN (code-numbered 24100), had been posted to the Station when Lisbon was a relatively unimportant backwater. He was an amiable drinking companion for the British expatriates in Portugal, but he had little ability to manage the SIS outpost in what was to become a virtual espionage capital. In desperation Menzies applied to Sir Vernon Kell for the services of an experienced MI5 officer, and he was recommended Richman Stopford. Stopford had previously been the personal assistant of Major T.A. (Tar) Robertson, the Security Service case officer who had nurtured Arthur Owens (code-named SNOW), the first of MI5's important double agents. Stopford's involvement with SNOW had led him to Mrs Mathilde Krafft, an Abwehr paymaster operating from Bournemouth, and William Rolph, a former MI5 officer who killed himself when confronted with evidence of his work for the Abwehr. Menzies accepted the offer of Stopford's services and he was duly dispatched to Lisbon as the Financial Attaché with his MI5 secretary, Mary Grepe.

By the end of 1940 the Lisbon picture looked rather more impressive. Stopford was Head of Station (with Walsh remaining in an advisory capacity). His staff included two European Station veterans, Rita Winsor (from Berne) and Ena Molesworth (from Berlin); Bobby Johnstone, a pre-war stockbroker; Mike Andrews; and Trevor Glanville, who had previously been evacuated from Belgrade where he had been working for the chartered accountants Price, Waterhouse & Co. In March 1941 the Station acquired a Section V representative, Ralph Jarvis (the 'Assistant Financial Attaché', a cover which was believable because he had been a merchant banker with M. Samuel & Co. before the war). In the spring of 1941 Stopford was posted to Lagos and replaced by Commander Philip Johns RNVR (previously Arnold–Forster's assistant in Section III and before that in a post at the Brussels Station). During Johns's tenure the Station experienced a number of bitter disputes which, as we shall see, resulted in Johnstone being recalled to London and Johns, in December 1942, being posted as Head of Station Buenos Aires. His successor was Cecil Gledhill, one of Dansey's wartime recruits and the only SIS officer fluent in Portuguese.

The third important centre of SIS operations in Europe was Switzeralnd, where, before the war, Dansey had been particularly active and had built up a sizeable Z-network. In addition, there was a CPO based in Geneva, Acton Burnell (code-numbered 42100), who had been banned from operating in Berne by the British Minister, Sir George Warner.

Burnell's pre-war organization had been combined with the local Z-network and consisted of Frank Nelson in Basle (as the British Consul) and

Richard Arnold-Baker in Zurich (in charge of the 'Visa Department of the Consul-General'), who had an SIS staff of four. When Dansey returned to London in November 1939, Pearson took over as Burnell's principal assistant and established a wireless set in Geneva. Unfortunatley the radio could only receive, so outward messages were sent via the Swiss post office. Other SIS personnel in Switzerland included Andrew King, a young Cambridge graduate who had worked under a pre-war London Films cover, courtesy of Alexander Korda; Hugh Whittall in Lausanne; Tim Frenken in Basle; Lance de Garston in Lugano; Edge Leslie and Rita Winsor in Zurich.

In February 1940 the CSS appointed a new CPO to Geneva, Victor Farrell, and also appointed a special representative at the Legation in Berne (under 'press attaché' cover), Major Freddie Vanden Heuvel. Vanden Heuvel, known as Fanny to his friends, had been educated in Switzerland and spoke fluent Schweitzer-Deutsch. He had once been a director of Eno's Fruit Salts Ltd and, during the Great War, he had worked for SIS and had been compromised. Under his direction the Berne Station was to become the principal SIS base for obtaining information from Germany. The British intelligence operation in Switzerland was complex. Intelligence of a direct, military nature was the responsibility of the Air Attaché, Air Commodore Ferdinand West MC, VC, who, for a brief period after the Great War, had been the air liaison officer at SIS headquarters in London. Before his posting to Berne, West had been the Air Attaché in Rome, where the wooden-legged air ace had done valuable work plotting air targets for Allied bombers.

The British Military Attaché, Colonel H.A. Cartwright, had made a successful escape from captivity during the Great War. He also doubled as the local representative of an MI6 offshoot, MI9, which received escaped Allied prisoners and evaders from whom it was able to obtain valuable information for forwarding to London about conditions inside Germany. However, Cartwright's high public profile made him an obvious target for the Abwehr, so he was constantly on the watch for *agents provocateurs*, and in one incident he had a 'walk-in' volunteer thrown into the street. This particular agent later turned out to be one of the Allies' most valuable sources.

The activities of the Stations in Berne, Lisbon and Stockholm will be looked at again later in closer detail, but first the order of SIS battle in the rest of the world should be examined, especially in the important centres of Gibraltar, Tangiers and Madrid.

In fact Gibraltar, being British territory, was officially in the parish of the Security Service, and after the fall of France MI5 had strengthened its local presence by appointing Colonel H.C. (Tito) Medlam as the Defence Security Officer. His staff undertook the counter-espionage and counter-sabotage roles normally associated with MI5, but the Rock's geographical location presented special counter-intelligence problems, not the least of which was the steady trickle of British (and, for that matter, German) agents fleeing from occupied territory. Because of these unique local conditions the Governor, General Sir Clive Liddell, agreed that SIS could establish a Station, and office space was made available in MI5's premises, at the central police station, known as the Irish Town headquarters. The man appointed by the CSS to head this Station was Major Donald Darling, but his arrival on the Rock was delayed until he had completed a temporary attachment to the Lisbon Station. In the meantime, the burden of work fell on Medlam and his deputy, Philip Kirby Green. Medlam, who was a chartered accountant and a pilot, had been born in Chile and was fluent in both French and Spanish. He had served on General Templer's BEF intelligence staff and, after the French collapse, had been transferred to MI5. Kirby Green's background was quite different: he had been a member of the Metropolitan police until his recruitment by MI5 in 1941.

As well as being home to both MI5 and MI6, Gibraltar had a further strategic importance to SIS headquarters in London. Under normal circumstances Madrid would have been the obvious regional centre, being both neutral and geographically closer to enemy-occupied territory. This, however, was not to be the case, largely due to the British Ambassador there, Sir Samuel Hoare. Hoare had been appointed to Madrid by Churchill in May 1940, and the former Air Minister held Anglo-Spanish relations in high regard. He, therefore, decreed that SIS should exercise restraint and do nothing to embarrass him. The local SIS Head of Station (code-numbered 23100) was Hamilton-Stokes, who had taken over from Edward de Renzy-Martin, the pre-war incumbent. Hamilton-Stokes was assisted by a Section V representative, Kenneth Benton, who had previously served in Vienna, until the Anschluss, and Riga.

Benton's efforts in Madrid were supplemented by the Spanish-speaking Naval Attaché, Lieutenant-Commander Alan Hillgarth RN, who had been the British Vice-Consul in Palma during the Spanish Civil War. It was there that he had met Admiral Godfrey, the Director of Naval Intelligence appointed in March 1939. At the time of their meeting Godfrey was Captain of HMS *Repulse* and was on a mission to the beleaguered city of Barcelona. The job was a risky one because the town was under constant aerial bombardment by Italian planes operating from Majorca. Somehow Hillgarth persuaded the Italian commander to suspend operations whilst the *Repulse* completed her mission. Godfrey was impressed and sent Hillgarth to Madrid to co-ordinate NID, SOE and MI6 operations. Furthermore, Hillgarth was authorized to report directly to both the CSS and the Prime Minister.

The Iberian region as a whole was watched over by a Section I case officer in London (Basil Fenwick, the former Z agent) and a Section V representative, a certain H.A.R. (Kim) Philby, who was later to be succeeded by Tim Milne. The chain of command stretched from Broadway, via the SIS transmitters in Bedfordshire, to Lisbon, Madrid, Gibraltar and Tangiers.

The Head of Station in Tangiers, Colonel Toby Ellis, liaised closely with the other Iberian Stations and was assisted by Colonel Malcolm Henderson, Neil Whitelaw and Paddy Turnbull. This network, which effectively covered the western end of the Mediterranean, continued further south with both SIS and MI5 representatives along the west coast of Africa. Among the more celebrated Heads of Station in the area was Graham Greene, who was based in Freetown, Sierra Leone.

SIS representation in the rest of the world was minimal. In the United States the Passport Control Office was presided over by Captain Sir James Paget RN, a retired naval officer and Baronet, whose financial wrangles with the American Internal Revenue Service caused some embarrassment to the Foreign Office. He was assisted by Miss Stewart-Richardson, the Station's senior cipher clerk.

The CPO's staff were housed in lower Manhattan, next to the British Consulate-General, but political considerations were to result in the PCO being closed down and a new organization being created under William (Little Bill) Stephenson which, as we shall see, was named British Security Co-Ordination. BSC was to take on responsibility for all SIS, NID and SOE operations in the western hemisphere in July 1940, and its personnel were drawn from all the British secret departments.

SIS coverage elsewhere was virtually non-existent, or was left to either MI5 or the navy. Perhaps the most obvious gap in the SIS organization was in the eastern Mediterranean and the Middle East, where SIS was almost completely 'blind' until December 1939 when a Balkan Intelligence Centre was created in Istanbul by the Military Attaché, Brigadier Allan Arnold OBE, MC. Its existence, which was supposed to be highly secret, was announced in a German news broadcast within a week of its inception. This unsatisfactory situation improved when the Director of Naval Intelligence appointed Commander Wolfson RNVR to the post of Assistant Naval Attaché in Istanbul with special responsibility for improving the quality of local British intelligence gathering.

In fact, it was not until June 1940 that Menzies made any serious attempt to improve a very dismal situation. In that month he sent one of his two Assistant Chief Staff Officers, Captain Cuthbert Bowlby RN, to Egypt to liaise with the local organization, Security Intelligence Middle East (SIME). This was eventually to lead to the establishment of a permanent SIS office in Cairo, operating under the cover of the Inter Services Liaison Department (ISLD). Bowlby's deputy in this endeavour was Bill Bremner, one of the pre-war 'G' officers.

This depressing picture of the British intelligence scene was reflected at

Broadway where the CSS and his pre-war staff were battling against rival organizations and the Whitehall bureaucracy to maintain their somewhat shaky position.

7

War
1940

The fall of France meant a disastrous collapse in the volume of intelligence being circulated to the Services and to the Government. Czechoslovakia, Austria and Poland had already succumbed; Norway, Denmark, Holland, Belgium and the Balkans soon followed suit. SIS was left with its few Stations in neutral territory in Europe and with the possibility of using what remained of the networks of Allied governments taking refuge in London. Menzies now had to fight hard in the Joint Intelligence Committee and elsewhere to prevent SIS from being dismembered.

When Churchill formed his War Cabinet on 10 May 1940, he created a finely balanced political coalition, but it was to have serious implications for the Secret Intelligence Service.

The Labour ministers in the new War Cabinet had strong reservations about the supervision and conduct of Britain's secret organizations, reservations that dated back to the political controversies of the 1920s and 1930s, which many in the Labour Party believed (with good reason in some cases) were caused by the Machiavellian activities of MI5 and SIS.

A number of Labour MPs had clashed with MI5, although none of the senior Labour politicians actually went so far as to believe that Kell, the Director-General of the Security Service, was in the pocket of the Tories, in spite of the Zinoviev Letter incident. It was, however, common knowledge that Kell had once ordered the removal of hundreds of compromising files soon after Labour's first administration took office in 1923.

During the early months of the year the Labour back benches echoed with accusations of City figures being appointed to cosy niches inside secret organizations. One particular target was Slaughter & May, the firm of City solicitors. Practically all their senior personnel at one time or another were recruited to wartime jobs that could be classified as 'secret'.

The resulting suspicion of all such secret bodies was voiced during the first of the coalition War Cabinets, principally by Dr Hugh Dalton, who had been created Minister of Economic Warfare on 15 May 1940, and Clement Attlee, who had become Lord Privy Seal on 11 May. Dalton had been at Eton at the same time as Menzies and was a graduate of King's College, Cambridge. He was on the Left of the Labour Party and was a well-informed critic of SIS. He had previously served in the Foreign Office as Parliamentary Under-Secretary of State (1929–32) and was well versed in the departmental manœuvrings of SIS. From the beginning of the coalition Dalton and Attlee insisted that at least one of the secret organizations be overseen by a Labour minister. The Whitehall structure of May 1940 obviously precluded such a concession because the Home Office, which was responsible for the Security Service, was in the hands of Sir John Anderson (who doubled as Minister of Home Security), and the Foreign Office was headed by another Tory minister, Lord Halifax. To give either of these two important posts to anybody outside Churchill's immediate circle of trusted friends would have been unacceptable.

Nevertheless, the Prime Minister was acutely aware of the need to breathe new life into SIS and MI5. At the second full War Cabinet of his administration Lord Hankey submitted his interim report on the structure of Britain's intelligence services. His report had been commissioned originally the previous December by Chamberlain, who had been obliged to field a number of complaints from his ministers concerning SIS's alleged ineffectiveness. Chamberlain had called on Hankey, his Minister without Portfolio, to investigate the complaints and deliberate on the requests for additional finance from Menzies. Indeed, on his own authority Menzies had spent a further £400,000 on top of his budget of £700,000. Hankey undertook a detailed review of SIS (including Section D) and GC & CS, and on 11 March 1940 submitted an interim report. He had still not yet had time to deal with MI5 in any depth. The Hankey Report made several proposals, but they did not extend to any major restructuring of SIS.

On 10 June 1940 Churchill actually increased his political hold over one of the secret organizations, MI5, by sacking the long-standing Director-General, Major-General Sir Vernon Kell, and instituting the Security Executive. This entirely new body was headed by Lord Swinton, a senior Tory who had been Air Minister in Chamberlain's Government. SIS had no direct interest in this development except to the extent that Menzies took the opportunity to increase his influence over the Security Service. It was agreed that one of the permanent members of the Executive (which effectively would be temporarily running MI5 in spite of the appointment of the Director of 'B' Division, Brigadier Jasper Harker, as Acting Director-General) Valentine Vivian, should be the Head of SIS's Section V. This appointment was eventually to prove invaluable when the Prime Minister sought the Security Executive's advice on the appointment of a permanent Director-General in the place of Harker.

The Security Executive was an uncomfortable escalation of political control in the eyes of the Labour Party, and its fears were increased when, in August, the Prime Minister declined to discuss the subject during question time in the House of Commons, when word had spread of the new institution. A belated attempt to calm the Executive's critics was then made by co-opting Isaac Foot (the former Liberal MP) and Alf Wall, a trade unionist, onto it.

The net result of these moves was to harden the opinions of Attlee and Dalton. Both men were perfectly aware that the formation of a new Service directorate was under consideration. The scheme favoured by the new Director of Military Intelligence, Paddy Beaumont-Nesbitt, centralized control over SIS, MI(R) and Electra House, with liaison arrangements with naval and air intelligence and the Foreign Office. All these units have been mentioned before in this book except for Electra House. Here, as far back as 1938, Sir Campbell Stuart had set up a propaganda unit to create misleading information, which would be released in such a way that it would appear to have originated in enemy countries or in enemy-occupied countries. It had been responsible jointly to the Ministry of Economic Warfare, the Foreign Secretary and the Ministry of Information up until now.

Beaumont-Nesbitt's proposal was turned down, but Churchill accepted the principle of introducing a co-ordinating body and instructed Lord Hankey to investigate further. On 13 June 1940 Hankey called in Laurence Grand, the Head of Section D, and John Holland, his opposite number in MI(R), to discuss the idea of a new department under a separate minister. Both concurred that the strategic consequences of a French collapse made such a development both necessary and desirable. This view was reinforced shortly afterwards by the Chiefs of Staff. Hankey duly reported back to the War Cabinet, and on 1 July Lord Halifax called a summit meeting in his office in the Foreign Office of all the interested parties to take the matter a step further. Menzies attended, as did Beaumont-Nesbitt, Hankey, Sir Alexander Cadogan (with his secretary, Gladwyn Jebb), Desmond Morton, Geoffrey Lloyd (the Colonial Secretary, now Lord Geoffrey-Lloyd), and Hugh Dalton. At the conclusion of the meeting Halifax wrote a report for the Prime Minister recommending the creation of a completely new organization, entirely independent of the War Office machine. The only problem remaining (apart from a few dissenting voices from the 'irregulars') was the question of control. Dalton and Attlee insisted that political control of the body be vested in a Labour minister, and on 16 July Churchill acquiesced by offering the post to Dalton. Dalton accepted and a charter for Special Operations Executive was drawn up by Neville Chamberlain, then Lord President of the Council. The paper announced Dalton's chairmanship and stated that Sir Robert Vansittart would assist him. On 22 July 1940 the document received the approval of the War Cabinet and SOE came into being.

The Prime Minister charged Dalton's new organization with responsibility for setting Europe ablaze. It was initially divided into two: SO(1), to be run by Sir Campbell Stuart, incorporating the propaganda staff of Electra House; and SO(2), to be headed by Sir Frank Nelson.

In Dalton's vision this new secret department would undertake 'unavowable' operations all over the world. To smooth the considerably ruffled feathers of the Whitehall Establishment, he appointed Cadogan's former Private Secretary at the Foreign Office, Gladwyn Jebb, as his chief executive and right-hand man.

The first Chief of SO(2), Sir Frank Nelson, was a former Tory MP for Stroud who had been the Z-network's man in Basle. He had held the post until the fall of France, when he had made his way back to London. He had been educated at Heidelberg and in 1926 had led a delegation of four Unionist MPs to the Soviet Union. Nelson acquired two Chiefs of Staff, George Taylor and Colonel F.T. (Tommy) Davies, and proceeded to reorganize Britain's capacity to pursue 'irregular warfare'.

Neither Taylor nor Davies were new to secret service work. Davies had been a director of Courtaulds until the outbreak of war when he was recruited into MI(R), the obscure War Office unit created by that early exponent of guerrilla warfare, Colonel John Holland. MI(R) had been principally concerned with promoting irregular operations behind enemy lines and had come under the jurisdiction of the War Office. Its personnel had operated in military uniform which distinguished them from other embryonic groups with similar aims. In one of MI(R)'s last missions in Europe, Davies had led a raiding party on a Courtauld factory in Calais and had succeeded in removing a large quantity of platignum from under the noses of the advancing Germans. Taylor, on the other hand, was an Australian who had previously been the head of Section D's Balkan division.

Nelson's acquisition of these two key officers effectively brought both MI(R) and Section D, with its staff of 140, under his control. This fact had not escaped the notice of the Head of Section D, Laurence Grand, or, for that matter, of Menzies, who complained bitterly that he had not been consulted about the take-over. The net result of this episode was that Grand returned to his regiment, and the Secret Intelligence Service was granted control of SOE's communications.

SIS's own communications were excellent. This success was largely due to one man, Richard Gambier-Parry, who, during the late 1920s and 1930s had been the BBC's public relations officer. Recruited from the Pye electronics firm in 1938, this Old Etonian and former Royal Welch Fusilier transformed Section VIII, the SIS communications unit, in just eighteen months. By mid-1940, and aided by his principal assistant, Major Maltby, he was presiding over the SIS transmitters at Hanslope Park and was organizing the building of special suitcase wireless sets at neighbouring

Whaddon Chase, for the use of agents in the field. At the outbreak of war most of the important SIS Stations around the world had their own short-wave radio equipment, enabling them to send messages direct to Hanslope Park without relying on the regular Foreign Office channels. At Hanslope the messages were passed to dispatch riders for delivery to London. Later in the war secure teleprinter lines were built to Broadway.

Nelson now took over Section D's old quarters in the St Ermin's Hotel and began reorganizing in earnest. Taylor took responsibility for the operational side, which consisted of forming individual country sections, whilst Davies initiated a transformation of the administrative structure, which included training, supplies and stores.

Overall direction for SOE was provided firmly by Dalton, who was by now expanding the Ministry of Economic Warfare in its new premises in Berkeley Square. Besides Gladwyn Jebb, he obtained the services of Philip Broad from the Foreign Office and Robin Brook from the City. Brook was an immensely successful businessman who was later appointed a director of the Bank of England.

The new management quickly proceeded to alter Section D's arrangements. Arthur Goodwill, D's representative in Cairo, was replaced by a barrister, George Pollock, and (Sir) Charles Hambro was placed in overall charge of the Norwegian and Danish country sections. The Polish section was given, briefly, to Bickham Sweet-Escott, who was then succeeded by Colin Gubbins, both early Section D and MI(R) recruits. On the recommendation of the new Director of Personnel, George Courtauld, responsibility for France was given to Leslie Humphreys, formerly Section D's representative in Paris. In December 1940 he was succeeded by Mr H.L. Marriott, a director of Courtaulds' French company. Later in the war he too was replaced, this time by Maurice Buckmaster, once a manager with the Ford Motor Company in France.

The new country section heads now began recruiting for agents in the field and constructed a system of stations overseas in direct parallel with SIS. Thus in November 1940 Jack Beevor was sent to Lisbon to represent SO(2) with the cover role of 'Assistant Military Attaché', and Tom Masterson went to Belgrade, the capital of neutral Yugoslavia.

SOE's creation was unquestionably a matter of political expediency, but it also acknowledged the urgent need for the capability to use unconventional warfare. The Nazi *Blitzkrieg* had swept across Europe and had left the British Isles seemingly defenceless. In the summer of 1940 it seemed that no regular units would be able to operate on the Continent for the foreseeable future, so everything would depend on harrying the enemy behind his own lines. In the intelligence field the options were equally limited. Menzies was naturally anxious to rebuild the lost pre-war networks, but in practical terms this could only be managed from the few remaining

SIS Stations in Europe, now effectively reduced to Stockholm, Lisbon, Madrid and Berne. This, in turn, placed a heavier burden on the peripheral Stations in Tangiers and Istanbul. Although all of these Stations had their star agents and their favoured sources of information, none could provide the ready-built networks on offer from the London-based secret services in exile.

The Czechs, who had been in London since March 1939, were quartered in two hotels in Victoria. They kept in contact with Prague through Harold Gibson; then when he moved to Istanbul, they worked through Captain Rex Howard RN until L. Fitzlyon took over as SIS liaison officer. In strategic terms the Czechs were particularly important because of Paul Thümmel, A-54, the senior Abwehr officer who continued to send out information for the first two years of the war, first through Frantisek Moravec, the head of Czech Military Intelligence, and then through Czech agents whenever he visited a neutral country. As soon as Gibson reached Istanbul, he contacted him there. It is difficult to exaggerate Thümmel's contribution during the months immediately before, and during, the first two years of the war.

Gibson's principal assistant in running this vital operation was Eric Gedye, a former *Times* Central European correspondent who had been based in Prague before the German occupation. Gedye's contact with A-54 was, however, to be jeopardized by Thümmel's promotion in late 1941. His new Abwehr position in Prague required him to obtain special permission before travelling outside the Reich, in spite of his privileged Party Gold Badge and his friendship with such senior figures as Canaris and Himmler. This threatened to seriously restrict the flow of intelligence from him, and accordingly a conference was hastily arranged in Istanbul with Moravec's deputy, Colonel Strankmueller, and Gibson. It was agreed that Thümmel should in future communicate through the Czech resistance movement, UVOD, and use the code-name FRANTA. His identity would further be protected by the cover-names of Dr Holm and Dr Steinberg. This decision to put him in the hands of the UVOD, despite the precautions, inevitably meant widening the circle who knew of A-54's existence and eventually led to Thümmel's arrest in February 1942. Thümmel was court-martialled but, incredibly, he was acquitted and released. In his defence he claimed he had tried to infiltrate the UVOD for patriotic reasons, a claim which, though implausible for a man in his position, was accepted. A more probable explanation is that Canaris protected him, perhaps by blackmailing Reinhard Heydrich, the SS governor of Bohemia, about his Jewish antecedents. In any case a plan was prepared in London, code-named ANTHROPOID, to extract him from Czechoslovakia. The rescue attempt failed, thus compromising Thümmel further, and he was rearrested on a charge of treason. A-54 spent the next three years in a fortress at Terezin, where he was murdered in April 1945.

Some of the Allied secret services exiled to Britain required a minimum of SIS supervision: the Norwegians were a case in point. Their Military Intelligence Service, headed by Thor Boye, was assigned Commander Eric Welch RN as SIS liaison officer. Welch was married to a Norwegian and, before the war, had been the manager of the International Paint Company's factory in Norway, so his detailed, first-hand knowledge of the pre-war Norwegian scene enabled him (and thus SIS) to manœuvre through the minefield of local politics and deal equally with Boye's service and the rival Milorg resistance group under the leadership of Captain John Rognes. One of the first results of the Norwegian/SIS relationship was the acquisition of several fishing boats and high-powered motor launches so contact could be maintained with the embryonic stay-behind networks in Norway. This service was to become famous as the 'Shetland Bus', the first of a number of 'irregular' NID/SIS operations run by Captain Frank Slocum RN, the Chief's former Assistant Chief Staff Officer. Slocum was given the naval intelligence cover title 'Deputy Director Operations Division (Intelligence)', and placed in charge of 'NID (C)', the cover-name for his section. Initially the unit lacked both French-speaking, personnel and suitable equipment, but Slocum, who had been recruited by Sinclair from the Royal Naval Tactical School in 1936, quickly set about acquiring both.

For the greater part of 1940 this embryonic private navy was responsible for running almost all the SIS missions into occupied territory. Later in the year its operations expanded and further bases were established at Dartmouth and Lerwick in the Shetlands.

Slocum's fishing boat section was to become a vital link with the Continent, not least because of SIS's dearth of alternatives. The Royal Navy was unable to provide any fast motor torpedo-boats until 1942, and the Air Ministry was equally ill equipped to meet the SIS's clandestine requirements. In fact, just one air mission was achieved between the evacuation from Dunkirk in May 1940 and the end of the year. The operation, which took place in November, consisted of a Westland Lysander aircraft, piloted by Flight Lieutenant Wally Farley of 419 Squadron (Special Duties), being sent to France to collect an SIS agent, Phillip Schneidau. The plane returned safely, and both men reported how well the Lysander had performed. This was the first of many SIS (and SOE) flights conducted by the 'Moon Squadrons', based at Tempsford in Bedfordshire and Tangmere in West Sussex.

The Poles exiled themselves first to France. Within a month of being chased out of there by the Germans, they had established themselves in London, in the Rubens Hotel in Buckingham Palace Road, under the leadership of Colonel Stefan A. Mayer. Mayer later became head of the Polish military training school in Glasgow, when he was succeeded by

Colonel Gano, who was assisted by Major Zychon. Commander Wilfred Dunderdale RNVR, an excellent linguist who had served in the Paris Station since 1926, became their link with SIS. Dunderdale had joined the Paris Station (then headed by Maurice Jeffes) after a four-year stint in Istanbul. He had attended many of the pre-war tripartite intelligence conferences, organized by the Poles and the French, as Sinclair's representative and was therefore a familiar face to the Poles.

Dunderdale had been one of the two pre-war principal SIS case officers for France (the other being Kenneth Cohen, the former Z-network organizer), and the strength of the Polish networks in France had led him to develop close relations with the Polish Deuxième Bureau in the 1930s. Information exchanged had mainly been about cryptography because Warsaw had not been regarded as a promising base for operations against the Nazis. As the Polish intelligence chief, Colonel Mayer, was to comment after the war, it seemed that the SIS Head of Station in the Polish capital had primarily been interested in the Soviet Union. This was true, but a good relationship had also been established with the Polish code-breakers which was eventually to be all-important in the Allied effort to defeat the German Enigma coding machine.

In spite of having been uprooted twice, the Polish Deuxième Bureau maintained good wireless links with its stay-behind agents in their own German-occupied home territory, and these networks quickly became the sole SIS sources in the region, another symptom of the collapse of the SIS rings in Europe. The Poles also provided valuable information from their other European rings. Predominant among these was the famous INTERALLIE organization based in Paris. This group, under the leadership of Wing-Commander Roman Garby-Czerniawski, continued to operate until November 1941. SIS's reliance on the Polish rings led to a unique bargain: the Poles could operate from England with complete freedom and use their own independent ciphers and transmitters (which were located in Woldingham, Surrey); in exchange, Colonel Mayer agreed to share all their information with SIS, with the sole exception of material deemed to be concerned with Poland's internal political affairs.

The Anglo–Polish relationship was to remain a happy one, which is less than can be said for the Anglo–Dutch. The evacuation of The Hague Station in May 1940 was executed by a similar removal of the Dutch Military Intelligence Service to London. Its Chief was General von Oorschot, the man who had been so involved with the events which led to the Venlo fiasco. Relations between him and the Head of Station, Lionel Loewe, cooled considerably in the aftermath of the kidnapping, and both were perfectly aware that the German excuse for invading the Netherlands was the claim that the Dutch were covert Allies of the British and had collaborated by allowing the British to operate freely on Dutch territory. There was, of course, an element of truth in this and, as a result, the government-in-exile in London found itself beset with problems with its intelligence services.

The first such service was the Centrale Inlichtingendienst (Central Intelligence Service) headed by Superintendent François van t'Sant, the former Commissioner of Police in The Hague. Van t'Sant enjoyed very useful connections, in that he had worked with Henry Landau in Holland in the Great War (when he had been in charge of the river police in Rotterdam) and had been instrumental in achieving Queen Wilhelmina's escape from the Germans. She was later to appoint him her private secretary. The SIS, painfully aware of van t'Sant's difficulties, appointed an SIS veteran, Colonel Euan Rabagliati, as its official SIS liaison officer. Rabagliati, who held the Military Cross and the Air Force Cross, had distinguished himself in the Great War (on 16 August 1914) by being the first British pilot to shoot down an enemy aircraft in aerial combat. As head of the Dutch country section he was assisted by his deputy, and future successor, Captain Charles Seymour.

Van t'Sant established his headquarters in 77 Chester Square, while the Dutch government-in-exile, led by Professor Gerbrandy, took over Stratton House in Arlington Street. In addition, a number of Dutch escapees were informally recruited by Rabagliati and given accommodation in Chester Square Mews. This division of labour was to prove very unsatisfactory, for the Dutch seemed to be more interested in sorting out their own political differences than helping Rabagliati.

Unfortunately, the very first joint SIS/Dutch operation attempted went badly wrong. A young Royal Netherlands Navy officer, Lieutenant Lodo van Hamel, was parachuted into occupied Holland near Leyden on 28 August 1940 with a transmitter and instructions to link up with one of the developing Dutch resistance organizations. Van Hamel arrived safely and proceeded to create no less than four local rings, each equipped with home-made transmitters. However, two months later, when he was summoned to his rendezvous with a seaplane on the North Sea coast for his flight back to England, he was denounced to the Germans and arrested near Zurig. The Germans also managed to arrest three of his travelling companions, all of whom were connected to an embryonic Dutch resistance cell. Professor Becking, one of the leaders of the Orde Dienst resistance group, survived the ordeal, as did his two couriers, but van Hamel was tried by court-martial and executed the following June.

This disaster served to confirm to the Dutch that the British were thoroughly unreliable, and relations went from bad to worse. By December 1941 Rabagliati and van t'Sant had infiltrated five agents into occupied Holland, but only one, Aart Alblas, was left at liberty. He too was soon to be arrested and executed at Mauthausen in 1944. SOE attempted to improve matters when it created a Dutch section under Richard Laming and Major Charles Blunt (later Head of SOE's Italian section), but there was no persuading them to co-operate. One particular bone of contention was the CSS's insistence that all contact with Allied agents in enemy-occupied territory should be handled exclusively by SIS, and that communications should only use ciphers provided by SIS.

The Dutch strenuously opposed this policy, but eventually complied, albeit reluctantly, when Rabagliati made it clear that there would be no compromise on the issue. This was to have unpleasant consequences later in the war when breaches in SOE's security resulted in the deaths of a number of Dutch SOE agents who were lured to Holland by enemy-controlled transmitters.

On 14 August 1941, after many internal disagreements, van t'Sant resigned as head of the Centrale Inlichtingendienst and was replaced by Dr R.P.J. Derksema, a young lawyer from Zutphen who enjoyed SIS's support. He did not last long, and the Dutch government-in-exile later set up a new intelligence organization, the Bureau Militaire Voorbereiding Terugkeer (Bureau for the Military Preparations for the Return), under the leadership of a Netherlands Royal Marines officer, Colonel M.R. de Bruyne. De Bruyne also found it difficult to co-operate with the British, and before Rabagliati passed his liaison job to Charles Seymour he commented at his amazement that the Dutch, who spent so much time fighting among themselves, had any time left to fight the Germans.

If the Dutch were less than enthusiastic about SIS, the problems encourtered by Rabagliati were minimal compared to the crises experienced by Claude Dansey and Kenneth Cohen in their dealings with the French.

By the end of 1940 there were no less than five separate British intelligence sections attempting to conduct joint intelligence operations with the French. SIS had two, one based on its contacts in Vichy (run by Commander Cohen using a number of code-names, including DUNCAN, and the more familiar Z-network covers of Keith Crane and Robert Craig), and the other, headed by Commander Dunderdale, tried to liaise with de Gaulle's Free French groups. For its part, SOE had established an 'RF' section, under the leadership of Eric Piquet-Wicks, who worked closely with Captain Andre Dewavrin and his deputy, Captain Lagier (code-named BIENVENUE), and an 'F' section, which operated entirely independently of the Free French, much to the latter's chagrin. Added to these four units was MI5's 'E' Division country section, headed by Kenneth Younger.

When they arrived in London, the two French pre-war intelligence organizations, the Deuxième Bureau and the Service de Renseignements, had been replaced by de Gaulle's Free French contingent with a new organization, headed by Dewavrin, and a Service Action under Captain

Raymond Lagier. In January 1942 both these secret departments were combined by General de Gaulle to form the Bureau Central de Renseignements et d'Action (BCRA), which was based at 10 Duke Street, in the West End of London. De Gaulle's candidate for the leadership of BCRA was Captain Andre Dewavrin, who also called himself 'Colonel Passy'.

The French enjoyed their proliferation of secret services, and expended a considerable amount of effort infighting with both their rivals and their Allies. It should be recognized that there were, at the time, an unlimited number of opportunities for embarrassing misunderstandings. One such example is an incident which took place in January 1941. The Chief of Security at the Free French headquarters in Carlton Gardens, Commandant Howard (a *nom de guerre*) had persuaded MI5 that de Gaulle's deputy, Vice-Admiral Muselier, was in fact a Vichy agent in touch with the enemy. His proof was a number of compromising letters. When MI5 informed Churchill, the Prime Minister exploded with rage and ordered Muselier's immediate arrest.

After Muselier had spent a very disagreeable week in gaol (Pentonville, followed by Brixton), de Gaulle indignantly protested the innocence of his deputy and proceeded to demonstrate how MI5 had been duped into thinking the 'Muselier Letters' were genuine. In fact, they had been forged by Commandant Howard and Adjutant Collin. Muselier was promptly released, but the damage to Anglo-French relations was incalculable. De Gaulle himself was always profoundly suspicious of all British intelligence agencies and bitterly resented the fact that SIS exercised overall control of his links with France.

Further damage to the Anglo-French relationship was incurred by what became known as the Dufour incident in December 1942, when a French former SIS agent was arrested by BCRA and detained at its camp near Camberley. Dufour escaped and made his way to London, where he applied to the High Court for a writ against Dewavrin and his deputy, alleging torture. On this occasion the complainant was given a substantial cash payment to drop the case. Relations with the Free French were further complicated in 1942 when de Gaulle appointed Jacques Soustelle as his intelligence supremo. Both MI5 and SIS had obtained considerable evidence that suggested Soustelle was a Soviet agent.

Internal wrangling was by no means confined to the French intelligence services. The Brussels Station, consisting of Colonel Calthrop (who was confined to a wheel-chair), Barnes-Stott and Mr Crowther, had been obliged to make a hasty withdrawal in the face of the German advance in May 1940. The Belgians arrived in London with their security department, Sûreté d'Etat, headed by Baron Fernand Lepage, and the Deuxième Bureau, led by Henri Bernard and Colonel Jean Marissal. These two organizations were, in effect, organs of the Belgian government-in-exile and there was, inevitably, some rivalry between them. There was, however, a third Belgian group, the Armée Secrète, a coalition of various different political interests, all united in their resistance to the Nazi occupation. The Armée Secrète was commanded by General Jules Pire, and his Chief of Staff was Jean de Marmol, a controversial character held in disfavour by the Belgian government-in-exile. The man appointed head of the Belgian section of SOE (later the 'LC', Low Countries, section) was Major Claude Knight, and he was assisted by Major Hardy Amies.

The business of intelligence gathering and 'irregular operations' in Belgium was left entirely to SOE, although Nicholas Vansittart, Lord Vansittart's brother, advised on political matters. Late in 1943 an SIS officer, Commander Philip Johns (formerly Head of Station in Lisbon, Rio de Janeiro and Buenos Aires), was sent to replace Knight.

The rest of the Allied secret services had less complicated backgrounds. The Danes, for example, had already provided temporary refuge for Frank Foley and his Berlin Station, and tolerated the less than neutral activities of Bernard O'Leary, one of Copenhagen's livelier characters who had been Head of Station until the end of February 1940 (when he was replaced by Sidney Smith). It soon became clear that SOE's Danish organization was producing excellent information on its occupiers, and it was therefore agreed that SIS would delegate its responsibility for the acquisition of intelligence to SOE. This meant running operations from the British Legation in Stockholm, already a thriving intelligence centre with both an SIS Station and an SOE Mission.

The Dutch, Belgian, Norwegian and Danish governments-in-exile were all grateful (in varying degrees) for the chance to regroup in London. One cause of friction with de Gaulle was the fact that he was not officially recognized as the leader of a government-in-exile. Nevertheless, SIS took the opportunity with each to improve its political standing and to take a share of its guests' incoming intelligence. From the foreign secret services' point of view, this arrangement seemed very attractive. They were provided with accommodation in London, training and other facilities in Scotland, and the use of equipment to communicate with their stay-behind networks at home. All believed that SIS enjoyed the benefit of numerous networks of its own, but this was not actually the case. In fact, without the exiled organizations SIS would have been largely ignorant of events taking place in enemy-occupied Europe. Virtually SIS's only covert advantage was in the development of signals interception and analysis, known as SIGINT.

Although SIS and the Foreign Office had been party to the formation of SOE, neither liked seeing a new secret service department growing under the control of another ministry, challenging their authority. However, Menzies was no doubt able to take some consolation from the fact that Frank Nelson, the first Head of SOE, had been the Z-network's man in

Basle and was, therefore, particularly close to Claude Dansey. Menzies also saw to it that he retained complete control over the communications of the newcomer. Initially also, SIS controlled all communications from London to their home bases of the exiled Allied intelligence departments, with the exception of Poland, for the Poles were superb decrypters and vital to the success of the Government Code and Cipher School at Bletchley.

Since the opening of hostilities in 1939 GCHQ had grown considerably in its new home at Bletchley Park, an ugly Victorian mansion in Buckinghamshire. The entire estate had been bought by Admiral Sinclair in 1938 from its owner, Sir George Leon. Now Leon's gardens were almost entirely occupied by rows of wooden barrack huts hastily constructed to house the ever-increasing GCHQ staff.

GCHQ's first major operational success took place in January 1940 when the Luftwaffe's Enigma cipher keys were broken for the first time. The Enigma cipher machine was the principal system of encrypting and decrypting messages used by all the German armed forces. The machine itself, resembling a bulky portable typewriter, was a development of a commercial machine, the Scherbius, patented in 1923 by a private company in Germany, Chiffriermaschinen-Aktiengesellschaft (The Cipher Machine Corporation). Five years later, in August 1927, the company registered a similar patent in London. In 1926 the German navy adopted the machine and two years later it was followed by the Wehrmacht. The Luftwaffe had no use for cipher machines until after 1933, when Hitler authorized their illicit expansion.

As soon as use of Enigma entered widespread military service in Germany, the Poles and the French began work on how to 'break' the system. The challenge was immense, for mere possession of a machine did not mean the ability to decrypt German messages. In fact, the various different modifications to the Enigma between 1926 and 1939 included the introduction of a fourth 'wheel', the adjustable disc which scrambled the text between the typewriter keyboard, where the operator entered his text, and the external cable which took the enciphered message to the transmitter. The wheels and the connections in between were variable and the German units using the machine changed the settings at regular intervals. Units dealing with the more sensitive material altered the wheels every twenty-four hours. If one did not have details of the current wheel setting, one was faced with many millions of possible permutations ... an apparently insoluble task.

The pioneer of Enigma decryption was the head of the French Service de Renseignements, Colonel Louis Rivet, who appointed Captain Gustave Bertrand to run his cryptanalysis unit, Section D. Rivet and Bertrand were aided in their search by a German, code-named ASCHE, who volunteered his services to the French Legation in Berne and subsequently sold several hundred documents describing the Enigma's operation. During the course of nineteen covert meetings held all over Europe, ASCHE provided some of the Enigma keys used by the Wehrmacht in 1932 and 1933. ASCHE is believed to have been Hans-Thilo Schmidt, an employee of the Wehrmacht's cipher department. In 1934 he was transferred to a Luftwaffe communications unit and continued to operate Enigma machines there. ASCHE's information was valuable to the French, but it proved priceless to the Poles who had been working in parallel to Bertrand and had collaborated with him. The Poles, led by Colonel Stefan Mayer, also ran a cipher bureau, the Biuro Szyfrow, which had simply purchased the commercial Enigma machine in 1932 and tried to convert it to the German military version. By combining their resources the French and Poles successfully reproduced an Enigma system, complete with the necessary keys, and thereafter Colonel Mayer's organization succeeded in constructing its own military Enigma machines at the Ava factory in Warsaw. By the time the Germans invaded Poland, it had built a total of fifteen facsimiles. The problem of finding the current keys proved more difficult, and a team of Polish mathematicians were put to work building an electronic computer, or *bombe*, to race through all the possible combinations. In 1937 they perfected the system and were able, for the very first time, to read intercepted German radio messages. This breakthrough was short-lived because the Germans, who were then only changing the wheel settings every three months, introduced a monthly alteration, and then a daily setting.

In spite of this disappointment the Poles had shown that the Enigma was not totally secure, and in December 1938 the French arranged a conference at their headquarters in the rue Tourville, Paris, to discuss the latest developments with GC & CS. The British were aware of Germany's reliance on the Enigma machine, but apart from a brief period during the Spanish Civil War (when Franco's forces had used the commercially available version) GC & CS had failed to make any progress. Indeed, the official attitude was that the German navy's Enigma machine was impossible to 'break'. Nevertheless, they handed over their intercepts and the direction-finding calculations to Bertrand in case they helped his research.

The first joint three-day conference took place in Paris on 7 January 1939. The Poles sent Colonel Gwido Langer and Major Maksymilian Ciezki and the British sent Commander Alistair Denniston and two assistants. The conference served to cement the basis of future meetings: the free exchange of information among the three allies. It was also agreed that to improve communications a secure teleprinter link would be installed between the three allies. Six months later a second conference was arranged on 25 July at a secret Polish signals intelligence unit at Mokotov-Pyry, some ten kilometres south of Warsaw in the Pyry forest. On this occasion Denniston was accompanied by Dillwyn Knox, one of the original GC & CS recruits from Room 40, and Stewart Menzies, representing the CSS. To preserve his identity Menzies adopted the cover of 'Professor Sandwich of Oxford University'. The conference proved to be one of the most important events in GCHQ's history, for the Poles announced that they had decided to give one of their replica Enigmas to each of their French and British colleagues.

The three British representatives returned to the Hotel Bristol in Warsaw and then continued their journey by air back to London. Meanwhile, Bertrand sent the two Polish gifts to Paris via a diplomatic messenger and contacted the SIS Station in Paris. At that time the Station consisted of Commander Wilfred (Biffy) Dunderdale and his assistant, Tom Greene. The Station itself was based in Dunderdale's flat in the rue Joubert. Liaison with the Russian émigré community was maintained by an SIS officer named Parkinson, and from time to time Kenneth Cohen, John Codrington and Claude Dansey made appearances on behalf of their Z-network agents.

On 25 August 1939 Bertrand, Dunderdale and Greene travelled by train to London with the replica Enigma and were met by Menzies at Victoria Station. Menzies promptly returned to Broadway with his prize and presented it to Denniston, who occupied an office in the same building, two floors above his. Denniston then took it to his technical staff at the Post Office Research Station at Dollis Hill in north London where Alan Turing, a mathematical genius, had been working on a British version of the Polish *bombe*. In addition, a contract was given to the British Tabulating Company at Letchworth to reproduce the Enigma's electrical circuits.

The immediate effect of this windfall was the capability to decrypt the accumulated German wireless traffic. The current traffic, however, remained unreadable because the relevant keys were still unobtainable.

When the Germans invaded Poland the Biuro Szyfrow began to move north and east, but on 17 September 1939 the Soviet Union also launched an invasion, thus forcing the Polish Government to seek refuge in Romania. On 25 September three experienced Polish cryptanalysts made their way to France, where they were joined a few days later by Colonel Langer with a contingent of their colleagues. They continued their work at a château near Vignolles under Bertrand's protection until mid-June 1940, when they were obliged to retreat. The CSS requested that the entire French–Polish organization be moved to the safety of England without delay but, characteristically, the French refused. They also declined an invitation to establish a tripartite cryptanalysis headquarters in France. Instead, a compromise was reached: the French and Poles were to concentrate on breaking the keys, while the recently renamed GCHQ was to attempt to develop quicker mechanical methods of achieving the same goal. As well as the existing landline teleprinter links, communications were improved by the posting of a British liaison officer, Captain Kenneth Mac-Farlan, to Vignolles.

MacFarlan was a linguist and a member of Colonel Jefferys's small staff in Section IX. He had done valuable work on Italian hand ciphers during the Spanish Civil War and it was his task to link Vignolles to Broadway and GCHQ.

The first key to fall to GCHQ was that of a Wehrmacht cipher broken early in the New Year of 1940, and this was quickly followed by a Luftwaffe key. Then, in February, the capture of U-33 yielded three Enigma wheels. All these three events led to renewed optimism about Bletchley's prospects, although the news from Vignolles continued to deteriorate. When France fell on 23 June 1940 Bertrand led his staff from Vignolles, via Paris and Toulouse, to Algiers in North Africa. Kenneth MacFarlan succeeded in escaping to Bordeaux, where an RAF transport collected him and returned him to England.

From SIS's point of view, the situation was catastrophic. All the combined experience of the French and Polish cryptanalysts was lost, and GCHQ was left to pick up the pieces. The overall intelligence picture in the summer of 1940 could hardly have looked bleaker.

Part Two

1940-45

The British, for their part, would have liked to see us simply send over agents with instructions to gather, in isolation, information about the enemy with reference to defined objectives. Such was the method used for espionage. But we meant to do better.

CHARLES DE GAULLE, *War Memoirs: The Call to Honour*
1940–42

8

European Developments
1940

One of Britain's most startling near disasters in the war was now about to occur. Intelligence which General Eisenhower called 'priceless', which was to save 'thousands of British and American lives and, in no small way, contributed to the speed with which the enemy was routed', very nearly never got off the ground because SIS's past history had been so equivocal.

By the spring of 1940, SIS had an unexpected bonus: it had broken some of the Luftwaffe Enigma keys and was able to read current traffic, but this raised problems of how this top-secret material was going to be distributed to those to whom it would be useful without giving away how it had been obtained.

During the Great War there had been very little Allied signals intelligence activity on the battlefield because the Germans had restricted their use of the wireless to the lowest levels of command and to their overseas communications. GCHQ at Bletchley, therefore, believed, fighting the next war closely on the basis of the last, that it would witness a dramatic reduction in enemy radio traffic. Inexplicably, the reverse happened, and even the internal security authorities in Germany turned to their own Enigma machines to transmit messages from one centre to another. GCHQ was, therefore, on the receiving end of an extraordinary windfall of raw intelligence, but it did not have the means to distribute it effectively. It was not until late in 1940 that teleprinter terminals were installed at Bletchley to cut out the time-consuming (and potentially hazardous) use of dispatch riders. When the trend of increasing enemy wireless activity became clear, Menzies authorized Denniston greatly to increase his staff at Bletchley and created a distribution system for the resulting information based on Special Liaison Units (SLUs).

The need for special security precautions to deal with the GCHQ decrypts was immediately obvious to Menzies, who suggested a suitable scheme to cover the source. He simply invented an apparently well-placed agent, code-named BONIFACE, and decreed that all the SIGINT material would enjoy the same code-name. By keeping the real source a secret, Menzies unwittingly devalued it, for SIS's credibility in Whitehall was all but lost. The appearance of yet another SIS agent was greeted with understandable scepticism by the Services, who had all been led astray by SIS in the past. To rely on the mysterious BONIFACE was too much to ask and, as a consequence, the Services ignored the material. When Menzies realized that the decrypts were being treated like the rest of the SIS advice, he scrapped the BONIFACE cover and introduced a more impersonal system which involved the use of a prefix 'CX' on the SIS intelligence summaries. This system remained in use until June 1941, when a new security classification, ULTRA SECRET, was brought in. Inevitably, ULTRA has since become the generic term for all the Enigma decrypts.

To say that the first Enigma decrypts were being thrown into waste-paper-baskets is undoubtedly going too far, but the result was similar. Much time and valuable information was lost through Menzies's use of the code-name BONIFACE and his sudden *volte-face* was not greeted with much enthusiasm either. Was Menzies unaware of the importance of the material or had he not realized how the SIS information was viewed in Whitehall?

After BONIFACE, he had no excuse for not recognizing the truth: that SIS's performance during the first six months of the war had been bad. Menzies was now obliged to take up defensive positions on a whole range of issues. In contrast, MI5's performance had been excellent and this served to deepen the existing divisions between the two organizations. Eventually relations deteriorated so much that Menzies was forced to request the creation of an MI6 section within the counter-espionage division of the Security Service. This plan was approved by Kell's successor as Director-General, Sir David Petrie, and accordingly Mark Oliver, formerly SIS Head of Station in Rio de Janeiro, was accommodated in MI5's temporary headquarters in HM Prison Wormwood Scrubs. Oliver's diplomacy brought an immediate improvement in the MI5–MI6 relationship and gave MI6 a useful ear in the rival camp. MI5 had scored several important intelligence successes, such as the recruitment of Klop Ustinov and Wolfgang zu Putlitz in the German Embassy in London, and its wireless interceptors in the Radio Security Service had also stolen a march on GCHQ.

The Radio Security Service, which operated under the cover military intelligence designation MI8(c), originally consisted of a group of amateur radio hams who scanned the airwaves seeking and locating illicit wireless transmissions. In fact, there were none to find, so the organization tuned in to various interesting German broadcasts. One such source proved to be a set operating from a ship in the North Sea, which appeared to be conducting the Abwehr's operations in Norway. What made the ship's transmissions so interesting was the nature of its codes. Instead of relying on the Enigma machine, the Abwehr was using a hand cipher. This was to MI5's advantage because a similar hand cipher had been given to B Division's principal double agent, a Welshman code-named SNOW. SNOW had been run briefly by an SIS case officer, Edward Peal, but it was believed that the agent had deliberately compromised himself with his German contact. His case had, therefore, been abandoned in 1938 and his file passed to the Security Service, MI5. SNOW's MI5 case officer was Tar Robertson of B Division, who turned an unpromising espionage suspect into his star double agent. As a result, B Division was able to provide its RSS colleagues with enough information about Abwehr hand ciphers to let them break the North Sea traffic in December 1939. This event proved to be a turning point for the RSS, who then concentrated all its resources on the Abwehr. Not surprisingly, MI6 felt that this was its parish and Menzies began a long struggle with the RSS head, Colonel J.P.G. Worlledge, to take control of his operations. As we shall see, the Chief met stern resistance.

There was trouble for Menzies on other fronts as well. In May 1940 the newly appointed British Ambassador to Madrid, Sir Samuel Hoare, arrived in the Spanish capital with a number of prejudices against SIS and imposed severe restrictions on the activities of the local Head of Station, Mr Hamilton-Stokes. Hoare had served as an intelligence officer in Russia shortly after the revolution and invariably quoted this fact whenever his opinion was challenged. Hamilton-Stokes had recently taken over from de Renzy-Martin and the Ambassador was anxious not to let SIS get itself involved in any anti-Franco plots. The Head of Station was livid at Hoare's interference and telegrams flew to and from the Spanish capital. However, as a former Home Secretary, Hoare's political influence invariably won the day and the Madrid Station virtually ceased to operate. As we shall see, the Station had eventually to rely on the Americans to execute its less acceptable secret operations.

SIS's early miscalculations about German military strengths were compounded by further mistakes during the summer of 1940. The French military strategists had observed the German mobile columns sweeping through Poland and had concluded that such tactics could not be employed against a defended frontier. The Polish border had been virtually defence-less to the German invasion and this, the French claimed, had been the key to the so-called *Blitzkrieg* campaign. The Deuxième Bureau noted that the Maginot Line, which was a continuous line of fortifications from Basle on the Swiss border to Belgium in the north, would present a formidable obstacle to the German motorized forces. This proved to be a terrible error and one that had been circulated in London on SIS appreciations. It is, therefore, not surprising that the Services continued to build their own intelligence resources in preference to listening to Broadway's opinions. The Air Intelligence Branch, for example, which had begun the war with a staff of just forty officers, had quadrupled in size, as had the Military Intelligence Directorate at the War Office which had employed just forty-nine officers.

This increase of manpower meant more staff to study captured documents, more interrogators to question captured prisoners of war and more technicians to examine such crashed enemy aircraft as there were, but it did little to improve the acquisition of secret intelligence. In fact, the extra personnel had had very little to work on. For the first few months of the war the Air Intelligence experts had seen only one crashed enemy aircraft, a Heinkel 111 that had been shot down near Dalkeith in Scotland. As for captured documents, the only examples were some maps which the Brussels Station had acquired from its contacts in the Belgian Sûreté. The maps had been recovered from a Wehrmacht spotter plane that had made a forced landing near the German frontier. They were marked with a plan to invade Holland and Belgium and the Head of Station in Brussels, Colonel Calthrop, sent them to Broadway with his deputy, Captain John Bygott. The maps were ridiculed as obvious forgeries, and it was not until the end of May 1940 that Broadway realized that they were genuine.

Other excellent information was also doubted. SIS had few remaining secret sources left by now: paradoxically its main one was the Abwehr, which was responsible for much useful data although SIS did not realize this at the time. For example, the Dutch Assistant Military Attaché in Berlin, Major Gijsbertius Sas, had established very friendly relations with Colonel Hans Oster, the deputy head of the Abwehr. For motives that were then unclear, Oster had given last minute warnings to Sas about the German invasion of Poland on 23 August 1939. Sas had passed them on to Foley's Station in Berlin and the French Deuxième Bureau had been alerted. This action had caused a short delay in the launching of the German offensive and had served to authenticate Oster's credentials, although Oster had originally given the date of the attack as 26 August.

In May 1940 Oster told Sas that Hitler was about to attack neutral Holland and Belgium. This vital information was disbelieved by Oster's immediate superior in the Dutch military intelligence service, Colonel van de Plassche, because two previous warnings given by Oster earlier in the year had proved to be false. The Dutch were understandably wary of such messages from the Germans in view of their experience at Venlo, so no action was taken. The British too were reluctant to listen to Oster, and they believed they had good reason. In the mid-1930s an unknown agent had offered to sell Foley what was claimed to be a complete order of battle for the Luftwaffe. The price had been £10,000, so Foley had consulted the CSS, Sinclair, and after much discussion the purchase had been authorized. Squadron Leader John Perkins, from Section IV, had been sent to Zurich to close the deal, but the information proved to be worthless. Thereafterwards there was a lingering suspicion that the money had been spent to finance the modern Abwehr.

This experience, combined with the pre-war fiascos in Holland, gave the Abwehr an unjustified reputation for duplicity, and SIS took the collective view that volunteered intelligence should be treated as suspect. This attitude is the explanation behind Broadway's verdict on what was to become known as the Oslo Report.

Late in October 1939 the British Naval Attaché in Oslo, Captain Hector Boyes, reported to the local Head of Station, Commander Newill, that he had been offered some unspecified technical data by an anonymous donor. His instructions, which had arrived by post, had suggested a slight alteration in the usual introduction to the BBC's news in German. Newill passed the note on to Broadway and Menzies, who was then Acting Chief, authorized the necessary request to the BBC. It will be recalled that a similar signal had been demanded in Holland to establish Stevens's credentials before Venlo. The BBC broadcast the suggested variation, and on 3 November 1939 a small packet was hand-delivered to the Oslo Embassy. It contained ten pages of detailed technical information on a variety of topics, ranging from the development of experimental pilotless aircraft at Peenemünde to the introduction of radar along the German coast and advances made in the manufacture of bomb fuses, an example of which was enclosed.

The Oslo Station sent the packet to Broadway, where it was received by Section IV. This was justified on the grounds that the air section was the only SIS section with any technical knowledge, but while Winterbotham and his deputy, Major Adams, both spoke German, neither had a scientific background. The problem was solved by borrowing the services of a young scientist then working for the Air Ministry's Directorate of Scientific Research, Dr R.V. Jones. Jones had recently performed a valuable service for Broadway. On 19 September 1939 Hitler had made a widely reported speech in Danzig in which he appeared to refer to his 'secret weapon'. Jones had been asked to speculate on the nature of this weapon, but when he read the text of Hitler's speech he realized that it had been translated badly and that the 'weapon' comment had been made in connection with a previous reference to the Luftwaffe. Much to everyone's relief Jones had eliminated a non-existent weapon. Now Winterbotham asked him to perform a similar job on the Oslo Report. On this occasion Jones could not oblige. He studied the document and sent the fuse for testing, and came to the conclusion that all the information was genuine and that the Report was of the highest importance. Unfortunately, no one else shared his opinion and he was informed that no single person could have been so well informed on such a wide range of technical subjects. The Report was an obvious 'plant', and when he protested that some of the checkable information had proved true, he was gently told that it was a standard procedure to include a little genuine material to make all the rest appear authentic. Like the map found by the Belgians, the Oslo Report in time proved itself. However, the initial unfavourable verdict from SIS meant that the anonymous author was never pursued. By May 1940 the Oslo Head of Station's principal concern appears to have been extracting £289 compensation for the capture of his Vauxhall saloon, which had fallen into German hands during the Norwegian Campaign.

Germany's sudden success in overrunning so many countries so quickly had taken SIS by surprise: it had no contingency plans for such an eventuality. There were no secret networks *in situ* with radios ready, primed, and there had been no time to set up stay-behind ones at the last minute. Heads of Stations, officers and personnel had just upped and gone back to England or to neutral territory. Now SIS must use the networks of its exiled allies, for the prospects of infiltrating agents back into occupied territory were, to put it mildly, exceedingly bleak.

At this stage of the war there were not even any aircraft available to fly agents into Europe, although a special squadron, 419 Flight (Special Duties), was set up at Tempsford, Bedfordshire, in July 1940, for exactly this purpose. A neighbouring manor house, Farm Hall, was requisitioned to house agents in transit and strict security was imposed around the squadron's headquarters. 419 Flight's drawback was that it was not equipped with aircraft until November 1940, when it first began to receive Westland Lysanders. The Lysander was originally designed as an artillery spotter-plane and was extremely slow. Powered by a single 890 horsepower Bristol Mercury radial engine, it had a comfortable cruising speed of 165 mph. When fitted with extra fuel tanks it had a range of 1,150 miles, and it could take off and land on the smallest of fields. However, it was not until November 1940 that 419 Flight undertook its first mission to occupied France to evacuate an SIS agent, Phillip Schneidau. SIS's pre-war air fleet was limited to a single Lockheed 12A, which was anyway fully committed to photo-reconnaissance missions.

In the absence of any substantial help from the hard-pressed RAF, Menzies turned to SIS's traditional partner, the Royal Navy, and asked his Assistant Chief Staff Officer, Frank Slocum, to create what amounted to a private navy. Slocum's principal lieutenants were Daniel Lomenech, a French refugee whose parents ran a fish cannery in Brittany, and Steven Mackenzie, a French-speaking yachtsman who had previously been a liaison officer with Admiral Darlan, Commander-in-Chief of the French navy. Slocum's first vessel was a Newhaven trawler, *N51*, which had been requisitioned by the navy and was being used as a coastal patrol boat. The *N51* resembled a typical Breton fishing boat, so it was given false colours and registration and pressed into service running agents across the Channel. It was crewed by six volunteer trawlermen from Lowestoft who were armed to the teeth, and was even equipped with a German ensign in case there was ever a need to pose as a German patrol vessel. The *N51* was eventually joined by two other converted trawlers and a fast motor torpedo-boat. Together they formed the 'Inshore Patrol Flotilla', Slocum's cover-name for his unit. All the vessels were based in the River Helford in Cornwall, where a large private yacht, the *Sunbeam*, provided headquarters facilities and sleeping accommodation. Later in the war, as we shall see, the SIS navy was expanded, but during the summer of 1940 Slocum was obliged to rely on slender resources. Nevertheless, he did achieve a 'regular service' between the Scilly Isles and Brittany.

Indeed, there appeared to be a shortage of virtually everything SIS needed to continue the battle. Portable wireless transmitters suitable for clandestine use were scarce and there were virtually no trained operators available for work in enemy-occupied areas. In retrospect it seems there were only two faint sources of encouragement. The first had been plucked from the recent defeat of the British Expeditionary Force.

With defeat and a possible invasion staring it in the face, SIS turned to innovation. Claude Dansey, whom Menzies had appointed his Assistant Chief, argued that ten per cent of the BEF had been captured by the Germans; several thousand soldiers were, presumably, still at large in France, all making their way home as best they could. Each would, consciously or unconsciously, carry important intelligence from the Continent. Since there were virtually no SIS networks left, why not collate the material brought home by the returning men? In suggesting this, MI6 was going further than other ideas in this field.

Before Dunkirk, MI5 had set up limited preparations to interrogate refugees and, as early as December 1939, the War Office had created a special unit to teach a simple coding technique to officers and NCOs. In the event of capture by the enemy, and if they had important information to send home, they should bury their message in seemingly ordinary letters addressed to their families. Any letter which possessed two special clues would be diverted to a new organization, MI9, and the clues were: the dating of the letter numerically, for example 16/5/40, as opposed to the more usual English system of spelling out the month; and the underlining of the signature. These two signs would alert the London authorities that a secret message lay in their seemingly innocuous letter.

MI9, the escape and evasion service, was headed by a former MI(R) officer, Major Norman Crockatt, and one of his first acts was to set up a school in Highgate and a special unit in the Intelligence Training Centre at Matlock in Derbyshire to explain the secret message system to men about to go on active service. Crockatt's code, devised with help from C.W.R. Hooker from SIS, was easy to remember and brought quick results, especially from the NCOs who, unlike the officers, were often permitted to work outside their prisoner-of-war camps. This had the potential of turning every prisoner-of-war camp into a useful source of intelligence for MI9 and its SIS colleagues. The length of the message was obtained by counting the number of letters in the first two words (after Dear ...) and multiplying them together. The text was constructed from a simple code known as 'HK' which, for added security, had numerous variations. The messages often took a long time to construct, but time was a commodity in plentiful supply in the camps.

As soon as the first indoctrinated BEF personnel had settled into the prisoner-of-war camps in Germany, they began to communicate with London. Now MI6 wanted to expand this system, first to BEF soldiers at large in occupied Europe and then to any other people with useful information who could be expedited home and relieved of such material. To speed this flow of data up even further, MI6 wanted to have officers inside Europe obtaining information from escapers and evaders as fast as possible. To do this, MI6 first transferred oficers to MI9, then it had them posted as MI9 representatives overseas. The first such reception officer was Major Donald Darling, a former member of the Z-network in Paris. He was posted to Madrid to receive BEF escapees, until the hostile Ambassador, Sir Samuel Hoare, ordered him to Lisbon. Later he was posted to Gibraltar (with the code-name SUNDAY) and other MI9 officers were established in Madrid, Lisbon, Berne, Stockholm and Cairo.

From SIS's point of view, 1940 was a complete shambles. It had lost credibility over BONIFACE; it had been upstaged by MI5; its Madrid Station had had to take on a low profile; it had misinterpreted the concept behind Hitler's *Blitzkrieg* and believed in the Maginot Line; it had doubted vital information from excellent sources and lost its most important European Stations and networks. It had not laid on any contingency plans in case of German invasion in any European country; it had no networks in enemy-occupied areas and no means of infiltrating agents back. It now had to call upon the RAF, the navy and exiled allies to help it, otherwise it was dependent for information on prisoners of war, evaders, escapers and the Abwehr.

At this bitter moment for SIS, at the nadir of its fortunes, an outstanding new source was offered to it through Switzerland. This ray of hope turned out to be one of the most startling aspects of intelligence in the war.

In order to explain how this new source of information was obtained, it is necessary first to consider the events that had taken place at the SIS Berne Station since 1939.

As soon as war had been declared the SIS Station in Switzerland had taken on a special significance. Dansey had been firmly in control, but when news of Sinclair's death reached him in Lausanne he had taken the first train back to London, leaving Acton Burnell as the Chief Passport Officer in Geneva (with the code-number 42100) and Sir Frank Nelson and Tim Frenken as his representatives in Basle.

After Kendrick, the SIS Head of Station in Vienna, had been arrested in 1938, Dansey had switched his Z-network operational base to Switzerland. This was thought to be safer because one of his main agents, R. G. Pearson, happened to be married to Kendrick's sister-in-law. Just in case he had been compromised, Pearson was given courier duties between London and Geneva and was made responsible for delivering the Geneva CPO's wireless receiver. Dansey's other informants included Hugh Whittall in Lausanne and three distinguished journalists: Frederick Voight, the Central European correspondent of the *Manchester Guardian*, (Sir) Geoffrey Cox of the *Daily Express* and Eric Gedye of *The Times*. In spite of this concentration of effort, Dansey's organization had little to show in the way of useful agents inside Germany. In fact, before December 1939, its best source was a semi-independent branch of the Swiss intelligence service.

Swiss military intelligence had been in the hands of Lieutenant-Colonel Roger Masson since 1937. It was a small outfit, even by 1939; Masson only had a staff of ten, divided into three Bureaux, D, F and I, covering Germany, France and Italy respectively. Even at the height of the war, Masson only employed 120 staff. There was, however, a second, unofficial intelligence organization based in a private house in Kastanienbaum near Lucerne. This was headed by Captain Hans Hausamann, an anti-Nazi reserve officer and the press secretary for the Union of Swiss Officers. His privately funded Büro Ha was essentially a press cutting agency, but it enjoyed useful contacts with various Social Democratic groups in Germany. When war was declared Masson posted a liaison officer, Captain Max Waibel, to Hausamann's office and encouraged him to continue his work. Hausamann's main preoccupation was monitoring the activity of Nazi sympathizers in Switzerland, but it was his links with Germany that attracted SIS's attention. Sir Frank Nelson, who had been educated at Heidelberg, was then operating as the British Consul in Basle, and he began to cultivate Hausamann as a source in the hope that the Büro Ha would share some of its information. Hausamann turned out to be an enthusiastic Anglophile and gave Nelson some useful intelligence. Gradually, as Hausamann's confidence in Nelson grew, he trusted him with his most valued product: a series of teleprinter flimsies which had, he claimed, originated from the Wehrmacht's High Command headquarters in Berlin. According to Hausamann, a group of Social Democrats were employed in the communications department there and they apparently passed the stolen flimsies via couriers who worked for the German railways. Contact with the group had originally been made by Max Waibel when he had attended a staff college in Germany. Waibel's courier network was code-named VIKING and stretched from Berlin to Basle.

The VIKING line proved extremely valuable, but in December 1939 a second, potentially more important, source suddenly materialized. By this date Acton Burnell had been evacuated to London and his place had been taken, temporarily, by Pearson. The new source had been offered to the CSS by Colonel Tadeusz Wasilewski, and it proved to be Admiral Canaris, the head of the Abwehr.

This remarkable development had come about through an intermediary, Madame Halina Szymanska, the wife of Colonel Antoni Szymanski, formerly the Polish Military Attaché in Berlin. It seemed that Madame Szymanska had appeared at the Polish Legation in Berne late in December 1939 where she had been interviewed by Captain Szczesny Chojnacki, the senior Polish intelligence officer in the Swiss capital. According to Chojnacki, Madame Szymanska and her three young daughters had been conveyed from Poznan, across Germany, and into Switzerland on the personal authority of Admiral Canaris. Furthermore, Canaris had already paid her a clandestine visit and was proposing to see more of her once she was settled in her new home. The Poles had checked her story and found that her husband, who was the Polish General Staff's German expert, had been arrested in Berlin and then imprisoned in Russia.

As an intermediary between Canaris and the CSS, Madame Szymanska's appearance was of the highest importance, and Menzies promptly sent his personal representative, Fanny Vanden Heuvel, to Berne to act as her case officer. The unco-operative British Minister, Sir George Warner, was also replaced, by David Kelly, a former Great War intelligence officer. Vanden Heuvel took up residence in Berne early in February with Press Attaché cover and called himself Z-1. Andrew King, who had been part of the Z-network in Vienna and Lausanne, was appointed his chief assistant and stationed in a Passport Control Office in Zurich with the code-number Z-2. He too was granted diplomatic status and was formally appointed the British Vice-Consul. Madam Szymanska was introduced to Vanden Heuvel, who designated her Z-5/1, and thus contact was established with Canaris, albeit indirectly. Madame Szymanska was given a part-time cover job as a typist at the Polish Legation and given further financial support by the new Head of Station. She was also promised that eventually a home would be provided for her and her three children in England. The whole arrangement was considered so secret that the identities of those involved were only known to Vanden Heuvel's immediate staff and Menzies in London.

The net result of Vanden Heuvel's contact with Canaris was an agreement that a trusted Abwehr representative should be sent to Switzerland under diplomatic cover to protect Z-5/1 and supply her with information. This move was made with surprising speed, and Hans Bernd Gisevius took up his appointment as Vice-Consul at the German Consulate-General in

Zurich at the end of February 1940. Gisevius was Canaris's trusted aide and he had also served in the Gestapo, which meant that he had the all-important confidence of some of his former colleagues. He was, however, an extremely conspicuous individual, being very well built and some two metres tall. In spite of this handicap, Gisevius and Canaris began a nocturnal routine of visiting Z-5/1 and delivering top-grade political intelligence for onward transmission to the Berne Station and London. This conduit was to prove vital later in the war, but during the summer of 1940 Broadway was rather more preoccupied with the Battle of Britain and the threat of invasion than with news of political manœuvres in Berlin.

In the meantime Madame Szymanska was issued with a diplomatic passport by the Polish government-in-exile at Angers, and MI6 manufactured a French identity card, number 596 and apparently issued on 5 June 1940, which described her as Marie Clenat, a French subject born in Strasbourg and resident at an address in Lyons. Almost every detail was incorrect, but it enabled Madame Szymanska to visit Paris to meet Canaris. She also used her Polish diplomatic passport to attend a rendezvous with him in Italy. Her travel arrangements were made by Gisevius, who called at Madame Szymanska's apartment at 10 Schonemweg in Berne.

In spite of its neutrality, Switzerland was by no means immune from the effects of the war, and that was especially true in the weeks surrounding the fall of France. The collapse of the French army led to a dramatic increase in tension and there was a genuine fear of a German invasion. Large numbers of French and Polish troops crossed the frontier during May and June 1940, especially around Geneva, and many observers believed that Hitler might take the opportunity, citing 'hot pursuit', to occupy at least the western end of Switzerland. It was this fear of attack that was the motivation behind Colonel Masson's secret co-operation with SIS through the cut-out of the Büro Ha. It later transpired that Masson had good reason to suspect that Hitler would ignore Swiss neutrality.

On 16 June 1940 the Wehrmacht discovered an abandoned railway wagon in a siding near La Charité-sur-Loire. Inside were dozens of French General Staff documents describing secret contingency plans drawn up jointly by French and Swiss officers which were to be used in the event of a serious and prolonged German violation of Swiss territory. The maps clearly demonstrated how the French 8th Army proposed to lend assistance to the Swiss. If Hitler had thought the Dutch had failed to observe their own neutrality by collaborating with an Allied power, was this not an example of the Swiss doing the same thing? In any event, the prospect of a German invasion was taken extremely seriously and there were several false alarms during the summer. On one occasion the entire Zurich PCO was evacuated late in the evening and removed to Berne, only to return the following day, and the out-Station in Basle was withdrawn each night to the safety of Solothurn. At one stage the situation appeared to be deteriorating so fast that the CPO staff asked for a general evacuation, but Dansey, who retained overall control of the Swiss Stations from London, refused the request. Instead, it was agreed that the secretaries should travel to Geneva and then make their own way to England as best they could. Four eventually made the epic journey, which included bicycling from Vichy to Bordeaux. Vanden Heuvel, Lance de Garston, Hugh Whittall and Andrew King all decamped to Geneva and resumed operations.

One important figure already in Geneva at this time was Victor Farrell, an experienced SIS officer who had previously served in Budapest and had then replaced Kenneth Benton in Vienna in 1938. Farrell had been appointed to head the Geneva Station in place of Pearson, and had succeeded in recruiting an extremely valuable local source of German intelligence. Farrell's agent was Rachel Dübendorfer, a middle-aged Polish Jewess who was then working in the League of Nations' International Labour Office as a secretary and translator. She had taken up this job in 1934, two years after she had married Henri Dübendorfer, a local mechanic, to get Swiss citizenship. They had parted almost immediately after the marriage and Rachel had then set up home with a German journalist, Paul Boettcher, who was an important Soviet agent. Boettcher had been the Social Democratic Minister of Finance of Saxony in 1923, but had been expelled from Germany in 1929. After fighting with the International Brigade in Spain, he went underground in Switzerland and adopted the identity of 'Paul Dübendorfer'. As a husband and common-law wife team the Dübendorfers built up an impressive ring of informants within the International Labour Office, and eventually made contact with another major Soviet ring based in Switzerland.

This second ring was largely supported, unwittingly at first, by the Büro Ha. In the summer of 1939 the Büro Ha had recruited a German political refugee, Rudolf Roessler, as a useful source. Roessler had made his home in Lucerne in 1933 and, the following year, he started a small publishing house, which the Büro Ha considered ideal cover for espionage. Gradually the flow of intelligence reversed and Roessler began to receive rather more information from the Büro Ha (which, in the main, had come down the VIKING line from Berlin) than he was contributing. Anxious to sell the VIKING material to the Russians, Roessler approached a translator at the International Labour Office, Christian Schneider, who, in turn, gave it to Rachel Dübendorfer. Code-named SISSY by Moscow, Rachel Dübendorfer served both the Soviet and British causes until her arrest by the Swiss Bundespolizei in April 1944.

By July 1940 the situation in Switzerland had calmed and the immediate danger of a Nazi invasion appeared to diminish. The PCO staff made a gradual return to Basle, Berne and Zurich, and Vanden Heuvel developed his contact with Gisevius through Z-5/1. In the meantime, there had been developments elsewhere, and Sir Frank Nelson had been recalled to London to head one of several new covert organizations, Special Operations Executive. The other new intelligence branches of MI6 founded that summer included British Security Co-ordination, in New York, and the Inter-Services Liaison Department in Cairo.

9

Overseas Developments

This chapter will deal with the detailed setting up of British Security Co-ordination in New York, with the creation of Security Intelligence Middle East and with the growth of Section V's counter-espionage work under Cowgill.

British Security Co-ordination was, in fact, none other than an alternative title for the SIS New York Station (code-numbered 48000), which had been run under Passport Control Office cover since the first CPO, Maurice Jeffes, was appointed on 1 September 1921. Since that date the Station had been headed by only three other SIS officers: Captain Henry Maine, Commander H.B. Taylor RN and Captain Sir James Paget RN. Both the latter two CPOs were retired Royal Naval officers who had been appointed to the Passport Control Office in Whitehall Street, New York, by Admiral Sinclair.

The New York Station had always been regarded as an anomalous post. When Jeffes was first sent out, there had been the usual discussion with the Foreign Office over the exact status of the CPO and his two assistants. At first it was thought that Jeffes ought to have a consular rank, but this idea was rejected as 'it was clearly impracticable to appoint as acting Vice-Consul an officer responsible for issuing instructions to senior consular officers in an important branch of their work', so 'Jeffes was regarded as nominally attached to the Embassy' in Washington. His Assistant PCO was Henry Maine. Surprisingly, Maine was granted acting vice-consul rank while he was Jeffes's Assistant PCO, and he retained it when he succeeded Jeffes.

When Taylor was recalled to London in 1935 to become a 'G' officer, Sinclair appointed James Paget to New York. Paget's two assistants were Mr D. Loinaz and a young London barrister, Walter Bell. In 1938 Paget's father, Sir John (the second baronet) died and James Paget succeeded to the title as he was born a couple of minutes earlier than his twin brother, Major George Paget. Paget soon discovered that his two Assistant PCOs were actually senior in consular rank to him, and an attempt was made to give the CPO some diplomatic status, but once again the Foreign

Office intervened ('the position is anomalous but the arrangement seems to work') and Paget remained until July 1940.

Unlike most of the other twenty-one SIS Heads of Station in 1939, Paget did not have a local secret intelligence organization with which to liaise. The closest the Americans had to such a thing was the FBI, so Paget had to content himself with developing a link with the FBI's office in Manhattan which was led by Percy J. Foxworth, known to all as Sam.

The Director of the FBI, J. Edgar Hoover, had prevented the formation of an American secret intelligence service by taking responsibility for all intelligence liaison duties himself. This was achieved by posting FBI officers to American Embassies and Legations under the semi-transparent cover of 'Legal Attaché'. It was only in South America that the Bureau actively engaged in espionage, and its networks were considered so extensive that SIS largely ignored the continent although a Station did exist in Buenos Aires, headed by Mark Oliver. The position of the CPO in New York was considered highly sensitive, for Hoover, who had been appointed the FBI's Director in 1924, exercised strong political influence and would not tolerate any act of espionage on American soil. Hoover had always been cautious about SIS, but he had long maintained a profitable relationship with MI5 via Herschel V. Johnson, then the First Secretary at the American Embassy in London. Johnson was particularly close to Guy Liddell, then deputy Director of MI5's B Division, the counter-espionage department, and for much of the early part of 1940 both men were engaged on a joint investigation of a leak from the Embassy in London. This resulted, in May 1940, in the arrest of an American cipher clerk, Tyler Kent. Hoover was perfectly prepared to co-operate with the British when it was a matter of American security, but he drew the line at any British counter-intelligence activity in New York or Washington aimed against the Germans.

Recognition of the United States' special position had been given in 1917 when Smith-Cumming had asked Sir William Wiseman to represent MI 1(c). With this precedent in mind, the Prime Minister authorized Menzies, in June 1940, to replace Sir James Paget with William Stephenson, with effect from 1 July.

Stephenson was a wealthy Canadian entrepreneur who had flown, with distinction, with the Royal Flying Corps during the Great War. Between the wars the diminutive Stephenson had amassed several fortunes and had wide interests in broadcasting, film-making, manufacturing and heavy industry. It was his role as a director of Pressed Steel Ltd that first brought him into contact with the Industrial Intelligence Centre, an off-shoot of the Committee of Imperial Defence, headed by Major (Sir) Desmond Morton. One of Morton's special interests was the strategically important Swedish iron ore deposits, and as Pressed Steel purchased large quantities of this ore Stephenson was particularly well placed to supply the IIC with information.

Germany's high-grade steel works needed iron ore with a high phosphorous content which was to be found in the Gällivare mines in the north of Sweden. From here the ore was sent by train across Norway to the northern port of Narvik. In summer the ore could be sent by the more direct route to Luleå on the Gulf of Bothnia, but when the port was iced up in winter the freight carriers were obliged to take their cargoes around the ice-free Norwegian coast. This presented the Royal Navy with the opportunity to intercept the ore carriers after they had left Narvik and starve the German steel industry, but the Foreign Office voiced objections to the plan. For a start, they pointed out, any naval action carried out in Norwegian waters would be a violation of Norway's neutrality; and the Admiralty's scheme to lay a minefield to force vessels into international waters was also vetoed. Fortunately the SIS and NID coast-watchers reported that during the winter of 1939 very few ships attempted the northern route from Narvik. Apparently, the mere threat of a naval intervention had been enough to keep the freighter crews in port. More disturbing, however, were reports from John Martin at the Stockholm Station that the Germans had foreseen this eventuality and had stockpiled supplies of ore near the ice-free Swedish port of Oxelösund in the south of Sweden. If the Germans succeeded in loading the ore in Oxelösund, they could easily take their cargoes to the Ruhr via the Kiel Canal. The Ministry of Economic Warfare, then headed by Ronald Cross, enlisted the help of two influential businessmen with strong Swedish connections, Charles Hambro and Lord Glenconner, but their intervention had little effect.

Desmond Morton of IIC concluded that the only way to prevent this route being used was to sabotage the ships in Oxelösund, and Stephenson agreed to help Section D obtain access to the port and place the necessary explosives. The operation was code-named STRIKE OX and Alexander Rickman, a Section D demolition expert, volunteered to accompany Stephenson to Sweden. The explosives themselves were sent to the British Legation in Stockholm in the diplomatic bag at the end of November 1939. However, soon after Rickman and Stephenson had arrived in Stockholm the operation was cancelled. The Swedish authorities learned of the plan when the two saboteurs had tried to recruit some local helpers. The King of Sweden, Gustav V, wrote a personal letter to King George VI asking him to guarantee the safety of Swedish ships in Oxelösund, thus forcing Menzies to recall Stephenson. The Canadian caught the next train to Narvik and made his escape, but the CSS's order arrived too late to save Rickman who was arrested by the Stockholm police. This abortive mission was to cause considerable complications for the SIS Station in Stockholm and compromise future relations with the head of the Swedish security police, Martin Lundquist.

In spite of this fiasco, Stephenson's safe return was welcomed in London by Desmond Morton, who had taken on the role of Churchill's unofficial intelligence adviser. However, to the astonishment of Menzies, Churchill announced his intention, in June 1940, to send Stephenson to America as his intelligence supremo. Menzies attempted to resist, but in the end he capitulated and Stephenson was sent to New York to replace Sir James Paget. As well as representing SIS, Stephenson's Station would also include liaison officers from MI5 and SOE. Before Stephenson's appointment, MI5's activities in the western hemisphere had been limited to three small offices in Ottawa, Bermuda and Trinidad, where Defence Security Officers liaised with the local police. Under the proposals for the new organization the New York Station would take responsibility for all security and counter-espionage work in the region, including postal censorship and contraband control. Instead of reporting to Security Service headquarters in London, the Defence Security Officers would communicate directly with British Security Co-ordination, the New York Stations's new title. Accordingly, William Stephenson was formally appointed the Passport Control Officer at New York with a salary of £870 per annum, a local allowance of £600, and the code-number 48100.

Although Menzies was bowing to the new Prime Minister's wishes in accepting Stephenson's appointment, he ensured that he retained maximum possible control over BSC New York by appointing an experienced SIS officer, Major C.H. (Dick) Ellis, as his deputy, and seconding several other SIS personnel to his staff. Ellis was an Australian who had been recruited as an SIS agent in 1924 after he had studied French at the Sorbonne in Paris. His introduction to the Paris Station, then headed by Major T.M. Langton, had been made by his future brother-in-law, Alexander Zelensky, who had many contacts in the White Russian community in the French capital. In 1923 Ellis had been attached briefly to the British High Commission in Istanbul, and from there he had been posted to the Berlin SIS Station with the rank of acting vice-consul. In addition to his work for SIS, he had contributed articles for the *Morning Post*. In 1938 he returned to Broadway and, as a German linguist, participated in a telephone tap placed on Ribbentrop's supposedly secure direct line to Berlin.

Also on the staff on British Security Co-ordination, which vacated the old Passport Control Office in lower Manhattan and moved into new premises in the Rockefeller Center on Fifth Avenue, was Ingram Fraser, the SOE representative, Bill Ross-Smith, an Australian businessman recruited by Dick Ellis, and Major John Pepper, from the Thames Sand and Gravel Company. However, before describing BSC's operations, we should turn our attention briefly to a second SIS organization taking shape in Cairo, the Inter-Services Liaison Department.

The one geographical region that had been neglected by Sinclair before the war had been the Middle East. Much of the region had been under British control since the end of the Great War and was therefore the responsibility of the Security Service and its military intelligence colleagues attached to the local Commander-in-Chief's staff. In any event, Sinclair simply had not had the funds available to build an SIS network similar to the system in Europe. In the early 1920s, as a result of the economies forced on Sinclair, only two Stations remained in operation: Beirut (Captain E.G. Thomson) and Istanbul (Major Gibson).

Throughout the 1920s SIS had concentrated its limited resources on the Balkans, where it had maintained Stations in Bucharest (Edward Boxshall), Sofia (Alex Elder), Prague (E.G.P. Norman) and Athens (Captain F.B. Welch). By 1939 the position was largely the same, although the Heads of Station had all changed and Stations in Budapest (W.T. Hindle) and Belgrade (Captain Clement Hope) had been opened. There were other Stations in Bucharest, Sofia (Mr Smith-Ross), Prague (Victor Farrell, then Mr Fitzlyon) and Athens (Mr Crawford). Elsewhere, in territories within the British sphere of influence, MI5 provided an impressive quantity of intelligence in the form of weekly summaries from its local staff, the Defence Security Officers. In addition, a considerable amount of secret intelligence of a political nature was channelled to Broadway by the dozens of British Arabists who travelled in the area, such as Freya Stark.

MI5's organization was both efficient and economic to run. The Commanders-in-Chief in each theatre were asked to select a suitable DSO to supervise intelligence and security matters. This became a much sought-after job, partly because it was an escape from the tedium of garrison duties, and partly because it was considered so secret that no one ever dared challenge the behaviour or activities of the DSO once he had been appointed.

The DSO system was, however, somewhat haphazard, and the quality of intelligence reaching London inevitably reflected the individual DSO's enthusiasm for his post. Some were outstanding, as was the case with the first DSO Egypt, Colonel Raymund Maunsell, while others produced less satisfactory results. The dangers of relying completely on part-time or amateur intelligence officers in such a sensitive theatre as the Middle East was well recognized, but until the Joint Intelligence Committee began its work in February 1937 there had been little opportunity for anyone to make improvements. The JIC proved to be an effective forum for debating such matters and in the summer of 1939, after prolonged discussion on the subject of intelligence gathering in the eastern Mediterranean, a Middle East Intelligence Centre was formed in the Semiramis Hotel in Cairo under the leadership of General Wavell's senior intelligence officer, Brigadier Walter Cawthorn. His task, according to the Committee of Imperial Defence, was two fold:

1. To furnish the Commanders-in-Chief and representatives of the civil departments in the Middle East with co-ordinated intelligence and to provide the joint planning staff in the Middle East with the intelligence necessary for the preparation of combined plans.

2. To provide the JIC in London for the information of His Majesty's Government with co-ordinated intelligence in respect of the area allotted to it.

Before the establishment of the MEIC, these responsibilities had fallen on MI5's Defence Security Officer in Egypt, Colonel Raymund Maunsell. At the age of only thirty- four, Maunsell had been appointed to this important post. For the previous five years he had served at GHQ in Cairo, having originally been transferred in 1930 from the Royal Tank Corps to duties with the Transjordan Frontier Force.

Within six months of formation, MEIC had grown to a considerable size and became the responsibility of Cawthorn's Arabic-speaking deputy, Colonel (Sir) Iltyd Clayton. Clayton had spent seven years on attachment to the Iraqi army during the 1920s and, after the war, was appointed Head of the British Middle East Office. The MEIC, however, proved to be short-lived and, after a long political struggle, was replaced by a new organization, Security Intelligence Middle East.

SIME, as it became known, began work in December 1939 under the leadership of Maunsell. In his place Colonel G. J. Jenkins, a former British officer serving in the Egyptian police, was appointed DSO Cairo. Maunsell immediately began a search for suitable German-speaking intelligence officers, because there was a wealth of German language material awaiting processing. His first recruit who filled the bill was Captain William Kenyon-Jones, a young Welsh regular officer who had recently completed a staff course in Cairo. Maunsell persuaded Kenyon-Jones to become his deputy.

In order to accommodate the ever-increasing staff of SIME, premises were obtained at the GHQ building in Cairo. A number of staff transferred from MI5 in London to help develop the existing networks of agents and, at the same time, monitor the activities of enemy agents. Among this group of experienced counter-intelligence personnel was Janet Smythe, an old MI5 hand, and the redoubtable Miss Paton-Smith, who had previously been in charge of MI5's Registry. This was the central collection of files and dossiers which, with the aid of a Hollerith punch-card sorter, cross-referenced every suspected enemy agent in England. Miss Paton-Smith's task in Cairo was to recreate MI5's Registry system and log the particulars of every suspected German agent. Largely thanks to her efforts, SIME's collection of individual dossiers became a powerful weapon, and was wielded with much effect by J.W. Marcham who succeeded Miss Paton-Smith as Head of Registry.

Other SIME staff included Patrick Wilson, son of General (Sir) Henry Maitland Wilson, Dan Sandford (who had previously served on MEIC),

James Robertson, Tony Simmonds, Geoffrey Seligman, Evan James Simpson (who later wrote a biography of James I) and Professor George Kirk, an eminent archæologist who later became a senior academic at Harvard University and wrote a controversial history, *The War in the Middle East.*

Within six months of its creation, SIME had established representatives at all of the important centres in the Middle East. This achievement was in part due to the support of the Middle East Force's DMI, Colonel (later Brigadier) John Shearer. Most operated under the familiar cover of Defence Security Officer and included the ex-Conservative MP for Derbyshire, Henry Hunloke, who was DSO in Palestine; Major Bertram Ede, the DSO Malta; Guy Thompson, the DSO Cyprus (and later the SIME representative in Istanbul); Colonel C.D. Roberts, the DSO Lebanon; Squadron Leader Hanbury Dawson-Sheppard, the DSO Persia; Major Joseph Penney, the DSO Ethiopia; and Colonel John Teague, the DSO Iraq. In Syria, which was then under French control, the SIME representative was Colonel (Sir) Patrick Coghill, Bart, a regular officer from the Arab Legion who headed a 'British Security Mission'. When the Allies occupied Syria in 1941, Coghill's team was replaced by a new DSO, Douglas Roberts, who was later to head SIME.

Under the direction of Raymund Maunsell, SIME reinforced the DSO system by making further appointments in Syria and Iraq. Extra DSOs were also posted to the important military centres within Egypt. Thus Major Guy Thompson became DSO Alexandria and Major Gerald Baird, DSO Mersa Matruh.

This remarkable network was reinforced in December 1939 by the introduction of an Inter-Service Balkan Intelligence Centre under the British Military Attaché in Ankara, Brigadier Allan Arnold. By June the following year the military situation in Europe had deteriorated, causing a general evacuation of the Balkan Stations. This resulted in a dramatic expansion of the Istanbul Station, which rehoused the displaced Stations. Fortunately, the recently appointed Head of Station in Istanbul was Harold Gibson who had, until the German take-over of Czechoslovakia, been running the Prague Station.

Gibson, who was now dubbed 18100, had been transferred to Istanbul so that he could maintain his profitable contact with A–54, the Abwehr officer who had been passed to SIS by the Czechs. A–54 had been transferred to the Abwehr outpost in Dresden, and Istanbul was judged to be the safest and most convenient neutral territory in which to meet. Gibson had other useful qualifications for his new post. He was thoroughly steeped in Balkan affairs, as indeed was his brother Archie who was to work for SIS in Cairo. Harold enjoyed excellent local connections, having previously headed the Istanbul Station between 1919 and 1921, and his family had married into the two principal British merchant families in the area, the Lefontaines and the Whittalls. His predecessor as Head of Station had been Dick Lefontaine, the British Consul.

The new Istanbul Station initially co-ordinated the efforts of no less than four British secret intelligence organizations: Special Operations Executive (for sabotage, led by Gardyne de Chastelain), SIS (for espionage of a wider variety), the Naval Intelligence Division (which monitored enemy shipping movements, headed by Commander Wolfson) and, of course, SIME.

Like the few remaining neutral countries in Europe, Istanbul quickly developed into a centre of espionage and, as the geographical meeting-place between Asia and Europe, its main industry became international intrigue. Gibson, who was known to his staff simply as Gibby, gathered around him an unlikely collection of displaced SIS officers to help him, including Bernard O'Leary (a huge Irishman who had been Head of Station in Copenhagen), Teddy Smith-Ross, Christopher Jowitt and Kenneth Jones. In addition there were two newly established country sections to liaise with the exiled DMIs of the countries concerned: a Romanian section, headed by Arthur Elrington, and a Yugoslav section, headed by a White Russian named Roman Sulakov. Others included Adrian Endhoven and Elena Erskine.

Apart from this concentration in Istanbul, the Secret Intelligence Service had only minimal representation in the rest of the Near and Middle East. This position was rectified when the CSS appointed his second Assistant Chief of Staff, Captain Cuthbert (Curly) Bowlby RN, to open a Station in Cairo. Bowlby was accompanied on his mission by Bill Bremner, who became his deputy in their new organization which operated under the cover-name 'Inter-Services Liaison Department'. By the time ISLD had found premises in Cairo (which were conveniently located directly above SIME in the 'Grey Pillars' GHQ compound), it had acquired a promising list of potential double agents from its security colleagues. ISLD and SIME worked very closely in Cairo (a cause of considerable gratitude among the male SIME staff – the SIS had a well-earned reputation for employing only the prettiest of secretaries) and were given access to SIME's lists of suspected German and Italian agents. This enabled Bowlby to recruit a number of double agents, so he created a B section of case officers, including Desmond Doran (who had previously served in the Berlin Station) and Eric Pope, to handle their increasing number. Other ISLD headquarters' staff were John Bruce Lockhart, Archie Gibson and Major (Titters) Titterington, King Farouk's personal chemist who was placed in charge of ISLD's technical section (which had responsibility for forging passports and other documents).

ISLD also posted personnel to the various offices in the Middle East already established by SIME. The largest of these was based in Beirut and was headed by Peter Chandor. His staff included Michael Ionides, a desert irrigation expert with considerable experience in the region. (Ionides had the distinction of being the son of a nun. Apparently his mother had been in a closed religious community in Khartoum when the Mahdi took over the city; among his more extraordinary directives to the Europeans was one insisting that all nuns should marry. The large Greek population offered to assist one particular order by supplying husbands; Ionides's father was amongst them, although he evidently failed to keep his undertaking not to consummate the marriage!) Michael Ionides's colleagues in Beirut included John Wills (from SIME) and Charles Dundas. Major Giffey, the pre-war Head of Station in Tallinn, was appointed ISLD representative in Baghdad. His staff included Reg Wharry and Ronald Croft, of whom more will be heard later. Another important joint SIS/MI5 office was located in the British Colony of Aden, under the direction of Major E.J. Howes.

Having established the basics of the SIS order of battle in the Middle East in 1940, we should return to England and take account of major developments in Section V.

Section V of the Secret Intelligence Service had had very little opportunity to preach the virtues of counter-intelligence until the general collapse of the SIS networks in the summer of 1940 forced Menzies to reassess his strategy. Section V had, of course, been drafted in to deal with such major breaches in security as the suicide of Dalton and the Venlo fiasco, but there had been little appreciation of the possible lessons to be learnt from these incidents. Much of the troubles experienced by SIS before the war could be attributed to the intervention of the Abwehr or its Nazi counterparts, the Sicherheitsdienst. If prevention was better than cure, might there not be advantages to be gained from mounting a counter-offensive against the opposition's military intelligence organization?

Before the recruitment of Felix Cowgill in March 1939, it is a remarkable, but none the less true, fact that no one at Broadway had conceived of counter-intelligence as being a function of the Secret Intelligence Service. Colonel Valentine Vivian had accepted responsibility, in the broadest terms, for counter-espionage and security, but the SIS intelligence gathering system simply did not cater for what was regarded as essentially MI5's work. Section V's brief was to liaise with the Security Service, and inevitably the work tended to concentrate on Indian affairs and the Comintern. Section V had taken only a passing interest in Germany's intelligence structure.

The SIS machine had been geared to operate along naval lines, something hardly surprising for an organization that had been run by naval officers for some thirty years. Each overseas Station had a ship, helmed by a Head of Station, with a cost-efficient staff that knew only how to execute their duties alone. If the registry clerk suddenly fell ill, no one in the Station could take over as a temporary measure. There were, of course, advantages. Security within the Station was supposed to be absolutely watertight.

The traditional role of the overseas Station was simply the acquisition of intelligence; once collected, it became the job of the headquarters' staff to analyse it and distribute it to the right consumers or clients. The greatest criticism of SIS during the first months of the war came from the receiving end, the Services, who all complained that they were getting a minimal quantity of information. What they did get, they claimed, was either irrelevant, out of date, or simply untrue. SIS had built a reputation for supplying unreliable intelligence, and this is why the BONIFACE material was ignored until Menzies authorized additional people to be indoctrinated into Bletchley's successes.

Cowgill's entry into SIS had marked a significant development. As one of his protégés was later to comment, 'Cowgill's disadvantage was that he saw everything in terms of cases, never in terms of problems.' Cowgill was an experienced Indian intelligence officer. He had probably studied the problems of Soviet and Communist subversion more closely than any man alive. Two volumes of *India and Communism** bear testimony to this. The original book is nearly 400 pages long and is packed with thoughtfully documented case histories which illustrate every facet of pre-war leftist attempts to undermine the Empire and the Indian constitution.

Cowgill's background was not that of a plodding Indian police officer. He was an intelligence officer who had grasped the fundamental rules of intelligence which had eluded his naval colleagues in Broadway: advance information of an enemy's intentions is worthless unless tight security is maintained. Surveillance, penetration and ultimately control of one's opponent's sources of intelligence will reap untold rewards.

The Secret Intelligence Service had some of the technical infrastructure in place to cope with war when it came. Sinclair had purchased Bletchley Park and so ensured SIS of a fall-back position for the day when London might have to be evacuated, and he had moved the communications section with its transmitters to Hanslope Park. The preparations had been made hastily, but they were adequate. The spanner in the works was the nature of the enemy and the extraordinary mobility of his forces.

The collapse of the Passport Control Office system on the Continent placed a burden of responsibility on the Z-network with which the latter had been ill equipped to cope. Nevertheless, the Dutch catastrophe was not a symptom of one single Station. It was evidence of the Germans' mastery of counter-intelligence techniques and weakness of the semi-overt system of Stations. Cowgill, who pinpointed points of weakness rather than broader problems, was the classic example of the right man at the right time. His first attempts to convert the machinery to recognition of counter-

* Restricted publication, Government of India Press, 1933, 1935

intelligence failed. His first proposal was to by-pass the established order by appointing Section V officers to all the Stations. This idea was an anathema to the 'G' officers and, unintentionally, had the effect of insulting the ability of the individual Heads of Station. It was, though, a necessary step and Venlo proved the point most forcibly.

In 1939 Section V consisted of Vivian, then aged fifty-five, Mills and Cowgill. On the outbreak of war they acquired two houses, Glenalmond and Prae Wood, on Lord Verulam's estate near St Albans. Both properties were large and had the advantage of being approximately half way between Bletchley Park and Broadway. During the course of 1939, Section V had recruited Rodney Dennys in The Hague and Keith Liversidge in Brussels. Stevens had been replaced temporarily in The Hague by his deputy, Harry Hendricks. On 1 May Lionel Loewe had taken over from him. Both officers had realized, through bitter experience, that SIS knowledge about the opposition was less than adequate. In Brussels Colonel Calthrop was sufficiently enlightened to recognize the very high level of interest taken in his Station by the Abwehr.

Section V had succeeded in gradually establishing the principle of assigning officers to particular targets, thus reversing the traditional method of handling intelligence. Instead of waiting for agents to report developments, Section V assigned personnel to particular tasks. Soon the idea, and the Section, grew, though part of the expansion can be attributed to the prevailing view in Broadway that Section V represented a convenient dumping ground for over-enthusiastic officers who might not fit into the establishment system. Thus two vital members of the counter-intelligence staff, Ralph Jarvis and Sir Robert Mackenzie, found themselves posted to St Albans. Both had served in General Gerald Templer's intelligence organization and, after Dunkirk, the British Expeditionary Force had no further need for them. Templer had been determined that the talents of two such able officers should not be wasted, so he virtually forced them on SIS. Broadway had them sent straight to St Albans.

Jarvis, who had worked in the City before the war, had excelled at identifying and turning enemy agents in France. Mackenzie was the twelfth baronet of a title dating back to 1673. His background could hardly have been more conventional: Eton and Trinity College, Cambridge, and an underwriting Member of Lloyds. He had succeeded to the title on the death of his father in 1935 and had joined Templer's staff four years later. Templer had been one of the few regulars to appreciate receiving Cowgill's early Section V counter-intelligence summaries. Jarvis and Mackenzie had rushed around the French and Belgian countryside discovering enemy agents and recruiting friendly ones, and Templer had been so taken with the idea of 'knowing the enemy' that he had pinned photographs of the opposing Wehrmacht generals on the sides of his tent in Arras so as to get to know them. He too found the regular SIS channels completely unresponsive to his particular needs, which inevitably changed from day to day. When the Germans launched their offensive in May 1940, he had communicated direct to St Albans in a special code, known as COWGILL/HILL-DILLON.

At first Cowgill assigned his staff the task of discovering the order of battle for the Abwehr and SD, based on the meagre information currently available. It is worth noting that in a letter dated 14 February 1940 MI5's contact in the American Embassy in London reported to the State Department:

This informant is said to be not only in touch with Jankhe but is in constant touch with Vice-Admiral Panaris [sic], who the British say is certainly head of the German Naval Secret Service and probably head of the entire German Secret Service. Of the latter they are not sure.

It would appear from this letter that some people working in British intelligence still had a severely limited knowledge of the Abwehr. The letter makes clear that, even if the spelling mistake of Canaris's name is American in origin, there was still doubt about his exact role.

Having obtained an (albeit reluctant) acceptance of the possible advantages of aggressive counter-intelligence, Cowgill went on to develop the concept of geographical sections. This left an individual case officer to become an expert on the enemy's activities in a certain theatre. Because Section V was so short-staffed, it was impossible to create country sections in parallel with the rest of the Secret Intelligence Service and Special Operations Executive. Instead, officers were assigned geographical regions. In the weeks after Dunkirk this was a relatively straightforward exercise, and each officer became known by a special Section V code-name. Thus Mills, Vivian's assistant, became V(a), with responsibility for a Belgian section which consisted initially of a repatriated agent named Duvivier (who became V(b)). The transport section was in the hands of Captain Blake-Budden, known as V(c). From 1942, an administration section operated under the leadership of a barrister from the Inner Temple, Roland Adams, and the officer who later became SIS's Chief Administrator, Harald Peake. Keith Liversidge, who joined Gerald Templar's staff after the evacuation of the rest of Colonel Calthrop's Station, dealt with Scandinavia; Mackenzie was assigned France, Jarvis dealt with Iberia, O'Brien with the Middle East and Dennys with the Netherlands. Staff passed to Section V from redundant European Stations, whom even Section V found it difficult to keep busy, were posted to the geographical section responsible for 'The Americas'. In this last category were Evelyn Sinclair (recently repatriated from Berlin) and Robert Carew-Hunt, of whom more will be heard later. Because of the acute logistical problems, the MI5 officer responsible for security in the western hemisphere, Colonel W.T. (Freckles) Wren, doubled as Section V's man and the Defence Security Officer.

Ironically, Section V only began to realize its full potential after MI5 had developed an agent rejected by SIS. At the end of 1936 Colonel Edward Peal, the SIS case officer, had been informed by MI5's Edward Hinchley-Cooke that one of his main agents in Germany, a Welshman named Arthur Owens, was playing a double game. Owens had been recruited by Naval Intelligence and had been passed to Peal, who had given him the code-name SNOW. As soon as Hinchley-Cooke disclosed that SNOW had been writing to an address in Hamburg which appeared on MI5's stop list, Peal abandoned the case and handed him over to MI5's B Division. Tar Robertson took over SNOW and ran him as a thoroughly successful double agent. The question of 'turning' agents in peacetime had never been considered by the CSS, who had viewed SIS's role in terms of intelligence acquisition, not intelligence *per se*.

When SNOW had been given the chance to operate his Abwehr wireless set under MI5 control in September 1939, he seized it and, in due course, SNOW was promoted by the Germans to the leadership of a substantial network. In March 1940, during the course of Robertson's radio contact with SNOW's Abwehr case officer in Hamburg, he had learned of the Abwehr spy ship cruising in Norwegian territorial waters. The location of the vessel had been passed to the Radio Security Service cryptanalysts at Arkley, near Barnet, and they had succeeded in recording the coded Morse messages. SNOW, of course, had already been provided with his key to the code, so the RSS had experienced only minimal trouble before reading the Abwehr traffic. The person responsible for this decoding was Oliver Strachey, brother of Lytton Strachey, and it was decided that his work was so secret that henceforth all his summaries of Abwehr traffic would be known as 'Intelligence Service Oliver Strachey', or ISOS. It had been a breakthrough, but there was little material of a direct, strategic nature in the decrypts. It related, in the main, to Abwehr intentions and specific cases, so the ISOS information was passed to Glenalmond for further detailed study.

Although most of the SIS Sections had been relocated at Bletchley Park, the Registry, under Bill Woodfield, had been transferred to a separate building in King Harry Lane, close to Prae Wood and Glenalmond near St Albans. This house, named Brescia, was very convenient for Section V and enabled the ISOS summaries to be logged and analysed with meticulous detail. The officer assigned this tedious job was a former Ceylon Special Branch police officer named Ferguson, who had been recruited from MI5. He was later assisted by Frank Foley after the latter had evacuated his Station in Oslo. Together Ferguson and Foley created a card-index of every Abwehr case officer and agent mentioned in the wireless traffic. When the information on the card-indices was combined with the additional information provided by the files from the Allied secret services, Section V was able to build a comprehensive picture of the Abwehr's order of battle for the latter part of 1940.

By December 1940 Section V's knowledge of the enemy had begun to impress even the 'G' officers, and Vivian obtained agreement to an ambitious plan which would, once again, allow Section V to place its own officers in the Stations overseas. The plan also gave the Section V staff the right to an independent channel of cipher communication, code-named 'XB'. Like most things in SIS, there was a struggle to make progress, but once Menzies's consent had been obtained the bureaucracy had difficulty in keeping up the pace. Further personnel were needed urgently for the expansion. Recruitment was enhanced in early 1941 by the transfer of a number of MI5 officers, and the absorption of a Field Security Wing from the Territorials. This particular wing was composed of units from various public schools, and as a result a number of schoolmasters found themselves in SIS. Among later recruits were Peter Falk and Martin Lloyd from Rugby, and Peter Mason from Cheltenham. Another addition was Aubrey Jones, from *The Times*, and Charles de Salis.

The New Year of 1941 also saw the inception of a committee to co-ordinate the activity of the growing number of double agents and the supply of specially prepared information for the consumption of the Abwehr. This group, which became known as the Twenty Committee after its double-cross 'XX' Roman symbols, was chaired by J.C. Masterman at its first meeting, which took place on Thursday, 2 January 1941. The Committee's secretary was John Marriott of BI(a), the MI5 section responsible for the running of all double agents on British territory, and the MI6 delegate was Martin Lloyd of Section V. The Committee got off to an excellent start with none of the problems that had dogged previous inter-departmental meetings. In fact, the prospects for Section V looked so good that on 15 January 1941 Vivian handed control of the Section over to Cowgill and moved his office back up to London. Although Vivian was to retain an interest in Section V, his new, somewhat ambiguous, post was that of Vice-Chief of the Secret Intelligence Service (VCSS).

This is an appropriate moment to review the few Stations remaining in Europe at the end of 1940. It will be recalled that the Helsinki Station (Harry Carr) and the Baltic Stations (Nicholson) had been combined with Stockholm (John Martin) when the Russians had attacked Finland. The Stations in Brussels, The Hague, Paris and Oslo had also been evacuated. Warsaw, Prague, Berlin and Vienna had long since disappeared, and the Balkan Stations had decamped to Istanbul. The Sofia Station followed suit in March 1941. Four Stations – Stockholm, Madrid, Lisbon and Berne – were all that remained. They were the only neutral capital cities left in

Europe, and it was correctly assumed that all would become centres of the Abwehr's operations. All would therefore need to have experienced Section V officers.

However, Section V was short of experienced manpower: if an officer was transferred to a neutral territory from headquarters, it would leave an entire geographical region without an expert in charge. Furthermore, so much of Section V's work had depended on the highly secret ISOS material that there was a perceptible risk in sending indoctrinated personnel into possibly hostile territory. It was now considered safe to assume that one consequence of the arrests of Kendrick, Stevens and Best was the Abwehr's identification of most of the pre-war SIS Station personnel. There was little point in sending a counter-intelligence officer to foreign parts to penetrate the opposition's structure if the individual concerned had been compromised before he could even begin operating. The solution to these problems was determined by Dick White, the Assistant Director of MI5's B Division.

MI5 had undergone a dramatic expansion during 1940 and had (in theory) only employed staff after 'stringent checks' had been carried out. After prolonged negotiations, a group of Security Service officers moved to Section V, led by Dick Brooman-White from B21 (MI5's Iberian Section) and Richard Comyns Carr.

Brooman-White, who later became Conservative MP for Rutherglen, had been initiated into the Iberian sub-section of Section V by Ralph Jarvis, who then flew to Lisbon to establish an office at Cintra, a town some miles north of the Portuguese capital. In September of 1941 Brooman-White recruited a further officer to his new section, this time from SOE. The officer was a journalist who had spent some time in Spain during the Civil War. His name was H.A.R. Philby; he was known to everyone as Kim. He subsequently brought his younger sister, Helena, to work in Section V.

The Iberian sub-section of SIS consisted of four important Stations: Madrid, Lisbon, Gibraltar and Tangiers.

SIS Madrid was headed by Hamilton-Stokes, who, as we have seen earlier, had left Warsaw in June 1936 for a spell of duty in London. He had then been sent briefly to help Hindle in Budapest and, in 1940, was appointed to Spain with Togo McLaurin who became his deputy. Hamilton-Stokes ran a staff of fourteen in the Passport Control building in the Monte Scinta, most of whom were registry staff recruited among the local British community. They included a nanny, the wives of two British diplomats and even Joan Bethell, the sixteen-year-old daughter of the Vice-Consul in Cartagena! In addition to the Station staff in Madrid, Hamilton-Stokes operated a network of twenty-two consular posts located in Spanish ports. All made regular reports to Madrid and tried, whenever possible, to obtain copies of the passenger lists of the transatlantic liners and the names of all hotel guests staying in their territory. All this information was entered on card files kept at the Station and helped to monitor the movements of suspected German agents. This was not such a difficult task as the Abwehr's agents tended to travel in wagons-lits and stay in only the very best hotels. Thus a retainer paid to a friendly concierge or railway steward produced a useful supply of information. Also in Madrid were representatives of the other British intelligence agencies. David Muirhead and David Babington-Smith headed the SOE contingent and Michael Cresswell took over MI9's responsibilities after Donald Darling had been sent to Lisbon. There was also a Naval Intelligence office, run by Captain Alan Hillgarth, who doubled as the Embassy's Security Officer.

The work of all these officers was greatly inhibited by Sir Samuel Hoare's desire to maintain good relations with Franco, but in spite of the restrictions placed on their activities the Madrid Station did manage to run some 168 agents and sub-agents throughout Spain. Many of these agents were insignificant but, as we shall see, a few were to provide some very valuable intelligence. The Station also succeeded in bribing a number of Franco's military advisers, thus helping to keep Spain from joining the Axis.

The Section V officer selected for the Madrid post was Kenneth Benton, who had previously served in Vienna and Riga. The Riga Station, headed by Leslie Nicholson, had been a fairly uneventful posting. The Station's star agent, code-name SACK, had proved very disappointing. He had been provided with a wireless transmitter by Major Maltby (from Section VIII), but when he was eventually activated, after the Station's evacuation, his coded messages had proved completely unreadable. On his return to London, Benton had been transferred to Bletchley as an assistant to Captain Edward Hastings, Menzies's personal representative at GCHQ. In the spring of 1941 Benton volunteered for Section V and was posted to the Spanish capital. However, as soon as he arrived at the Embassy, he was ordered home by the Ambassador who had apparently not been informed of Benton's arrival by Hamilton-Stokes. Telegrams flew between Madrid and London, and eventually Hamilton-Stokes won the day. Benton was allowed to stay provided he did not compromise Hoare's diplomatic mission. We will return later to the Madrid Station's operations, but first we should deal with the other Section V postings.

Portugal had always been regarded as something of an intelligence backwater. In the early 1920s, when SIS was undergoing a period of financial stringency, the Station in Lisbon, then headed by Mr W.G. Chancellor, had been closed down. In September 1939 the CSS had hurriedly reopened it under the leadership of Commander Austin Walsh RN, who was given the code-number 24100. At that time the Station consisted of one room in the British Consulate.

Suddenly, with the fall of France, the Lisbon Station acquired a special importance and new accommodation was rented at 37, rua Emenda. Menzies also modified the 'G' officer system and introduced 'Controls' to which the individual Heads of Station would report. The Iberian Control was Basil Fenwick, an oil executive from Shell. New SIS personnel were also drafted in to the Portuguese capital: Richman Stopford, from the B1(a) section of the Security Service, was appointed Head of Station; Ena Molesworth (from the Berlin Station) and Rita Winsor (from Switzerland); Graham Maingot (formerly the Z-network's man in Rome); Trevor Glanville (from Belgrade), Mike Andrews and Bobby Johnstone. In March 1941 Ralph Jarvis arrived as Section V's representative with Phoebe Orr-Ewing as his secretary. In addition, there was Donald Darling (from MI9) and Jack Beevor (from SOE), who doubled as the Embassy's Security Officer.

The Portuguese were officially neutral, but Dr Salazar's Government held a definite pro-German bias. The dreaded local secret police, the Polícia Internacional e de Defesa do Estado (PIDE), was headed by Captain Lourenço, who was considered pro-Nazi. He also had close links with the Spanish security service, the Seguridad. Yet in spite of PIDE's attentions, Jarvis and his Section V staff succeeded in identifying and turning virtually every Abwehr spy in the capital.

Basil Fenwick's Iberian Control extended from Lisbon down to Gibraltar, where the Defence Security Officer, Tito Medlam, reported to both MI5 and MI6. It was not until 1942 that John Codrington (from the old Z-network) was sent to the Rock on behalf of MI6 with the code-number 5100. Codrington had been evacuated from Bordeaux, along with the rest of the Paris Station, on board HMS *Arethusa*. On his return, he had assisted Kenneth Cohen in the running of SIS's French country section. When he was posted to Gibraltar, he took with him two Section V officers: Desmond Bristow (who had worked for de Beers before the war) and an ex-monk named O'Shagar. His other staff included a former Communist named Cavanagh, Sergeant McNeff who acted as the Station's secretary, two cipher clerks and Hans Vischer, the half-Swiss who had at one time been Head of Station in Zurich. The local Naval Intelligence representative was Commander Grenville Pyke-Nott, and Hugh Quennell ran SOE with Harry Morris.

Iberian Control was completed by Toby Ellis's Station in Tangiers. He was assisted by his deputy, David Thompson, Colonel Malcolm Henderson, Neil Whitelaw, Paddy Turnbull and a Scottish expatriate, Teddy Dunlop; SOE's local man was a mining engineer, Edward Wharton-Tigar, who was later succeeded by Barbara Salt.

We will return to MI6's operations in the Iberian theatre later, but first we should complete the description of Section V's development. Two further European Stations on neutral territory have yet to be examined: Berne and Stockholm. The Berne Station was regarded as a special case for two reasons. Firstly, Dansey had retained a special interest in Switzerland and had, in effect, become a one-man Control for the country although his ambiguous, official post was Assistant Chief. Secondly, Vanden Heuvel's relationship with the local Abwehr was such that there was little need to mount a counter-intelligence offensive. Furthermore, such an escalation of SIS activity might well prejudice the close relationship between the Swiss DMI and the Station. The consensus view was that nothing should be allowed to endanger Anglo–Swiss relations which, incidentally, had developed to such a point that a well-placed diplomat at the Swiss Legation in London had volunteered his services to MI5.

The Stockholm Station, on the other hand, was obliged to operate in a relatively hostile environment. Its Section V officer, Peter Falk, was unable to reach Sweden until March 1943 because of the Station's geographic isolation.

By the end of 1941 Cowgill had achieved his aim and established a Section V representative at all the important overseas Stations and, indeed, a few less vital ones: Graham Greene had been sent to Freetown; Malcolm Muggeridge to Lourenço Marques; Benton to Madrid; Bristow to Gibraltar; Trevor-Wilson to Algiers; and Wren to New York. Later, as Section V began to show results, Rodney Dennys was sent to Cairo and Nicholas Elliott went to Istanbul. All communicated in their unique 'XB' cipher (signed by their numeric code-number, which was always 500 added to the country numeral) direct to St Albans, where their information was collated by a Section V headquarters staff that had grown to around 120. The Iberian sub-section, headed by Kim Philby, had been expanded with the recruitment of Tim Milne. Other new sub-sections included a Middle East section (O'Brien), a Dutch section (Lord Reay), a Scandinavian section (Keith Liversidge) and a Belgian and French section (Bobby Mackenzie). Cowgill had, in effect, created a second secret service within the first and, in doing so, had outmanoeuvred the old 'G' officers who, originally, had failed to see Section V's potential.

By the spring of 1941, largely thanks to Section V's efforts, the Secret Intelligence Service had been transformed from a near-moribund organization staving off total collapse to an aggressive, two-tiered structure ready to take on the Abwehr and, indeed, its critics. Menzies can take considerable credit for this for two reasons: his operational decision to encourage the development of Section V, and his political astuteness which had enabled him to retain control of GCHQ's product, the ULTRA decrypts, and so undermine SIS's critics.

Certainly there was no shortage of the latter, and Menzies was obliged to make some politically expedient compromises to ensure SIS's survival. At one point in November 1940, the Prime Minister actually asked the Chiefs of Staff to report to him about the possibility of creating a new, unified intelligence structure that would serve (and satisfy) all three Services.

Menzies was in danger of losing his autonomy and traditional immunity from supervision and inspection. As the Official History commented: '... the ability of the SIS to acquire reliable information had not improved, and in some areas markedly declined.'

The erosion of confidence in SIS meant a growing reluctance in the Services to recognize its role and co-operate by granting Service facilities. As a result, SIS was short of wireless transmitters and almost totally lacked air transport. Menzies could only improve the situation by making compromises. One such compromise concerned his relations with the Foreign Office which had reached a low ebb in the tense months following the fall of France, and Menzies had been obliged to take a very defensive position in Whitehall on virtually every issue. His solution was ingenious. The Prime Minister's favour was assiduously cultivated by Menzies who endeavoured to hand the daily crop of GCHQ decrypts to Churchill personally. The Head of Section IV, Fred Winterbotham, arranged for Menzies to have a continuous supply of GCHQ's product; Denniston did the same with the diplomatic traffic; the intercepted messages were then delivered to the War Room in a special box, and Menzies ensured that it was his organization that got the credit for what Churchill later described as his 'most secret source'. The majority of this material was Luftwaffe intercepts, but Menzies took care to mix in some spicy decrypts. These varied from day to day, but generally included a summary of the Abwehr traffic (prepared by the Radio Security Service), some German police signals (annotated by GCHQ's experts), a few diplomatic telegrams and whatever good quality naval decrypts were available. Menzies rounded off his daily delivery with a personal commentary on GCHQ's current progress. It all made impressive reading. The entire package was designed to establish a close bond between Menzies and the Prime Minister, and it certainly succeeded. The contents of the box were tailored to Churchill's taste, and if a particularly interesting decrypt arrived at Broadway Menzies might even make a special journey to the War Room. The overall effect was to inspire the Prime Minister's confidence in SIS. It also gave him the opportunity to baffle his senior advisers by quoting some recent titbit of intelligence that had failed to reach them. There was nothing he liked better than winning a debate by demonstrating his knowledge of a subject. In this Menzies acted as his collaborator.

In another masterly move Menzies won over the Foreign Office by agreeing to attach a permanent Foreign Office official to his personal staff. The Foreign Office's nominee was (Sir) Patrick Reilly, a career diplomat who had been educated at Winchester and New College, Oxford. Reilly had joined the Foreign Office in 1933 and, after two years in London, had been posted to Tehran. In 1938 he returned to London and on the outbreak of war was seconded to the Ministry of Economic Warfare. In September 1940

1 21 Queen Anne's Gate, the elegant headquarters of the Passport Control Office and the London residence of the CSS. The rear of the property was connected to Broadway Buildings, the office block which housed both the pre-war MI6 and GC & CS.

Seniority	Rank	Name	Nature of Service

K.C.M.G. C.B. (Gazette 22/6/14)

(30.6.14)

Sir **Mansfield George Smith.** Smith-(Cumming)

Born 1 Apr 59
Entered Jan 72
Passed R.N.C. Sept 18__
Gunnery 2 Cl (£80) 13 Apr 80

20 June 78, act sub Lieut
Sub Lieut

Bellerophon — Come home in 20th Force = 23 Dec 78
Duke of Well = Cole. Jan 79 — 13 Oct 79
Vulture — 2 Apr 80 Thetis — Dec 1880 Granted
Perak Medal = 1 July 81 Victoria & Albert Transferred

14 Sept 1881 Lieutenant

30 Septem 1881 President as 2d Lt for R.N. College
14 June 82 Daring — See letters from Capt. Jenkins
stating he had allowed him to be attached temp'ly to
Ruby from 1st August — Appointed to join Daring 25 Aug 82

23 Feb 76. Gazetted for services as a.d.c. to
Capt Buller in operations of Naval Brigade
against Malay pirates = Hecla SNO Dec 80 Judgm't & Knowledge G.
other qualities V.G. L.V.G. speaks French = ...

2 The official Royal Naval service record for Mansfield George Smith-Cumming, the first Chief of the Secret Intelligence Service.

3 Major-General Sir Stewart Menzies KCB, KCMG, DSO, MC, Chief of the Secret Intelligence Service 1939–53. For much of the war one of his regular weekend guests, Friedle Gaertner (and a relation by his younger brother's marriage to her sister), was in touch with the Abwehr and acting as a double agent for the rival organization, MI5, operating under the code-name GELATINE.

4 The British Passport Control Office in a quiet suburb of The Hague, the scene of a number of MI6's scandals. In September 1936 the Head of Station, Major Hugh Reginald Dalton, committed suicide in his first-floor flat after having been caught embezzling MI6 funds. His successor, Major Monty Chidson, proved unsatisfactory and his replacement, Major Richard Stevens, was kidnapped by the Germans in November 1939. It was alleged that many secret MI6 documents were recovered intact by the Abwehr when it occupied the building in June 1940.

VÖLKISCHER BEOBACHTER

Kampfblatt der national-sozialistischen Bewegung Großdeutschlands

Verräter Otto Strasser das Werkzeug des englischen Geheimdienstes

Wiederholte Anschläge auf den Führer

Die britische Mordverschwörung

Strassers Auftrag, den Führer zu beseitigen

Der gedungene Mörder

Die Mittelmänner

Die große Pleite des Intelligence Service

Der gedungene Mörder und seine Hintermänner

Das gekaufte Werkzeug
Georg Elser

Die Leiter der britischen Mörderzentrale für Europa
Kapitän Stevens

Mr. Best

A German newspaper headlines the Venlo incident, implicating, for the purpose of propaganda, Captain Sigismund Payne Best and Major Richard Stevens in the attempted assassination of Hitler at the Munich Beer Cellar.

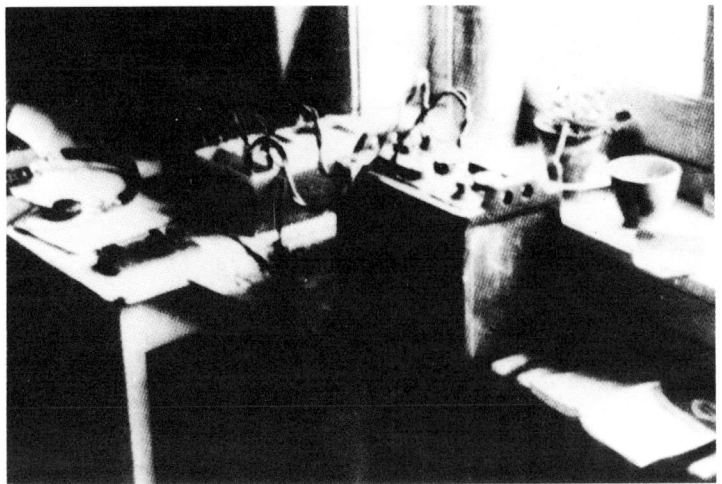

6 One of MI6's first battery-powered 'portable' wireless transmitters pictured in Holland while the Dutch operator prepared to make contact with Whaddon Chase, the MI6 radio station near Bletchley. Later the Section VIII experts developed a less cumbersome model.

7 A remarkable group photograph taken in May 1940 at the Château de Vignolles, the headquarters of the French decryption service. Among those pictured are Major Gustave Bertrand, the head of the organization (5th from left); Captain R.C. (Dick) Pritchard from GC & CS (6th from left); Colonel Gwido Langer, head of the evacuated Polish decryption service (8th from left); with Kenneth MacFarlan, the MI6 liaison officer (extreme right).

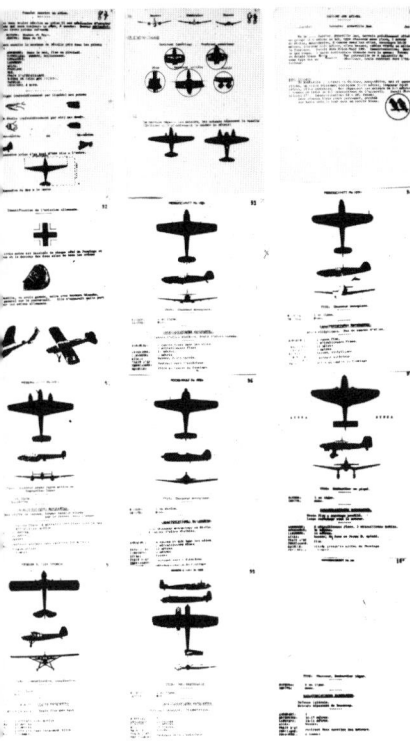

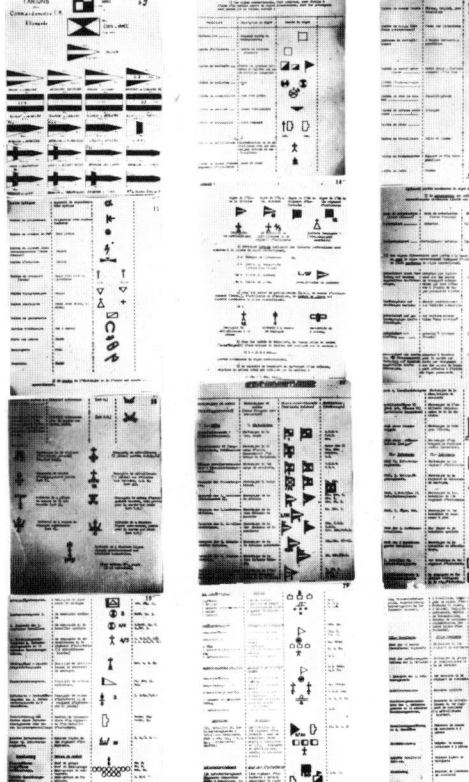

9 Pages of an intelligence manual provided by
Kenneth Cohen's French country section of MI6
for use by agents of the ALLIANCE network.
Guidance on aircraft recognition and the proper
construction of an agent's report are included
among the pages.

10 A vessel of MI6's private navy based in the Helford Estuary. The converted trawler was disguised as a French coastal fishing boat and crewed by volunteers. Headed by a former 'G' officer, Captain Frank Slocum CMG, OBE, RN, the organization was the only means of infiltrating agents into German-occupied France, until late in the summer of 1941 when the RAF established a Special Duties Squadron equipped with Lysanders to fly agents across the Channel.

11 Admiral Wilhelm Canaris, pictured shortly before his arrest in 1944.

12 Madame Szymanska's Polish diplomatic passport granted to her in Angers in France in April 1940. The passport is stamped with numerous entry and exit visas, including two relating to her rendezvous with Admiral Canaris in Italy in April 1941, at which he disclosed details of Hitler's imminent attack on the Soviet Union.

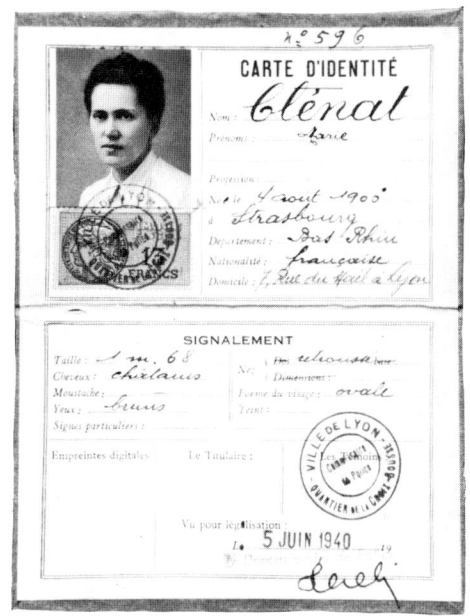

13 Madame Szymanska's French identity card, which identifies her as Marie Clenat, a French subject born in Strasbourg in August 1906. The document, which purported to have been issued in Lyons in June 1940, was a forgery manufactured by MI6 by its printing expert, Mr Adams, at his secret press at Potters Bar. Madame Szymanska used this *carte d'identité* when meeting Admiral Canaris in German-occupied France.

14 Sir Claude Dansey, founder of the Z-network and subsequently Assistant Chief of MI6.

15 Lieutenant-Colonel Monty Chidson, one of MI6's most experienced pre-war Heads of Station, pictured in Cairo in 1941, shortly before taking up his new appointment as Security Officer at the British Embassy in Ankara.

16 Brigadier Raymund Maunsell CBE, the first Defence Security Officer, Egypt, and subsequently the founder of Security Intelligence Middle East (SIME).

17 Colonel Euan Rabagliati MF, AFC, the first Head of MI6's Dutch country section.

18 Captain Cuthbert Bowlby CMG, CBE, DSC, RN, one of MI6's four 'G' officers until his appointment as Head of Station in Cairo in 1940.

19 Colonel Charles Howard (Dick) Ellis CBE, CMG, in Washington in 1941.

20, 21 The silver Gestapo warrant forged by MI6 to help Hans Bernd Gisevius escape to Switzerland from Berlin after the failure of the bomb plot to kill Hitler on 20 July 1944.

he moved into Broadway with the title Assistant Chief Staff Officer and joined Menzies's personal entourage which, at that time, consisted of David Boyle and Peter Koch de Gooreynd. His principal role was that of peacemaker between the Foreign Office and SIS.

Reilly's appointment succeeded in reducing Foreign Office criticism of Broadway's intelligence summaries, but did little to silence the complaints all the three Service intelligence directors voiced in the Joint Intelligence Committee. Once again Menzies defended his position by inviting the Director of Naval Intelligence, the Director of Military Intelligence and the Director of Air Intelligence to recommend candidates to fill three new co-ordinating posts which, Menzies suggested, would be known as Deputy Directors. This ploy effectively undermined the critics of SIS and led to the introduction of a further management layer on the distribution side of SIS. John Godfrey proposed a marine, John Cordeaux, to represent the interests of the NID, while Davidson proposed Brigadier W.R. Beddington and Archie Boyle suggested Air Commodore ('Lousy') Payne. These three candidates were accepted and later came to be known irreverently as 'the commissars' because of their obviously political role.

Another strategically important move made by Menzies concerned the Americans. Although he had initially resisted Stephenson's appointment to head a British intelligence set-up in New York, he did realize the advantages to be gained from American co-operation if and when they joined the Allies. However, they had no intelligence structure with which he could liaise, but as soon as anyone appeared who might be useful Menzies seized his opportunity.

It came because Churchill now asked Stephenson to try to obtain the transfer of fifty destroyers from the United States Navy's mothball fleet to the Royal Navy. In addition, Stephenson was to invite President Roosevelt to send a special envoy to England to see the situation at first hand and report directly to the White House, thus bypassing the Anglophobe American Ambassador Joseph Kennedy. The President eagerly accepted the invitation and asked Colonel William J. (Bill) Donovan to represent him. Bill Donovan was a veteran of the Great War and a highly successful lawyer. When Stephenson arrived in New York in July 1940, Donovan was giving evidence to the Senate's Military Affairs Committee in Washington. Stephenson delivered Menzies's invitation to the Secretary of State for the Navy, Frank Knox, and he conferred with both the President and Donovan. All agreed that Donovan should take the mission and, accordingly, on 14 July 1940, Donovan flew to Lisbon aboard a Flying Clipper. If Donovan's report was favourable, the President would release the fifty destroyers.

Donovan arrived in England at the height of the Battle of Britain and stayed until 4 August. Menzies arranged his itinerary and ensured it included all the sights. Donovan had an audience with the King, met the

Cabinet and was taken on a (carefully planned) tour of England. An official report later commented: '... he was initiated into the mysteries of the British organizations which dealt with secret intelligence and the various elements of unorthodox warfare.' To put it mildly, Donovan was treated to a rare experience. His itinerary included MI5, MI6 and the Prime Minister, but it did not involve Joseph Kennedy. The consequences of Donovan's visit to London will be described in chapter fourteen.

While Stephenson was busy exerting his considerable influence over Donovan, the FBI agreed to send two of its agents to London to work at Broadway. Once again Menzies took the opportunity to impress the Americans with the scope of SIS's activities and indoctrinated them into some of GCHQ's secrets. Both agents reported to Hoover, in tones approaching adulation, that the British had cracked all the Axis codes. This was, of course, something of an exaggeration, but it had the effect of cementing Hoover's co-operation. By the summer of 1941, arrangements had been finalized for a complete exchange of military intelligence. SIS interpreted this, with Donovan's consent, to mean using American consular facilities for running agents. This collaboration was of enormous assistance to SIS and grew month by month. As an illustration it is worth citing the experience of one American Consul. Between January and November 1942 the American Consul in Casablanca dealt with no less than 193 separate requests for help from SIS, ranging from the delivery of wireless sets to the payment of agents.

Before finally turning to SIS's wartime operations, we should briefly cover what remains of the SIS organization abroad. Only two Stations are left to describe. In the Far East SIS had long maintained small, one-man Stations in Shanghai and Yokohama. Both had been abandoned in the face of the Japanese advance. In Shanghai, Tom Barton was arrested and died of illness. In Tokyo, Harry Steptoe (who had previously headed the Shanghai Station) was interned by the Kempetai, the Japanese secret police. Luckily for him his SIS connections were never discovered and he was exchanged in 1941 in East Africa, along with other British diplomatic internees. The fall of Singapore in February 1942 removed the base of a joint intelligence unit, Combined Intelligence Far East (CIFE), a NID/MI5/MI6 organization created in 1938 in Hong Kong under Captain Bill Wiley RN. CIFE was relocated in Kandy, Ceylon, under an MI5 officer, Courtney Young, but was not, initially, in a position to run individual agents. Nevertheless, Section V appointed a former *Times* journalist named Horler as its Far East representative to Ceylon.

With great determination, SIS was putting its house in order, setting up new Stations in the Middle and Far East and co-operating in America, strengthening a second tier of operations through Section V, building up its teams in neutral countries and taking every advantage it possibly could from its possession of GCHQ Bletchley and the ULTRA decrypts.

10

Wartime Operations in France and North Africa

SIS wartime operations will be covered geographically rather than chronologically, beginning in this chapter with France and North Africa. Chapter eleven will cover Norway, Sweden and Russia, chapter twelve will deal with Holland, Belgium and Portugal, and chapter thirteen with the Middle East.

As the SIS had no European intelligence networks of its own, it had to make the best use it could of those belonging to others. Biffy Dunderdale had previously been SIS Head in Paris, where he had come into contact with the Poles. Now he was made liaison officer with the French exiles in London, the only Head of Section allowed to continue with his former hosts, all the other Section Heads being posted far afield. He soon discovered that the Poles were running a network in occupied France through Colonel Gano, the Polish intelligence head who was living at their headquarters in the Rubens Hotel, Buckingham Palace Road.

The organizing spirit behind the Polish network was the Polish Deuxième Bureau's representative in Paris, Colonel Wincenty Zarembski, who had been attached to the Paris Embassy under Commercial Attaché cover. He had remained in southern France after the evacuation of the Polish General Staff to help the many hundreds of Polish stragglers escape to Spain. He was based in Toulouse where he had, by coincidence, found two stranded Poles, Maslowski and Dulemba, who had been wireless operators in the Polish Foreign Ministry. Zarembski persuaded them to build a primitive transmitter, and by the late summer of 1940 he had made contact with the Polish Embassy in Madrid. A regular schedule was then arranged with the exiled Polish DMI in London who gave Zarembski the SIS code-name TUDOR. Initially the TUDOR group was restricted to the unoccupied area of France, which was governed by Marshal Pétain from Vichy. However, TUDOR succeeded in recruiting a number of Polish officers in the German-occupied region, which included Paris, and principal among these was a Polish air-force officer, Captain Roman Garby-Czerniawski, codenamed VALENTIN.

VALENTIN had opted to remain in Paris after the fall of France and had adopted the identity of his French mistress's late husband, Armand Borni. Late in December 1940 he took delivery of an SIS wireless set from TUDOR. This was the first of its kind and had been built at Whaddon Chase by Section VIII. It was a portable, combined receiver-transmitter and was small enough to fit into a suitcase. Its journey to Toulouse had been overland via a series of couriers from the Madrid Station. The first message from VALENTIN's new radio was received on 1 January 1941, when he announced that his group would henceforth be known as INTERALLIE. His operator, named Gane (and code-named KENT), was a young Pole who had been taught to use a radio in the army before the war; he transmitted from a top-floor flat near the Trocadéro. The five-figure code to be used was based on a common French/Polish dictionary, *Kielski*'s, but the first attempts to establish contact with London proved unsatisfactory. The signal strength was too weak, so London sent out a second operator, named Wlodaurczyk (code-named MAURICE), to Toulouse (via Madrid) to help build a more powerful transmitter.

The new transmitter proved highly effective and, by May 1941, it was on the air four times a day, sending up to a hundred groups on each occasion. It was assumed that the plethora of German broadcasts in the French capital would provide suitable screen to hide the illicit signals. Having made the radio link, the INTERALLIE circuit proceeded to recruit new members. The occupied territory was divided into fourteen sectors, each with its own couriers and head agents. They passed military intelligence to VALENTIN, who collated it and then had it transmitted to London. For SIS the INTERALLIE network represented a tremendous advance. Most of the circuits were Polish and were, therefore, immune from the political rivalries paralysing the rest of the Resistance. Perhaps more significantly, the majority of the head agents had received military training and, therefore, knew exactly what to look for and report. Thanks to the Polish Deuxième Bureau-in-exile, SIS was receiving regular, high-grade messages from behind enemy lines. The intelligence included observations made by nearly 120 INTERALLIE agents located near French channel ports, Luftwaffe airfields and industrial centres. By the summer of 1941 a further three transmitters had begun working.

The INTERALLIE network proved so successful that in September 1941 VALENTIN was invited to London to attend a joint SIS/Polish Deuxième Bureau conference to discuss its future. On 11 October a Lysander, piloted by Flight-Lieutenant Phillipson, collected VALENTIN from a small airfield near Compiègne. The field had been a pre-war aeroclub, but it was too small to be used by the Luftwaffe. The pick-up was executed faultlessly and the journey back to Tempsford was uneventful. The following day VALENTIN met Dunderdale for the first time and was introduced to Colonel Gano at the Polish headquarters, and his deputy, Major

Zychon. The Polish Commander-in-Chief, General Sikorski, decorated VALENTIN with the highest Polish award for gallantry. After nine days of discussions VALENTIN was ready to return to France, and on 21 October he was parachuted 'blind' into the Loire valley. When VALENTIN returned he found that his cipher clerk, a volatile French nurse named Mathilde Carré, had quarrelled with KENT and that relationships at his base in Paris had deteriorated sharply, in spite of the brevity of his absence in London. Much later VALENTIN learned that he had been betrayed to the Abwehr by a trusted sub-agent in Cherbourg, Raoul Kiffer, who was in charge of one of INTERALLIE's northern sectors. As well as betraying twenty-one of his own helpers, Kiffer gave the Abwehr VALENTIN's address in Paris. Early in the morning of 17 November 1941 VALENTIN was arrested in bed at his flat in the St Germain-en-Laye district. The Abwehr recovered a quantity of documents from the flat and it was eventually able to identify and arrest the entire network in just three days. It was helped in this by Kiffer and Mathilde Carré, who became the mistress of one of the Abwehr investigators.

Mathilde Carré's decision to collaborate with the Abwehr was disastrous for SIS because she alone was in a position to supply details of all four INTERALLIE wireless stations. She knew their locations, their transmitting schedules, their codes and, most importantly, the hidden security checks embedded in the texts of messages which indicated that they were not being sent under control. The operators in England failed to spot that Abwehr personnel had taken over the sets, and the French country section at Broadway noticed no change in the management of its star network. To allay any possible suspicions, Carré belatedly reported VALENTIN's arrest and announced that she would be taking over the network. She proposed to call herself VICTOIRE, and London approved.

INTERALLIE's apparent continuing success pleased SIS, and it was decided that since SOE was still experiencing considerable difficulties communicating with its circuits, VICTOIRE should be used to channel messages to London. Understandably the Germans were delighted with this proposal, and VICTOIRE met her first SOE contact at dinner in Paris on 26 December 1941. He was Pierre de Vomecourt, one of SOE's first F section agents who had parachuted into France near Châteauroux the previous May. Unfortunately, most of his circuit had been arrested, and he was left in Paris with little money and no means of communicating with SOE. As soon as he heard of INTERALLIE's existence, he got an introduction to VICTOIRE and renewed his link with London. This was regarded as a very favourable development by SOE until, in mid-January 1942, it learned from SIS that all was not entirely well with INTERALLIE.

Exactly what made SIS suspicious remains unclear, but certainly Pierre de Vomecourt had grown suspicious of VICTOIRE. She seemed to have limitless facilities and, on one occasion, produced an impressive selection of identity cards and other travel documents for the remaining members of his circuit. Vomecourt decided the best course was to request a Lysander pick-up. This VICTOIRE did, with the consent of the Germans. They had decided to send their double agent to London as well so that she could infiltrate SOE. SIS and SOE concurred with the plan to extract VICTOIRE, Vomecourt and two other stranded SOE agents, Roger Cottin and Major Ben Cowburn. Two pick-up operations were arranged and then cancelled because of bad weather, and it was finally agreed that a motor launch would be sent to rendezvous with the three near Locquirec in Brittany. While these tense negotiations were continuing, Vomecourt challenged VICTOIRE about her access to genuine identity cards and she suddenly told him the whole story. Vomecourt realized that both he and his fellow agents were entirely in the hands of the Germans, but he decided to play along with the German plan in the hope that they would all be allowed to escape.

At midnight on 11 February 1942, an SIS motor torpedo-boat (MTB) arrived at the prearranged rendezvous and proceeded to disembark two new SOE agents equipped with radios. Suddenly the Germans emerged from the darkness and closed in on the group on the beach. The Royal Naval officer in one of the two rubber dinghies, Lieutenant-Commander Ivan Black, flashed an ambush signal to the MTB, which promptly headed for home at full speed. In the confusion that followed, VICTOIRE and her two companions escaped, but Black, Claude Redding and his wireless operator, G.W. Abbot, were all arested.

News of this disaster reached SIS as soon as the MTB docked at Dartmouth. Yet, astonishingly, Abbot's radio was soon on the air reporting a safe arrival. Undaunted, two further MTB pick-ups were arranged without success and then, on the night of 26/27 February, a well-armed party from the MTB made contact with VICTOIRE and Vomecourt on the beach near Pointe de Bihit. In the meantime, Cowburn had embarked on the first stage of his own escape over the Pyrenees to Madrid. Cottin had decided to go to ground in Paris.

Although SIS was by now fully aware of VICTOIRE's duplicity, it was decided to leave her at liberty in London and to continue the contact with the Abwehr-controlled INTERALLIE wireless sets. As well as taking the double game a step further, it was argued that the lives of Abbot and Redding might rely on the arrangement. The charade was continued until April the following year, when Vomecourt returned to France by parachute to organize a new circuit. He was arrested weeks after landing and was eventually given to VICTOIRE's lover for interrogation. The Germans tried to prevent news of Vomecourt's arrest from leaking out, but SOE quickly obtained confirmation from another of its networks.

Virtually all the participants of the VICTOIRE trap survived the war. Black, Redding and Abbot were sent to prisoner-of-war camps in Germany; VICTOIRE was handed over to the Security Service and spent the remainder of the war in Aylesbury Gaol. After the Liberation, she was handed back to the French authorities and was tried on a charge of collaborating with the enemy. She was convicted, sentenced to death, reprieved and was released from prison in September 1954. Ben Cowburn reported to the British Embassy in Madrid and was repatriated; he then successfully completed three further missions for SOE into France. Roger Cottin also survived the war in spite of being caught by the Abwehr in Paris in April 1942.

Gradually messages from INTERALLIE dried up and SIS was left to consider the lessons of the episode. The German manipulation had only been made possible by the network's poor security procedures, which had allowed a key figure, VICTOIRE, to learn all its secrets. Minimal compartmentalization had enabled Kiffer to betray VALENTIN, and SIS's decision to share its facilities with SOE had endangered further lives.

There was, however, an extraordinary sequel to the story. In October 1942 VALENTIN turned up at the Madrid Station and asked to be taken to England. The Germans had offered him a unique deal: if he went to London and spied for the Abwehr, they guaranteed to treat the imprisoned members of INTERALLIE as prisoners of war. If he failed them, they would all be executed. VALENTIN had little choice but to accept the offer; however, once he had been cleared into London, he volunteered to work for MI6 as a double agent. MI6 turned him over to MI5's B1(a) section and he was run (with the Security Service code-name BRUTUS) by Hugh Astor until January 1945, thus saving the lives of his network.

The INTERALLIE experience was a bitter one for SIS, although it must be said that for twelve vital months from November 1940 the network provided an unprecedented volume of valuable information and helped confirm to the management at Broadway that its Abwehr opponents were extremely skilled at running double-agent operations.

Biffy Dunderdale not only worked with the Poles building up INTERALLIE during the late autumn of 1940, but also helped the Free French groups and those with de Gaulle. An outline of the main French groups with whom SIS was dealing in London has been given in chapter seven. Suffice it to say here that French politics were so complicated, and the warring factions among the exiles so fierce, that SIS had divided French networks into those with de Gaulle and those operating independently. On the whole, the latter were mainly assisted by Kenneth Cohen, who was particularly interested in making approaches to those with contacts with Vichy.

At the end of July 1940, de Gaulle in London asked Captain Andre

The Interallie Network, Autumn 1941

HEAD OF INTERALLIE

CODING	
VIOLETTE	Renée Borni

ASSISTANT	
CHRISTIAN	Bernard Krótki

COURIERS	
RAPIDE	Stanislaw Lach
JEAN	G. Lurton
STEPHANE	Stefan Czyż
ANTONIO	N. Mateo

WIRELESS SERVICE	
Admin: KENT	Fernand Gane
Techn: MAX	Max Desplaces
Oper: MAURICE	Eug. Wlodarczyk
Oper: MARCEL	Henri Tabet

SECRETARY, CONTACTS	
LA CHATTE	Mathilde Lily Carré

STUDIES	
Army: RENÉ	René Aubertin
Air: VOLTA	George Boucier
Press: PAUL	Lucien de Roquigny
Industry OBSERV	W. de Lipski

PARIS GROUP	
YAG	B. Jngiellowicz
CHON	Mad de Jankowski
ETTE	Paulette Porcher
LYDIA	Lydia de Lipski
WANDA	Wanda Choińska
YARD	W. Nowiński
MARIE	Maria Bradkowska
OSCAR	
YOLE	René Legrande
YIN	
YVES Railways	Henri Busset

POLICE (R) GROUP	
ROLAND (BOB)	Charles Lejeune
ROBERT	
RAUL	
RAYMOND	
ROGER	

'PATRIE' (P) GROUP	
PHARAON (MARC)	Marc Marchal
PROMETHÉ	(explosives)
PILATE	(Potez)
PANDORE	Railways, Nord
PARQUE	Railways, East

LETTERBOXES	
NOEUD	R. Hugentobler
MIREILLE	Mireille Lejeune
LA PALLETTE	Mme Gaby
BERLITZ School	(office)

'LA LIBERTE' GROUP
Group of Vichy anti-German officers

SECTORS (Field Organization)

SECTOR A	
AOUTA	Mono Deschamps
ALBERT	Jean Lejeune
APOLLO	Paul Angelman
ANGELO	Paul Maillet
ANTONIO	N. Mateo

SECTOR B
BERTRAND
BERNARD
BASILE
BAPTISTE

'Boat-to-submarine' link org. by Baptiste

SECTOR C	
CHARLES	T. Burlot
COCO	J. Collardey
CLEMENT	
CASSIS	
CELESTIN	
CASIMIR	
CHRISTOPH	
CONSTANT	
COURAGEUX	
CHATEAUX	
CHARLOTTE	

SECTOR D	
DESIRÉ (KIKI)	Raoul Keiffer
DANIEL	
DENIS	
DEDÉ	
DAMIEN	
DOLLY	

SECTOR E	
EDGAR	
E-ORION	Madeleine Lequelec

SECTOR F
FERNAND
FRANC
FELIX

EASTERN SECTORS

SECTOR S	(Zone Annexed)
SIXTE	

SECTOR Q	(Belgium)
QUINTEX	

SECTOR G
GEORGES

SECTOR H	
HONORÉ	Paul Martin
HECTOR	Defly
HERCULES	
HARVEY	

SECTOR I	
IRENÉE	Jean Boudon
ISIDOR	Gilbert Lefevre

SECTOR J	
JEAN	G. Lurton
JANINE	

SECTOR K	
KLÉBER	Fernand Butler
KAROL	

SECTOR L	
LOUIS	Henri Gorce
LOUDOVIC	
LEONARD	
LES LOUPS	

Dewavrin to run a new fledgling French intelligence service based on a small office in St Stephen's House. Dewavrin had been evacuated from the Allied invasion of Norway in June 1940 and had been landed at Glasgow. From there he had sailed to Brest with his commando unit and had arrived in time to learn of the armistice signed at Compiègne. Dewavrin tried at first to rejoin the French army in North Africa, but the only ship he could find was bound for Southampton. Once there he transferred to Trentham Park. He was then subjected to two conflicting loyalties: Marshal Pétain's officers were ordering troops back to France; de Gaulle was urging resistance from London. Dewavrin decided to report to de Gaulle's headquarters.

Dewavrin's first move after de Gaulle had asked him to run the new Service de Renseignements was to open negotiations with SIS. Claude Dansey offered him the same terms as he had offered to other Allied intelligence organizations: training, accommodation, transport and communications in exchange for shared information. Dewavrin agreed, and the first agents were recruited for missions back to France. Most of those chosen adopted *noms de guerre* to protect their families at home and some of the earliest personnel chose the names of Paris Métro stations. Thus Dewavrin became Passy, and Maurice Duclos, who had served in the abortive Norwegian Campaign with Dewavrin, became St Jacques. By the middle of July 1940 Dewavrin was compiling lists of suitable agents.

The official SIS view of Dewavrin and his network was coloured by caution, bearing in mind that many French political factions were seeking to represent themselves as *the* resistance organization with the largest following. There was also an uneasy relationship between the political Left and de Gaulle's supporters, which had to be taken into account. As the Left frequently pointed out, some of Dewavrin's earliest recruits, including Maurice Duclos and Pierre Fourcaud, were known to have been members of a group of anti-Communist (and occasionally pro-Fascist) secret societies known collectively as La Cagoule. According to some, membership of La Cagoule was inconsistent with being anti-Nazi. Dewavrin took the view that the only qualification he wanted to be sure of was committed anti-Germanism.

SIS had enjoyed excellent close relations with the pre-war Deuxième Bureau; these people had now regrouped at Vichy and seemed to be ostensibly loyal to Marshal Pétain. Churchill would have no truck with them, but the United States had opened diplomatic relations with Pétain. Kenneth Cohen too thought that they were well worth contacting and might prove a useful line of entry into war-torn France.

The reconstituted Deuxième Bureau in Vichy was headed by Colonel Louis Baril, who had already made himself known to the American Embassy in Vichy as an anti-German. He had also sent a courier to the Secret Intelligence Service Station in Geneva with a message of support. His other helpers included Colonel Louis Rivet, who headed the Service de Renseignements, the French overseas intelligence service, and the head of the counter-espionage section, Captain Paul Paillole. The complicated intelligence structure at Vichy consisted of Paillole's undercover military organization, based in Marseilles, which called itself Travaux Ruraux (Rural Construction), and Commandant Rollin's civilian counter-espionage service, the Direction de la Surveillance du Territoire. All of these units were official departments of the Vichy Government and, as such, were empowered to operate anywhere south of the demarcation line between occupied and unoccupied France. The Vichy regime also employed a small internal security office headed by Colonel Georges Groussard; he, too, had volunteered his services to London and had been dubbed ERIC by SIS.

All of these officers were prepared to re-establish their pre-war links with SIS, but the question remained of quite how to do it. The first solution was offered by Dewavrin, who proposed to send a trusted lieutenant, Pierre Fourcaud, to Vichy via Spain.

Fourcaud's instructions were to contact Commandant Georges Loustaunau-Lacau, a controversial French army officer who had been court-martialled for criticizing the General Staff's conduct of the war. He had been wounded in action, captured and then released from a German military hospital for rehabilitation. In August 1940 he had taken over a hotel in Vichy and transformed it into an unofficial reception centre for convalescing soldiers. At the same time he was publishing an anti-Communist newspaper, *L'Ordre National*. Loustaunau-Lacau, who had adopted the *nom de guerre* Navarre, had already been in touch with London with ideas for starting a national resistance movement. His first communications to London had been sent via a Canadian diplomat in Vichy named Dupuy, and early in November 1940 he sent Jacques Bridou to London with a plan to set up an intelligence organization based on the Vichy Deuxième Bureau.

Bridou made his way to Tangiers, and from there caught a ferry to Gibraltar where he had made himself known to the authorities. He was placed aboard a troopship, but when he arrived in England he was taken into custody by the Port Security staff. Bridou promptly produced the names of two English references: Jeavons, his English father-in-law, whom he had never met, and a naval officer recommended by Navarre. Unfortunately a letter from Bridou's English wife to her father had failed to arrive, so when he was approached by MI5 to confirm his son-in-law's credentials he refused. Eventually a confrontation was arranged and Mr Jeavons was able to establish that Bridou was who he claimed to be. Meanwhile, the naval referee had alerted his cousin, Kenneth Cohen, and he also made a timely intervention.

Bridou was particularly welcome to SIS because Navarre had already made it clear that he was not prepared to be subordinate to de Gaulle. He was perfectly willing to work in parallel with the Free French, but this was unacceptable to de Gaulle. This enabled Cohen to recruit Bridou for his French country section, and he was parachuted back into Vichy territory near Clermont-Ferrand in March 1941 with a wireless operator named Laroche.

Bridou's safe arrival back in France was a turning point for SIS. It was agreed over this radio link that Navarre should operate direct to London, independently of Fourcaud, and that the intelligence product would be shared by SIS with the Bureau Central de Renseignements et d'Action. SIS, of course, was delighted with this arrangement, and Cohen arranged to hold a meeting in Lisbon with Navarre. A rendezvous point was made by the tomb of Vasco da Gama in the Church of Santa Maria de Belém, and the two men continued their negotiations for three days. Cohen, using his old Z-network cover-name of Keith Crane, produced a new wireless transmitter and a set of radio schedules. Henceforth, Navarre's network would be known as ALLIANCE; its radio call-sign was to be KVL. Navarre himself would be known as N1 and his chief assistant, Marie-Madeleine Meric, was to be POZ 55. All the other members of the network were given three-letter and two-numeral identifications (COU 25, for example). At the end of his discussions with Cohen, Navarre returned to Vichy. Navarre's own standing with the Pétain regime was so good that the French Ambassador in Lisbon unwittingly aided the transmitter's journey to Vichy by suggesting that Navarre carry the diplomatic bag on his return journey, thus freeing him from customs' inspections.

SIS believed that it would be too dangerous to use KVL from the town of Vichy itself, so it was established in the the town of Pau, with its operator, Lucien Vallet. The plan was for couriers to carry encoded messages from Vichy to Pau, where Vallet would transmit them on a regular schedule. Helped by this direct link with SIS, ALLIANCE expanded rapidly and recruited agents in the occupied territories. As well as providing a channel of communication for the Deuxième Bureau, it also developed sources in Paris, Brittany and, indirectly, North Africa.

It was the North African link, and Navarre's ambitious plan to foment a revolt in the French army there, that led to his arrest in May 1941. Navarre had always regarded himself not as a spy but as an activist waiting for the right moment to organize overt military resistance. His scheme was to recruit sympathetic army officers garrisoned in North Africa, persuade them to revolt against Vichy, and thus deny the region to any German occupation. Navarre travelled to Algiers to join his conspirators, but he was betrayed soon after his arrival and arrested by French military police loyal to Vichy. When he was searched he was found to be carrying a number of incriminating documents, some of which compromised other members of ALLIANCE.

This setback threatened the entire ALLIANCE group and forced the evacuation of the KVL set from Pau to Marseilles, where the network enjoyed considerable support from within the police. POZ 55 took over control of the organization, but within a few days Navarre turned up. The police commissioner in Algiers turned out to be sympathetic and had allowed Navarre to escape.

Navarre's miraculous return signalled a new stage in ALLIANCE's development. As he was now obliged to operate underground, he had more time to devote to running his circuits, and soon ALLIANCE requested a further three SIS transmitters. He established BAY in Monaco, MED in Marseilles and moved KVL back to Pau. The fourth, call-sign LUX, was held in reserve. All were carried into France by Jean Boutron (ASO 43) who, conveniently, had been appointed Vichy's Assistant Naval Attaché in Madrid. ASO 43 duly reported to the Madrid Station, which took copies of Vichy's diplomatic seals. Thereafter, whenever ASO 43 was assigned courier duties, the Vichy diplomatic bag was opened at Pau and then resealed. This gave ALLIANCE the advantage of examining the contents of the bag and inserting its own material.

On 17 July 1941 Navarre was arrested for the second time. Once again, he had been caught by police loyal to the Pétain regime. He was incarcerated in Pau prison, and ALLIANCE prepared for the worst. KVL was moved to a hotel in the town centre, but the expected wave of arrests never materialized. Instead ALLIANCE grew larger and became the main source of reception committees for SIS airdrops. Once a rendezvous had been agreed over KVL, a group of volunteers would mark a dropping zone and flash a visual signal to the 161 Squadron men as they approached. This system proved far more effective than SOE's early policy of dropping its agent blind.

On 5 August 1941 another operator, SHE, was parachuted into ALLIANCE, destined for Normandy, but within twenty-four hours of his arrival it was learned that he was suffering from appendicitis. As his condition worsened POZ 55 ordered that he should be taken to the hospital in Pau, accompanied by another member of the network who posed as his wife. The wireless operator, who was a Londoner who had spent most of his youth in France, underwent a successful operation, but he needed constant supervision by his relatives: he talked in his sleep ... in English. Eventually SHE was declared fit and he moved on to his destination in Normandy.

By the autumn of 1941 ALLIANCE had acquired two further transmitters: VAL in Lyons and OCK in Paris. The network was going from strength to strength and to date only one of the radios had been lost, although there had been many close calls. On one occasion the police had raided the homes of several ALLIANCE agents in Pau and had arrested more than a dozen people, including N1's wife and son. At POZ 55's headquarters they found her chief assistant, COU 73 (a young air-force officer named Maurice Coustenoble), but KVL had been saved. Unfortunately, the agent who removed KVL panicked and threw it into the River Gave.

Shortly before Christmas 1941 the French country section invited POZ 55 to London for a conference, but it was not until she reported to the Madrid Station that it was realized that she was a glamorous thirty-two-year-old mother of two! For unknown motives Cohen's deputy, travelling under the cover-name Richards, flew to Lisbon and met her there. POZ 55 had experienced a rather more uncomfortable journey from Pau; most of the time she had been hidden in the boot of ASO 43's Citroen, covered with bulky diplomatic bags. His news was depressing. London believed that only MED (in Marseilles) and BAY (which had moved from Monaco to Nice) were operating freely. There had been other complications as well. SHE had suffered from some technical problems and had taken over OCK in Paris. This news came as a considerable surprise to Richards, who had believed that SHE was still based in Normandy. At the root of the problem was the cell system adopted by SIS, which prevented separate radio operators communicating with one another. All the messages had to be channelled through London, and it now became clear that neither London nor POZ 55 had realized how deeply their organization might have been penetrated. To help speed up the flow of messages, especially within ALLIANCE, ASO 43 was given a transmitter, which he installed in the roof of the French Embassy in Madrid. With typical bravado he told the official Vichy operator that he too was sending messages back to Pétain!

The December conference in Lisbon broke up with Richards giving POZ 55 two further wireless sets for what remained of ALLIANCE. Over the next few weeks reports arrived daily of fresh arrests. Then, quite unexpectedly, a message smuggled from Lucien Vallet in Fresnes prison arrived. Vallet had been arrested several weeks earlier. He claimed that his Abwehr captors had just handed him OCK to repair ... yet OCK was apparently being operated in Paris by SHE. POZ 55 immediately signalled London that their first wireless operator was almost certainly working for the Abwehr. London's reply was brief: 218 FOR POZ 55: EXECUTE SHE.

This was rather easier said than done, considering that SHE was obviously working hand in glove with the Germans. In fact, it was not until September 1942 that SHE reappeared. He was spotted in Marseilles railway station by an ALLIANCE operator named Crawley, who happened to have been on a radio course with SHE at the SIS training centre in Sloane Square. They made a date to meet in a bar and, when they did so, SHE was arrested by two ALLIANCE members posing as French detectives. As Crawley looked on, SHE identified himself by his real name and explained he was an Englishman living in Paris. He also gave them a telephone number to ring to confirm his identity: the number was that of the Abwehr's headquarters in Paris. SHE was taken to a flat belonging to ALLIANCE's head of operations, Commandant Leon Faye, and interrogated by him and his butler, Albert. Once SHE realized he had been duped, he admitted his guilt and a signal was sent to London. SHE claimed he had always been a Fascist sympathizer and had deliberately offered himself to the Abwehr soon after he had recovered from his appendix operation. The French country section sent its congratulations to ALLIANCE and confirmed the execution order.

POZ 55 agreed that the simplest method of carrying out the order was to give SHE a couple of the 'L' (for lethal) capsules thoughtfully provided by SIS for use by agents who could not face torture. It had been claimed in London that the poison worked in seconds, so the contents of two capsules were poured into some soup. SIS's information was evidently exaggerated because SHE drained the soup . . . and then asked for more. Two further 'L' pills were put into a mug of tea, but after he had drunk most of it he realized that it had contained a drug and commented to Faye that it 'couldn't be much fun for an officer to have to do this sort of thing'.

The poison still had not taken effect two hours later and POZ 55 was called in to decide what to do. She recommended another dose of poison, only this time it should be administered in a cold drink. The capsules were dissolved in a glass of whisky and handed to the prisoner. He paused, announced that the Germans intended to invade Vichy's unoccupied territory on 11 November (as indeed they did), and drained the whisky in one gulp. He promptly dropped dead.

POZ 55 continued to operate ALLIANCE until 18 July 1943 when, reluctantly, she was flown to Tangmere in a Lysander piloted by Flying Officer Peter Vaughan-Fowler. ALLIANCE was later to suffer many losses, with more than 150 agents being rounded up later in the year. At the peak of ALLIANCE's operations it ran some 3,000 agents and thirty wireless sets, all reporting to SIS's French country section.

The Secret Intelligence Service's link with the Vichy Deuxième Bureau, via Madrid, was to pay dividends, and the quality of information between March 1941 and July 1943 was considered excellent. This, of course, is not to say that all the ALLIANCE reports were acted on by the Services. Two weeks before the break-out of the German battleships *Scharnhorst* and *Gneisenau* from Brest in February 1942, an ALLIANCE agent in the dockyards had warned of their imminent departure. He had provided regular situation reports on the status of both battleships and they had proved a useful supplement to the RAF's occasional photographic reconnaissance flights. His crucial message was routed through Madrid to London, but apparently little action was taken. As a result, both ships, accompanied by the heavy cruiser *Prinz Eugen*, slipped into the Channel soon after midnight on 12 February and, in a little over twenty-four hours, had successfully negotiated the Straits of Dover and reached the safety of Wilhelmshaven.

The Deuxième Bureau retained its ambiguous loyalty to the Vichy regime, but this did not prevent it from channelling information into ALLIANCE. Colonel Groussard (ERIC), of the Groupe de Protection, made no less than three secret visits to London before his arrest on 16 July 1941. After a successful escape, Groussard was sent to Geneva to continue his contact with the Resistance. On 24 January 1942 Groussard was followed by Captain Paillole. Paillole's Travaux Ruraux had absorbed most of the pre-war Deuxième Bureau's German section and was, therefore, well positioned to monitor German espionage, although in theory its job was directed against the Allies and the Free French. One important sub-section of Travaux Ruraux, headed by Colonel Bertrand, was the cryptographic department that had collaborated so closely with GCHQ before the war. It had been evacuated to Oran on the fall of France, but had later been repatriated and stationed in the fortress of Les Fouzes, near Nîmes. Bertrand's team included fifteen Poles, under the command of Colonel Langer, most of whom had worked on the first Enigma *bombes*. Thus, within easy reach of the Germans, the Vichy Deuxième Bureau harboured a combined interception and decryption centre which was, in part, staffed by the Polish army. Even more remarkably, this covert establishment initially escaped the attention of the Abwehr, who really believed it was a construction firm! SIS dubbed the centre CADIX and supplied the organization with ten transmitters, which formed the basis of a circuit headed by Michel Thoraval. Paillole escaped to England via Spain and Gibraltar in January 1942, and the CADIX centre continued operating until the following October when the Germans traced its location. Most of the cryptographers, including Bertrand, succeeded in escaping to England, where they participated in an independent Polish cryptanalysis unit based at Boxmoor in Hertfordshire.

The French country section's relations with Dewavrin's Service de Renseignements remained on the whole good, although de Gaulle was never reconciled with SIS's independent role. In January 1942 the Service de Renseignements was amalgamated with Captain Lagier's Service Action, which had liaised closely with SOE's RF section. Three months later they moved into new offices at 10 Duke Street, in the West End of London, and were established as the Bureau Central de Renseignements et d'Action. Occasionally there were hiccups. In one incident shortly before Operation TORCH, the Allied landings in North Africa in November 1942, a BCRA officer, Lablache Combier, approached ASO 43 in Madrid offering details of Operation TORCH to the Vichy authorities. ASO 43 immediately alerted his contact in the local Station, Kenneth Benton, and Combier was lured into a trap. He was invited to see the British Naval Attaché, Alan Hillgarth, but when he arrived he was literally sandbagged with a sock filled with sand. Unfortunately, the officer wielding the weapon did so with such ferocity that the sock burst and the office was covered with sand! A plan had been agreed whereby Combier would be drugged, driven to Gibraltar, and then sent back to London in custody. The Embassy doctor administered an injection to the unconscious BCRA officer and he was then deposited in the boot of the Naval Attaché's car for the drive to Gibraltar. The doctor explained that the effects of the drug would wear off during the journey, so a second dose was given to Combier half way to Gibraltar. When the car arrived in Algeciras, Combier was found to be dead. Importing a corpse into Gibraltar in wartime proved to be a complicated affair, even with the help of the recently arrived Head of Station, John Codrington. Eventually, after the intervention of the Governor, Sir Mason Macfarlane, Combier was allowed in and was given a secret burial.

The full details of this incident were never admitted to the French, but complaints were made to Dewavrin concerning his organization's poor security. A much stricter regime was introduced in London to improve matters, and this indirectly led to an embarrassing incident in Duke Street. On 9 January 1943 a man using the name Paul Manoel was found hanged in the basement of Dewavrin's headquarters. Manoel was suspected of being a German agent and had been undergoing a hostile interrogation at the hands of the BCRA. It was only after SIS's intervention that the local police were persuaded to drop the matter.

Kenneth Cohen's French country section had taken responsibility for Vichy's intelligence service and, in particular, for running the ALLIANCE ring. Meanwhile, Dunderdale's other French country section had created an entirely new network, following the collapse of INTERALLIE.

Dunderdale's new organization was a Catholic network run by a Jesuit based in Bordeaux, Father Arnould. Arnould had adopted the *nom de guerre* Colonel Claude Ollivier (he was known as Le Colonel) and had acquired another Catholic, Philippe Keun, as his chief assistant. Keun's *nom de guerre* was L'Amiral, and together they formed a *réseau* code-named AMICOL. AMICOL's headquarters was the convent of the Sisters of St Agonie in the rue de la Santé in Paris, and in the months before D-Day the resourceful Father Arnould supplied Dunderdale with information from more than a thousand Catholic sub-agents, each reporting to a head agent identified only by the name of a gemstone. One particular circuit, JADE/AMICOL, had links with railwaymen at all levels of the French national rail system, and was able to provide valuable information on German troop movements.

Shortly before D-Day Philippe Keun returned to London to be briefed at Broadway, but he was betrayed in July 1944 and was executed two months later. Nevertheless, the AMICOL network transmitted many hundreds of messages over the invasion period and the main wireless set, hidden in the attic of the convent, remained undetected until the liberation of Paris.

The INTERALLIE, ALLIANCE and AMICOL networks were small compared to those established in France by SOE; but considering the relatively small numbers of headquarters staff devoted to the SIS country sections at Broadway, it is remarkable that they managed to achieve such an extraordinary volume of intelligence with such relatively few casualties.

John Codrington, as we have already seen, had been a key figure in the Z-network and, on the outbreak of war, had helped combine the organization with Dunderdale's Paris Station. After his evacuation from Bordeaux, he joined Kenneth Cohen in the new French country section. (Later Codrington was sent to Algiers as the chief British Liaison Officer to Jacques Soustelle's Free French intelligence organization in North Africa.) In 1942 the Defence Security Officer in Gibraltar, Tito Medlam, appealed for help in running both MI5's and MI6's local headquarters. Codrington was himself anxious to move closer to the scene of operations in the south of France, so he was appointed Head of Station, Gibraltar, with the cover of the Governor's Chief of Staff and the code-name FISHPASTE.

After the German occupation of the Vichy 'Free Zone' in November 1942, Codrington's Station became an important operational base for infiltrating agents into the south of France. While Medlam had been responsible for the Rock, his duties had been chiefly of a defensive nature: identifying and arresting German agents. The MI9 representative, Donald Darling (code-named SUNDAY), had recently been transferred from Lisbon to receive and debrief the growing number of escapees. Codrington and his Section V staff pursued a more aggressive policy and recruited a network of agents along the Spanish coastline. His best agent was Jean Ruthven, Lady Monckton's sister, who had married into a family of wealthy Spanish landowners, the Larious family.

SOE was also represented on the Rock (by Hugh Quennell and Harry Morris), but its activities had been somewhat limited. Its original mission, code-named MAD DOG, was to plan the sabotage of Spanish roads and railways in case of a German invasion (in spite of Sir Samuel Hoare's objections), but as that had not materialized it was limited to liaison duties. It was further restricted by an unfortunate incident in March 1942, in which an SOE limpet mine destined for a French dredger in North Africa exploded prematurely. The accident had sunk the Gibraltar ferry in Tangiers harbour with considerable loss of life: thirty-nine civilians, including five Britons and the diplomatic courier who had been carrying the mine in the official pouch, were killed. The Governor, Lord Gort, had taken exception to the role played by SOE and had demanded Hugh Quennell's recall.

Codrington was aided in his agent infiltration operations by a local branch of Frank Slocum's private navy, which initially consisted of two, 20-ton, Spanish fishing boats, known as feluccas, named *Seawolf* and *Seadog*. The boats were operated by a pair of Polish lieutenants, Buchowski and Kadulski, who had narrowly escaped arrest when their INTERALLIE cell had been betrayed. A later addition to the SIS fleet was a former Portuguese trawler, HMS *Tarana*. The *Tarana* had seen service in the Channel during the invasion summer of 1940 as an Auxiliary Patrol Vessel. Frank Slocum's organization acquired her during 1941, reconditioned the engine, fitted concealed machine-guns and moved her to the Mediterranean. She was skippered by Lieutenant-Commander E.B. (Nobby) Clark RNR and crewed by three Lowestoft fishermen, Douglas Sowden, Dickie Draper and Dierks Morris.

All three vessels had the appearance of typically scruffy members of a coastal fishing fleet. All flew Spanish flags, except when they made their final approach (always in darkness) to Gibraltar's naval dockyard, where they were kept out of sight of inquisitive eyes across the frontier. A routine agent pick-up or drop involved a round trip of some 1,500 miles and took the best part of a fortnight. As the number of trips built up with the success of the SIS (and SOE) networks in France, extra personnel were recruited in London by Slocum's deputy, Patrick Whiney, to assist the two intrepid Poles. Among them were Lieutenants T. Maxted and Francis Cosens, who each took alternate command of the feluccas, and a member of the Polish navy, Lieutenant Marian Lukas.

This flotilla of 'irregular' ships proved highly successful in the western Mediterranean, and none were lost to enemy action although the Luftwaffe frequently buzzed them, not realizing that the men aboard, apparently occupied by mending nets, were SIS agents on their way to a clandestine rendezvous.

One particular development in the Straits of Gibraltar which caused great concern in London was the discovery, shortly before the TORCH landings, that the Germans had constructed a 'burglar alarm' across the Straits. The Admiralty had always assumed that, provided their ships steamed in and out of the Mediterranean at night, there was little chance of the Germans knowing exactly how many ships were in the vicinity. However, according to Section V, the Germans had built two infra-red devices on either side of the ten-mile-wide Straits, which would detect heat from the smoke stacks of passing ships. Whether the ships negotiated the narrows by night or day was immaterial.

Section V's information had been culled from a number of sources and is a good illustration of how different pieces of an intelligence jigsaw can add up to a development of considerable strategic importance. In December 1941 the Radio Security Service succeeded in breaking the Enigma key used by the Abwehr for communicating between Berlin and the Abwehr's principal out-stations in neutral countries. This was a crucial breakthrough and, as SIS had taken control of RSS the previous May, Section V was ideally situated to take advantage of it. By February 1942 the RSS had cracked the keys for the Enigma traffic between the various Abwehr sub-stations around the Straits of Gibraltar and Berlin. Most of the intercepts concerned the routine coast-watching activities of the local agents, but Section V's attention was drawn to one particular code-name ... BODDEN.

This is an opportune moment to describe the sequence of events that led SIS to take over RSS and so enable Section V to intervene in apparently mundane events in the western Mediterranean. At the beginning of the war, as we have seen, the RSS was primarily concerned with isolating and identifying illicit wireless signals in England. Contrary to expectation, there were none, and RSS adopted a counter-intelligence role (as opposed to its original counter-espionage brief) and began to monitor the Abwehr's radio traffic. The first successes were achieved with the hand ciphers used by agents in Norway, and SNOW's own code book had provided a convenient starting point for the RSS cryptographers. Success bred ambition, and RSS turned its attentions to the Abwehr Enigma keys. At this point Section V detected the possibility of RSS (and, therefore, MI5) straying into what was indisputably its territory: Abwehr operations in foreign countries. A struggle for control of RSS ensued, and Menzies triumphed. Richard Gambier-Parry's nominee from Section VIII, Major Ted Maltby, replaced Colonel Worlledge as Head of RSS, and a more direct link was established between Arkley, where the RSS analysts were located, and St Albans. To preserve the peace between Section V and MI5, a B division officer, Kenneth Morton Evans, was appointed Maltby's deputy.

Under the new arrangements, the Abwehr signals were intercepted at Hanslope Park and sent to GCHQ for decryption. The raw intelligence was then passed to RSS for analysis. The resulting intelligence summary was then delivered to St Albans for operational distribution on a geographical basis. All material concerning the Iberian region was dealt with by Dick Brooman-White and his two assistants, Kim Philby and Tim Milne. Their procedures never varied: they recorded any new information on a card-index and cross-referred any code-names with previous mentions. If a new personality appeared, he was rewarded with a card and a copy would go to the Section V representative in the relevant country. If the code-name represented an operation or betrayed a future intention, the local Station was informed so as to take the appropriate measures. In this particular case, the word BODDEN was in the context of an operation (as opposed to an agent) and files on the personalities mentioned suggested some kind of a technical operation. BODDEN itself was interesting because that was the name of the sea around Peenemünde, which had already been identified in the Oslo Report as a centre of important scientific developments.

Having established the broad nature of the threat, Section V officers in Madrid, Gibraltar and Tangiers were informed of a possible Abwehr technical operation in their area and requested to report any unusual Abwehr activity. It will be recalled that the Section V representatives in each Station were solely concerned with their opposite numbers, and not necessarily with the collection of other intelligence which was left to their Station colleagues.

Once a possible case had been identified in this way, it was only a matter of time before the Station reports started flowing in. Madrid reported the movements of a number of unidentified German personnel; Gibraltar signalled the covert purchase of several secluded Spanish beachfront properties by known German middlemen; Tangiers noted the arrival of some technical equipment; a senior source in the German Legation in Tangiers, Curt Reiss, mentioned a possible new radio station right on the North African coast. By the time the file had been passed to Dr Jones in Section IV, the answer to the conundrum leapt at him from the pages: the Germans were working on a system of infra-red searchlights or detectors, or both. On his recommendation the RAF undertook a photo reconnaissance flight along both coasts and the photo analysis staff at Medmenham were briefed on what to look for. Once the sites had been spotted, there only remained the question of what counter-measures should be taken.

For an appreciation of the possible consequences of allowing the scheme to proceed, the growing BODDEN file was passed to the Director of Naval Intelligence, Admiral John Godfrey. He sought the opinion of the First Sea Lord, Sir Dudley Pound, and compiled a report recommending that the scheme should be stopped with expedition. Both men were perfectly aware that plans for TORCH would be jeopardized if the Germans were allowed to develop their idea further. The Joint Intelligence Committee concurred and further deliberations followed over what action should be taken. The Admiralty was inclined to shell the sites identified by the RAF, but the Foreign Office advised that this would undoubtedly force Spain to join the Axis. Sir Samuel Hoare was also bitterly opposed to any military-style solution.

In such circumstances Menzies invariably counselled caution to give his staff time to create a useful counter-measure which might offer an intelligence advantage, but in this instance the time factor, combined with ignorance over BODDEN's exact state of operational readiness, left little alternative. Menzies was authorized to instruct the Station in Tangiers to prepare a suitable plan.

The SIS Station in Tangiers consisted of Toby Ellis, a former Indian army oculist, who operated under Press Attaché cover in (Sir) Alvery Gascoigne's Consulate-General, Malcolm Henderson and Neil Whitelaw. The Station ran several useful networks among the local British expatriate community, and among the various groups of anti-Nazi refugees, but the Spanish authorities were extremely vigilant and pro-German. As a result, Ellis had been obliged to restrict his activities to monitoring the Spanish garrison and making contingency plans for MAD DOG.

Ellis's agents were instructed to survey the site of the suspect German infra-red station, which was identified as a newly purchased villa at 4, rue de la Falaise. The villa itself was in an isolated position, perched on the edge of the cliff-top. It was poorly guarded and there appeared to be a cliff path passing almost directly underneath. The agents reported that, if a large enough explosive charge could be placed against the foundations of the villa, there was every chance that the whole structure might topple into the sea. SIS passed the plan on to the Foreign Office, but Sir Samuel Hoare raised the strongest objections to it. Nevertheless, further preparatory work was completed and a suitable bomb was constructed by SOE in Gibraltar and delivered to Edward Wharton-Tigar, the sole SOE representative in Tangiers. As the former manager of a lead and zinc mine in Yugoslavia, Wharton-Tigar was well qualified to supervise what had become known as Operation FALAISE. He was attached to the Consulate-General as a cipher clerk, and it was believed that the Spanish authorities had not 'blown his cover'.

Eventually, on 11 January 1942, Sir Samuel Hoare bowed to mounting pressure and reluctantly gave his consent to FALAISE. The following night two SOE agents, a Spanish Communist and a Jewish barman, pushed thirty-eight pounds of plastic explosive through the bars of the German villa's basement window and retreated. Minutes later the charge went off and the entire building slipped majestically into the sea below. The following morning the Consul-General informed Wharton-Tigar that Sir Samuel had had second thoughts about the operation over the weekend and had cancelled it.

The Spanish police rounded up most of Ellis's networks, but everyone connected with the Station had established alibis and were, therefore, released after a brief spell in custody. Wharton-Tigar was decorated with an MBE and transferred to SOE's headquarters in China.

When the Ambassador in Madrid was informed that FALAISE had been successful, he furnished the Spanish Foreign Minister with photographic evidence of the Abwehr's infra-red site on the Spanish mainland. GCHQ reported a sharp increase in the signal traffic between Madrid and Berlin, and the Gibraltar Station spotted the dismantling of scientific apparatus in its target site. Operation FALAISE was, therefore, marked down as that rarest of commodities: a ninety-eight per cent intelligence success and an object lesson in inter-departmental co-operation. The success was not judged to be total because, as a result, Toby Ellis had come under suspicion.

Once the invasion of North Africa had been executed, the intelligence war in the western Mediterranean changed dramatically in nature; but before dealing with these events we should first return to developments in northern Europe.

II

Wartime Operations in Norway, Sweden and Russia

On Tuesday, 9 April 1940, shortly before dawn, the German cruiser *Blücher* sailed up the Oslo fiord towards the Norwegian capital and was sunk by two well-aimed torpedoes from a shore battery. 1,600 German seamen were drowned and the German officer in command of the invasion forces, General Nikolaus von Falkenhorst, who was also on board, narrowly escaped death and swam through the freezing water in full uniform. This unexpected setback so early in the operation delayed the capture of Oslo for at least ten hours, and enabled the Secret Intelligence Service to save the life of the sixty-seven-year-old King Haakon VII.

The Oslo Station was manned by the Head of Station, Commander J.B. Newill; he was assisted by Frank Foley, who had been evacuated from the Berlin Station just seven days before the outbreak of war the previous September. Foley had brought with him to Norway his former secretary in Berlin, Margaret Reid. When news reached the Station of the German attack, Foley's agreed task was to secure the Bank of Norway's gold reserves and the royal family. The King, however, had other ideas and, while the Government debated the question of calling for French and British assistance, he was preparing to decamp to the north of his country to organize resistance to the invasion. The King was taken to Tromsö by HMS *Glasgow*, but as soon as he left the capital Oslo Radio, which was in German hands, announced that he had fled to Britain. In fact, he remained on Norwegian soil until 10 June, by which time the German take-over was all but complete and the Swedish authorities had confirmed that the royal family would be interned if they tried to flee eastwards. There was little choice but to accept the Royal Navy's offer and take the cruiser HMS *Devonshire* to Scotland.

When the Norwegian government-in-exile was established in London, Frank Foley was recommissioned and attached to the staff of General Carl Fleischer, the Commander-in-Chief of the Norwegian forces. Fleischer, aged sixty-nine, had taken control of what was left of the Norwegian army from General Otto Ruge, who was himself aged seventy-two when made a prisoner of war by the Germans. Virtually his last operational decision before being taken prisoner was his appointment of Captain John Rognes as the head of Milorg, the military intelligence wing of the resistance.

The Milorg organization was to form the basis of the resistance movement in Norway, but during the late summer of 1940 communications proved extremely difficult. Contact was maintained by the so-called Shetland Bus, the shuttle service of fishing boats which operated between occupied Norway and Lerwick on Shetland, under the sponsorship of Frank Slocum's private navy. The first such mission took place on 10 August 1940, when an SOE wireless operator named Andorsen was sent to link up with Milorg and provide it with a channel of communication with London. His signals, and those of the operators that followed him, were received either at SIS's principal receiving station at Whaddon Chase (opposite Hanslope Park) or at SOE's Special Training School 052 at Thame. Later in the war, Slocum's clandestine supply line from Lerwick was operated by fast motor torpedo-boats which could complete the 600-mile round trip in around twenty-four hours. But to begin with the journey took up to four days one way and was undertaken by slow inshore fishing boats at considerable risk. The incoming vessels would carry volunteers destined for one of SOE's Special Training Schools; outgoing ships contained food, weapons and ammunition.

For the first six months of the war SIS's interest in Norway was limited to coast-watching for the Naval Intelligence Division. These operations, which were similar to those of the Great War, were executed with the tacit approval of the neutral Norwegians. Norway had no established military intelligence organization for the simple reason that there had never been any need for one. SIS was, therefore, left entirely to its own devices, an arrangement, it must be admitted, that suited it.

The general evacuation of June 1940 changed the entire picture and the Norwegian government-in-exile, aided by Frank Foley, saw the need for creating an intelligence agency to liaise with the SIS Norwegian country section, which was initiated by the CSS under the leadership of Commander Eric Welch. Although SIS took responsibility for the acquisition of secret intelligence, it was SOE's Scandinavian section which had the much larger task of regrouping the Norwegian army and co-ordinating the resistance. The first Head of the Scandinavian section was (Sir) Charles Hambro, who was destined to succeed Sir Frank Nelson as SOE's Chief. His section included his colleague from Hambro's Bank, Harry Sporborg, Lionel Neame (a former Finnish timber merchant), Commander Frank Stagg and the Hon. Robert Gathorne-Hardy, who both spoke Norwegian and had strong pre-war business connections in Norway. SOE's Norwegian sub-section was headed by Colonel Jack Wilson. While SIS supervised the Norwegian radio links and the fishing boats in Shetland, there was only a minimal need for intelligence collecting operations. In strategic terms Norway was relatively unimportant in the intelligence war and, provided SOE harried the occupation forces and sabotaged Germany's supply of iron ore, there was little need to concentrate SIS's tiny resources on setting up networks of agents. However, the prospect of tying up large numbers of German forces in Norway appeared very attractive later in the war, and there were to be many deception plans to encourage the Wehrmacht to keep a large garrison there. When, early in 1941, Keith Liversidge was appointed the Section V representative to the Norwegian country section, his role was primarily that of overseeing the distribution of the regional Abwehr decrypts, code-named ISK and ISOS.

This strategic assessment was altered dramatically by the escape, in September 1941, of Professor Leif Tronstad to Sweden. Tronstad was a senior member of the Institute of Technology in Trondheim and had been responsible for channelling industrial intelligence to SIS during the occupation. Before the war he had done research work at Cambridge. Much of his information concerned developments at the nearby Norsk Hydro Hydrogen Electrolysis plant at Vemork. As well as being a sophisticated hydro-electric complex, the Norsk Hydro was unique for its capability to produce large quantities of an extraordinarily rare commodity, heavy water.

Heavy water has exactly the same chemical characteristics as ordinary water, with one important exception: its hydrogen atoms consist of deuterium, the hydrogen isotope that contains one proton and one neutron instead of a single proton. This abnormality can be found in minute quantities in all water, but extraction and isolation is an expensive, time-consuming technique requiring vast amounts of plain water. When any significant quantities of the commodity are accumulated, it is found to be approximately ten per cent heavier than ordinary water. It also enjoys a special attraction for physicists: its molecular structure enables atomic fission to take place in a uranium pile. Pre-war atomic research had confirmed that a slow chain reaction might be achieved by creating the fission process in a Uranium 235 isotope. Theoretically, if such a chain reaction could be made to occur, it would release immense power. There was also a possibility that such power might be turned into a bomb.

Possession of heavy water was irrelevant unless combined with access to large quantities of uranium oxide, and the Germans had achieved this by occupying Belgium. Europe's largest stocks of uranium oxide were stored by the Union Minière in Belgium. Germany, therefore, was known to have the two necessary ingredients for developing an atomic bomb. These scientific considerations were not entirely lost on SIS's Norwegian country section, for Eric Welch had had technical training; indeed, he was the only SIS officer with a science degree. He agreed with Section IV's scientific advisers that the Norsk Hydro was of paramount strategic importance. Tronstad had been able to supply details concerning the production levels of heavy water in the plant, thus enabling the physicists in England to monitor the progress of the Germans' atomic research programme. Tronstad had always limited his information to statistics on the grounds that technical information might be passed to his research competitors at ICI. His arrival in England in October 1941 had been prompted by German suspicions about his industrial espionage and a dramatic increase in German demand for heavy water. Soon after their capture of the Hydro, orders were given to increase production to 3,000 pounds per annum. By the end of 1941, it was learned that more than 10,000 pounds were required by the Reich.

This disturbing new was assessed by the Section IV advisers, and Dr R.V. Jones recommended that every effort should be made to acquire the Vemork heavy water before the Germans shipped it to their laboratories. Tronstad, therefore, wrote to his contact inside the plant, Dr Jomar Brun, suggesting that a plane land on one of the frozen lakes above Vemork, pick up the heavy water and take off again for England. Brun, who was manager of the Norsk Hydro plant and supervisor of the heavy water extraction unit, vetoed the idea as impractical. Several plans were suggested, but all were extremely risky. Instead, Section IV's scientific staff offered an alternative: sabotage the heavy water stocks by adding small quantities of castor oil. This was done as it was a relatively simple exercise, but it did not destroy the water's special property; instead, it caused the water to froth in the high concentration cells, which baffled the German supervisors who invariably shut down the entire production system to investigate the mysterious phenomenon. All castor oil did, therefore, was to delay production.

While new plans were being thought up, Welch was appointed to the directorate of TUBE ALLOYS, the cover-name given to the British atomic bomb research programme, so that he could keep abreast of developments. Then more drastic measures were suggested using RAF Bomber Command, but the Norwegians made fierce objections. At their insistence it was agreed that any plan would try to minimize civilian casualties, and a sabotage plan was, therefore, put forward, code-named FRESHMAN.

On 18 October 1942, after two false starts had been cancelled because of technical failures and weather conditions, FRESHMAN got under way. The plan was for an advance party of SOE saboteurs, trained at the Scandinavian section's Special Training School STS 026 (located at Glenmore Lodge, Aviemore), to establish a base on the Hardanger Plateau, a 3,500-square-mile uninhabited wasteland above Vemork. Once the preparations had been completed, the advance party, led by Jens Poulsson, was to signal Scotland and a pair of gliders filled with British commandos would take off from Wick and land on a specially lit strip of snow. On 9 November 1942 Poulsson made his first radio contact and confirmed the position of the landing zone. A bizarre security check was introduced into the exchange to confirm that the SOE transmitter had not fallen into enemy hands. The operator, Knut Haugland, was asked: 'Who did you see in the Strand in the early hours of 1 January 1942?' The correct answer was 'three pink elephants'.

FRESHMAN was launched on the night of 19 November. Two Halifax bombers towing Horsa gliders, loaded with a force of heavily armed volunteers from the First Airborne Division, took off from Wick and headed across the North Sea. The weather deteriorated as they neared their target, so the pilot of the first aircraft opted to fly under the cloud cover until they reached the Norwegian coast. Once landfall had been made the pilot increased altitude, but the glider failed to clear the first ridge of mountains. It crashed into the mountain side, killing all aboard. Moments late the bomber suffered the same fate. The pilot of the second bomber and glider chose a higher altitude, but, after he had overshot the landing zone twice in heavy cloud and fog, decided to return to base. Almost as soon as he turned for home the iced tow-line snapped, and the glider and bomber crash-landed onto a snow-covered mountain top. Eight commandos were killed instantly, the remainder all suffered injuries of varying severity. The crash had attracted the attention of the Germans, and by the time two of the more able-bodied of the survivors had reached a doctor the local security forces were closing in. The Germans took four of the more seriously injured men to Stavanger hospital, where they were treated briefly before being delivered to the Gestapo. The other five soldiers were sent to the notorious Grini concentration camp, some thirty miles north of Oslo.

The details of what occurred next were only established after the war. It seems that the Wehrmacht requested that all the survivors should be put in its custody as prisoners of war, but the Gestapo insisted on interrogating them, claiming that they were spies and that Hitler had decreed that all 'irregular' Allied forces should be treated as terrorists and shot. As part of the original FRESHMAN plan involved an escape to Sweden after a successful operation, each commando wore civilian clothes under his uniform. The Gestapo took this as confirmation that the soldiers were spies and injected the five injured survivors with poison. Their weighted bodies were then sunk in a fiord. Their five companions were kept in solitary confinement at Grini and then shot.

News of the double crash was radioed to England on 20 November by the reception committee and caused deep depression in London. FRESHMAN was the first major operation of its kind attempted in Norway and had turned into an appalling catastrophe. Welch consulted Section IV's scientific adviser, Dr R.V. Jones, and it was relucantly decided that a second attempt should be made to sabotage the Norsk Hydro. It was also agreed that the next operation would be left entirely to SOE.

While SOE planned a new operation, SIS concentrated on another angle to the same problem: it was too late to prevent uranium and, apparently, heavy water from falling into German hands. The next best thing was to deny the Germans access to the human resources needed to develop an atomic bomb. Welch, therefore, took advice on the personalities left in occupied Europe who might be in a position to advance the German research. This was not a particularly arduous task as only a very limited number of physicists around the world had worked on atomic projects. Unfortunately, the most distinguished of them all, Professor Niels Bohr, was still at his post in German-occupied Copenhagen.

Bohr had won the Nobel Prize in 1922 for his pioneering research into atomic fission. When the Germans invaded Denmark, Bohr was President of the Danish Royal Academy and Director of the Institute of Theoretical Physics. He was also completely unaware of the Nazi interest in the atomic bomb. Communicating with Copenhagen presented no particular problem for Welch, and a message was sent to Bohr inviting him to continue his work in England.

Delivering the message to Bohr was a relatively straightforward affair. In the autumn of 1940 SIS had concluded an agreement with SOE whereby the SOE representative in Stockholm, Ronald Turnbull (the former Press Attaché at the Legation in Copenhagen), adopted a dual role for both organizations in Denmark. Turnbull's main link with Copenhagen was via an underwater telephone cable, which the Germans believed had been disconnected. In fact, it terminated in Malmö, in southern Sweden. Soon after the German invasion of Denmark in April 1940, the Danish General Staff's tiny Intelligence Department had formed a resistance cell known as Prinserne (the Princes). This became the basis of a nationwide resistance group, and one that SOE encouraged and supplied. It was so well organized that SIS had no need to operate in the country and SOE limited its involvement to logistical support.

Welch's invitation was signalled to Turnbull, who passed it on to Captain Gyth, a senior member of the Prinserne. When Gyth approached Bohr, the physicist resolutely refused to discuss the matter without positive evidence that Welch's offer was genuine. This eventuality had not been foreseen, so Welch went to Sir James Chadwick, one of Bohr's close friends and pre-war collaborators, and one of Britain's foremost scientists, at his laboratory at Liverpool University and explained the position. Chadwick agreed to write a letter to Bohr appealing to him to flee occupied Denmark. His letter, which was concealed in a hollow door key, was delivered to Bohr by Gyth at the end of March 1943. Bohr instructed him to return the following day for a reply. It was a polite refusal. Bohr's letter was reduced photographically and then inserted into a courier's denture for the journey to Stockholm.

Bohr's refusal was greeted with astonishment and disbelief in London. The Danish scientist denied that it had been possible for the Germans to have made significant advances in the atomic field and declared that his duty was to remain in Copenhagen. A week later a second letter from Bohr confirmed that the Germans had indeed stepped up demand for Uranium 235 and heavy water, but he insisted that there was little chance of an atomic bomb being built.

Bohr's attitude was to change radically during the summer of 1943. At the end of September he learned that he and his family were to be arrested in a general round-up of Danish Jews. He, therefore, appealed to the Prinserne for help and was smuggled to Limhamn in Sweden on 30 September 1943 aboard a fishing boat. He was then placed under the protection of the Swedish police until arrangements had been made to fly the physicist to Scotland in an RAF Mosquito. There was one false start when, on 11 October, the Mosquito developed engine trouble and had to turn back to Bromma airport. He finally made the journey the following night. As soon as he had recovered from his ordeal, Bohr was entertained to dinner at the Savoy by Menzies, Welch and a group of senior British scientists.

While SIS had been trying to persuade Bohr to escape to London, SOE had been planning and executing another assault on the Norsk Hydro, code-named GUNNERSIDE. The plan, hatched by SOE's Scandinavian section, was much less ambitious than FRESHMAN. It involved six Norwegian volunteers from STS 026 and STS 017 (located at Stodham Park, near Petersfield), led by Lieutenant Joachim Runneberg. After several false starts the six volunteers parachuted into the Hardanger Plateau at one o'clock in the morning of 17 February 1943. They all landed safely and linked up with an SOE reception committee. Ten days later, on Saturday 27 February, they broke into the Vemork plant and laid demolition charges against all the high-concentration cells and the canisters containing the German stocks of heavy water. All six men wore British uniforms and were equipped with 'L' pills, but the operation went very smoothly. They retired from the plant undisturbed and heard the muffled sound of their delayed-action explosives going off before making good their escape to their base camp on the Hardanger Plateau.

The Germans estimated that the British must have used a force of 800 men and, led by an enraged SS General Wilhelm Rediess, launched a search throughout the entire region. More than 10,000 troops were called in to trace the saboteurs, but all of Runneberg's men got clean away and signalled their success to England. They eventually skied to Sweden, where they were briefly interned before being released and flown back to Scotland.

GUNNERSIDE was hailed as a tremendous success, but five months later, on 8 July 1943, the Milorg organization reported that the Germans had worked night and day to repair the damage in the Vemork plant, and that heavy water production would be back to normal by mid-August. This depressing news was received badly in London, for previous messages had indicated that the Germans had greatly strengthened their security arrangements in the area. Another sabotage attack was out of the question, so a precision air strike was planned without informing the Norwegian government-in-exile. On 16 November 1943, 460 Flying Fortresses and Liberators of the USAF 8th Bomber Wing flew to southern Norway to bomb targets around Oslo and Stavanger. A third group of aircraft was scheduled to destroy the Vemork plant during the workers' lunch-hour. Unfortunately, the Americans arrived over their target eighteen minutes early, so they turned away, circled over the sea and returned. By this time they had lost the element of surprise and the entire Rjukan valley was obscured by clouds of smoke released as a precaution by the Germans. The bombers released their load on what they believed to be their target and turned for home. In fact, they had dropped over 250 bombs on a nitrate plant located further up the valley than the hydro-electric works, and had killed twenty-one Norwegians. A twenty-second, a lone skier, later died of bomb splinters when one bomber jettisoned its cargo over the Hardanger Plateau.

The Norwegian government-in-exile reacted angrily when they learned of the raid and delivered a strongly worded protest to both the British and the Americans. It was not until February 1944 that the threat from heavy water was removed, once and for all. On 20 February the Germans removed their remaining stocks of the commodity from Vemork and dismantled a large amount of their technical equipment. The decision had been made in Berlin to transport Vemork's facilities to Germany. SOE arranged to intercept the train carrying the valuable cargo. The train itself was protected by a very high degree of security, so SOE and Milorg recruited an agent with access to the ferry which would carry the train across Lake Tinn. A time bomb was placed in the bilges and, when the Hydro reached the deepest part of the lake, the bomb went off. Four minutes later the ferry, the train and twenty-six Norwegian civilians had disappeared into 1,200 feet of water. Germany's atomic bomb research programme was at an end.

The Secret Intelligence Service had been forced through circumstance to leave responsibility for most wartime intelligence gathering in Norway and Denmark to SOE. There was no pre-war organization to speak of in either country and the local military intelligence structures appeared well able to cope with what was essentially an opportunity to harry the enemy through irregular warfare.

In Sweden, however, the position was somewhat different. The evacuation of the Baltic Stations and Harry Carr's Station in Helsinki lent Stockholm a special importance. There was practically no SIS coverage of the Soviet Union, so SIS's resources were concentrated in the Swedish capital. Unfortunately, the military situation precluded Broadway from building up the Stockholm Station to any significant strength. The pre-war Head of Station, John Martin, continued at his post until September 1942, when a former timber merchant, Cyril Cheshire, relieved him. Others in the Station included John Sillem (a former manager of a brewery in Riga before the war), Martin's two secretaries, Peggy Weller and Miss Swindall, David McEwen (whose contact with certain German youth leaders had proved useful), Vic Hampton (who shared responsibility for Denmark with Ronald Turnbull), and two Station clerks, named Whistondale and Appleby.

Initially Martin's Station, which was located on the Birger Jarlsgatan in the city centre, fought a defensive role, trying desperately to re-establish contact with hastily prepared stay-behind networks in Finland and the Baltic states. It soon became clear that almost all the rings had either been penetrated by the local security forces or had simply gone into hibernation. After the collapse of Norway, the Station was kept busy by a constant stream of Norwegian refugees anxious to get to England so that they could join the Norwegian army. Most were obliged to wait in internment camps until winter night flights to Scotland were introduced in the latter part of 1941. When a volunteer appeared, he was referred to the Norwegian Legation, which was controlled by the government-in-exile, where he was vetted by Asbjorn Bryhn (later the Milorg representative, John Lyng). This co-operation eventually became the basis of a joint Anglo–Norwegian Security Service, which achieved some considerable success in compiling a blacklist of collaborators and suspected Nazi agents. Its task was made easier by unofficial assistance from the Swedish Director of Military Intelligence, Count Bonde. By the end of the war, more than fifty Norwegians were detained in Sweden as known infiltration agents from the Sicherheitsdienst in Oslo. A separate joint operation with the local Polish Deuxième Bureau representative, Captain Edmund Piotrowski, acted as a link between the SIS Station and the Polish underground stay-behind networks.

The Stockholm Station boasted a staff totalling eight, including the two secretaries, and was only in a position to go onto the offensive after the arrivals of Cyril Cheshire in September 1942, and Peter Falk in March 1943. An illustration of the Station's geographical isolation is given by the journey undertaken by Ronald Turnbull when he arrived in Stockholm early in 1941 on behalf of SOE. He went by ship from Liverpool to South Africa, where he caught a plane to Cairo. From Alexandria he travelled overland to Istanbul and then sailed to Odessa. There he transferred to a train and continued to Leningrad via Moscow; from Finland he crossed into Sweden. The trip covered some 10,000 miles, all to reach a destination less than 1,000 miles from London. This enforced isolation created a unique spirit of camaraderie among the diplomatic community, and it must have been an odd sight to see personnel from the German, Japanese and British Legations all visiting the seaside together on Sundays during the Swedish summer.

Martin had been withdrawn from Sweden when two of his chief agents,

Emery Geroe and Carl Christian Ellson, were arrested by the Swedish security police on a charge of espionage. Geroe was a Hungarian poster painter with useful contacts among Sweden's artistic community. His friend Ellson posed as a Nazi sympathizer and worked as a journalist sending news reports to radio stations in neutral countries. He was also paid by the Abwehr to insert German propaganda into his reports, and this co-operation enabled him to travel widely in occupied Europe. His arrest as one of Martin's agents was unfortunate, but it did lead the Swedish authorities to seize an illicit German transmitter in the Radio Mundial building in Stockholm.

This setback compromised Martin, but the popular British Naval Attaché, Captain Henry Denham, remained in close contact with the Swedish intelligence authorities and continued to operate his coast-watching cells without interference. Indeed, his friendship with Colonel Bjoernstierna of the Swedish Combined Intelligence Bureau led the Germans to assume that Bjoernstierna was a British agent. The Germans, therefore, arranged to discredit him and have him replaced with a pro-German Swede.

Stockholm's easy-going wartime atmosphere had changed by the time the Section V representative, Peter Falk, arrived. Falk had been a schoolmaster at Rugby and had been drafted into the Intelligence Corps along with a number of colleagues from other public schools. He had a knowledge of Icelandic, so he was posted to a Field Security unit scheduled to maintain security on the island during the British occupation in May 1941. His first brush with espionage took place when he was introduced to the case of SPIDER. SPIDER was a Spanish seaman, who had been taken off a neutral vessel visiting Reykjavik. The agent quickly confessed that he had been trained by the Abwehr in Lisbon to report sightings of any British shipping. The interrogation was conducted by a Field Security officer named Seddon (who later distinguished himself in SOE) and the Conservative MP for Smethwick, Alfred Wise.

The Spanish seaman proved extremely co-operative, so much so that he was 'turned' into a double agent and given the code-name SPIDER. SPIDER was flown back to England for extra wireless training to improve his standing with the Abwehr, and Harold Blyth, from Section V, replaced him during the absence. Evidently the Abwehr case officer responsible for recruiting him failed to notice any difference, and SPIDER became an agent of considerable importance. Falk's role in the SPIDER case was reported by Blyth, and Falk was transferred to St Albans in June 1942. His knowledge of Scandinavian history made him an ideal candidate for Keith Liversidge's Scandinavian section based at Glenalmond, and when, the following year, a Section V representative was needed in Stockholm, Falk agreed to go. By the time he went to Sweden, Falk was fully briefed on Section V's progress with the Abwehr codes.

During the previous two years Section V had achieved some spectacular successes, and most of the Abwehr's machine and hand ciphers had succumbed to GCHQ. The machine ciphers were those created by the Enigma machine, and this method was used by the Abwehr to communicate with its branches (known as Abstelles) in neutral and occupied countries. Radio messages to individual agents relied on a variety of similar book ciphers which had to be encoded by hand. The Enigma decrypts were known as ISOS (after the leading Abwehr cryptanalyst at Bletchley, Oliver Strachey), and the hand ciphers were identified by the code-name ISK (standing for Intelligence Service Knox, after Dillwyn Knox).

The Radio Security Service had completely mastered the hand ciphers thanks to the growing stable of double agents operating under MI5's control. The machine codes, which were reset each day, were only slightly more trouble. One particular double agent, run by B1(a)'s Hugh Astor, kept a regular wireless schedule every morning, sending a weather report to Germany. Its format was the same every day: temperature, barometric pressure, cloud cover, etc., so it was relatively easy to monitor the broadcast and then watch the Abwehr's receiving station recipher the message on the Enigma for onward transmission to Berlin. Knowing the exact content of the message made decryption easy, and enabled Bletchley to make the necessary adjustment to its replica Enigmas. It was this knowledge of the current Enigma setting that had enabled the RSS to advise Section V about SPIDER's imminent arrival in Iceland. Not surprisingly, ISK and ISOS remained closely guarded secrets even after details of ULTRA had been made public.

Peter Falk was indoctrinated into the mysteries of ISK and ISOS and flown to Stockholm with his secretary, Bridget Pope. She had been Admiral Limpenny's secretary in Section VI and had a special interest in going to Sweden: her brother was believed to be imprisoned at Colditz, and she was anxious to find friends in the Swedish Red Cross so that she could make contact with him. Falk's arrival caused something of a stir in the Swedish capital, for there was little justification for an increase in the British Passport Control Office, given the fact that there was only one flight a week to Scotland. The British Minister, Victor Mallet, succeeded in silencing the Swedish criticism and Falk's appointment was confirmed. Fortunately, Mallet enjoyed a close friendship with the King and played tennis with him once a week.

As the Section V resident in Stockholm, Falk's task was to penetrate the enemy's intelligence organization. Even before he had arrived, Asbjorn Bryhn's contacts in Oslo had already made significant progress in Norway. It was Bryhn's boast that the Abwehr in Oslo could not operate without his support, and that everything that happened in the Abwehr's office was known to him within three days ... the length of time it took one of his couriers to reach Swedish territory. Falk's German opposite number in Sweden was the Passport Officer, Hans Wagner. Wagner had formerly been the Abwehr chief in Bucharest and drove his staff hard. His secretary, Alice Fischer, was rumoured to have committed suicide after one particularly brutal confrontation. He was so unpopular that one of Fraulein Fischer's colleagues, a secretary in the German Legation's press department, took revenge. She was a member of an old Prussian family and managed to obtain a complete order of battle of the German Legation staff.

Wagner certainly did not pose a threat to the Allies, but his inactivity gave little opportunity for mounting counter-intelligence operations. If, perhaps, Wagner suddenly stumbled over an apparently useful source (thoughtfully provided by Section V), it was unlikely that his information would be treated very seriously in Berlin. Most of his convoy intelligence was three months out of date, and the rest of his signals traffic was trivial in the extreme. This position changed dramatically in September 1943 with the arrival of a new Air Attaché, Karl-Heinz Krämer. Section V's analysis of ISOS was so effective that the Stockholm Station was warned of Krämer's impending arrival a fortnight before he turned up.

According to St Albans, Krämer was an important Abwehr officer, so Falk placed him under surveillance to build up a knowledge of his personal habits. Meanwhile, Bridget Pope received a visit from a German woman who was married to a Swede and was now resident in Stockholm. The woman's fear of the Gestapo had made her distraught, but she imparted one vital piece of information: her best friend, who was an Austrian, had been hired as Krämer's maid. The maid was an anti-Nazi and, more importantly, anti-Mrs Krämer. She was promptly enrolled by Falk as agent number 36704. (For administrative reasons Falk was assigned 36700, unlike the more usual Section V number of 500 after the country identification number.)

36704 began her work by reporting gossip from the Krämer household and supplying the contents of his waste-paper-basket. She then told Falk about a locked drawer in Krämer's desk. He carried the key on his person and never let it out of his sight. This challenge appealed to Falk, who provided the maid with half a pound of butter. In a carefully planned and rehearsed operation, she kept the butter in Krämer's fridge until she had an opportunity to take an impression of the key. One evening, when Krämer was taking a bath, the maid slipped into his room and pressed both sides of the key into the slab of butter. She then replaced the butter in the fridge overnight and passed it to Falk. A member of the British Legation staff, who happened to be an architect, was commissioned to make an exact drawing of the key from the impression in the butter. A Norwegian refugee, working as a locksmith in Stockholm, completed the job, and a few days later Falk was able to give the maid a duplicate key which fitted the drawer perfectly. Inside she found Krämer's passport, which showed that he had once spent ten days in England and had left London on 3 September 1939. She also discovered a quantity of other useful papers, later estimated to be about a quarter of Krämer's output of signals. In intelligence terms, it was a gold-mine, even though a high percentage of his information seemed to have been gleaned from newspapers. Krämer was also reported by a Norwegian agent to have been seen buying aircraft manuals in a Stockholm bookshop. Section V concluded that it had little to worry about from the Air Attaché, but anyway began working on identifying Krämer's sources.

The first of Krämer's agents to be identified was a Frenchman, known simply as 27. Little was known about him except that his information, though low-grade, was generally accurate. Krämer seemed to run agent 27 personally, and by tracking Krämer's reports of his agent's movements it was possible to narrow the source down to the Free French Assistant Air Attaché. He was recalled to London and interrogated by Dewavrin's BCRA, but he admitted nothing. Guilty or not, Krämer's source dried up. One possible explanation was that Krämer had simply claimed to Berlin that the Attaché was his source, and quoted his travel arrangements to substantiate the claim. Another agent was a Finnish journalist, who was invited to visit London by the British Council. It was only minutes before the Finn was due to board the aircraft at Bromma that Bletchley signalled a warning and his visa was cancelled. Evidently Krämer had boasted to his superiors about his agent's trip.

Another of Krämer's agents run from Stockholm was the former Estonian Director of Military Intelligence, who was also supposed to be working for an SIS case officer. He was discovered through 36704's access to Krämer's signal traffic. On one occasion the Head of Station compared a report from the Estonian with the text of a long message transmitted to Berlin by Krämer. The contents were identical, and contact with the Estonian was discontinued.

Krämer's most important source was an agent code-named JOSEFINE, who appeared to enjoy remarkably good sources in London. She was able, for example, to give Krämer details of telegrams passing between Churchill and Roosevelt and seemed to have a particularly well-placed informant, code-named HEKTOR, in the Foreign Office. Much of JOSEFINE's material was sent to Berlin by teletype along a landline, thus rendering useless Bletchley's interception efforts. 36704 was the only way of tapping into Krämer's product, and Falk was urged to obtain as many clues as possible about JOSEFINE. At first there was a suspicion that Krämer might be manufacturing the information himself, but there were indications that he had indeed established a reliable ring in London. His workload always increased after the arrival of the Swedish courier Dakotas from England, and he became very concerned when one of the

RAF's bi-weekly Mosquitos *en route* for Bromma was shot down over the Skagerrak.

The prospect of a major Abwehr network operating in London filled MI5 with dread. Many of its double-agent operations relied on there being no independent agents at liberty, and several important strategic deception plans were likely to be endangered if the Germans had the capability to double-check their information. Krämer's information appeared authentic and, on occasion, enough to jeopardize major operations. For example, shortly before Operation MARKET GARDEN, JOSEFINE predicted an airborne assault on one of five targets. Included on the list was Arnhem. Was Krämer guessing wildly, or did he have solid information? The Security Service was justifiably alarmed by Krämer's network and selected one of its ablest B division officers to identify JOSEFINE. The officer worked in B1(b) section and had spent more than two years dealing with the ISK and ISOS decrypts. He was an expert on the Abwehr's order of battle and was, therefore, in a good position to review all the JOSEFINE material and advise on lines of investigation. The officer was Anthony Blunt.

Blunt's inquiries led him to conclude that JOSEFINE was probably one single informant, as opposed to an entire network, and that most, if not all, of the material originated from the Swedish Naval Attaché in London, Colonel Count Johan Oxenstierna. HEKTOR was almost certainly William Strang, then an Assistant Under-Secretary of State at the Foreign Office. Strang underwent a painful interview with MI5, and the Swedish Naval Attaché was provided with some plausible, but false, information. Sure enough, the 'barium-meal' appeared in a report attributed to JOSEFINE. Colonel Count Oxenstierna was requested to return home and JOSEFINE ceased to operate. The curious aspect to the case was the fact that Oxenstierna was not in the least pro-Nazi. An investigation led by the Swedish intelligence authorities later established exactly what had happened. Oxenstierna had made his routine reports to Stockholm, but Krämer had gained access to them after they had arrived at the Foreign Department of the Swedish Defence Staff. Krämer had succeeded in recruiting a secretary who was responsible for filing the Naval Attaché's dispatches. Oxenstierna was cleared of any misconduct and MI5 sent an apology to Strang. (After the war, Krämer was arrested in Denmark and interrogated by MI5 at Camp 020. He confirmed that JOSEFINE's reports had been gleaned from the Naval Attaché's dispatches.)

At the end of September 1944, Falk's surveillance of Krämer's activities was made complete by a 'walk-in' who volunteered his services. He was a cipher clerk in the German Legation who had a Danish mother. Once he had begun passing Section V all the teleprinter signal traffic, the Station's task was virtually completed. Copies of all the German Legation's secret telegrams were delivered to Falk on a daily basis. He enciphered them on

Auswärtiges Amt

r.Krämer   Stockholm, den 17.8.1943.
Tagebuchnr.40/43.

An das Oberkommando der Wehrmacht
Amt Ausland Abwehr I Luft/E
z.H.Herrn Oberstltn.i.G.Kleyenstüber o.V.i.A.
Abdruck: Auswärtiges Amt, Berlin   1x nebst Anlage.
         Deutsche Gesandtschaft, Sthlm.   1x nebst Anlage

G e s e h e n .
Stockholm, den 17.August 1943.
Der Deutsche Gesandte
gez. Thomsen.

liegend wird überreicht: Mantelbericht Nr.40/43

Anl. 1) Produktion von Spitfire im Juni 1943.
     2) Produktion von Lancaster im Juni 1943.
     3) Produktion von Halifax im Monat Juni 1943.
     4) Produktion Hawker Hurricane im Juni 1943.
     5) Produktion von Typhoon im Juni 1943.
     6) Produktion von Short-Stirling im Juni 1943.
     7) Produktion von Wellington im Juni 1943.
     8) Produktion von Miles Training Flugzeugen im Juni 1943.
     9) Produktion von Mosquitos im Juni 1943 bei de Havilland.
    10) Produktion von Cygnet und Owlet im Juni 1943.
    11) Bristol-Produktion im Juni 1943.
    12) Produktion von Sunderland im Juni 1943.
    13) Produktion von Bombay und Flamingo im Juni 1943.
    14) Produktion von York im Juni 1943.
    15) Produktion von de Havilland Schulflugzeugen im Juni 1943.
    16) Brief an Abw.I Luft/E.

One of the JOSEFINE reports prepared by Karl-Heinz Krämer in August 1943.
Peter Falk, the Section V representative in Stockholm, also had access to them via
Krämer's maid. The information contained in the reports was so accurate that MI5
appointed Anthony Blunt to identify the source.

his one-time tables and transmitted them to England over the British Legation's wireless. He provided a complete list of Wagner's agents. He gave it to Bridget Pope and, although the list proved to be accurate, it was unimpressively short. It was subsequently passed on to the Swedish security police.

The Stockholm Station was arguably the most successful of the war. It experienced minor losses in 1942 with the arrest of two useful agents, but no lasting damage had been suffered. The Head of Station received minimal co-operation from the host intelligence service and, although many of the old Jacobite families which had originated in Scotland were sympathetic to the Allied cause, the Swedish aristocracy was generally pro-Nazi. From Section V's point of view, its operations in Stockholm had proved extremely worthwhile and more than justified its specialist role.

Before turning to SIS operations in the remainder of Europe, we should take this opportunity to look briefly at another SIS Station in the vicinity, and one that could be described as the least profitable of all: the Moscow Station.

The Moscow Station opened for business in June 1943 and was headed by George Berry, a very experienced SIS hand who had previously served in Riga before replacing Kendrick in Vienna in 1938. He had been evacuated from Vienna shortly before the outbreak of war and had since been immersed in administrative duties at Bletchley. His appointment to Moscow coincided with the return of the Embassy from its temporary home in Kuibyshev, where most of the foreign diplomatic missions had been evacuated to during the German advance on Moscow.

As we have seen, Moscow had not possessed an official SIS Station since Boyce's temporary imprisonment in 1918. The absence of a Station was justified by the strict security regime in the Soviet capital. There would have been little chance to recruit and run agents, and it would have been far too dangerous to contemplate using Russian territory as a base from which to send agents into neighbouring countries. Three successive CSSs had been satisfied by using the northern Stations (Helsinki, Stockholm and the Baltic states) as spring-boards into the Soviet Union, with additional help from the émigré communities in Warsaw and Paris. For its part, SOE appointed George Hill as its representative in Moscow.

George Berry's assistant in the Moscow Station was a relative newcomer to SIS, Cecil Barclay. Barclay had been recommended to Admiral Sinclair by his stepfather, Sir Robert Vansittart, then Chief Diplomatic Adviser to the Foreign Secretary. Barclay's father, Sir Colville Barclay, had been British Ambassador to Lisbon. With these impeccable qualifications Barclay was apprenticed in a G section to learn the ropes and was then posted to Section VIII (communications) at Bletchley to assist Henry Maine.

Maine had joined SIS from Buckingham Palace in 1922 and had run the SIS communications organization single-handed until the arrival of Richard Gambier-Parry in 1938. This triumvirate of Maine, Gambier-Parry and Barclay had obtained the co-operation of the Head of the Foreign Office's communications department, Harold Eastwood, and had transformed Whaddon Chase's small short-wave net into a worldwide radio system. It was an extraordinary achievement considering the limited resources available to them.

Barclay's role in Moscow was principally one of liaison. It was his job to provide his Soviet counterparts with selected ULTRA intelligence without compromising the source. His chief contact was General F.F. Kuznetsov, who attended regular meetings at the British Embassy to discuss developments in the intelligence field. Also in attendance was Arthur Birse, the Station's interpreter. At one of their first meetings Kuznetsov produced a captured Luftwaffe code book and asked Barclay to ensure that it got into the right hands. In spite of this and other broad hints from Kuznetsov that he was well aware of GCHQ's function, Menzies insisted on keeping up the charade of disguising the true source of the ULTRA material. No doubt the Soviets, who enjoyed the loyalty of any number of indoctrinated MI5 and MI6 officers, found the pantomime entertaining.

12

Wartime Operations in Holland, Belgium and Portugal

SIS's relative success in Scandinavia demonstrates that the roles of intelligence gathering and irregular operations were quite distinct and were best conducted by separate organizations. This certainly appeared to be the lesson from GUNNERSIDE and FRESHMAN.

SIS's Colonel Euan Rabagliati maintained an excellent relationship with the Dutch Central Intelligence Bureau headed by t'Sant and also, after his resignation in August 1941, with his successor Captain R.P.J. Derksema. SOE's Netherlands section (later known as LC for Low Countries) concentrated its efforts on a rival Dutch group run by Colonel de Bruyne. That the groups were rivals might not have mattered if SIS had been dealing solely with the acquisition of intelligence; but by 1941 both SOE and SIS were engaged in military resistance as well and, as a result, friction and suspicion between the two groups was exacerbated. Certainly the results achieved were catastrophic: between May 1940 and September 1944, 144 Allied agents were infiltrated into Holland, of whom only twenty-eight survived the war.

The first of Rabagliati's recruits to return to occupied Holland were betrayed very quickly. Lodo van Hamel, C.H. van Brink and W.B. Schrage were all arrested in 1940. Rabagliati then decided not to rely on embryonic Dutch resistance cells, which were evidently heavily penetrated by Gestapo informers. Instead, he opted for a 'blind' mission, for which he chose a Dutch naval cadet, Hans Zomer. After Zomer had completed his wireless training, he was dropped on the Dutch coast by one of the fast motor gunboats (MGBs) Slocum had, based on Felixstowe and Great Yarmouth. Zomer successfully made contact with a wealthy Bilthoven businessman, Jan Sickinga, and set up a transmitter in a shed in the garden of Sickinga's villa. On 31 August 1941 Zomer was betrayed, and both men were arrested by the Abwehr. Unfortunately, the raiding party also discovered a number of Zomer's old signals, and from them the Germans were able to reconstruct his code. Worse still, they discovered his security check. Although this alerted the Germans to the existence of security procedures, it did not enable them to play Zomer's wireless back because Zomer was completely unco-operative and SIS quickly spotted that he had been taken into custody. Nevertheless, there was one important consequence. The SIS Dutch section was relying on one particular code. Zomer's arrest meant that the other SIS radio in the field, call-sign TBO, operated by Aart Alblas, would have to be given a new code.

Rabagliati replaced Zomer with Johannes Ter Laak at the end of September, but his radio was badly damaged in the parachute jump. He was followed on 21 November 1941 by William van der Reyden, a Royal Dutch Navy signalman who arrived by MGB 320 from Great Yarmouth after no less than eight false starts. He was the first of many to use the 'Scheveningen ferry', which involved landing agents on the beach in full evening dress. It was known that the Palace Hotel on the esplanade at Scheveningen had been turned into an officers' mess by the occupation forces and that the area was filled by boisterous late-night revellers. The plan was for individual agents to paddle ashore from the SIS ferry armed with an empty champagne bottle. If challenged by a sentry, the agent was to pretend to be a drunken guest from the mess taking some fresh air. Unfortunately, van der Reyden's arrival was not entirely successful. MGB 320, captained by Peter Loasby, set off from Great Yarmouth on the afternoon of 21 November and arrived off Scheveningen soon after midnight. But as the agent paddled towards the beach, his transmitter was accidentally tipped into the sea. However, he did manage to hold on to a new code for TBO, based on Goethe's poem 'Der Erlkönig'. This was delivered without incident, and when he made contact with Ter Laak the latter was able to repair the damaged set.

In the absence of a third transmitter Ter Laak and van der Reyden were obliged to work together for the next few months. Clearly this was a breakdown of the compartmentalized 'cell' system and a dangerous breach of security. Rabagliati, therefore, made strenuous efforts to send Erik Hazelhoff to Scheveningen with two more sets. Peter Loasby had, by this time, been replaced by Lieutenant-Commander Hall RN, but MGB 320 still failed to make their rendezvous until 18 January. This delay enabled the Germans to learn more about SIS's methods of infiltrating agents; they had discovered that Radio Orange, the BBC radio station run by the government-in-exile, always spoke the nightly rendition of the Dutch National Anthem, the Wilhelmus, instead of singing it, when an agent was due to land. On the one night that MGB 320 did manage to complete the crossing without engine trouble, there was no reception committee. The Germans had arrested them off the beach, but had failed to wait for the bigger prize: the MGB.

Eventually, on 13 February, disaster struck, and Ter Laak and van der Reyden were arrested during a routine Gestapo search on their host's home in Wassenaar.

The Germans took this opportunity to try working van der Reyden's wireless back, but they met with only limited success. Van der Reyden omitted one of his three security checks, and the SIS operator in England followed the established procedure and failed to acknowledge the signal.

The Germans were apparently undaunted by this setback and, with the aid of direction-finding equipment, concentrated their efforts on finding where an SOE radio using the call-sign RLS was working from. (RLS was based in The Hague and was in communication with PTX, otherwise known as STS 053, near Bicester.) The Germans narrowed their search down to a particular house and arrested Hubert Lauwers, an SOE trained operator who was found to be carrying three coded messages in his pocket. Lauwers was imprisoned in the Gestapo wing of the prison at Alkemadelaan in Scheveningen while the Abwehr deciphered his three messages with the aid of the code found on Zomer weeks earlier. The text of one read: 'GERMAN BATTLESHIP PRINZ EUGEN LYING UNDER REPAIR IN SCHIEDAM DOCK'.

After a week of skilful interrogation Lauwers agreed, on 12 March 1941, to keep a radio schedule and transmit three coded messages to England. In each he omitted the prearranged security checks and even managed to insert the English word CAUGHT into one of the preambles. To Lauwers's consternation, the receiving operator ignored the warnings and acknowledged his signal. He concluded, incorrectly, that his capture had been noted and that the British had their own reasons for wanting to maintain the contact. This was to begin more than two years of Abwehr deception, which completely fooled both SIS and SOE and cost the lives of more than a hundred volunteer agents. The majority were lured to dropping zones, where they were met by reception committees of Abwehr and Gestapo officers. It has been estimated that the Germans were responsible for 'between two and four thousand' wireless messages received by the Dutch sections of SIS and SOE. The Abwehr code-named the entire operation NORDPOL. Its scale was extraordinary. At its peak, NORDPOL ran seventeen transmitters and thirty dropping zones. According to German sources, it received a total of 570 separate containers holding: 3,000 Sten guns, 5,000 assorted small arms, 300 Bren guns, 2,000 hand-grenades, 75 radio transmitters, 100 signal lamps, 40 bicycles, 15,200 kilos of explosives, and half a million rounds of ammunition. Large quantities of food, clothing and currency were also dropped directly to the enemy.

Of those arrested by the Germans during NORDPOL, forty-seven were shot in the infamous quarry at Mauthausen concentration camp on 6 and 7 September 1944.

After the war, the Dutch Government set up a Parliamentary Commission of Inquiry under the chairmanship of Dr Dronkers to ascertain exactly what had taken place during the operation known to the Germans as NORDPOL. Beginning on 3 October 1949 three SIS officers, Euan

Rabagliati, Charles Seymour and John Cordeaux, gave evidence to the Commission which took a week to present. The Commission concluded that the entire affair had been caused by 'serious blunders'. For its part, the British Foreign Office spoke of 'errors of judgement'. The Commission recorded that:

Investigations were held at various periods after the original penetration had begun, but in each case a decision was taken to continue the operations. These decisions were reached after taking into consideration the personalities and characters of the agents, and with the knowledge that the security checks had been proved in other cases to be inconclusive as a test.

It was later realized that the decision to continue the operation was mistaken.

It was the SIS Dutch section's poor security which allowed NORDPOL to start in the first place, and allowed it to spread to SOE's circuits; and once the operation had got under way, it proved extremely difficult to obtain independent corroboration about events in German-occupied territory. Furthermore, the Germans exploited NORDPOL so skilfully that they were able to use it to infiltrate SOE networks further afield, including France and Belgium. To SIS's credit, however, is the fact that it was Rabagliati's successor, Charles Seymour, who first realized that the SOE networks had been penetrated.

The Abwehr was, in part at least, able to continue its deception because of political rivalries in London. The experienced François van t'Sant resigned in August 1941 and was replaced by Captain Derksema, who, in turn, was to be deposed by Colonel de Bruyne. Erik Hazelhoff, author of *Soldier of Orange*, who worked closely with van t'Sant and Rabagliati, later commented on de Bruyne's insistence that his organization supervise all Dutch intelligence operations:

The point at issue was whether to put our agents in direct contact with the established Dutch resistance organizations. I objected to it. My experience under the Occupation had shown the established organizations to be too large to avoid Gestapo infiltration; they posed unacceptable risks for our people. Right or wrong, this was my conviction, and only sound arguments – of which de Bruyne failed to produce a single one – could have budged me from it. Van t'Sant and Rabagliatti [sic] might be ruthless secret service types, yet they had taught me to regard the trust of an agent behind enemy lines as a sacred responsibility immune from considerations of primitive discipline.*

Van t'Sant's departure heralded Charles Seymour's take-over of SIS's Dutch section and the introduction of a new country section case officer, John Cordeaux. Cordeaux was a regular Royal Marines officer, who had been transferred to the Naval Intelligence Division on the outbreak of war. Shortly afterwards, he was the Director of Naval Intelligence's choice for

* Erik Hazelhoff, *Soldier of Orange* (Holland Heritage Society, 1980).

the post of Deputy Director (Navy). His arrival in the Dutch section coincided with Queen Wilhelmina's creation of yet another Dutch intelligence agency, the Bureau Inlichingen, which was headed by Major Broekman for a few months, after which he was forced by ill health to hand over to Major J.M. Somer. Somer's first initiative was to distance his organization from both SIS and SOE.

German infiltration of SOE's Dutch networks was so extensive that each time London sent an independent agent to check on a particular circuit, the agent would be scooped up and played back. The SOE networks were primarily concerned with armed resistance, so manipulating the wireless traffic was easily accomplished. Consignments of arms would be gratefully acknowledged and reports of successful operations would be transmitted. SIS, on the other hand, dealt in raw intelligence, which was more complicated to re-process. The Germans, therefore, tried to avoid running SIS agents and simply eliminated them without further explanation whenever they appeared. In the spring of 1942, for example, William Niermeyer ran short of funds and requested additional finance. SIS turned to SOE for assistance and provided their next parachutist, Aat van der Giessen, with a torch filled with local currency. Van der Giessen was met by an Abwehr reception committee and arrested. The substitute who duly appeared at Niermeyer's home produced the authentic identification material and was accepted. Niermeyer was promptly arrested and his wireless set moved into the Gestapo's headquarters.

It was not until May 1943 that SIS began to supect that SOE's networks might be badly infiltrated. Charles Seymour gave SOE its first warnings, but it was not until later in the year that confirmation appeared in the form of messages sent by imprisoned members of NORDPOL who had managed to escape. When the first two escapees, Pieter Dourlein and Johan Ubbink, evaded a huge German manhunt and made their way to Switzerland, their version of NORDPOL was disbelieved. In the meantime, the Germans had sent reports warning of the duo's collaboration via their controlled sets. It took the two men five months to travel from the Gestapo prison in Haaren to Berne and finally to England via Madrid. When they reached England, they were imprisoned at Brixton for helping the enemy.

In November 1943 further escapees revealed the truth and the two SOE men were released from prison. As the full picture emerged, the Dutch carried out a purge of their organization in London. Colonel de Bruyne's unit was closed down and the head of SOE's Dutch section, Major Bingham, was transferred to the Far East. The new Dutch Bureau voor Bijzondere Opdrachten (Bureau for Special Services) was led by one of SIS's oldest friends, General van Oorschot, the former Dutch Director of Military Intelligence who had presided over the Venlo fiasco. Oorschot was brought out of retirement in Farnham, Surrey, to head the new organization, but he usually left most of the day-to-day affairs to two aides: Major E. Klijzing and Major de Graaf. Eventually, in March 1944, the Germans abandoned their last NORDPOL wireless, but not before they had completed a final message to SOE complaining that their 'sole agency' status had been removed, and warning that any attempts to renew the 'business' without German assistance would be sure to fail. It was the final humiliation.

As well as souring relations with the Dutch, the NORDPOL fiasco had led the Abwehr to other SOE circuits in Belgium and France.

In May 1944 a senior American intelligence official, Captain Ray Brittenham, complained:

At the present time the Belgian Sûreté is bound by certain very firm agreements with the British to which they are holding which prevent them from having relations with other intelligence services. One of these is that they will tell the British of every agent who goes in and comes out of Belgium. The British apparently have complete control over all communications between the Sûreté here and the underground now in Belgium. The underground networks are directed from London, much of the direction and control being done by the British.

The substance of this complaint was, indeed, true. Before the war Colonel Calthrop had developed the closest of relations between the Brussels Station and Baron Fernand Lepage, the head of the Belgian Sûreté d'Etat. This ensured a warm welcome for him and his staff when they arrived in London in 1940, but it did not take account of the political ambitions of the Belgian Deuxième Bureau, the military intelligence service headed by Colonel Jean Marissal. Marissal was a regular officer, who presided over the many different strands within the Belgian resistance movements. They ranged from the Mouvement National Belge, on the political Right, which consisted mainly of the police and the gendarmerie, to the Milice Patriotique, which was largely dominated by the Left. Neither would co-operate with the other, but both were equally determined to oppose the Nazis.

SIS took the view that the local politics were so complicated that the business of liaison should be left to SOE. Accordingly, Colonel Calthrop was transferred to Baker Street to cope with the different factions. Virtually the only direct SIS link with Belgium was via CLARENCE, a ring operated by a veteran of a Great War network, Walther Dewe. SOE enjoyed a less fruitful relationship with the Belgians, which is not entirely surprising considering that the first SOE agent destined for Belgium was parachuted by mistake into a prisoner-of-war camp ... in Germany. Henri Spaak, the Foreign Minister of the Belgian government-in-exile, eventually lost confidence and broke off all contact with SOE in August 1942. The situation improved the following year, but all the resistance networks suffered heavy German penetration. Among those who were arrested by the Gestapo was

Colonel Jules Bastin, the first commander of the Armée Secrète. Even after Belgium had been liberated, the political divisions within the country threatened to erupt at any time. The Allies looked to the Armée Secrète to harass the enemy after D-Day, but once Brussels had been taken, the resistance was promptly disarmed.

Lisbon's sudden prominence in the intelligence world on the outbreak of war certainly took SIS by surprise. Richman S opford had been sent to take over the Station from Austin Walsh early in 1   ), but he had failed to shake the Station out of its pre-war backwater style. urthermore, he had clashed badly with Captain Arthur Benson RN, the Shipping Attaché. The situation deteriorated so badly that Broadway assumed that the Head of Station was waging war on the other locally based British personnel. Certainly most of his telegrams contained complaints about the lack of co-operation offered by Benson and the Naval Attaché, Captain Dorset Owen RN.

After the fall of France, the Lisbon Station had acquired a special strategic importance. In some respects it could be regarded as SIS's last operational post on the Continent, for the Stations at Stockholm and Berne had become increasingly isolated by the German military advance. The Madrid Station was the only other Station remaining on the continental mainland, and there the Ambassador had placed strict limits on the Station's activities. The Head of Station in Madrid was Colonel Edward de Renzy-Martin, a veteran of the Great War who had spent seven years as Inspector of the Albanian Gendarmerie before joining SIS in 1934. Neither he, nor his successor in 1940, Hamilton-Stokes, were able to go onto the espionage offensive. In spite of Hoare's restrictions, the Madrid Station pulled off two major intelligence coups in conjunction with the Naval Attaché, Alan Hillgarth. The first was to bribe a group of Spanish generals, led by General Aranda, one of Franco's top military advisers, to keep Franco from joining the Axis. This was done through Aranda's secret bank account in New York. The Station's second achievement was to bribe Alcázar de Velasco's male secretary.

Alcázar de Velasco was a senior official in the Spanish military intelligence service and, as the sometime Press Attaché to the Spanish Embassy in London, was thought to be responsible for supervising many of the Abwehr's agents. The Section V officer in Madrid, Kenneth Benton, arranged for de Velasco's secretary to receive £2,000. In return, he agreed to allow his employer's safe to be opened. The operation was successful, and the safe's contents were photographed and then sent to St Albans by King's Messenger. There they were examined by experts who came to an astonishing conclusion: de Velasco was so short of reliable agents in London that he was concocting fictitious reports for the Abwehr. He was, therefore, allowed to continue his activities undisturbed.

These two covert operations in Madrid were virtually the only breaches of the Hoare ban on SIS operations. The chief effect of the ban was to place a further burden on the increasingly pressed Lisbon Station, which was unable to cope. This was not entirely surprising, considering that Stopford's previous experience had been limited to MI5: he had been Defence Security Officer in Lagos, Nigeria, and had then done a spell in B1, then MI5's section dealing with German espionage.

The Station in Lisbon consisted of the Head; his deputy, Robert Johnstone (in peacetime a City stockbroker); Ralph Jarvis, the Section V representative; Rita Winsor, who had been evacuated from the Berne Station; Graham Maingot, formerly Dansey's chief Z-agent in Rome; and Austin Walsh, who had remained to fulfil the role of Chief Passport Officer. Two late arrivals were Trevor Glanville, from Belgrade, and Michael Andrews. The remainder of the staff was made up of secretaries, cipher clerks and two wireless operators.

At the end of 1940 the CSS concluded that Stopford should be recalled, and in his place Menzies appointed Philip Johns, a relatively inexperienced SIS officer who had previously been Colonel Calthrop's deputy in Brussels. Johns's official diplomatic posting was that of Financial Attaché, a fairly transparent cover since Johns had only spent a few months working in a bank, some twenty years earlier. His inexperience of intelligence work was more than made up for by his holding a naval rank and he would, therefore, be able to get along with his prickly senior Service colleagues in Lisbon. This, indeed, turned out to be true.

Under Johns's direction, the Station began tapping two important sources of intelligence: reports from refugees from occupied Europe and the local Anglo-Portuguese community. Throughout the war, there was a constant stream of weary travellers who had crossed the Pyrenees to escape to Spain. Very often, if these escapees were of military age, the Spanish authorities would intern them at such camps as the notorious Miranda de Ebro. Those evaders that managed to continue their journey ended up at Gibraltar or Lisbon and became the responsibility of the Repatriation Office, the cover for MI9. Here the MI9 staff would interrogate the recent arrivals, to weed out the Abwehr agents, and then debrief them to obtain up-to-date intelligence about conditions in German-occupied France.

Johns's particular success was in mobilizing the local expatriate British colony for SIS. Many of the most influential trading families in Lisbon enjoyed strong British links, and the Station recruited several for wartime attachment to the Embassy and Consulate-General. They provided a useful network of informants and were more successful than the regular SIS staff at avoiding the constant surveillance of the pro-Nazi, local Portuguese secret police, PIDE.

Information accumulated by the Lisbon Station was transmitted to Broadway and to the relevant 'G' officer, Basil Fenwick. In common with other Stations, the Section V representative reported directly to the Iberian sub-section in St Albans. By the end of 1941, the signal traffic between Lisbon and Broadway had reached an unprecedented volume, greater than any of the other SIS Staions worldwide. The pressure of work on the Station was immense and, eventually, led to a rift in relations between the Head of Station and the controlling 'G' officer. Fenwick made more and more demands on the limited facilities available at the Station and Johns objected. One particular request, which was resisted, involved the cultivation of several influential members of the Portuguese banking community. Johns argued that most of the bankers suggested were known to be pro-German and that, anyway, he himself was fearfully ill equipped for the task because he knew next to nothing about banking. If the Portuguese spotted the Financial Attaché's ignorance, his cover would be jeopardized and he would most probably be declared *persona non grata*. Johns also pointed out that he had been in Lisbon for twelve months already and that to suddenly start developing banking contacts would look distinctly odd. Broadway disagreed and, in December 1941, he was recalled to London and replaced, early the following year, by one of Dansey's recruits, Cecil Gledhill. Johns was subsequently appointed Head of Station in Buenos Aires to relieve Rex Millar. Robert Johnstone opted to return to his regiment.

Under Gledhill's leadership the Lisbon Station scored several important successes, including the positive identification of two British traitors, Duncan Scott-Ford and Oswald Job, who were both executed. Ralph Jarvis of Section V also contributed to the transformation of Lisbon into the key link in the Iberian chain of Stations. By the end of the war, his registry contained files on 1,900 confirmed enemy agents, 350 suspected enemy agents and 200 Germans with known intelligence connections. In addition, some forty-six businesses in Iberia were identified as commercial covers for enemy espionage.

Gledhill had lived in Brazil before the war and spoke Portuguese fluently. In the absence of Johns and Johnstone, the Station's 'acrimonious disputes'* were reduced, although Gledhill's severe editing of agent reports from Rita Winsor and Graham Maingot became an issue of contention. Unfortunately, the Station's reputation at Broadway led to several important reports being ignored. One in particular was to prove significant. In early 1942, an escaped slave labourer reported that he had until recently been employed at a secret German rocket research establishment on the Baltic. His information was transmitted to London, but Fenwick, who had not been indoctrinated into the Oslo Report, failed to attach any importance to the information. He had never heard of Peenemünde and instructed the

* See Hinsley's *British Intelligence in the Second World War*, Vol. 1 (HMSO) p. 275.

Station to consider the information as a plant. When Broadway did make the necessary connection, the labourer had disappeared.

Section V's chief target in Lisbon was the local Abwehr office and, in November 1942, Graham Maingot reported a promising contact with a Lufthansa official, Dr Otto John. John professed to be a liberal lawyer with close contacts with a group of anti-Nazi Abwehr officers. His position within Lufthansa's legal department allowed him considerable freedom of movement, and he explained that he had been selected to act as a link between the Allies and the anti-Hitler conspirators. Once John's credentials were checked, he received a cautious but cool welcome from the Station. As Graham Maingot pointed out, several Wehrmacht officers had protested their opposition to the Nazi regime before the war, but nothing had come of it. Indeed, the generals had been doing rather too good a job. SIS would need a tangible demonstration of John's good faith if the contact was to be continued. Dr John returned to Berlin to pass this message on.

John returned to Lisbon early in February 1943 and, in Maingot's absence, was met by Rita Winsor. John described how his contacts were preparing a coup, but the SIS officer gave him some depressing news. She outlined Broadway's view that there was little point in dealing with any alleged German opposition movement while Hitler was still in control, and that anyway to encourage such contacts might unnecessarily alarm the Russians. Her instructions were to break off the discussions.

Once again John returned to Berlin to report to his fellow-conspirators. They decided to take action and, on 13 March 1943, placed a bomb in Hitler's private aircraft. The attempt failed when the detonator (part of a captured SOE stockpile) malfunctioned. The only consolation was that the bomb never went off and was, therefore, never discovered, thus leaving an opportunity to try again. Following this incident John turned for help to Colonel William Hohenthal, the American Military Attaché in Madrid. He repeated the Allied policy on contact with German dissidents and, accordingly, a further attempt was made on Hitler's life on 20 July 1944.

On the Monday following the abortive coup, Dr John flew to Spain on a scheduled Lufthansa flight, determined to put as much distance as possible between himself and the inevitable Gestapo investigation. Once safely established in the Palace Hotel in Madrid, the SIS arranged to transport him to Lisbon via Vigo. Once in Portugal, Dr John adopted the identity of an RAF pilot and was given temporary accommodation in an MI9 safe-house while awaiting further instructions from Broadway. At this point the Portuguese secret police, PIDE, intervened, raided the safe-house and incarcerated John in the notorious prison fortress of Aljube. In the interrogations that followed John was obliged to discard his cover story, and word of his arrest leaked to the German Embassy which promptly demanded his extradition on grounds of treason. The Germans also prepared an elaborate assassination plan, but this was entrusted to a senior Abwehr official, Fritz Cramer, who was himself nurturing pro-Allied sympathies. (Cramer finally defected in the spring of 1945.) He tipped off the SIS Station, where Rita Winsor prepared a strong note of protest to Dr Salazar's Government. If anything happened to Otto John while he was in Portuguese custody, the Allies would view the matter extremely seriously. John was promptly released into Miss Winsor's custody and placed on the next British plane out of Lisbon. It so happened that it was destined for Gibraltar, but John was bundled aboard anyway with an emergency British passport. Bad weather forced the plane to return to Lisbon a few hours later, and the German was obliged to spend a further night in the Portuguese capital. The following day, he caught a flying boat to England and was met at Poole and escorted to Camp 001, the Oratory School in Chelsea. Here he underwent a routine interrogation and debriefing lasting a fortnight, and was then offered a job with the Political Warfare Executive's black propaganda organization. He was posted to Woburn Abbey, the base used for the preparation of programmes on the Soldatensender Calais radio station, and put to work aongside SIS's first major German defector, Wolfgang zu Putlitz.

Dr John's successful escape, thanks to the timely leak from the local Abwehr office, served to undermine the confidence of the German spymasters in Lisbon, but SIS did not always have it its own way. One of the many Allied intelligence organizations represented in Lisbon was that of the Czech government-in-exile. Its networks into occupied France provided the SIS Station with a mass of apparently interesting material, especially in the months before D-Day when large groups of Czech labourers were drafted into the Todt Organization to build the so-called Atlantic Wall. Fritz Cramer later identified the second-in-command of the Czech network as a long-term Abwehr agent. As soon as Section V realized that the officer, code-named ALEXANDRE, was reporting directly to the Abwehr, it eased him out of his sensitive position. He was then promptly hired by the Americans!

Cecil Gledhill remained the Head of Station in Lisbon until the end of 1943, when 'Togo' McLaurin, from the Madrid Station, took over. Soon after the D-Day landings, Hamilton-Stokes was recalled from Madrid and was replaced by Colonel W.T. (Freckles) Wren, formerly the Defence Security Officer in the Caribbean.

Both SOE and SIS accomplished some amazingly successful feats during their wartime operations in Europe and North Africa: they both had their share of failures too. When looking at their roles, it is important to remember that their functions were different: SIS was the information gatherer who felt that its role was to 'watch enemy troops crossing a bridge', whilst SOE's brief was sabotage, 'to blow up the bridge to prevent army movements'. SIS was responsible to, although separate from, the Foreign Office, whereas SOE was answerable to the Minister of Economic Warfare. Although relations between individual SOE and SIS officers were generally good, there was considerable antagonism between both organizations at higher levels. Menzies was opposed to the principle of separate units dealing with special operations; Dansey accepted that they were necessary, but believed they should be controlled by SIS. For its part, SOE thought that SIS was in no position to criticize its very limited role.

Without the help of the secret intelligence organizations of the Allied governments exiled in London, SIS would have found it difficult to gain footholds in German-occupied Europe; but with the assistance of locally run networks, it was able to gain a great deal of useful intelligence. However, it was the detailed material coming through ULTRA, ISOS and ISK which had the most profound effect.

13

British Secret Intelligence in the Middle East

The chief problem associated with the turning and running of double agents is the question of their intelligence product. If a double agent provides worthless information to his masters, they may abandon him; if he supplies genuine material, he is a risk to his new controllers. The wartime solution to this conundrum was the Twenty Committee, which co-ordinated the activities of all the double agents based in the United Kingdom; ensured that all the relevant parties were involved; and consulted about developments in what was to become known as the double-cross system. The Committee was also instrumental in refining the practice of strategic deception into a practical weapon. In Cairo, the management of deception operations was similar, with a Thirty Committee, chaired by Colonel Oliver Thynne co-ordinating those involved. In July 1942 Thynne was succeeded by Michael Crichton, who was himself replaced by Terence Kenyon in July 1943.

By the time Cuthbert Bowlby had established the Inter-Services Liaison Department in Cairo, the counter-espionage experts at Security Intelligence Middle East had, on their own initiative, begun a localized double-cross system of turned agents. In addition, Kenneth MacFarlan, from Section VIII, had duplicated the Radio Security Service's effort and was intercepting and distributing a Middle East version of ISOS, code-named TRIANGLE.

An Italian Jew named Renato Levi, who had arrived in Egypt via Istanbul in 1940, had originally been recruited as a spy by the Italian Servizio Internazionale Militare (SIM), who appeared to have miscalculated Levi's hatred of fascism. In any event, Levi had made a tentative approach to SIS's Rome Station before diplomatic relations had been broken off between Britain and Italy and had been instructed to make himself known to the British authorities if he was ever put to work as an Italian agent. This he did in Cairo, and he was promptly handed over to Major Kenyon-Jones at SIME. Levi's proposal was utterly straightforward: he would transmit to his Italian controllers, with British assistance, in exchange for British citizenship and a one-way ticket to Australia after the war. Kenyon-Jones accepted the offer and gave Levi the code-name CHEESE. Just to be on the safe side, CHEESE was detained temporarily in secure accommodation in the Abassia Barracks. CHEESE's wireless set, however, presented a problem. It was supposed to have been delivered to CHEESE in Cairo, courtesy of the Hungarian diplomatic bag, but it failed to materialize. Instead, a signals expert, Staff Sergeant Ellis, constructed one and CHEESE was allowed to travel to Istanbul to inform his controller of his operating wavelength. Much of CHEESE's first messages were concocted by a SIME case officer, Evan Simpson. It was Simpson's inspiration to pursue the development of CHEESE further by inventing a completely bogus sub-agent, whose role was taken on by an officer named Beddington. No sooner had CHEESE made contact with the Italians than an Abwehr spy in Cairo volunteered his services. This individual, code-named STEPHAN, was an Austrian Jew named Klein. He produced a transmitter which, in the hands of Corporal Shears, established contact with the Abwehr in Athens.

Both the Italians and the Abwehr acknowledged their respective agents, and it was from this firm base that the Thirty Committee attempted to duplicate the successes of its counterpart in London, who had over forty double agents under its control.

The next step in the development of CHEESE was his recruitment of a completely fictional White Russian named Nikitov. In reality, Nikitov, code-named LAMBERT, was the inspiration of a senior SIME case officer, James Robertson. According to CHEESE, Nikitov was a prosperous businessman who gambled heavily and was a Nazi sympathizer. The Italians were delighted and so was SIME. The fourth agent to join the Thirty Committee was a parachutist who was intercepted soon after he landed near Haifa in Palestine in September 1941. During the course of his subsequent interrogation, the spy explained that he was partly Jewish and had joined the Abwehr as a means of escaping persecution. This story was accepted at first, but a stool-pigeon, reporting to the Director of Military Intelligence, Brigadier John Shearer, discovered his real identity: before his recruitment he had been a senior Nazi official in Mannheim. This made him an extremely unsuitable candidate for turning, so he was imprisoned. In later interrogations he gave enough details of his radio instructions to tempt SIME to try and make contact with the Italian recieving station at Bari. The Italians responded favourably and congratulated him on his notional employment ... as a waiter in an officers' mess in Cairo. The link proved highly successful and was maintained even after the Nazi had been shot dead during a futile bid to escape.

The Thirty Committee's purpose in running these agents had three levels: the overall control of the enemy's networks; the creation of a conduit through which misleading information could be fed to the enemy; and, finally, the identification of hitherto undiscovered spies. Overall control was something that was particularlly difficult to determine, and could only really be established with post-war debriefing of enemy intelligence personnel. The deceptive element was of inestimable value, and by the time the Thirty Committee had got into its stride an entire organization, known as A FORCE, was conducting sophisticated deception operations to mislead the enemy about Allied intentions. As a counter-espionage weapon, the Thirty Committee contributed some important discoveries.

One such discovery, in June 1942, was the arrival in Cairo of a senior Abwehr agent, Johannes Eppler. Eppler was the son of a German family which owned a hotel in Alexandria. Soon after his birth in 1914, Eppler's father had died and his mother had married a prominent Egyptian, Salah Gaafar. In 1937 Eppler had been recruited by the German Military Attaché in Cairo, who had suggested that Eppler might avoid the mandatory two years of military service in the Fatherland by undertaking intelligence missions for the Abwehr. Eppler had consented to the arrangement and, in the following few years, became an accomplished agent, engineering such coups as the escape of Haj Mohammed Amin el-Husseini, the Grand Mufti of Jerusalem, after the failure of the Arab Revolt.

In May 1942 ISOS intercepts showed that Eppler, who was referred to by the code-name CONDOR, and a German East African named Sandstetter were about to embark on a mission to Cairo code-named SALAAM. Instead of risking capture along the heavily defended Egyptian coastline, Eppler and his radio operator were to infiltrate into British territory overland, across the inhospitable desert. The Abwehr had acquired the services of a renowned Hungarian explorer, Count Laszlo Almasy, to guide them over the treacherous terrain. CONDOR was equipped with papers identifying him as Hussein Gaafar, his late stepfather's son, and Sandstetter carried an American passport in the name of Peter Monkaster, an oil prospector. They arrived in Cairo on 10 July 1942, having entered Egypt at Asyut, and completed their journey on the Luxor–Cairo Express.

Soon after his arrival, CONDOR moved into a houseboat on the Nile, close to the Zamalek Bridge, with his mistress, Hekmat Fahmi, who was a belly dancer in a local cabaret. Throughout his brief time at liberty in Cairo, CONDOR was kept under constant surveillance by James Robertson from SIME (who took up residence in a neighbouring houseboat) and a detachment of the Field Security Police led by Major Alfred Sansom. Even Almasy's regular progress reports on his epic 1,700-mile journey had been monitored. On 12 August CONDOR took delivery of a radio transmitter from a member of the extremist Moslem Brotherhood and then began contacting a group of dissident officers in the Egyptian army. Two of those identified by Eppler, Anwar el-Sadat and Gamel Abdel Nasser, were subsequently arrested for subversion.

Operation SALAAM ended in mid-September 1942, following an unfortunate success in the desert. A company of New Zealand troops overran a forward German signals post at Tel el-Eisa and, in the process, eliminated a link in the communications chain between CONDOR and the Afrika Korps. The Germans naturally assumed that, because the wireless station had been captured intact, the agents reporting to it were automatically compromised. In fact, this was not exactly the case. The basis of CONDOR's cipher, Daphne du Maurier's best-selling novel *Rebecca*, had indeed been found, but the German signals officer in command of the detachment, Captain Seebohm, had been killed during the fighting. It would have been almost impossible to have identified Eppler from such a vague clue as an English edition of *Rebecca*, but the ISOS intercepts confirmed that the Abwehr assumed that Seebohm had been captured alive and had betrayed CONDOR. In these circumstances, SIME reluctantly raided Eppler's houseboat and arrested Eppler and Sandstetter. Both were detained until the end of hostilities, when they were deported to Germany.

The SALAAM case was not entirely wasted, because the Thirty Committee was able to achieve some short-term deception objectives by supplying CONDOR with bogus military intelligence which neatly confirmed messages from CHEESE and STEPHAN. In particular, CONDOR had supplied reports which had deliberately underestimated the British strength at Ruweisat Ridge. On the basis that the Eighth Army had one, not three, armoured divisions at Alam Halfa, Rommel pressed home a disastrous attack, which cost the Afrika Korps nearly 5,000 men and some fifty tanks.

Surprisingly, the failure of SALAAM forced the Abwehr to launch a further operation to refinance its original trio: CHEESE, LAMBERT and STEPHAN. Under interrogation Johannes Eppler admitted that he had been entrusted with more than £50,000, which had been supposed to go to these other agents. Eppler had learned that most of the currency supplied to him was counterfeit, so he had decided against distributing it. This was a little awkward for the two real (and one notional) spies, who were all, in theory, mercenaries. When CHEESE and STEPHAN complained that their funds were running low, their controllers were obliged to dispatch a courier.

In late August 1942, the Abwehr in Athens decided to send in a team of three: a Greek air-force officer, George Liosis, who had been in touch with the SIS Station in Athens before the war; a Greek Gestapo agent named Bonzos, who had been compromised in his own country; and the mistress of an Italian intelligence officer, Anna Agiraki. The team arrived on the beach near Beirut by caique from Greece and were promptly arrested by the local police. They were then handed over to the Defence Security Officer in Beirut, Douglas Roberts, who initially assigned them to a case officer named Cleary-Fox, and later to John Wills. Before the war Wills had been the Paris representative of the Federation of British Industries. He was a competent linguist, but his asthma had prevented him from joining his regiment. Instead, he had been recruited into SIME, and the arrival of the three German agents provided him with a rewarding occupation.

All three were interrogated in prison, and all expressed (in varying degrees of enthusiasm) the desire to co-operate and escape a firing squad. Liosis was given the code-name QUICKSILVER and placed in secure accomodation just outside Beirut, in a location which led the Abwehr to believe that its agents had taken up residence in Damascus. The thug from the Greek Gestapo (code-named DINOS) was considered rather less reliable, so he was made to transmit a message to his Abwehr controller explaining that he had joined the Royal Hellenic Navy as a rating. This, it was agreed, would keep his case active and, at the same time, adequately explain why he could communicate only rarely. DINOS's cover-story was later complicated by the loss of the ship that he was notionally serving on. Arrangements were hastily made (and communicated to the Germans) that DINOS had been transferred to a (non-existent) new ship. When DINOS's cover-story got too dangerous to sustain, it was alleged that he had been involved in a brawl and had been sentenced to a term of imprisonment. The female member of the team, code-named GALA, was more promising. She acquired a series of well-informed (but notional) lovers, including Papadopoulos, a building contractor in the port of Beirut, and several British officers. The QUICKSILVER network was reinforced in November 1942 by the PESSIMIST ring, another group of German agents led by an Egyptian Greek named Demetrios whose family lived in Zamalek. Demetrios himself was kept in custody with QUICKSILVER, and his two companions, Costa and Basile, were also imprisoned, although the Abwehr in Sofia remained confident that all three were at liberty. According to the ISOS intercepts, the QUICKSILVER network was held in high regard by the Abwehr in Athens and, by the end of 1942, its work had merited an off-shoot of Cairo's Thirty Committee ... the Thirty-One Committee. Until July 1943 this was chaired by Rex Hamer from A FORCE, and consisted of Wills (from SIME), the 3rd Viscount Astor (from the Naval Intelligence Division), Michael Ionides and Peter Chandor (both from the Inter-Services Liaison Department Station).

While John Wills was busy manufacturing the sordid details of GALA's exotic love life, the SIS Station in Istanbul was beginning to develop its own ring of double agents. The first, code-named CRUDE, was actually the janitor of the British Consulate who had dutifully reported an approach from the Abwehr. CRUDE was encouraged to continue the contact and, under the direction of his case officer, Michael Ionides, was persuaded to recruit a useful (notional) source, ALERT. ALERT was alleged to be resident in Aleppo, and Ionides had created a particularly colourful motive for his espionage activities: he told the Germans that his mother had been raped in the Great War by an Australian sergeant-major. ALERT passed on minor snippets of intelligence in letters written in secret writing. He then delivered them to the Abwehr in Istanbul. Another of Michael Ionides's agents was SMOOTH, a senior Turkish customs officer and occasional Abwehr agent whose lack of financial probity had led him to ask the British for financial support. ISLD took him on with some reluctance because he was a neutral and, therefore, its only hold over him was the threat to denounce him to his Turkish employers. SMOOTH's link with the Abwehr enabled ISLD to identify two important spies in Alexandretta, Paula Koch and her Armenian son-in-law, Joseph Ayvazian. Both unwittingly became significant contributors to the Allied deception effort. ISLD extracted a further advantage from SMOOTH by the invention of an important recruit, HUMBLE, who was described as a greengrocer in Aleppo who supplied provisions to various army camps in the area. (According to David Mure's *Practise to Decieve* [William Kimber, 1977] two American OSS officers were so convinced of HUMBLE's existence that they spent several weeks in Aleppo trying to track him down!) HUMBLE's credentials were accepted by the Abwehr in Istanbul, and he was authorized to recruit three sub-agents, KNOCK, WIT and WAIT, who were equally notional.

The activities of all these agents were co-ordinated by the relevant Thirty Committee and, as the war progressed, their importance as a weapon of strategic deception became recognized. Elaborate cover plans were prepared for German consumption, some with short-term objectives. The most comprehensive plan of all was ZEPPELIN, which was designed to keep German reserves pinned down in the eastern Mediterranean, thus preventing their transfer to the invasion area in France. One part of the plan was WANTAGE, a completely fictitious Allied order of battle which exaggerated the size of the British forces in the theatre. Reports from agents controlled by SIME and ISLD were backed up by the appropriate signals traffic and camouflage. Aircraft and tanks made of plywood also played an important part in deceiving the enemy's aerial reconnaissance cameras.

The success of the Twenty Committee in London, and the hidden advantage of the ISOS intercepts which enabled the case officers to monitor the enemy's perception of individual agents, encouraged ISLD to enter the double-agent game on a more ambitious scale. In January 1943 Ronald Croft recruited an Indian army officer named Gulzar Ahmed and had him transferred to censorship duties at the British Consulate in Istanbul. In August Ahmed reported an approach from the Abwehr and from that moment he became OPTIMIST, one of the more successful double agents of the war. Some, like DOMINO, were not entirely reliable. DOMINO was a wagons-lits steward on the Taurus Express who also happened to hold the reserve rank of major in the Turkish army. He was initially recruited in Istanbul, but he was later passed on to John Bruce Lockhart who discovered that, as well as working for the Abwehr and the Italian SIM, DOMINO also had occasional contacts with the Hungarian and Japanese secret services. Another unsatisfactory agent was ODIOUS, a German Swiss con-man who suddenly acquired a special importance when he was instructed by the Abwehr in Istanbul to deliver 200 gold sovereigns to QUICKSILVER, who operated under SIME's control. SIME knew that ODIOUS had once been friendly with the Belgian Consul in Beirut, who was considered somewhat suspect: it was, therefore, anxious not to compromise QUICKSILVER. The ISLD representative in Beirut, Charles Dundas, shared SIME's misgivings about ODIOUS and encoded a now-legendary telegram to Istanbul: 'PLANS WHICH APPEAR WELL PREPARED AT YOUR END SEEM HALF BAKED AT OURS.'

Reluctantly the DSO Beirut, Douglas Roberts, agreed to let ODIOUS into his territory, but he regretted giving his consent when it was learned that ODIOUS had taken advantage of ISLD's protection by smuggling a consignment of watches into the country. ODIOUS was promptly thrown into prison, much to the dismay of the Istanbul Station's Section V.

According to the ISOS intercepts, the Germans were soon reconciled to the loss of ODIOUS and their faith in QUICKSILVER remained intact. QUICKSILVER himself was aware of these developments, but he remained in custody and in wireless contact with his controller until August 1944, when he became Provost Marshal of the Greek air force in Egypt.

In addition to the deception committees already mentioned, there were others located in the region. The Thirty-Two Committee in Baghdad, chaired by David Mure, with the head of the ISLD Station (Frank Giffey and later Reg Wharry), ran a network inside the Moslem Brotherhood, code-named SAVAGES. The Thirty-Three Committee in Nicosia was chaired by the DSO Cyprus, Guy Thompson, and consisted of a single ISLD representative, Philip Druiff. Druiff ran two significant Greek wireless agents, LEMON and SENIOR LEMON.

There was, on paper, a Thirty-Four Committee in Tehran chaired by the local DSO, Colonel Joe Spencer, but in fact it never had any reason to operate as Spencer (and his successor, Squadron Leader Hanbury Dawson-Sheppard) were too busy chasing an elusive Abwehr master-spy, Franz Meier. Other deception committees included the Forty Committee in New Delhi, the Fifty Committee in Algiers and, eventually, the Sixty Committee in Rome.

As well as misleading the enemy, the double agents run by SIME and ISLD led to the identification of many other spies. It has been estimated that in Syria and Lebanon alone more than 400 people were arrested and detained on espionage charges. SIME was also responsible for liaising with the numerous groups of exiles which took up temporary residence in British-run territory to await the liberation of their countries. They included many Greeks, Poles, Yugoslavs and Jews, all of whom brought their own special security problems. SIME's relations with the Jewish Agency only began to improve late in 1943, when the Americans opened an Office of Strategic Services (OSS) liaison office in Cairo and signed an agreement to receive the Agency's intelligence reports. Unfortunately, OSS's first representative in the Egyptian capital, a former advertising director from the United Fruit Company, failed to gain the confidence of either SIME or ISLD and was soon replaced. Similar ructions were to occur in the espionage capital of the Middle East, Istanbul.

While ISLD headquarters in Cairo concentrated on persuading the enemy to retain as many troops as possible in the eastern Mediterranean theatre, the Istanbul Station was pursuing an ambitious policy of completely dominating the Abwehr's operations in the region. Initially, the Station had the Czech's agent, Paul Thümmel (A-54), to thank for its inside knowledge of the Abwehr's local order of battle. But Thümmel was arrested by the Gestapo in Prague on 22 March 1942, and thereafter the Station's Section V team was obliged to rely on ISOS and the manipulation of double agents. The Station's objective was the eventual elimination of the local Abwehr's complete organization.

The Station's first sign of success in this endeavour occurred at the end of December 1943, when an Abwehr officer, Dr Erich Vermehren, made two telephone calls to the British Legation in Istanbul. In both calls he identified himself as a German official, and eventually he was put through to the SIS Station, where it was suggested that a Section V representative met Vermehren for lunch. This was duly proposed, but never actually took place because the venue was badly chosen: it was next door to the German Legation and was popular with the staff. After this false start, Erich Vermehren and his wife were invited to the apartment of Nicholas Elliott, the Section V representative, for a meeting. Vermehren had twice been awarded a Rhodes Scholarship, but had been prevented from going to Oxford by the Nazi authorities who had confiscated his passport in 1938. He explained that he and his wife were devout Catholics and had been undergoing a crisis of conscience about continuing to work for the Nazi regime. Both were under suspicion of being anti-Nazi because of Elisabeth Vermehren's family connections, and her safe arrival in Istanbul on Christmas Eve had been in defiance of an official ban on her travelling beyond the frontiers of the Reich.

The Vermehrens were evidently extremely troubled by their dilemma. They did not wish to betray their country, but neither did they support

Hitler. Their position was made more complicated by the fact that Vermehren worked for a close family friend, Dr Paul Leverkühn, who was the head of the local Abstelle, and that he was related, by marriage, to the German Ambassador in Ankara, Franz von Papen. Elliott was sympathetic to their plight, partly because his own wife, Elizabeth, was also a strong Catholic, and eventually it was agreed that the British would receive the Vermehrens on their offered terms: neither would be required to assist the war effort; they would retain the power of veto on their future employment; and that their defection would be staged to look like a kidnapping. Elliott agreed, and the necessary plans were made.

The preparations consisted of the Vermehrens moving to a new apartment and their telling Leverkühn that the new address did not yet have a telephone installed. SIS calculated that if Vermehren pretended to fall ill on a Thursday morning, they might expect to have five days in the clear before the Germans were alerted to their disappearance. As double protection, the couple attended a cocktail party at a neutral embassy and left late. As they did so, two men leapt from a passing car and bundled them inside. This was for the benefit of witnesses, but in the event there were none. While the Vermehrens were recovering in an SIS safe-house in Izmir, von Papen turned up unexpectedly and asked to see his distant relatives. Someone was sent to trace the Vermehrens, but was unable to find their new apartment: Vermehren had left a deliberately inaccurate map to indicate where his flat was for just such an eventuality.

By the time the Germans finally realized what had happened, the Vermehrens were on the train to Aleppo with papers identifying them as a Yugoslav lieutenant named Vanneck and a British internee named Eva Maria Paton. They were accompanied on the seventy-two-hour train journey by six British commandos who had recently escaped from occupied territory. On their arrival in Aleppo, they were met by the local Defence Security Officer's representative, Sergeant-Major Christopher Kinniemouth. However, when Section V in Istanbul had signalled the Vermehrens' imminent arrival, there had been a slip up, and the cover-name 'Lieutenant Vanneck (General List)' had been corrupted to 'Lieutenant-General Vanneck (Yugoslavia)'. As a result, a British brigadier was requested to surrender his hotel room in Aleppo to what he took to be the more senior ally. After an unexpectedly comfortable night in Aleppo, the Vermehrens were escorted to Cairo.

The arrival of a senior Abwehr officer in the Egyptian capital took a number of people by surprise including, apparently, ISLD, and the Vermehrens were provided with separate, secure accommodation at the Combined Services Detailed Interrogation Centre. After three days of harsh confinement, Vermehren wrote a letter of protest to the Commandant, which eventually found its way to Major Patrick McElwee, a former housemaster at Blundell's School, then serving with SIME. He then arranged for the Vermehrens to be reunited at an ISLD villa at Mahdi. Here the pair underwent some four weeks of intensive debriefing, and Elisabeth Vermehren's health began to deteriorate.

When the debriefing had been concluded, Vermehren was provided with papers identifying him as Erich Vollmer and flown to Gibraltar via Benghazi. As the flight progressed 'Mrs Vollmer' fell ill, and when they finally arrived on the Rock a doctor diagnosed whooping cough, pleurisy and pneumonia. The local DSO, Philip Kirby Green, booked them into the Rock Hotel, but they were unable to continue their journey for another four weeks. As soon as they reached England, they were placed in Leslie Nicholson's custody, and 'Mrs Vollmer' was found a bed in the Naresborough Nursing Home. The SIS's controversial medical adviser, Dr Lankester, was called in, and, in spite of his efforts, Elisabeth Vermehren made a full recovery. (SIS maintained its own private hospital at Tempsford Hall, under the direction of Dr Henry Hales, but it was strictly for SIS personnel only.)

The Vermehrens' arrival in London posed several problems for SIS, for neither of the defectors had any means of support; nor were they prepared to contribute to the war effort. While Broadway pondered on what to do with the pair, a Section V officer, Kim Philby, offered to lend them his mother's flat in Drayton Gardens. Here they remained until eventually their case was handed to Blake-Budden, who arranged for them to join Sefton Delmer's black propaganda team at Woburn Abbey.

SIS had very little further use for the Vermehrens, and they were quickly abandoned. Nevertheless, their defection was to have grave consequences in Germany when the British decided, on 9 February (while the couple were still in Cairo), to release a press statement in America. This public loss of face was too much for Hitler who, on 12 February 1944 merged the Abwehr with Himmler's Sicherheitsdienst. Six days later Canaris was dismissed, and a purge began among the top ranks of the Abwehr. As a further result, Dr Leverkühn and several of his staff were ordered home.

This prompted the defection of several other important German officials in Istanbul. The next to arrive were Mr and Mrs Kleczkowski, a Jewish couple working for the Abwehr under journalistic cover, and Dr Willi Hamburger. All three had been recalled to Berlin to appear before an internal inquiry. Rather than face an interrogation at the hands of the Gestapo, they surrendered themselves to the Americans in Istanbul. Hamburger was an Austrian and was literally seduced into leaving the Abwehr by Adrienne Molnar, a glamorous Hungarian who also enjoyed the company of several influential Americans. Although SIS was delighted to see the enemy camp in chaos, there was only a minimal intelligence advantage to be gained by the defections. The British argued that any further approaches from the Abwehr would have to be refused unless the individual concerned was prepared to work his passage. The Americans agreed to close the door, but within a matter of weeks there was another defection.

On this occasion the defector was not from the Abwehr. She was Cornelia Kapp, who held the post of confidential secretary to the chief SD representative in Ankara, Ludwig Moyzisch. Nellie Kapp had spent several years in America before the war with her father, Carl Kapp, who had been the German Consul-General in Cleveland. While in Cleveland she had met and fallen in love with Ewart Seager, an American who subsequently joined OSS. Early in 1944 Seager was posted to Turkey and persuaded Miss Kapp to defect. When she did so, on 6 April 1944, she brought some startling news: Moyzisch was running a spy code-named CICERO in the British Embassy in Ankara. During a lengthy debriefing in Cairo, Miss Kapp volunteered a number of clues about CICERO, but she had never discovered his real identity. Security at the Embassy was tightened and the Ambassador, Sir Hughe Knatchbull-Hugessen, was warned of the leak. It so happened that the Embassy Security Officer was Monty Chidson, the experienced SIS officer who had been sent to The Hague Station after Dalton's suicide and had then joined Section D. He had, however, suffered a nervous breakdown after his removal of Amsterdam's diamond reserves in May 1940 and had been posted to Ankara as a sinecure. Broadway had already alerted Chidson to the possibility of a leak after some of the WOOD material from Berne (see chapter fourteen) had included information that could only have come from the British Embassy in Ankara. Chidson failed to identify the source, but the extra security measures tipped off the spy, who was the Ambassador's valet, Elyesa Bazna.

Bazna had joined Sir Hughe's personal staff in September 1943, although he had previously been employed by a German diplomat. Within a month of taking up his post in the residence, he had acquired copies of the keys to the Ambassador's private safe and dispatch box, and was busy photographing the contents of both. He then sold the unprocessed rolls of film to Moyzisch. In Berlin the coup was greeted with disbelief, for the entire story seemed too good to be true. Senior SD officials debated the merits of CICERO's haul and decided to continue the contact, but to pay him with counterfeit currency. They argued that if CICERO turned out to be a British *agent provocateur*, as seemed probable, little would have been lost.

As soon as CICERO realized that Chidson was imposing a stricter security regime at the Embassy and the residence, Bazna tendered his resignation and left Sir Hughe's service early in April 1944. Bazna's departure made the investigation all but impossible, and SIS reluctantly admitted to being baffled. The Foreign Office was appalled at the prospect of an unidentified spy at liberty in the Embassy and passed the file to William

Codrington,* the Chief Security Officer at the Foreign Office. Codrington dispatched his assistant, Sir John Dashwood, to Ankara, along with a detective from Scotland Yard's Special Branch, Chief Inspector Cochrane.

Dashwood examined all of the WOOD material delivered to Broadway from the Berne Station and noticed that one particular telegram concerning Churchill's visit to the Tehran Conference contained a typing error. By a process of elimination, he was able to trace the telegram to Sir Hughe. Thereafter, the investigation was relatively straightforward. He and Cochrane interviewed all the Embassy personnel and concluded that only Bazna (who had conveniently dropped from sight with some £200,000 in forged notes) had enjoyed the right access to the material. In his report to the Foreign Secretary, Dashwood described how Bazna

> succeeded in photographing a number of highly secret documents in the Embassy and selling the films to the Germans. He would not have been able to do so if the Ambassador had conformed to the regulations governing the custody of secret documents.

Later that same year Knatchbull-Hugessen was appointed Ambassador to Belgium, a post he held until 1947.

The CICERO incident was a unique German success, but fortunately the SD was always somewhat sceptical about the authenticity of his information. Bazna was later imprisoned for passing counterfeit currency, and Nellie Kapp ended up in an internment camp at Bismarck, North Dakota.

In fact, the CICERO case was not the only lapse in security in Turkey. On one memorable occasion Bernard O'Leary had inadvertently named Berlin as the capital of 12000 in a signal to London. According to Broadway, this was a grave breach of security and compromised SIS's entire coding system. O'Leary was ordered home in such disgrace that his Head of Station had not the courage to report a further embarrassing incident: a group of drunken German intelligence officers had later been heard to sing 'Zwölfland, Zwölfland, über alles' in Taxim's Casino in Istanbul. Yet, despite such rare humiliations, British secret intelligence in the Middle East could be fairly described as having been well organized and reasonably efficient. Certainly it initiated an impressive number of double agents, who misled the Abwehr and enabled SIME and ISLD to identify many important enemy agents.

By the end of the war, the Istanbul Station had opened 'personality' card files on 1,500 enemy agents in Turkey and had persuaded the Turkish authorities to intern some 750 of them. Altogether about fourteen were recruited by Section V as double agents, and a further nine volunteered information about their German controllers. Soon after D-Day Nicholas Elliott was recalled to London to take up a new appointment as Head of Station in Berne, and Keith Guthrie, Cambridge University's Public Orator, took over from him.

* Brother of John Codrington, then Head of Station in Algiers.

14

OSS: The Unsecret Service

When 'Little Bill' Stephenson arrived in New York aboard the *Britannic* on 21 June 1940 to head British Security Co-ordination, he had no less than three major tasks, all under the general heading of 'protecting British interests in a neutral territory'. He was to supervise the procurement of vital war material and investigate Nazi activities in the United States. He was also to exercise 'covert diplomacy to reassure [Secretary for the Navy] Knox and [Secretary for the Army] Stimson'.

Stephenson was needed to carry out all these different roles because there was no direct channel of communication between the Secret Intelligence Service and the Americans. The FBI, of course, had enjoyed a close peacetime liaison with MI5, and Hoover was perfectly aware of the true function of the Passport Control Office in Manhattan, but there was no American organization even remotely similar to SIS. As a result, Stephenson was obliged to combine the work of British Security Co-ordination with what amounted to covert political lobbying. Stephenson obtained an introduction to Hoover through Gene Tunney, the heavy-weight boxing champion, and his conduit into the White House was via a millionaire Wall Street lawyer, William J. Donovan.

At first glance Donovan must have appeared an unlikely candidate for presenting SIS's case in Washington. He was a fifty-seven-year-old, second generation Irishman from Buffalo, New York, and an influential Republican. President Roosevelt was a Democrat. However, on closer examination, Donovan emerges as a key figure in Stephenson's campaign to counter Nazi propaganda in the United States and promote the British cause. It was, in fact, Donovan's strong Catholic background that first brought him into contact with SIS during the Great War. In April 1916 Donovan had been in neutral Holland awaiting a visa to allow him to carry out famine relief work in German-occupied territory. He had crossed the Atlantic to supervise the delivery of badly needed supplies to Poland, but, initially at least, he only got as far as Belgium. While there, he was recruited by Cardinal Mercier into the WHITE LADY network as a courier. His American travel documents enabled him to travel in Belgium with relative freedom and for two months he had toured the countryside whilst ostensibly engaged on 'relief work'. He then went on to Germany and Austria, with brief visits to Rotterdam and Stockholm. Although he had originally intended to visit Warsaw, he never entered Poland. In June 1916, while in Berlin, Donovan received his American call-up papers and returned to the United States. The following year Donovan returned to England as an infantry officer and fought with distinction on the Western Front. He ended the war as one of America's most decorated heroes, complete with the coveted Congressional Medal of Honor.

In January 1936 Donovan came to SIS's attention for a second time when he volunteered a report to the Foreign Office in London on the Italian invasion of Ethiopia. Donovan had written the report after having received Mussolini's personal permission to visit General Badoglio and his troops. SIS's knowledge of the Italian Campaign had been embarrassingly meagre owing to the almost complete lack of intelligence resources in the area, so when Donovan offered to submit a report on his observations he was given encouragement from Whitehall. The report proved to be an impressive document, correctly forecasting a crushing Italian victory. After his unique tour, Donovan was better placed than anyone to provide an assessment of Mussolini's intentions, and his conclusion that the Suez Canal would not be directly threatened by the dictator was particularly well received in London.

In addition to his experience of military intelligence, Donovan possessed considerable political influence in Washington. Although he was politically opposed to the President, he had attended law school with him and had even been offered the job of Secretary for the Army. Donovan had turned him down, but each respected the other. Some believed that the Irish–American had greater ambitions, perhaps even to be America's first Catholic President.

As soon as he had checked into the St Regis Hotel in New York, Stephenson telephoned Donovan's law office and made a bold suggestion: would Donovan fly to London and judge the military situation for himself? Accommodation would be provided for him at Claridge's and he would be granted an audience with the King. This remarkable offer had few risks for either the Prime Minister or SIS since it was verbal, and anyway Stephenson was not due to take up his official position for another fortnight. The idea of Donovan undertaking an independent mission to England was greeted enthusiastically in Washington, where the administration had been receiving conflicting reports from the American Embassy in London. The Ambassador, Joseph Kennedy, had predicted an imminent British surrender, while the various Service attachés were less defeatist. If Donovan were granted the right access, his opinion would be invaluable to the White House. The invitation was accepted and on Saturday, 13 July 1940,

Donovan dined with the British Ambassador to Washington, Lord Lothian, and received the final details of his trip to England. The following morning he caught a Pan Am Clipper to Lisbon via Bermuda.

Donovan arrived in London on 17 July, having completed the last leg of his journey from Lisbon to Poole on a British flying boat. His schedule was a busy one. His first call was to Buckingham Palace, where George VI explained that there was no possibility of a capitulation. The British Government and the British people, he declared, were determined to fight on. During the following two weeks Donovan was treated to a unique tour of Britain's defences, as already mentioned in chapter nine. His carefully planned schedule was arranged by Stewart Menzies in conjunction with the American Military Attaché, Brigadier-General Raymond Lee. Wherever he went, he saw apparently well-equipped and well-armed troops preparing for an airborne invasion. The two fighter airfields he visited seemed to be in an advanced state of readiness to meet the Luftwaffe. Much of what Donovan saw was an elaborate deception to persuade him that Britain possessed the means to continue the fight. The King's performance had succeeded in convincing him of the nation's resolve; SIS's role was to persuade him that the country was logistically able to support its determination.

Donovan was also introduced to all the top personalities in the British intelligence community. Menzies personally briefed him on SIS's overseas organization; Colin Gubbins accompanied him to Norfolk to witness an exercise conducted by his Auxiliary Intelligence Officers, the embryonic secret resistance movement; the Director of Military Intelligence, Paddy Beaumont-Nesbitt, gave him a tour of the War Office and explained the German order of battle; Sir Frank Nelson received him at the Baker Street headquarters of SOE and introduced him to his senior staff; Desmond Morton described the Industrial Intelligence Centre's strategy of an economic blockade; John Godfrey showed him round the Admiralty and invited him to dine at his home in Sevenoaks. Finally, he was escorted into the maze of tunnels under Great George Street to meet the Prime Minister in the Cabinet War Room.

By the time Donovan joined the flying boat *Clare* at Poole for his flight home, he was thoroughly convinced that Kennedy was mistaken: Britain certainly possessed the morale and the determination to resist the Germans. On 6 August 1940, the day after Donovan landed at La Guardia, he reported to the Secretary for the Navy, Colonel Frank Knox. In short, he concluded that Britain would not suffer a military collapse in the style of the French if the United States administration provided logistical support. He also clarified another important point for the White House: there was little chance of the President being embarrassed by granting strategic aid to a power which then promptly succumbed.

Donovan's dramatic visit to England will remain one of the greatest intelligence triumphs of the war. On the basis of the opinions he expressed on his return, the President agreed to enter into Lend–Lease negotiations with Britain which resulted in the delivery of desperately needed equipment in exchange for leasehold agreements on British bases in Newfoundland, Bermuda and the Caribbean. It was an extraordinary achievement, and was to lead to still further American covert participation in the war.

In the three months following Donovan's return to Washington, he collaborated closely with Stephenson. Donovan was anxious to develop an American counterpart to the British institutions of SIS and SOE. Stephenson was equally anxious to undermine Nazi propaganda in the States and build up political support to protect BSC from the FBI. Having met Hoover, Stephenson was perfectly aware that the Director would not tolerate any foreign espionage on American soil, whether it be conducted by the British or anyone else. There were, however, important intelligence advantages to be gained among the embassies in Washington. Also at stake was vital shipping information. There was little point in procuring large numbers of American-made weapons if they were going to fall prey to German U-boats operating in international waters off the eastern seaboard. Thus, no sooner had Stephenson succeeded in purchasing war material, than he had to protect the cargoes from the German intelligence rings known to be operating in the dock areas of New York, Boston and Baltimore.

Once BSC and the Co-ordinator of Information (COI) were firmly established, Stephenson and Donovan prepared to travel to Europe together to cement the relationship further. On 6 December 1940 Donovan and a mysterious 'Mr O'Connell' flew from Baltimore to Bermuda. Ten days later they both arrived in London and kept a lunch appointment with the Prime Minister. Donovan now proposed, with help from SIS, to expand the role of the COI, and requested facilities to make a major tour of the Mediterranean and Central Europe. His plan, which had originally come from the President, was endorsed by Churchill, and on New Year's Eve Donovan set out on a ten-week journey, accompanied by Colonel Vivian Dykes, the Assistant Secretary to the War Cabinet. Donovan later commented that 'the red carpet was laid wider and thicker than I had thought it possible to lay'. Donovan was met by the senior British officers in Gibraltar, Malta and Cairo, and then made his own way through the Balkans from Athens. Unfortunately, this part of his tour was less successful. American press correspondents dogged him on most of his way and were inconveniently on hand when Donovan visited a night-club in Sofia and had his briefcase containing his diplomatic passport stolen. The American Minister in Belgrade, Arthur Bliss, intervened to persuade the Yugoslav authorities to allow Donovan to continue his journey. On 24 January 1941, the Germans broadcast an entertaining version of Donovan's misfortune on their English language radio service.

Donovan returned to London on 3 March and conferred further with Stewart Menzies and, for the first time, with the Security Service, MI5, who was responsible for intelligence and security throughout Ireland. This was Donovan's opportunity to repay SIS hospitality. Although isolated from the Continent, Britain was still vulnerable to the infiltration of German agents through the Republic of Ireland, and ISOS decrypts had already confirmed this to be a real danger. However, the authorities in Dublin had threatened to intern any British intelligence officer found in Eire, nor did they wish to liaise in any way with MI5. Now Donovan agreed to travel to Dublin to meet representatives from G–2, the Irish military intelligence department. Eire continued to refuse to link up with MI5's Irish section, but agreed to raise no objection if an American intelligence officer was posted to Dublin for liaison purposes. This arrangement was to prove exceptionally rewarding.

Having completed his European and Mediterranean mission, Donovan returned to the United States, landing at La Guardia on 18 March. Almost immediately he began a round of briefing sessions with influential figures in Washington, including the President. On 15 May John Godfrey flew to Washington to pursue some of the matters he and Donovan had discussed in London and made firm proposals concerning the exchange of information and staff ... 'not liaison but complete co-operation'. Unfortunately, Godfrey found that not all of Washington shared Donovan's views. As he recorded later, 'after a fortnight it became clear that I was up against a brick wall'. Sir William Wiseman obtained an interview with the President which provided the Director of Naval Intelligence with the opportunity to express his views, and he returned to London (with his Personal Assistant, Ian Fleming) well satisfied.

While Godfrey was in Washington, Stephenson and Donovan were collaborating to develop their relationship further. Donovan had been promised that, if he made a further trip to England, he would be let into one of the country's most important secrets. Stephenson explained that he did not have the authority to disclose the information, but he would accompany Donovan on a special military flight. On Sunday 1 June both men drove up to Dorval Airfield, Montreal, where they met a plane bound for Scotland. They landed safely at Prestwick and took a train to London. The object of the mission was to indoctrinate the American into two closely guarded secret weapons. The first was the massive black propaganda exercise operated by the Ministry of Economic Warfare from Woburn; the second was the existence of GCHQ.

Section VIII, headed by Richard Gambier-Parry, had developed a scheme, code-named ASPIDISTRA, to build a huge short-wave transmitter which would resemble 'a raiding Dreadnought of the Ether'. In the spring of 1941, SIS only had the use of four 7.5 kilowatt transmitters; it desperately wanted to acquire a gigantic 500 kilowatt, medium-wave transmitter which had been built by RCA in America. Beaming this radio across Europe would drown any German interference and prove a mighty weapon in the hands of the propagandists. Donovan was taken on a conducted tour of Woburn and promised to help Gambier-Parry. Donovan's second call was to Bletchley Park, where he was indoctrinated into some (but by no means all) of the secrets of ULTRA. Stephenson and Donovan then flew back to New York. This, Donovan's third visit to London, seems to have been of considerable significance. It is not unlikely that Godfrey's initial reports from Washington might have tipped the balance in allowing Donovan to be taken further into Menzies's confidence. In any event, the brief trip seems to have had the desired effect. RCA agreed to release its transmitter to SIS and Donovan began lobbying to obtain Federal funding for an American secret intelligence organization.

On 11 June 1941 Donovan submitted a report to the President outlining the creation of a 'Service of Strategic Information'; but as soon as the document was circulated among the military, it met heavy opposition. Accordingly, the President established the office of the Co-ordinator of Information within his own executive office and, on 11 July 1940, appointed Donovan to head it. The Presidential Order was vague in the extreme. Donovan was authorized

to collect and analyse information and data, which may bear upon national security; to correlate such information and data, and to make such information and data available to the President and to such departments and officials of the Government as the President may determine; and to carry out, when requested by the President, such supplementary activities as may facilitate the securing of information important for national security not now available to the Government.

The office of Co-ordinator of Intelligence was to be the foundation of America's new secret intelligence service. One of Donovan's first moves was to open a COI office in the American Embassy in London, and appoint a noted Anglophile, William D. Whitney, to head it.

The arrival of Bill Whitney in London at the end of October 1941 was an important step in the covert development of Anglo–American relations, which took place in spite of the restrictions of the Neutrality Act. A former Rhodes Scholar and New York lawyer, Whitney was popular with both SOE and SIS. He also held the rank of major in the British army and had served briefly with the BEF before returning to Washington to become Averell Harriman's Executive Assistant in the Lend–Lease administration. As a former British officer, he was therefore well placed to channel large quantities of secret intelligence to the COI headquarters in Washington. Accompanying Whitney to London was Colonel Robert Solborg, Donovan's new chief of the COI's Special Operations division. Solborg was a former cavalry officer in the Czar's army who had acquired American citizenship after the revolution. His task was to study SOE's methods and advise Donovan on the future structure for the COI's operational arm. This was the first time that an American had been allowed prolonged access to a secret British department, and by this date the exchange of information between British Security Co-ordination and the COI and FBI had been put on a more or less formal basis. As Desmond Morton commented on 18 September 1941 (not without some exaggeration):

... to all intents and purposes US Security is being run for them at the President's request by the British. A British officer sits in Washington with Mr Edgar Hoover and General Bill Donovan for this purpose and reports regularly to the President. It is of course essential that this fact should not become known in view of the furious uproar it would cause if known to the isolationists.

An illustration of this close relationship is the case of SCOUT, one of the Belgrade Station's six volunteer double agents.

SCOUT was a Yugoslav named Dusko Popov who, like his brother Ivo, had been recruited into the Abwehr during the summer of 1940. Both men had offered their services to the SIS Head of Station in Belgrade, St George Lethbridge, and he had accepted them. In November 1940, Dusko had been instructed to travel to Portugal to receive training as an Abwehr agent. SIS also provided him with the telephone number of the Lisbon Station so he could report his progress. This he did, and when on 21 December 1940 SCOUT flew on a commercial flight into Filton Airport, Bristol, MI5 was waiting.

SCOUT was accommodated at the Savoy Hotel in London and debriefed by both MI5 and SIS. The Security Service was delighted at the opportunity to interrogate a willing Abwehr agent and SIS was equally pleased to have been able to make such a meeting possible. The event proved so successful that MI5 took SCOUT onto its books as TRICYCLE and created an entire network around him. One of his sub-agents was Menzies's brother's sister-in-law, Friedle Gaertner. Stewart Menzies's younger brother Ian had married a glamorous Austrian, Lisel Gaertner, before the war. Lisel's sister, Friedle, was a cabaret performer in various London clubs and had also been an *agent provocateur* for MI5. Within a few weeks of TRICYCLE's arrival in England, he had got on close terms with Friedle Gaertner and had arranged, via MI5, to recruit her into his network, thus giving the Abwehr an informant within the CSS's family. Miss Gaertner, code-named GELATINE, continued supplying the Germans with information in secret writing until the end of the war.

Having established his credentials with both SIS and MI5, SCOUT returned to Lisbon in January and March 1941. On both occasions he met his Abwehr case officer and received special intelligence questionnaires.

When he returned to London in April, after his second rendezvous, SCOUT disclosed that he had been asked to travel to the United States and establish a new network of agents there. Apparently, the Abwehr felt vulnerable because most of its United States' informants were also members of the German–American Bund, a completely legal organization, but one which was thought to have been penetrated by the FBI. With the consent of SIS, SCOUT flew to Bermuda later the same month and was met by John Pepper (from British Security Co-ordination), who escorted him on the remainder of his journey to New York and introduced him to Charles Lehrman from the FBI. The FBI took an understandably cautious attitude to SCOUT, who was, after all, a self-confessed spy. Approximately one-third of his microdot questionnaire concerned the US naval base at Pearl Harbor, Hawaii, but the FBI was adamant that SCOUT could not leave New York. This handicap certainly reduced the effectiveness of his mission, but arguments about SCOUT's behaviour and status also distracted both the FBI and BSC from the true significance of the Abwehr's interest in Pearl Harbor. This only became clear on 7 December 1941, when the Japanese caught much of the US Pacific Fleet unawares in port.

SCOUT's apparent failure to complete his task in America surprisingly did not diminish his standing in the eyes of the Abwehr, and when, in October 1942, he returned to Lisbon and re-established contact with his case officer, he was made welcome and given a new assignment in London.

The Japanese attack on Pearl Harbor succeeded in bringing the United States into the war, and it also formed the basis of a top-level conference at the White House, code-named ARCADIA, attended by Churchill and President Roosevelt. Indeed, it was agreements formalized at ARCADIA that led to a joint undertaking to maintain 'the spirit of revolt in the occupied territories, and the organization of subversive movements' and undermine the Germans 'by air bombardment, blockade, subversive activities and propaganda'. Once the Joint Chiefs of Staff on both sides of the Atlantic had accepted the principle of such unorthodox means making strategic contribution to the war effort, it remained to Stephenson and Donovan to translate the accords into action.

For the following six months, BSC collaborated with the COI and was given what amounted to a free hand to conduct intelligence operations in the United States. However, such activities did not pass entirely unnoticed and, in March 1942, Senator Kenneth McKellar tried to introduce a bill specifically designed to force Stephenson to identify and register his agents. Such a development was unthinkable, especially since Bill Ross-Smith had recruited such a profitable network of ship-borne agents. Of the forty-two German agents arrested by the FBI during 1941 and 1942, thirty-six had been originally identified by BSC. The threat from McKellar was averted, but it caused BSC to transfer more of its intelligence gathering operations into the hands of the COI, which was at least a legal establishment.

BSC's headquarters in the Rockefeller Center had spread to cover the 35th and 36th floors, and Stephenson's organization had grown beyond all expectations. Initially, BSC had consisted of the original New York Station staff, with a few extra specialist personnel: Ingram Fraser to supervise SOE's representatives in South America; John Pepper to co-ordinate economic warfare; Cedric Belfrage to supervise British black propaganda; Freckles Wren to look after MI5's security interests; and Bill Ross-Smith to concentrate on building up a network of informers on neutral ships.

Two important developments account for BSC's growth: the desire of the American authorities to have selected men undergo SOE/SIS training, and the unforeseen number of intelligence opportunities available to the British in the western hemisphere. For example, poor postal security in Manhattan enabled BSC to extend its Empire censorship programme, based in Bermuda, to cover the rest of Europe. Virtually all the in-coming mail from Europe ended up being read illicitly by BSC. Every letter of interest was steamed open and, if necessary, photographed, before being returned to the mails. By the end of the war, BSC was employing several thousand people to undertake this work.

Another useful source of information was the network of observers recruited by Ross-Smith. By approaching individual American shipping companies, and by harnessing the services volunteered by Basque representatives, Ross-Smith ended up with observers on some 400 neutral vessels, including a dummy Red Cross ship based in the Azores.

It was information from one such ship-borne observer that led to one of BSC's greatest wartime triumphs. It was reported that the skippers of all Spanish merchantmen had been issued with a special leather wallet containing secret orders which had to be kept by them personally, at all times. Whenever a ship docked, its captain was obliged to produce the wallet at the local Spanish Consulate so that the elaborate seals on the wallet could be checked. According to rumour, the penalty for losing the wallet was death, and it could only be opened upon receipt of a secret coded signal from the Spanish Ministry of Marine. The daunting task of reading the contents of the wallet was given to Ross-Smith, who arranged for a Spanish skipper to be intercepted on his way back from his mandatory visit to the Consulate and entertained at Reuben's Restaurant on 58th Street. The captain was plied with alcohol while his precious wallet was removed and taken to BSC headquarters. There Dorothy Hyde carefully extracted the secret document, had it photographed and replaced it, a lengthy process, but one achieved without disturbing the elaborate Spanish seals. The wallet was then restored to its inebriated owner without him detecting its temporary loss.

The contents of the wallet turned out to be special, top-secret orders instructing the captains of Spanish merchantmen to change course to named ports upon receipt of a particular code-word. Evidently, this signal was to herald Spain's entry into the war on the side of the Axis. Once appraised of this information, BSC's Basque collaborators prepared a special message which was to be transmitted if Franco took this course. It simply informed the captains that the Allies were perfectly aware of the signal they had received only moments earlier, and offered them an alternative route ... to an Allied port.

A second, more elaborate, operation was later successfully carried out in Buenos Aires, when the Spanish changed the secret code-word. On neither occasion did Franco's Government realize that its contingency plan had been compromised.

Robert Solborg completed his study of SOE in January 1942 and returned to Washington. He had found 'a high degree of rivalry and, on occasion, jealousy, between the two British agencies' (SIS and SOE) and, therefore, recommended that the COI should consist of two branches, Secret Intelligence and Special Operations under one head, rather than two completely separate concerns like the British. He did not combine the two into one single unit however, because he thought two branches would ensure better relations with SIS and SOE. This idea was accepted and M. Preston Goodfellow (a Brooklyn newspaper publisher from the Hearst organization was appointed Chief of the COI's Special Operations Branch. Donovan's candidate for Chief of the Secret Intelligence Branch was David Bruce, then Chief Representative of the American Red Cross in London, and later (in 1961) American Ambassador to the Court of St James.

It was not until June 1942 that the COI was able to expand its London office from its original staff of Whitney plus nine others. In that month Stephenson escorted Donovan, Jim Murphy (one of Donovan's senior lieutenants and a colleague from his legal practice) and Preston Goodfellow to Montreal and then accompanied them on a transatlantic flight to England. For the next two weeks the COI representatives negotiated with SIS and SOE to conclude an agreement setting out the areas in which the Americans would be allowed to undertake secret intelligence operations. On 16 June Donovan was invited to address the War Cabinet on the subject of future Anglo–American co-operation, and this eventually led to a draft agreement on the subject. Certain areas were designated as being in an American sphere of interest, while other regions were to remain under British control. The final document, hammered out by Sir Frank Nelson's successor at SOE, Sir Charles Hambro, and Donovan was to form the basis of all future covert Anglo–American co-operation. Europe, India and East Africa would remain under British control. The Middle East and the Balkans would be shared, and America would dominate in North Africa, China, Manchuria, Korea, the South Pacific, Finland and the islands in the Atlantic. In addition, there were strict rules about protocol. The COI office in London, which had now grown to over 100-strong, was to limit its activities to liaison. No independent operations were to be mounted from England into France or anywhere else in Europe without British consent. In return for these undertakings, the COI would be granted access to SOE's training facilities and communications equipment. It would also be able to send its personnel on SOE courses at the Special Training School established by BSC at Oshawa, near Toronto.

The Hambro/Donovan accord was completed on 26 June 1942 and was confirmed by the American Joint Chiefs of Staff on 26 August. It did not, however, involve SIS, which held itself aloof from the proceedings. Instead, on 30 June, Donovan flew back to New York to continue his discussions with Stephenson. On his return, Donovan discovered that in his absence the COI had been wound up and that he was the head of a completely new organization, the Office of Strategic Services.

One unforeseen consequence of the new arrangements, and in particular the pact with SOE, was Bill Whitney's opposition. He objected strongly to the division within OSS between Secret Intelligence and Special Operations. From his viewpoint, on the sidelines of the SIS/SOE conflict, such a mistake was merely repeating an error invented by the British. He resigned as the London representative and, as his replacement, Donovan promptly appointed William Phillips, a former American Ambassador to Rome, Belgium and Canada.

The Secret Intelligence/Secret Operations split suited SIS perfectly, and Stephenson began recommending suitable candidates to fill the new American secret intelligence posts. His first suggestion was Whitney Shepardson, an Oxford- and Harvard-educated businessman who was later to become President of the Carnegie Foundation. Shepardson was installed as Chief of Secret Intelligence at the OSS's office in London, while another Oxford graduate (and hurdles blue), Arthur Roseborough, was declared the SI Chief in Washington.

Phillips's arrival in London on 18 July 1942 marked a turning-point for both SIS and the OSS. Phillips abandoned the old COI office in the American Embassy and took over two large houses on Upper Grosvenor Street, which had formerly been the headquarters of the French *couturier*, House of Worth. The new arrangement also gave Broadway a sense of security: the Americans it was dealing with would not be in direct communication with SOE. The first manifestation of this new climate of trust took place in November 1942, when George Bowden, one of Donovan's closest colleagues and a Chicago-based tax lawyer, was invited to visit SIS. Bowden had been the author of the original Lend–Lease bill, which had authorized the transfer of fifty US Navy destroyers to England, and was, therefore, particularly welcome in London.

Although Bowden was an attorney principally specializing in tax matters, he was also active in many leftist causes, including the radical National Lawyers Guild. This gave him an immediate entrée into some of the Left-orientated international labour organizations, such as the Industrial Workers of the World. Bowden, Murphy and Donovan agreed that such groups might prove to be fruitful areas of recruitment. Most of the organizations they had in mind were listed by MI5 as Communist fronts and, as such, were partly denied to SIS. Thus Bowden's visit to London had a dual purpose: he was to establish contact with the exiled trade union leaders and, at the same time, make a detailed study of SIS.

When Bowden arrived in London, the decision had already been taken at a high level to withhold nothing from him, except the identity of individual agents. After being briefed at Broadway on the worldwide structure of the Service, Bowden was invited to see Section V at work in St Albans. He was to spend nearly three months there learning most of Felix Cowgill's secrets. He was shown the German signals intercepted by the Radio Security Service and was allowed to visit Bletchley to see the raw material being decrypted and transformed into ISOS text. He spent a considerable amount of time at Arkley where various RSS experts, such as Hugh Trevor-Roper and Gilbert Ryle, analysed the English translations and prepared the vital ISOS summaries for distribution to MI5 and Section V. At St Albans the summaries were filtered into Section V's geographical sub-sections for entry on the card-indices. Each time a new personality was mentioned in a German message, a new card file was introduced, together with cross-referring entries in the Nominal Index, the relevant country index and the relevant Abstelle index. All combined, this involved a check against half a million separate cards. If a particular personality was already known in the system, then the relevant card was simply updated. Once all the information gleaned from the ISOS decrypts had been processed, it was reconstituted and delivered in the form of brief reports to those authorized to receive them in MI5 and the rest of SIS.

In addition to the ISOS material, there was also a constant flow of other important intelligence which was added to the Section V dossiers. Information came from such varied sources as the interrogators at MI5's Camp 020 (at Latchmere House, Ham Common), the captured document experts, the Letter Interception Unit and MI5's stable of double agents. When problems were posed by particular decrypts like, for example, the appearance of a previously unidentified agent in a certain town, a carefully worded questionnaire would be sent to the local Station's Section V representative, who would investigate and provide further information for entry on the card-indices.

The ISOS system gave the impression that as soon as, say, a suspect Spaniard arrived in Hamilton, Bermuda, by ship, the local Defence Security

Officer could be warned to intercept him. If no action was required, then the suspect's movements would simply be logged until he next came to Section V's attention. Bowden was suitably impressed and reported to Donovan that ISOS was an essential counter-intelligence weapon that the Americans could not hope to match. On the other hand, the British imposed such strict security conditions on all the ISOS material, even within SIS, that it seemed unlikely that SIS would share it.

As the OSS historian later commented: 'When the secret methods of the British agencies were fully understood, the importance of the security risk they took was appreciated as overwhelming.'

Accordingly, Donovan proposed the creation of a special counter-espionage branch within OSS to handle ISOS, and suggested that a small liaison unit be introduced in London to collect the material and ship it to Washington. Initially, Donovan's idea was that this unit would take sole responsibility for liaising with both SIS and MI5, but the FBI Director insisted that he retain his own independent link with MI5 through his Legal Attaché at the Embassy. Donovan agreed, and when, finally, SIS obtained the Prime Minister's consent to the scheme, an American counter-intelligence division was established on 1 March 1943 within OSS's Secret Intelligence Branch. The chief condition imposed by SIS was that it would supervise the transmission of ISOS, which would be made available at Stephenson's headquarters in New York. The material could not leave the building, so the counter-intelligence division, headed by Jim Murphy, rented a floor directly below British Security Co-ordination's office. As a further precaution, the use of the code-names ISK and ISOS was banned. OSS renamed them PAIR and ICE respectively. Murphy appointed three OSS officers to open the liaison office in OSS's office in Mayfair. Led by a crippled academic, Norman Holmes Pearson (also a Rhodes Scholar and Yale's Professor of Literature), the group included Hubert Will (a Chicago lawyer), Dr Dana Durand (another Rhodes Scholar), Robert Blum (a Professor of European History) and four secretaries. Section V found accommodation for them in Ryder Street, conveniently close to MI5's headquarters in St James's Street, but uncomfortably distant from Broadway, directly across St James's Park. Because of his immobility Pearson, uniquely, was granted the privilege of a desk in the room of the Chairman of the Twenty Committee, J.C. Masterman, in MI5 headquarters.

Pearson and his team started work at the end of March 1943, and it was quickly apparent that the arrangement was to prove extremely profitable to both sides. Pearson accepted an offer to sit in on the Twenty Committee, thus enabling him to learn the practicalities of strategic deception using double agents. His three colleagues concentrated on developing their links with St Albans. Within three months of opening for business, the small counter-intelligence division of the OSS group had become the single most important unit within the organization, generating much of the work conducted by the other sections within OSS. From SIS's point of view, the relationship was encouraged to flourish because it reduced the pressure on BSC and freed its personnel for investigative and other duties. Walter Bell, formerly on Sir James Paget's staff at the Manhattan PCO, was sent to London to liaise with the Americans, and Dick Ellis, Stephenson's deputy, stepped up his advisory role. Fortuitously, SIS had acquired an apparently bottomless pool of manpower equipped with limitless resources and limitless funds. SIS had suddenly been relieved of much of the counter-espionage burden in the western hemisphere. On 16 June 1943 the counter-intelligence division was redesignated Counter-Espionage (X-2) and elevated to full OSS Branch status.

Within a further three months this Branch had transferred its registry to Washington and was initiating ISOS inquiries for the first time. The rapid development of X-2, in fact, reflected the lessons that SIS had learnt from sometimes bitter experience dating back to the German penetration of The Hague Station. OSS was absorbing Section V's collective wisdom, but what price was being paid?

The question of X-2's relations with Section V remains, even today, a potentially sensitive subject. Kermit Roosevelt's official *War Report of the OSS*,* which was heavily censored at the request of SIS before it was released in 1976, admits that 'Misapprehensions as to the close relations between X-2 and the British services were not infrequent.' But he concedes that Section V 'demanded knowledge of Special Operations and X-2 operations and a degree of co-ordination which often amounted to complete control.'

In September 1943 Donovan himself expressed his concern over SIS's refusal to allow OSS's Secret Intelligence Branch to operate in Europe without direct British supervision. He protested that the draft agreement proposed by Dansey and his recently recruited Deputy Director (Army), General Sir James Marshall-Cornwall, 'suggests "co-ordination" and "agreement" but as employed here the word "co-ordination" means "control" and "agreement" means "dependence"'.

Invariably SIS won the argument with the implied threat that the ISOS traffic might suddenly dry up. In that event, OSS would have been powerless to protect itself or its operations against Axis interference. Certainly the flow of counter-intelligence information was one way. In another revealing comment, Kermit Roosevelt observed: 'SIS never co-operated extensively with OSS, and its security was so effective that it was rarely possible to determine with assurance where its agents were located.'

This is in contrast with the concern of the OSS Secret Intelligence

* Walker Publishing Company, New York.

Branch when informed that it had to submit the names of its recruits to vetting against the ISOS indices. The Branch 'feared the tracings would reveal its agents to the British services'.

While X-2 continued to expand, elsewhere in the world OSS was establishing itself as America's first secret intelligence service. Unfortunately, its high public profile did not lend itself being very secret, and its OSS initials were soon substituted with such titles as 'Oh So Social', a reflection of the large number of wealthy, East Coast establishment names in the organization. Security was so poor that a German short-wave radio station broadcast news of Donovan's appointment in 1941 almost before the rest of the American media had received the official press statement.

No such laxity was tolerated in London, where William P. Maddox headed OSS's Secret Intelligence Branch, and Preston Goodfellow ran the Special Operations Branch. Maddox had been a political scientist at both Yale and Harvard and he was required to exercise all his diplomatic skills for, although OSS had mirrored the SIS/SOE separation, it was not burdened by the rivalries which sometimes appeared to dominate the inter-Service relations of the British. Maddox's role was to liaise with SIS, and Goodfellow, for his part, was charged with bringing about the complete amalgamation of the Special Operations Branch with SOE. This eventually took place in January 1944, when a joint headquarters was established. No such joint arrangement was reached with SIS.

Because of the restrictions imposed by the Hambro/Donovan accord of June 1942, OSS concentrated its first field operations in the Mediterranean theatre. This arrangement was extremely convenient for SIS, which had made very little headway in North Africa. The quality of intelligence from the Stations in Tangiers and Algiers was minimal, and SIS operations in the Spanish zone were still subject to Sir Samuel Hoare's veto. More than one SIS officer in the region welcomed the arrival of OSS as an opportunity to circumvent Hoare.

The principal OSS representatives in Iberia were Robert Solborg in Lisbon, the White Russian adventurer who had written Donovan's first report on SOE. His colleague in Madrid was Donald Steele, a wealthy Chicago businessman who had fought the Russian Bolsheviks in the American Expeditionary Force in 1919. His indiscretions led to an official request for his removal from the local SIS Station. Steele was later replaced by H. Gregory Thomas, but in the long interregnum Solborg supervised all OSS operations in the peninsula. One particular plan developed by SIS involved the removal of Franco from power and his replacement by the Spanish Pretender, Don Juan, who was then in exile in Switzerland. The coup had been financed by SIS through a bank in New York, thus respecting Hoare's ban on subversive activities. The only direct British link with the plotters was Commander Hillgarth, the Naval Attaché who made contact with the conspirators on a regular basis to supply them with the code words that released their funds in New York. Although there was little prospect of a full-scale coup, the arrangement served to remind Franco's military advisers that if Spain joined the Axis the money supply would be cut.

An extension of the coup plot was a joint Anglo–American operation code-named BANANA, which involved the infiltration of a number of Republican networks into southern Spain. In July 1943 the first BANANA team was landed without incident by HMS *Tarana* near Malaga. The agents quickly established radio contact with the OSS base camp at Oujda, and a second landing to supply reinforcements and more equipment was scheduled for September.

The second BANANA operation was planned for 23 September 1943 and involved delivering a further five OSS-trained Spaniards to a reception committee on a beach near Malaga. Between July and September the BANANA network had supplied valuable information regarding local Spanish garrisons and a wealth of material relating to Spanish co-operation with the Axis. However, just as HMS *Tarana* was due to leave Algiers, the skipper received a signal from Gibraltar aborting the mission. Word had leaked to Sir Samuel Hoare of the joint Anglo–American plan and had forced the Foreign Office to cancel it. Because there was no radio schedule due, there was no time to warn the reception committee and, as a result, a group of Republicans gathered on the beach to await the SIS boat. It was later learned that a routine Spanish police patrol had spotted them and taken them in for interrogation. Under torture the group admitted the existence of the BANANA network and some 261 suspects were arrested, of whom a total of twenty-two were executed for plotting against Franco.

Although there were no political consequences for SIS, who had, after all, been indulging in such activities for years, the Americans were less understanding. The Spanish secret police, the Seguridad, recovered an impressive collection of American weaponry and communications equipment, and extracted a number of confessions from agents who had undergone training in the OSS base at Oujda. The State Department was outraged, and Colonel Solborg was recalled to Washington and relieved of his post. Two further casualties were Arthur Roseborough, the OSS representative in Algiers, and Donald Downes, the OSS liaison with the SIS Station. Although a US citizen, Downes had previously been employed by British Security Co-ordination in New York; he was transferred to other duties in the Middle East.

The BANANA disaster was written off by the Stations in Algiers and Tangiers as an acceptable loss, but OSS failed to comprehend the complex relationship between the Foreign Office and Broadway and simply blamed SIS for the withdrawal of HMS *Tarana*. SIS was unapologetic and continued to maintain a tight control on transport facilities granted to OSS by

Slocum's private navy. By the end of the summer of 1943, the OSS commanders in North Africa had begun to feel increasingly frustrated. By their agreement with SIS they were unable to launch independent operations from England. They were, therefore, limited to the Mediterranean theatre, which had proved, to date, to be completely lacking in promise. The American Ambassador in Madrid had imposed restrictions in the style of his British counterpart and the BANANA episode had reduced the availability of British vessels or aircraft. Meddling in local French politics was also fraught with danger, as the OSS chief in Algiers, Colonel William Eddy, discovered to his intense embarrassment when one of his more promising agents put his training to good use and assassinated Admiral Darlan on Christmas Eve, 1942. OSS was anxious to commence infiltrating agents into German-occupied territory, but, as a senior officer complained in August 1943, '. . . as long as the British control the only feasible means of transport into France from North Africa they control our operations there'.

The RAF's Special Duties Squadrons had taken many months to acquire their expertise and the United States Air Force had not yet developed an equivalent unit. Neither did OSS possess a private navy suitable for undertaking clandestine missions into hostile areas. Such facilities were the monopoly of the British, and they always seemed to be fully committed. SIS listened to the complaints, but invariably dismissed them on the grounds that there had been local misunderstandings, or that there was a shortage of suitable aircraft in the area. In fact, SIS had a variety of objections to OSS operating into France independently. Primarily, clandestine operations in France equalled political prestige among the local population. There was a fear that OSS's lack of political discrimination would result in it supporting some very undesirable resistance organizations. If OSS were to operate in France, then it must do so jointly with SIS so that such dangerous temptations could be curbed. SIS had neatly tied up the Belgian and Dutch intelligence organizations in written treaties that prohibited them from coming to understandings with other Allied agencies, and in particular the Americans. Unfortunately, however, France's southern flank left it vulnerable to independent operations from North Africa where OSS had been permitted a certain freedom of action. SIS reasoned that such independence should be tactfully discouraged. When Donovan confronted Menzies with all the problems he had experienced with the SIS Stations in Algiers and Tangiers, he learned two further British motives for frustrating the Americans: Menzies remarked that inexperienced OSS agents might jeopardize SIS missions, and that OSS's access to such large quantities of unvouchered funds might 'affect the recruiting market'.

As a compromise, Menzies agreed a liaison system in North Africa whereby the OSS Chiefs would discuss future plans with Trevor-Wilson, the SIS Head of Station in Algiers, and then send them to London for joint approval by OSS and Broadway. Once a plan had been accepted, it would be passed back to North Africa for implementation. As Donovan commented, somewhat optimistically:

This arrangement shall in no sense be interpreted as impairing the complete independence of either of the services concerned, but is intended to achieve what at this time seems a necessary co-ordination, in order to avoid possible confusion or duplication.

In other words, OSS had to advise SIS of all future independent operations.

SOE, of course, enjoyed its own routes into France, and it was not a party to the political intrigues apparently so enjoyed by Broadway. The local SOE mission, code-named MASSINGHAM, and headquartered in Algiers, was certainly aware of SIS misgivings about collaborating with OSS because the SIS Station raised hell every time it was learned that SOE had granted OSS any facilities. One memorable occasion was Operation PENNY FARTHING.

PENNY FARTHING was in part a manifestation of the frustration felt by virtually all the OSS Secret Intelligence staff in Algiers. By June 1943 OSS still had not achieved a single agent in the whole of France, and the Secret Intelligence Chief with responsibility for France, Henry Hyde, approached his opposite number in SOE, Colonel Douglas Dodds-Parker, for help in dropping two agents into an existing network that had previously been run by the Gaullists. Time was running out for Hyde because his two candidates were French subjects, so there was a danger that BCRA might want to reclaim the services of two such well-prepared men. Their training had lasted more than three times the length of the usual SOE course and, at the end of it, Hyde had no means of getting them to their operating area. He wanted to parachute them into France, but, unlike SOE and SIS, OSS had no Special Duties Squadron to call on. Neither did Hyde have any suitable boats. Dodds-Parker agreed to help and offered to fly the PENNY FARTHING team into France from Tempsford if Hyde could get them to England in time for the July full moon. Hyde grabbed at the chance and promised that he would personally deliver the two Frenchmen at the appointed time.

On 28 June 1943 Hyde and his two companions flew into Prestwick on an American aircraft and were promptly taken into custody by the Port Security staff. All three were wearing British uniforms, although they were not even remotely entitled to wear them, and none possessed a British passport. Hyde had neglected to give advance warning of his arrival to OSS headquarters in London, so it was some days before Hyde's credentials could be checked by MI5. He was eventually escorted to London, where he was given a cool reception from the OSS Chief in London, David Bruce.

Hyde explained the background to PENNY FARTHING and was then told that he would have to present himself at Broadway because his action had been in clear breach of the OSS undertaking not to operate independently in, or from, the United Kingdom.

Hyde was summoned to Broadway and given a dressing-down lasting ninety minutes by the combined forces of Claude Dansey and Marshall-Cornwall. Hyde defended himself by saying that PENNY FARTHING was not a London-based independent operation, but one run from Algiers. The SIS officers were unimpressed, but Hyde was allowed to deliver his two agents to SOE so that the operation could continue. When, on 16 July 1943, the two agents parachuted into France, they became the first independent OSS team to commence operations in German-occupied territory. (The first American to parachute into France was Peter J. Ortiz, an OSS officer [and former Foreign Legionnaire] who had been dropped by SOE the previous month.)

Although the PENNY FARTHING incident was a blatant (but understandable) example of OSS attempting to circumvent its agreed limits, it was by no means the only occasion OSS personnel were to undertake clandestine missions within the UK. Within weeks of the two Frenchmen making a successful landing in France, a number of OSS agents were evading the attentions of the West Sussex Constabulary in the small market town of Horsham.

The origins of this extraordinary development lay in a proposal made by Menzies to David Bruce on 29 May 1943. Bruce and the head of his Secret Intelligence Branch in London, William Maddox, had been pressing for some months for greater OSS collaboration in SIS operations in France. OSS was largely ignorant of the extent, or indeed the limit, of the SIS networks in France, but it assumed that both Cohen and Dunderdale were fully stretched. In fact, as we have seen, this was not strictly the case. The culmination of Bruce's gentle persuasion was Menzies's offer of OSS participation in an SIS French country section operation code-named SUSSEX.

SUSSEX was an extremely ambitious plan, which involved parachuting sixty two-man teams into northern France to undertake short-term intelligence gathering missions. Each team would be equipped with a portable wireless transmitter and would report military information to a special message centre, which would in turn relay the material on to the invasion forces. The teams would not require sophisticated cover since they would have specific, limited objectives, and would simply remain in position until the Allied forces overran them. The SUSSEX plan had originally been a joint Anglo–French project, but, in spite of some misgivings in Broadway, it was offered to OSS. Bruce accepted the invitation enthusiastically, and the SIS reservations seemed to vanish when Bruce threw in enough aircraft to equip two Special Duties Squadrons. A tripartite committee was formed to manage the operation, the members being Kenneth Cohen, representing SIS, Gilbert Renault, for the French BCRA, and Colonel Francis P. Miller for OSS. Miller was a Rhodes Scholar, had fought in France during the Great War and had been active in Democratic politics in Virginia. He had been one of Donovan's earliest COI recruits and, in December 1941, had joined the Secret Intelligence Branch in Washington. Almost as soon as he arrived in London, in September 1943, he was plunged into a series of conferences with SHAEF to determine which key points in France should be targeted for SUSSEX. Eventually, the SUSSEX planners drew up a list of bridges, railway junctions and other strategic centres to be kept under observation.

The SUSSEX operation got under way in November 1943, when the first of the agents attended a special training course at Milton Hall in Leicestershire. The course lasted a minimum of twelve weeks (with one week's leave towards the end) and included parachute practice, wireless operating, map reading, unarmed combat and a five-day survival exercise in hostile territory: the agents were given certain intelligence objectives in Horsham and the local police were alerted to look for enemy spies. Those agents that revealed their true identities to the police were dropped from the final part of the course.

When the SUSSEX school opened for business, there were no OSS agents on the course. OSS had agreed to supply half the 120 French-speaking agents needed, but it was unable to find enough suitable candidates. The SUSSEX agreement specified that the entire operation would be divided into OSSEX (the American teams) and BRISSEX (the SIS agents). Unfortunately, many of the first OSSEX recruits were French refugees who had fled France in 1940 and, after three years in America, had lost the sharp edge given to individuals who have experienced occupation by an enemy. They were also ignorant of many of the colloquial expressions, a handicap that might easily identify them as recent arrivals in France. Of the few who were recommended by OSS, most were rejected during a BCRA screening as politically unreliable. Time was against OSS continuing its search in America, so it enlisted the help of the OSS office in Algiers which supplied a group of candidates in December 1943. All failed the course.

In desperation OSS turned to the BCRA for help and, at the end of January 1944, Gilbert Renault began recruiting volunteers (with de Gaulle's consent) from the Free French forces in North Africa.

The first SUSSEX team to land in occupied France was an SIS 'path-finder' mission to locate suitable dropping zones for those who were to follow. Because SUSSEX was supposed to be entirely independent of any existing networks, the pathfinders, who parachuted blind into the

Châteauroux area on 8 February, were obliged to make their preparations with only minimal local help. Unfortunately, the group lost most of their equipment during the drop and, when they tried to contact their safe-houses, they learned that most had been raided by the Gestapo. In spite of this unpromising start, the pathfinder mission did succeed in locating suit-able dropping zones, but only with the help of local resistance organizations. Nevertheless, when the first wave of OSSEX and BRISSEX parties was dispatched on 9 April, almost all were met, conveyed to their prearranged posts and transmitted safe arrival signals. Of the fifty-two SUSSEX teams infiltrated between 9 April 1943 and 31 August 1944, only three OSSEX units were intercepted by the Germans. All six members were executed, including the only woman agent involved in the operation.

Once the first SUSSEX observation posts had been established, they kept a regular schedule with two wireless stations in England. The BRISSEX teams reported direct to Whaddon, but OSSEX communica-tions were kept separate. OSS's comparatively late arrival in the European theatre, and the SIS ban on independent operations, meant that OSS possessed very few trained personnel to handle the incoming signal traffic and virtually no suitable wireless facilities. Accordingly, a new signals unit was opened in March 1944, code-named VICTOR, and staffed with forty-six experienced British operators. Once VICTOR began receiving OSSEX transmissions, another problem emerged: the OSSEX recruits had been sent into the field with only minimal training on wireless procedures. This had been brought about by the last-minute scramble to find suitable OSSEX recruits. The all-important training course, therefore, had been re-duced to enable the teams to meet the deadline for the invasion. Further-more, VICTOR had only had time to conduct one full-scale exercise before becoming operational and had not had the opportunity to perfect its proce-dures. The OSSEX parties were also handicapped by the SIS security rule that agents should not transmit to their operational controls while in train-ing. These factors all combined to reduce the effectiveness of the OSSEX communications, and on D-Day itself there were only ten teams in position.

Although OSS was obliged to operate under what might be described as adverse conditions in London, there were no such restrictions placed on its activities in two important neutral cities in Europe, Berne and Stockholm.

The OSS office in Berne was headed by Allen Dulles, formerly Dono-van's representative in New York. In November 1942 he had been asked to assist David Bruce in London, but Dulles had reminded his chief that he had served in Switzerland as a diplomat during the Great War and was, therefore, better qualified to operate in Berne than London. Donovan agreed, and Dulles took up his post as Special Legal Assistant to the American Minister, Leland Harrison, on 8 November.

Dulles set up shop in an apartment building in the old quarter of Berne and placed a brass plate on the front door announcing his presence. His arrival prompted several newspaper stories concerning his special status at the American Legation, but in spite of this unorthodox approach to espionage he was welcomed by Vanden Heuvel, the SIS Head of Station, and given an extremely thorough briefing. Contrary to some other reports, the two Allied intelligence representatives enjoyed a good working relationship, although Vanden Heuvel took the precaution of planting an agent in Dulles's household to keep an eye on him. The agent was Dulles's doorman-cum-butler, who kept a careful log of his master's visitors. In February 1943 Dulles was contacted by Hans Bernd Gisevius, Canaris's link with Madame Szymanska. Initially Gisevius had neglected to mention his work for SIS, but when Vanden Heuvel's agent reported the unmistakable, shambling figure calling on Dulles late at night he arranged for OSS in London to send Dulles a routine circular warning that Gisevius was untrustworthy. Dulles ignored the warning and continued to see the Abwehr man. As their friendship grew, Gisevius confided to the American that the British had not lived up to his expectations. They were only interested in the information he could provide and had ignored his requests for help with his political testament, *To the Bitter End*.* Dulles immediately offered to supply him with a translator and a secretary, who would assist him to get his manuscript into a form in which it might be published after the war. Gisevius recommended two other Abwehr officers, Eduard von Waetjen and Theodor Struenck, to act as couriers between himself and Mary Bancroft, the typist suggested by Dulles. For the following twelve months von Waetjen (who was himself half American), and occasionally Gisevius, delivered additional pieces of manuscript to Mrs Bancroft. However, on 11 July 1944, Gisevius announced that he was returning to Berlin to take part in Hitler's imminent assassination. The attempt, which took place nine days later, failed, and Gisevius was obliged to go into hiding in the German capital. The wave of arrests that followed the attempt resulted in the arrest and execution of (among several thousand other suspects) Canaris and Struenck. Nothing more was heard of Gisevius until 17 August, when Dulles received a brief message describing the collapse of the plot and asking for help to escape.

To extract a wanted Abwehr official from Berlin was rather beyond the means of OSS, so SIS assistance was requested. Broadway's solution to the problem was to supply Gisevius with papers identifying him as a Gestapo official named Dr Hoffman. The cover was excellent because Gisevius had once been a member of the Gestapo and could, therefore, be relied upon to know exactly how to behave. The two remaining problems concerned the vital silver warrant carried by all the Gestapo, and the question of delivering

* Jonathan Cape, 1948.

it to him safely. The silver warrant (see plates 20, 22) was oval in shape and was made of an unknown alloy. The reverse face was engraved with an official number, which could be checked with one telephone call to any Gestapo office. SIS argued that few Germans would dare to challenge the authority of a Gestapo officer and that no one would be making a chemical analysis of the medallion-like identity disc. The bold plan was accepted and the necessary documentation was delivered to OSS in Berne. At the last moment it was discovered that a particular travel stamp was missing from Hoffman's forged German passport, so it was returned to London for the necessary alteration. Unfortunately, the OSS courier carrying it to London presented it to a military policeman in newly liberated Paris and was promptly arrested! Four valuable days were lost while OSS extricated its man and enabled him to continue his journey.

Gisevius eventually received his passport, medallion and identity papers on 20 January 1945 via a member of the Swiss VIKING line into Germany. The following day he bullied his way on to a train bound for Stuttgart and escaped recognition. On 23 January he flashed his Gestapo warrant at two bewildered customs officials at the frontier at Kreuzingen and crossed into Switzerland.

Soon after Gisevius had delivered the first 1,400 pages of his manuscript to Mary Bancroft in June 1943, another German approached Dulles with information, this time from the German Foreign Ministry. The story of Fritz Kolbe had really begun on 23 August 1943, when the middle-aged diplomatic courier had approached the British Military Attaché, through a friend, Dr Ernesto Kocherthaler, a Spanish Jew who happened to be resident in Switzerland. Dr Kocherthaler telephoned the British Legation and made an appointment for Kolbe to see Colonel Henry Cartwright. At the appointed hour Kolbe appeared at Cartwright's office and blurted out an extraordinary story. He explained that he was a highly placed member of the German Foreign Ministry and was at that moment an assistant to Karl Ritter, Ribbentrop's link with the Wehrmacht High Command. He offered the name of a family in South Africa who, he assured Cartwright, would vouch for him and his political views. He was, he claimed, a committed anti-Nazi. He also produced a sheaf of twenty telegrams classified as secret which, he alleged, he had purloined from his office in Berlin. He described them as mere samples of dozens more documents hidden in Berne.

Colonel Cartwright responded to the self-confessed thief by having Kolbe thrown out of his office. Once, long before the war, Cartwright had been posted in Trieste, where he had been responsible for vetting applications from Jewish emigrants wishing to settle in Palestine, and was, therefore, familiar with every kind of ploy used by the desperate. To Cartwright, Kolbe's admission that he had stolen information served to confirm the

German's untrustworthiness. It probably never occurred to him that there might be an intelligence advantage to be gained. At the very least Cartwright believed that Kolbe was an *agent provocateur* trying to stir up trouble for the Legation.

Kolbe was mystified by his reception and, on the same day, confided in a German refugee who happened to be acquainted with Dulles. He recommended that Kolbe pay Dulles a visit the following day. Dulles gave Kolbe a cautious welcome, but his caution evaporated when he examined Kolbe's collection of 183 'flimsy' file copies of what appeared to be original German Foreign Office telegrams. Kolbe promised to return with more when he got an opportunity, and promptly disappeared.

Dulles informed a sceptical Vanden Heuvel about his treasure trove and then signalled Washington. One major problem was the volume of material Kolbe had delivered. If he was an *agent provocateur*, as the British Station believed, there were considerable hazards in transmitting the full texts to Washington or London. The Germans might intercept the radio traffic and, already knowing the contents of the message, might easily break the American diplomatic code. Dulles, therefore, decided to wait until he had an opportunity to send it all via a reliable courier. In the meantime, he dubbed Kolbe GEORGE WOOD and asked Vanden Heuvel to examine the telegrams.

Kolbe reappeared in Berne on 7 October 1943 and produced some seventy-six telegrams on 200 separate flimsies, and it was this second batch of information that served to confirm Kolbe's *bona fides*. In the following sixteen months Kolbe made three further visits to Dulles's office and delivered more than 1,600 classified documents. For added security, each consignment was divided into two: one half was sent to Washington, the other was delivered to Richard Arnold-Baker, the Section V representative at the Berne Station, who had it delivered by courier to Broadway. After the war the GEORGE WOOD source was described (by James Angleton, Head of X-2 Italy) as 'one of the best secret agents any intelligence service ever had'. To its credit OSS was extremely circumspect in distributing the GEORGE WOOD material, and Kolbe never came under suspicon in Berlin. Indeed, in April 1945, Karl Ritter selected his trusted aide to escort his mistress, a beautiful opera singer, to Bavaria, away from the advancing Russian forces. Once Kolbe had delivered her to Ottobeuren, he continued his journey south and slipped over the border near Lake Constance into Switzerland.

After the war Kolbe gave evidence for the prosecution at the Nuremberg trials, as did Hans Bernd Gisevius. Kolbe and Gisevius emigrated to America. Kolbe opened a business with financial help from OSS, but was defrauded by his partner. He subsequently moved back to Germany and opened a shop selling power-saws. Gisevius also retired to Germany to concentrate on his writing.

The OSS office in Berne was unquestionably the most successful at recruiting agents, although the Stockholm representative, Bruce Hopper, a former Professor of Government at Harvard, also succeeded in obtaining a valuable source. Code-named RED, the agent was Eric Ericson, a Swedish oil trader who had been blacklisted earlier in the war for trading with the enemy. Ericson volunteered his services to OSS while on a visit to Washington; later, he offered the Germans the opportunity to build a synthetic oil plant in neutral Sweden. Believing Ericson to be a Nazi sympathizer, the Germans invited him on a guided tour of all the Reich's synthetic oil plants. The tour, in October 1944, lasted a week and provided valuable information for both OSS and SIS.

The last OSS office to be opened in a neutral country was Lanning Macfarland's mission to Turkey, which commenced business early in May 1943. It was to prove a disastrous venture.

Macfarland was a banker from the Midwest and, like many of the first COI recruits, active in American politics. Neither he nor his two principal lieutenants, Archibald Coleman (a correspondent for the *Saturday Evening Post*) and Jerome Sperling, an archaeologist, had any experience in intelligence operations. Nevertheless, somewhat belatedly, the trio entered the intelligence minefield of Istanbul. One of their first recruits was a Czech engineer, code-named DOGWOOD, who had previously enjoyed links with virtually every European intelligence service, including SIS. This was not much of a recommendation for him, but, as we have seen, Istanbul had developed into a major centre of espionage and the loyalty of agents had become a highly negotiable commodity, generally available to the highest bidder.

The advantage to OSS of dealing with DOGWOOD was that he came 'pre-packaged' with a particularly well-organized network that stretched into Austria and Hungary. Code-named CEREUS, the network boasted some impressive agents. They included an Austrian lawyer, Kurt Grimm; the Managing Director of the Semperit Rubber Company, Franz Josef Messner (code-named OYSTERS); a Dr Kraus, the General Manager of the Siemens radio factory in Austria; Professor Alexander Rustow (code-named MAGNOLIA), an economist of some standing; and Heinrich Maier (code-named CASSIA), a leftist priest who was a senior member of an Austrian resistance movement known as the Secret Committee of Fourteen.

Between June 1943 and February 1944 CEREUS provided no less than 730 messages from some fifty-three sub-agents. All reported to DOGWOOD who, in turn, passed the information on to his principal OSS case officer, Archibald Coleman. This arrangement was far from ideal, because neither Coleman nor his superiors knew the identities of any of the CEREUS agents. They were, therefore, unable to check them against the comprehensive dossiers held by the Section V registry at the SIS Station in Istanbul. Elsewhere in the world the Section V files had achieved recognition, showing that knowledge of identity was a vital weapon against enemy penetration. ISOS intercepts invariably gave advance warning of such penetration attempts, if identities were known, but Gibson's Station had no control over his American allies. The X-2 representative in Istanbul, Frank Wisner, did not arrive on the scene until October 1943. When he eventually learned of OSS's dependence on DOGWOOD, he demanded to know more about CEREUS and its sources. DOGWOOD refused to name his agents and Macfarland supported him. Wisner was obliged to back down.

CEREUS continued to provide adequate intelligence until September 1943, when the Hungarian Military Attaché, Colonel Otto Hatz, contacted DOGWOOD and was enrolled in the network as TRILLIUM. Although TRILLIUM was regarded as an extremely suspicious character and a known double agent, his 'bait' was attractive. He proposed a plan, code-named SPARROW, which would bring about Hungary's withdrawal from the Axis. In addition, TRILLIUM suggested that the Hungarian intelligence service in Europe might be placed at the disposal of the Americans. SIS was not privy to the details of SPARROW and, if consulted, would have denounced TRILLIUM as a fully paid-up Sicherheitsdienst agent. It might also have pointed out that the Hungarians had a strange way of showing their intention to co-operate: two SOE officers had recently disappeared without trace in Hungary. As the CEREUS material filtered through to Broadway, it was dismissed as 'undependable and much of it planted'. OSS security deteriorated so badly in the two months following TRILLIUM's recruitment that, in May 1944, Gibson convened a conference of all the British intelligence organizations operating in the region and decreed that there should be only minimal contact with OSS personnel in the future.

When DOGWOOD first accepted TRILLIUM, it appeared that he was going to treat the Hungarian with caution; but DOGWOOD's vanity had got the better of him, with the result that he overestimated his own ability to keep his new recruit at arm's length. The less generous explanation is that the wily Military Attaché compromised all the CEREUS network and then recruited DOGWOOD himself. Such is a classic double-agent tactic. Either way, the results were the same. On 19 March 1944 German forces occupied Hungary. Instead of SPARROW, exactly the reverse had happened. Even worse, the entire CEREUS network was rounded up, tortured and executed.

The CEREUS disaster was a major setback for OSS because the greater part of its Secret Intelligence effort in Europe had been channelled through Istanbul. One possible explanation was German inspection of captured

Hungarian intelligence records. This was entirely plausible, but the older hands, including the local SIS Station, claimed to recognize CEREUS for what it really was ... a hugely successful deception operation. X-2, in the person of Irving Sherman, was called in to conduct a post-mortem, and a bitter indictment of OSS methods in Istanbul resulted. The OSS officers responsible for supervising DOGWOOD (who conveniently disappeared) were 'directed in the first instance by mediocrities'. The organization was 'unwisely conceived and badly staffed'. Not even the X-2 representative, Frank Wisner, escaped without criticism. Sherman discovered that Wisner's chauffeur was in the pay of the Turkish secret police. Macfarland's conduct was roundly condemned, and his chauffeur was found to be a Russian agent. He was replaced in June 1944. To complicate matters further, X-2 failed to trace Colonel Hatz, who also disappeared, but it did turn up some evidence which suggested that he might have been serving the Russians rather than the Germans. One of the objects of CEREUS had been to provide a credible Social Democratic and anti-Communist leadership for the post-war era. The elimination of the network left the Communist resistance to operate without any significant competition.

One welcome consequence of the DOGWOOD fiasco was a resumption of good relations between OSS and Gibson's Station. A copy of Sherman's damning report was circulated and the wound was cleansed. OSS agreed to limit future intelligence gathering activities in Istanbul to participation in a joint debriefing board designed to extract information from travellers recently returned from German-occupied territory. It also led to a much greater exchange of information between Wisner's X-2 and the local Section V office.*

In spite of the political tensions which occasionally strained SIS/OSS relations, individual officers of both organizations developed strong bonds. This was especially true in London, where large numbers of OSS personnel had undergone various degrees of indoctrination into the British intelligence community. One direct result of this was to obtain the help, for the first time, of the Irish military intelligence department, G-2. Before 1944 G-2 had consistently refused to co-operated with MI5's Irish Section, B11, headed by Guy Liddell's younger brother, Cecil. But, as has been previously explained, when Donovan had come over in March 1941, he had arranged to send a liaison officer to Dublin. The Head of G-2, Colonel Dan Bryan, consented to take the OSS officer, Edward Lawler, into his confidence on condition that Lawler did not pass information directly to MI5. Lawler abided by the letter of the pact. G-2's intelligence was passed to Hubert Will of X-2, who was then able to reassure Cecil Liddell that the

---

* Wisner later became a senior CIA officer and was appointed Station Chief in London in 1959. He resigned from the Agency in 1962 after a breakdown and committed suicide in 1965.

Irish had indeed taken all the necessary precautions to control German espionage in Eire.

In January 1944 the Special Operations Branch of OSS had amalgamated with SOE and formed a Special Forces Headquarters. A month later MI5 made a formal agreement with X-2 and this led to further development: the creation of Special Counter-Intelligence (SCI) units composed of American and British officers.

The SCIs were spawned by ISOS references to various stay-behind networks in France prepared by the Germans in anticipation of a successful Allied invasion. The ISOS material gave considerable clues as to the identity and locations of the agents, but instant arrests might easily alert the Germans to the fact that their codes had been broken. The alternative was to scoop up each network and allow it to continue under control, in a continental version of the double-cross system. Once the Allied military commanders had given their consent to the idea, it only remained to transfer the necessary number of experienced case officers from MI5 and SIS to run the intercepted agents. Unfortunately, it was not quite as simple as that. The French, for example, insisted on being involved in the conduct of any French double agent. This was not an unreasonable request, given that MI5 and SIS were proposing to operate in France, but it was suspected that the BCRA's demand might be connected with a desire to administer some retribution after the agents had outlived their usefulness. The fact that many of the agents would be found in American combat sectors demonstrated the necessity of OSS involvement.

Under normal circumstances responsibility for intercepting enemy agents near the front would have fallen to the British Field Security Police and the American Counter-Intelligence Corps. However, owing to the demands of strict security, neither organization had been allowed to learn of the work of the Twenty Committee nor been indoctrinated into the ISOS secret. The aim of the SCIs was twofold: the elimination of all enemy intelligence assets and the manipulation of those allowed to survive. Late in April 1944, the first joint SCI units were given the opportunity to identify and turn opposition agents during a full-scale exercise held in Horsham, Sussex. The SCI's performance at sniffing out SOE wireless operators was impressive, but the experience led to an important communications gap between the various Allied intelligence services. This was subsequently bridged by the introduction of an SCI War Room, which monitored the work of the field units and distributed up-to-date progress reports. Liaison officers from MI5 and BCRA attended the SCI War Room to ensure its co-operation.

Three days after D-Day an SCI unit, complete with its own mobile signals section, was landed on OMAHA beach in Normandy. Two days later a second SCI unit landed in the south of France near St Tropez and, as the invasion forces gained ground in the north, a further SCI unit, designated the 62nd SCI, was sent in early in July 1944. The first agent to be located was a Portuguese dockyard clerk living in Cherbourg. When the 31st SCI unit arrested him, he wasted no time in volunteering a confession. Apparently, he had worked for the Norddeutsche Lloyd shipping line before the war and had agreed to spy in a stay-behind network when the Germans abandoned Cherbourg. According to ISOS he was known as EIKENS, and his wireless messages were to be received by the Abwehr in Wiesbaden and Stuttgart. The SCI case officers recruited EIKENS and code-named him DRAGOMAN, which fitted his new occupation. He was given notional employment as an interpreter in the US Army's Port Office.

DRAGOMAN's case officers began meeting his radio schedules on 13 July, but it was not for a further twelve days that they made contact with his Abwehr controllers. DRAGOMAN was accepted as completely genuine by the Abwehr and continued to meet his schedules until the end of the war. In all, he transmitted more than 200 separate messages.

On 25 August 1944 the first SCI units entered Paris and began mopping up the networks identified by ISOS. One of the SCI's principal targets was the Abwehr headquarters in the Hotel Lutetia, a familiar address to all those in Section V, but many of the records had been removed or destroyed before Paris could be liberated. Fortunately, an Abwehr NCO, who was later code-named JIGGER, volunteered his services to the SCI and described many of the Abwehr's stay-behind sabotage networks. He also accompanied SCI officers to various arms dumps, which had been left to equip these networks, and supplied several batches of files missing from the Hotel Lutetia. His help was so valuable that the Abwehr later tried to launch a mission to assassinate him.

Another important volunteer was KEEL, a French SD agent who had a long history of collaboration. He gave himself up on 28 August, but just a month later he was lynched by a French revenge squad. However, instead of terminating KEEL, the SCI unit concerned pretended that he had hurt his wrist in an accident (to explain the change in his Morse technique) and maintained contact with the Abwehr for a further seven months.

By the end of September 1944 the SCI units based in Paris were running six Abwehr wireless sets and were doing so with the benefit of knowledge acquired from ISOS, captured enemy documents and the statements of captured Abwehr officials who had been shipped back to England for interrogation at MI5's Camp 020.

At about the same time that the SCIs were being reorganized in Paris, DRAGOMAN was contacted by another German agent, code-named DESIRE. He was promptly arrested, but he proved too unreliable to turn. Nevertheless, he unwittingly compromised a third agent, code-named

SKULL, who was arrested on 26 August and transferred to Camp 020. SKULL was to prove one of the most important double agents of the war, and one of seven agents run from Le Havre by an energetic Abwehr officer, Friedrich Kaulen. Kaulen was well known to ISOS, but as soon as SKULL was placed in custody Kaulen's other agents began to be arrested and turned. By mid-December only two remained at liberty, the others having agreed to supply their case officer with information specially prepared by the SCIs.

SKULL himself resumed contact with the Abwehr on 27 November and was appointed Kaulen's paymaster in northern France. Ironically, one of the first of SKULL's payments was to DRAGOMAN in Cherbourg, an act that served to convince his 31st SCI masters that the Germans had accepted him completely. He was so highly regarded by the Abwehr that an elaborate operation, TRIPOD, was planned by the SCI to trap Kaulen. The idea was to lure the German case officer to Bordeaux, which was still in enemy hands, and then ambush him at a prearranged rendezvous. If the operation was successful, the 31st SCI would spread the news of the deaths of both Kaulen and SKULL. Kaulen agreed to attend the rendezvous with SKULL on the banks of the Gironde and, on 6 April 1945, accompanied his agent into a nearby field which was filled with French and American soldiers. Unfortunately, a torch was lit at the wrong moment and an American NCO panicked. In the ensuing chaos Kaulen was shot dead and SKULL was half-strangled. The only consolation that could be obtained from TRIPOD was the fact that every one of the agents referred to in the documents found on Kaulen's body was already operating under Allied control.

Not all the agents run by the SCI units were members of stay-behind networks. On 26 October 1944 two Frenchmen were parachuted into liberated territory near Verdun to report on Allied troop movements. Both men were quickly captured by the French authorities and handed over to the American Counter-Intelligence Corps. They interrogated them and alerted the local SCI unit, which decided to make use of the German wireless set. The radio operator, code-named WITCH, seemed anxious to co-operate and offered to report that his less compliant companion had been killed in the drop. Eventually, on 4 November, WITCH received an acknowledgement signal from his controller and became the first double agent to operate in north-east France. WITCH's mission had only had short-term objectives, so the SCI unit concentrated on the German routes across the front lines. WITCH asked for advice on which route to choose and the Allied authorities took the appropriate action to improve security in those sectors. One recommended route, via St Avold, resulted in a notional 'narrow escape' for WITCH, who transmitted a bitter complaint to his controller. The Germans abandoned the idea of evacuating WITCH and instead instructed him to make for Metz. This itself was useful intelligence to the SCI unit, which concluded, correctly, that this indicated that there were no other enemy agents in the area. WITCH was later rewarded with an Iron Cross for his valuable espionage and was sent several couriers, all of whom fell into the hands of the SCI. WITCH maintained his radio schedules until 29 April 1945, when his controllers signed off for the last time. When his controllers were later traced and interrogated, they steadfastly protected WITCH; evidently, they had never suspected that he had been operated by the Allies.

The SCI units based in France, Belgium and Holland achieved a success on a similar scale to that of the Twenty Committee in London. Through a combination of strategic deception and overall control of the enemy's networks, the Allied forces were able to mislead the German commanders about Allied intentions and provide the intelligence bureaucrats with a wealth of clues concerning the strengths of Allied military units. As the Germans gradually withdrew across the Rhine, and relied upon landline communications (in contrast to their previously heavy use of wireless signals), the SCIs grew in importance. The ISOS summaries were reduced in number and the intelligence war took on more of the characteristics of the relatively early, less sophisticated days of spring 1940, when everything seemed to depend on the human factor ... the conduct and credibility of individual human agents.

During the last few months of the war the political differences between OSS and SIS became more apparent. OSS, for example, became increasingly determined to infiltrate short-term teams of agents into Nazi-occupied territory. It was prepared to use volunteers from virtually any source and saw its agents as a means of securing influence in the area. SIS, on the other hand, took an entirely different view and, on occasion, deliberately obstructed OSS. One contentious decree from Broadway forbade OSS from infiltrating non-approved leftist agents into Germany along routes established and serviced by MI9. The suspicion that OSS was abusing this edict led to the SIS Station in Stockholm having to vet individual OSS agents before they were allowed to join one of the more safe routes into Northern Germany. Broadway justified its attitude by avoiding the political issue and repeating the claim that even the reduced volume of ISOS and ULTRA material made the human element too risky.

Certainly, in retrospect, it appears that many leftist organizations used OSS as a conduit to post-war political office. One talent-spotter eagerly recruited by the OSS Labor Office, which concentrated on finding help from within anti-Nazi union movements, was Professor Jurgen Kuczynski, an Oxford economist and self-confessed Soviet agent. He was responsible for recommending candidates to OSS, and many of his agents were infiltrated into Germany during the last days of the war. Once established, they possessed the best possible credentials to influence the post-war Allied administration.

The SCI effort in north-west Europe was matched by that in Italy, where OSS took the initiative and opened major offices in Bari and Rome. For its part ISLD took a less active role, but limited its activities to a new joint SIS/SOE base in Bari for operations into the Balkans. The Rome Station, which was scheduled to be opened by Cuthbert Bowlby and George Young after the Anzio landings in January 1944, had to be delayed, and the newly appointed Section V representative, Kenneth Benton (from the Madrid Station), took up residence in Ryder Street instead of the British Embassy in Rome.

The initial failure of the Anzio beachhead reduced SIS's opportunity to run operations in Italy. In any event, its reliance on ISOS and ULTRA had gradually reduced its involvement in the more dangerous business of recruiting agents and sending them into enemy territory. The interception of German and Italian signals made such risky adventures unnecessary. That is not to say, of course, that no SIS personnel indulged in such activities, although officers with any knowledge of ULTRA or ISOS were under strict orders not to risk capture by straying into combat areas. These limitations also applied to OSS, although Donovan himself visited the front on no less than four occasions. He did so in Sicily, Anzio, UTAH beach in Normandy (on 7 June 1944) and in Burma. He was never disciplined for what the OSS *War Report** called 'clearly outrageous' breaches and SIS never learned of the incidents.

If Menzies had discovered that Donovan had deliberately placed himself in a position where he might have been captured by the enemy, there might have been a major inter-Allied row. The only serious threat to the security of ISOS took place towards the end of September 1944 when an X-2 officer, Major Maxwell Papurt, was captured near the front in Luxembourg. Papurt was one of Donovan's earliest X-2 recruits and had been fully indoctrinated into ISOS. Fortunately, Papurt was able to conceal the fact that he was an OSS officer and was placed in a prisoner-of-war camp near Limburg. He was killed some two months after his capture during an Allied air raid.

In spite of the many hiccups in the 'special relationship', OSS and SIS ended the war the best of friends. This is demonstrated by the number of decorations OSS lavished on both its own personnel and that of SIS. Even Menzies was awarded the US Legion of Merit. 831 OSS personnel shared between them 2,005 decorations for gallantry and meritorious service. In contrast, the British authorities awarded just ten medals - one DSO, three MCs, three MMs and three OBEs - to members of OSS. Most SIS officers who came into contact with OSS received recognition: Walter Bell received

* Volume II, p. ix.

the Medal of Freedom; Kenneth Cohen, Harold Gibson and Biffy Dunderdale the Legion of Merit; Stephenson (who was knighted by George VI in 1945) received the Medal of Merit, and Dick Ellis the Legion of Merit. Claude Dansey, who had received his knighthood with Menzies in 1943, was excluded from these honours. His Deputy Director (Army), General Sir James Marshall-Cornwall, was made a Commander of the Legion of Merit.

15

Soviet Penetration

Once Paris had been liberated by the Allies, the intelligence war changed out of all recognition. Pressure on the Iberian Stations was reduced dramatically and the supposedly neutral regimes that had been hostile to SIS began to offer unofficial assistance. As the Allies moved eastwards, Special Counter-Intelligence personnel attached to the 21st Army Group re-established a presence in Brussels, The Hague and Copenhagen, where Leslie Mitchell reopened a full Station. Some of the more far-flung (and less popular) Stations, such as Freetown (which was surrounded by French West Africa) and Mozambique, were closed down and their personnel transferred to Europe.

The Head of Station in Lorenço Marques was Malcolm Muggeridge, who bridged the gap in the chain of British Security Intelligence Middle East/SIS representatives which stretched from Cairo to South Africa. Muggeridge's one-man Station was matched by an Abwehr officer, Leopold Wertz, who operated under consular cover, and the head of the local Italian SIM organization, a journalist named Campini. In the autumn of 1944 Muggeridge was transferred to Paris and the Portuguese, after some encouragement from the Americans, expelled Wertz and most of his staff. Graham Greene, meanwhile, was coping with French intrigues from his Station in Freetown. He was subsequently recalled to Ryder Street, where he took over responsibility for Section V's Portuguese sub-section.

There were changes too in the Middle East. At the end of 1943 John Teague took over the Inter-Services Liaison Department and Michael Ionides replaced Rodney Dennys as the local Section V representative. John Codrington, who had struggled unsuccessfully to liaise with Jacques Soustelle and keep apart the Vichy and Gaullist intelligence services in Algiers, was recalled to London and ended the war as a labourer in a Watney's brewery. Cuthbert Bowlby, who had by D-Day moved to Algiers, travelled to Italy to supervise the opening of a temporary Station in Bari. (Bowlby remained in SIS until 1960, when he retired as Director of Personnel.)

Bari became the focus of both SIS's and SOE's operations into Yugoslavia and Albania. The first major British Military Mission into Yugoslavia took place on 23 May 1943, when SIS and SOE flew a combined team to Tito's headquarters. The operation, code-named TYPICAL, consisted of (Sir) William Deakin from SOE and Bill Stuart, ISLD's resident Serbo-Croat linguist. Accompanying Stuart was a radio operator and a tough marine sergeant, John Campbell, who was to act as bodyguard. The radio operator was Peretz Rosenberg, a German Jew who had been recruited into ISLD from the Jewish Agency in Cairo. The team successfully linked up with the partisans but, on 9 June, Stuart was killed during a German air raid on Tito's headquarters. ISLD was unable to supply a replacement liaison officer until the end of August 1943, when Kenneth Syers arrived by parachute. The support given to Tito by SIS and SOE was to prove both controversial and decisive, but it ensured that the British Government maintained excellent relations with the partisan leader after he had taken power. When Tito took office in Belgrade, Deakin was appointed First Secretary at the British Embassy, a post he held for two years.

In territory 'liberated' by the Soviets, SIS encountered many difficulties in reopening old Stations. For example, in September 1944 the Russians ordered both the American and British Military Missions out of Bulgaria on pain of immediate imprisonment. Eventually, the Americans were allowed to return to Sofia, but the British were not. The local OSS X-2 man, Frank Wisner, was therefore the sole Allied representative from either Service. SIS also experienced problems in Romania, when an SIS Station was established there in October 1944. Even Harold Gibson received a frosty welcome when he returned to take up his old post in Prague. His wartime Station, Istanbul, was turned over to Cyril Machray.

Surprisingly, SIS made little attempt during the latter part of the war to infiltrate agents into Germany or Austria. This apparently casual attitude towards the enemy's home territory was something of a surprise for the Americans who had believed that the British possessed extensive networks in the Greater Reich. In fact, this was not the case and, as Kermit Roosevelt later commented, 'it is not believed that SIS had any W/T-equipped agent' in Austria in 1944.* The last British source was an SOE agent in Austria, who had been captured in November 1944. When the Americans decided to rectify the situation and proposed schemes to send OSS agents into Germany, SIS invariably turned them down. When the Americans tried an alternative approach and asked the Dutch for help, they too denied them access to their already-established resistance networks. SIS's attitude is simply explained by its profitable exploitation of the ULTRA material. SIS argued that it was pointless to risk the lives of agents when the interception of enemy signals was yielding a huge volume of operational intelligence. Furthermore, it claimed that experience had taught it that all good

* *War Report*, Volume II, p. 315.

rings depended to some degree on a local resistance organization and, after 20 July 1944, Hitler had eliminated such opposition groups as were left in Germany. With ULTRA providing high-grade intelligence, there was little necessity for agents to gather information, and aerial bombardment could take care of sabotage targets. SIS justified this approach by pointing out that civilian casualties among an enemy population were much more acceptable than those sustained in an occupied territory.

A review of the achievements of SIS's networks before D-Day makes brief reading. Of the three major SIS rings in occupied France, only one, JADE/AMICOL, survived beyond June 1944. The INTERALLIE network collapsed in November 1941 and ALLIANCE had largely been wound up in September 1943. In terms of scientific intelligence, the major contribution was probably made by the Abwehr in the Oslo Report. SOE can also claim credit for amassing a wealth of technical information, especially in connection with the V1 and V2 rockets, which was eventually passed on to Broadway. It will be recalled that Cecil Gledhill's early agent reports concerning Peenemünde were ignored by his 'G' officer. Outside Europe, as we have seen, agent reports were considered to be so unreliable that SIS concentrated on strategic deception and the management of double agents. Virtually the only direct contact with human sources inside Germany came from Gisevius and Canaris through Madame Szymanska, and Fritz Kolbe.

If SIS was not concentrating its effort on penetrating Germany, the question remains then, what exactly was it doing during the latter part of the war? It was changing direction and protecting its most valued source, GCHQ. The change in direction merely reflected the political map in Europe. The chief link between Broadway and the Foreign Office during the summer of 1943 was (Sir) Patrick Reilly. Late in September 1943 he was sent to Algiers, and Robert Cecil replaced him. It was the following summer that Menzies, consulting with his Vice-Chief, Valentine Vivian, and his Principal Staff Officer, Christopher Arnold-Forster, gave his approval to the creation of a new section, designated Section IX, to deal with Soviet espionage and subversion. Previously Section IX had been the cipher section under Colonel Jefferys, but his unit was amalgamated with the GCHQ sub-section that had been responsible for providing Broadway with one-time pads and other coding paraphernalia.

The creation of Section IX marked a significant turning-point for SIS. It was also a recognition that after the liberation of Western Europe, there might well be a prolonged struggle for the liberation of countries occupied by Soviet forces. By the end of 1944 the list was depressingly extensive: Lithuania, Latvia and Estonia had all but disappeared; Poland, Hungary, Bulgaria, Romania, Czechoslovakia and Albania were to fall into the hands of Soviet-backed Communist regimes. Section IX was planned to be the forerunner of a post-war Section V, designed to combat Russian espionage. Since the Security Service possessed a wealth of anti-Soviet talent, a senior MI5 officer, Jack Curry, was seconded to Broadway to head the Section. His SIS deputy was Harry Steptoe, SIS's expert on the Far East. Steptoe had been SIS's sole pre-war representative in the Far East and had endured many hardships during the course of his long service. He was eventually captured by the Japanese in Shanghai and was repatriated with other Allied diplomats through Lorenço Marques. Menzies's original intention had been to combine Section IX with Section V's facilities and expertise, once Germany had been defeated. Naturally this would have meant Felix Cowgill taking control, but such a development did not entirely suit everyone.

Cowgill's success at establishing Section V was recognized by many, but several of his colleagues resented his tough internal security policy. Section V had been at the forefront of SIS's struggle against the Abwehr and had protected ISOS from discovery. Its manipulation of ISOS over a four-year period was unparalleled; by the end of the war Section V had identified a total of 3,575 enemy agents, of whom 675 were arrested. Ten were subsequently released and thirty were executed. The remainder stayed in custody to await the post-war de-Nazification process. ISOS had also provided a complete enemy order of battle and had saved SIS's reputation with the Prime Minister and Whitehall. If SIS had not been able to rely on ISOS summaries, any number of inaccurate agent reports might have been believed and acted upon. In retrospect, it must be accepted that SIS's networks in enemy territory were of limited value and on occasion, as happened in Holland, were actually counter-productive. Cowgill had known SIS before the advent of ISOS and was, therefore, sharply critical of those who, in his view, jeopardized the motherlode by poor security. His preoccupation with security led to a number of internal rows and irritated members of both MI5 and the Radio Security Service. Cowgill took the view that ISOS should never, under any circumstances, be compromised. Others, including Hugh Trevor-Roper, believed that there were advantages to be gained from making more adventurous use of its information. Menzies often found himself arbitrating between Cowgill (advocating the continued protection of ISOS) and Vivian (presenting complaints of non-co-operation from MI5). When the question arose of a suitable personality to lead Section IX after Curry's retirement, several senior officers voiced reservations about Cowgill's political judgement. He was, they claimed, an intelligence bureaucrat with an excellent record, but not a suitable candidate for a supremely sensitive post-war job. Instead, on Vivian's recommendation, the job went to Kim Philby, one of Section V's brightest recruits.

In the light of Philby's (occasionally inaccurate) autobiography *My Silent War*,* it is apparent that Philby himself was instrumental in persuading

* MacGibbon and Kee, 1968.

Vivian to abandon Cowgill, whom he refers to as 'a prickly obstacle in the course laid down for me'. Cowgill retired from Broadway soon afterwards and was appointed to a senior post with the British military government in Germany. Tim Milne replaced Philby in the Iberian sub-section of Section V and, when Curry retired at the latter end of 1944, Philby succeeded him. Section IX exactly mirrored Section V's structure, with geographical sub-sections. Philby also recruited two important newcomers to SIS: Jane Archer, formerly MI5's expert on Soviet espionage, and Robert Carew-Hunt, an acknowledged authority on the Comintern who later wrote *The Theory and Practice of Communism*.* Carew-Hunt had previously headed, with Oliver Miller, Section V's sub-section dealing with North and South America.

Philby's new seniority also enabled him to influence SIS's long-term future. In 1945 the Cabinet appointed Sir Findlater Stewart to advise on Britain's requirements for covert services in peace, and he took evidence from the Joint Intelligence Committee's sub-committee which was then busy reorganizing SIS and dismantling SOE. The four old Production Sections were replaced by a system of Regional Controllers. Kenneth Cohen and Vanden Heuvel became Controllers, Central Europe, with three further area controllers: John Munn, the Controller Eastern Area (running Germany, Switzerland and Austria); Harry Carr, the Controller Northern Area (known simply as CNA); and Simon Gallienne, the Controller Western Area. In addition, in May 1945 British Security Co-ordination was closed down and Stephenson's deputy, Dick Ellis, was sent to Singapore to re-organize Combined Intelligence Far East. Liaison with the Americans, which had previously centred on BSC's headquarters in New York, was placed in the hands of a small SIS Station attached to the Washington Embassy and headed by Peter Dwyer, formerly the Head of Station in Panama. The individual SIS sections were renamed Requirement Sections, with R1 to R7 conforming to the old structure. R8 became SIS's liaison with GCHQ and R9 took responsibility for scientific intelligence.

SIS's resumption of its pre-war anti-Soviet posture can largely be said to date from the creation of Section IX, but the history of SIS's wartime operations cannot be described as complete until the matter of Soviet penetration of the organization is dealt with. Whilst reading this account, it must be remembered that Soviet Russia and Nazi Germany were allies from 1939 until 1941.

The first evidence of hostile penetration of SIS came in a remarkable captured German document entitled *Informationsheft Grossbritannien*, which was evidently prepared during 1940 for the then imminent invasion of England. The document contained two items of specific interest for SIS.

* Geoffrey Bles, 1950.

One was a general arrest list, the *Sonderfahndungsliste Grossbritannien*; the second was an eleven-page chapter entitled *Der Britische Nachrichtendienst*. A translation of part of this latter document is reproduced in the Appendix.

The arrest list was apparently designed to be used as a reference manual by the Gestapo when they took control of England. Each of 116 closely printed pages lists the names, addresses and personal details of an average of thirty individuals. Although many of the entries relate to prominent anti-Nazi politicians, journalists and others who might have been expected to be arrested by the Gestapo, an extraordinarily large number identify SIS staff and their agents. One, numbered 50 and typical of many, describes Christopher Rhodes, a junior SIS officer attached to The Hague Station at the time of the Venlo incident:

Rhodes, Christopher, 30.4.14 Gosport/England, brit. Offiz. d. Pass-Control-Office, zuletzt: Den Haag, vermutl. England (Taterkreis: Stevens/Best) RSHA IV E 4

For Acton Burnell (No. 264), the pre-war Head of Station in Geneva, the entry even listed the Swiss registration number of his car and one of his aliases:

Burnell, Albert Ernest Acton, 18.9.89 London. Brit. Cpt. Deckn: Brandon, zuletzt Genf, vermutl. England Kraftw. GE 21351 GB, RSHA IV E 4.

As for Stewart Menzies, whose name remained generally unknown from the public until 1962, when H. Montgomery Hyde disclosed it in his biography of Sir William Stephenson,* the document states that 'according to Stevens' Admiral Sinclair had been succeeded by 'Colonel Stuart Menzies (pronounced Mengis) a Scot, on November 4, 1939'. The summary of the British Secret Service identifies Broadway Buildings as the headquarters and even reproduces the passport photographs of many of its principal officers. A brief explanation of the Z-network and its staff (including Dansey and Cohen) is also featured along with some of its business covers. As well as accurately giving the SIS order of battle, it also states on which floors particular sections were located. Thus Section III, the naval section, is mentioned as being on the sixth floor and headed by Captain Russell.

This appalling breach of SIS security was the subject of a prolonged investigation early in 1945, and there were certainly plenty of clues in the text to indicate the source of the leak. The names of Captain Best and Major Stevens appear more than forty times. When describing Colonel Gambier-Parry's Section VIII (communications), the anonymous editor comments: 'Stevens says ... most of the staff have moved to Bletchley.' Best and Stevens themselves survived the war and, in April 1945, were found in Niederdorf, a small village in the German Tyrol, along with a group of other hostages from Dachau and Colditz known as the *Prominente*.† Best

* *The Quiet Canadian* (Hamish Hamilton, 1962).
† Among them was Gisevius's sister, Anneliese.

and Stevens were repatriated to England, where they underwent separate interrogation at the hands of MI5. Both admitted confirming various aspects of SIS's internal structure, but each insisted that he had done no more. SIS concluded that one had been skilfully played off against the other after their kidnapping in November 1939. No further action was taken against either man, although neither was offered further employment in SIS.

Close analysis of both captured documents discloses some interesting details. Fred Winterbotham is mentioned as the head of SIS's air section, and his deputy is named as Adams. This is particularly illuminating since Squadron-Leader Perkins took over from Adams in 1938. In other words, the German source for this particular item can definitely be said to be pre-war, and certainly pre-dates Venlo. Perkins's name does not appear, and there are some other curious omissions. There are entries for Dunderdale (Paris Station), Foley (Berlin), O'Leary (Copenhagen), Gibson (Prague), Campbell (Athens), Shelley (Warsaw), Nicholson (Riga) and Giffey (Tallinn); virtually every SIS officer that had served at the Berlin Station is listed, as one might expect, yet there is only a reference to one Ellis, a British journalist. The brief entry, numbered 36 on page 52, reads: 'Ellis, brit. Journalist, RSHA IV E 4'.

This seems curious since Dick Ellis was officially posted to Frank Foley's Station on 24 October 1924 as Assistant Passport Control Officer with the rank of temporary Vice-Consul. He remained on Foley's staff for the following fourteen years, although he undertook missions all over Europe during this period. The fact that the Abwehr appeared to have listed him as a journalist and failed to spot him as an SIS officer was later to prove significant.

Best and Stevens were regarded as being the most important sources for the opposition until Hermann Giskes, the Abwehr officer who masterminded the double-agent operation in Holland, identified Jack Hooper as a traitor. Hooper's fate remains unknown, but a further reassessment was made in September 1951 in the light of MI5's suspicion that Kim Philby had been a Soviet spy and had tipped of Donald Maclean to his impending arrest.

Since transferring from Section V to Section IX in November 1944 Philby had climbed the promotion ladder at Broadway. In February 1947 he had been posted to the Istanbul Station, where he had remained until the summer of 1949. In his absence Section IX was placed in the capable hands of Douglas Roberts, from SIME. In August Philby had returned to London for a briefing before taking up another senior position, that of Head of Station in Washington in succession to Peter Dwyer. Philby was still at his Washington post when he was recalled to London for a hostile interrogation and enforced retirement. That Philby was, or had been, a Soviet agent was disbelieved by many of his colleagues who, ignorant of the full facts, concluded that he had been treated shabbily by the CSS. It was not until his subsequent flight to Moscow in January 1963, after a confrontation with Nicholas Elliott, that everyone accepted the evidence. In the meantime, a number of other hostile agents had been identified, including no less than three who had been associated with or served in British Security Co-ordination in New York during the war.

The first to be identified was Cedric Belfrage, a pre-war member of the Communist Party of Great Britain, who gave evidence before the Committee on Un-American Activities in May 1953. Soon after his appearance another Briton, who had served at the British Embassy in Washington during the war, came under suspicion. A routine telephone tap on the Russian Embassy in London caught two Soviet intelligence officers boasting about a London-based publishing house which, they claimed, had been financed by a 'soft loan' from Moscow. The person concerned was interviewed by MI5's resident interrogator, Jim Skardon, but although he admitted having been a Communist Party of Great Britain member, he denied passing secrets to any Soviet contacts in America. His denials were not accepted and further interviews followed at various different times. No further progress was made with the case, although the probability was that the Soviets had developed an extensive ring within the Washington Embassy. At the very least MI5 knew that Donald Maclean, who had served there between May 1944 and January 1948, had betrayed every secret that had passed over his desk.

The escape of Burgess and Maclean in May 1951 was the first clue to the existence of Soviet 'moles' inside the British Establishment, although it was not until April 1954 that the Security Service could obtain confirmation that the pair had been long-term Soviet spies and had indeed fled to Moscow. In the investigation that followed their departure, two further individuals came under immediate suspicion. One was Anthony Blunt, who was to make no admission until April 1964 when he accepted an offer of immunity from prosecution. Blunt had been an MI5 officer during the war and had inevitably had close dealings with SIS and, in particular, Section V. The second suspect was a senior civil servant official named John Cairncross, who had left GCHQ in 1944 to join Section V in Ryder Street. Cairncross came to MI5's attention after he had been compromised by various documents recovered from Burgess's flat. When confronted with this evidence, Cairncross pointed out that none of the papers were classified and claimed that he had been an unwitting tool of Burgess. He maintained this line until March 1964, when MI5 interviewed him again. On this occasion Cairncross, who was living outside British jurisdiction, admitted that he had been supplying the Soviets with information since he had first been recruited at Cambridge by Guy Burgess. He had held regular meetings with his Soviet case officers while at GCHQ and Ryder Street.

The prospect of long-term Soviet penetration of the Secret Intelligence Service led to a review of all the evidence for more extensive wartime and post-war betrayal. Some of the leads had been cold for a long time. Harold Gibson, for example, was one. He had returned to Prague in 1945 and had then been posted to Germany in 1949. After a two-year tour of duty in Berlin, he went back to Broadway and then went to Rome as Head of Station in 1955. He retired on his sixtieth birthday in 1958 and remained in the Italian capital. On 24 August 1960 he was found shot dead in his apartment at 25 Via Antonio Bosio. The British and Italian investigators concluded that he had committed suicide. However, three years later, MI5 reopened the file following defector reports that the Soviets had indeed planted 'moles' in SIS, and that these spies had strong Russian backgrounds or Russian connections. Certainly Harold Gibson had these basic qualifications. He had been born in Russia and had been educated there. English was a second language to him and he had married two Russians. His first wife, Rachel Kalmanoviecz, was the daughter of an engineer from Odessa. She had died in 1947 and the following year he had married Ekaterina Alfimov. Apart from the suspicious circumstances of his death, there was nothing to suggest that Gibson had been anything other than loyal.

Another SIS personal file reviewed by the investigators was that of Dick Ellis. Ellis had been appointed Head of Station in Singapore in 1946 after the closure of British Security Co-ordination. He then succeeded Vanden Heuvel as Chief of Production in Europe, before handing the post over to Herbert Setchell in 1953 and retiring. During his retirement he returned briefly to his native Australia to advise the Australian Secret Intelligence Service.

Like Gibson, Ellis fitted the profile of a Soviet spy. He had been married four times, the first in 1923 in Paris to Lilia Zelensky, the daughter of a White Russian. Ellis recruited her brother, Alexander, as an agent, and continued to meet him in Paris even after his marriage to Lilia had broken up. In 1934 he married Barbara Burgess-Smith, from whom he obtained a divorce in 1947. After his retirement, in 1954, he married a widow, Alexandra Wood. After her death he married for a fourth time. The only curiosity about Ellis's four marriages is that he attempted to cover the traces of his first one, to Lilia Zelensky. In his *Who's Who* entry, Ellis (who wrote it) describes his marriage to Barbara Burgess-Smith as his first.

The investigators decided to inquire into Ellis's background further, and discovered an interesting link between the Abwehr and Ellis. According to a statement made by an Abwehr officer who underwent debriefing at Camp 020 after the war, much of the information used in *Informationsheft Grossbritannien* had come from a White Russian source in Paris. The former Abwehr officer was still alive and he was traced to Germany and interviewed. He confirmed that the SIS order of battle had come from Alexander Zelensky, who had in turn obtained it from an Australian married to a Russian. To make absolutely certain, the investigators traced the notes taken by the MI5 interrogator who had debriefed him in 1945. The notes even mentioned the name Captain Ellis. Evidently, an error in the translation had obscured the correct spelling of the surname. Ellis now came under suspicion of having been the Abwehr's source on SIS. A check in the *Sonderfahndungsliste* provided another clue. At the end of each entry was a departmental reference for the particular section (Amt) of the Reich Security Agency which had been responsible for requesting the arrest. The designation RHSA IV referred to the Gestapo and the sub-section responsible for journalists was VI G 1. The entry for Ellis was unique because, although he is described simply as a British journalist, the Gestapo section which supplied the information about him was IV E 4, the unit which dealt with SIS. In other words, the Gestapo had tried to obscure the fact that this 'journalist' was known to them as an SIS officer. In every other case the Reich Security Agency's entry reflected a person's true status as an intelligence officer. Hooper's entry number 173 on page 86, for example, describes him as a British agent:

Hooper, William John, 23.4.03 Rotterdam, brit, Agent, zuletzt: Scheveningen/Holland, vermutl. England (Taterkreis: Stevens/Best) Deckname: Konrad, RSHA IV E 4

Like all other SIS officers Ellis also used a cover-name, and his was Howard. A check on the two male Howards listed failed to find Ellis. One was Stanley Howard, with an address in Buckinghamshire, and the other was merely described as Captain Howard. Since the latter's address was listed as 144 Sloane Street and his aliases given as Hughes, the entry clearly referred to Captain Rex Howard RN, formerly Sinclair's Chief Staff Officer. The omission of Ellis's details was entirely circumstantial, but it lent weight to the evidence of the former Abwehr officer.

It was decided to confront Ellis with this evidence and it was learned that he was close at hand. He had recently been invited to return to SIS headquarters in London to assist in the 'weeding' of unnecessary Registry files, a not uncommon retirement job. Ellis was summoned to an interview and he was challenged about the kind of information he might have given his former brother-in-law. The investigator told Ellis that the Abwehr officer who had bought Zelensky's information was willing to fly to London to identify 'Captain Ellis'. At first Ellis denied the charge, but when he returned to SIS headquarters the following day for a second interrogation he admitted to selling the SIS order of battle to the Abwehr. When pressed about whether or not the Soviets had subsequently taken advantage of this lapse, Ellis insisted that he had never had any contact with the Russians. He also denied any further contact with the Abwehr after he had left Paris for the last time.

Some doubts remained in the minds of the investigators about the completeness of Ellis's confession, but it did at least serve to clear up one of the remaining mysteries of the war. Best and Stevens had indeed confirmed the details of SIS's internal structure to the Germans, but most of the information had already been in their possession for some considerable time. This, then, was the explanation for some of the outdated material included in the *Informationsheft Grossbritannien*.

The wheel had come full circle: the Victorians and the Edwardians had always kept a wary eye on Russia, so had the first head of SIS, so had his successor, and now the leading Section V had been augmented and turned into Section IX whose main aim would be to watch for Soviet subversion. But most of the other facets of SIS had changed greatly since 1909.

During the first forty-four years of its existence, SIS had only had three Chiefs: Mansfield Smith-Cumming from 1909 to 1923, followed by Hugh Sinclair until 1939, and then Stewart Menzies who stayed until 1953.

Mansfield Smith-Cumming had hardly begun to create an intelligence gathering apparatus before the Great War intervened; during this time he was somewhat overshadowed by the navy both in expertise, fieldwork and in manpower. Naval officers also predominated in SIS. Despite these drawbacks, he laid down the bare scaffolding of the Service, although this suffered from being moved from the aegis of the War Office to the Admiralty to the Foreign Office.

Hugh Sinclair, also a naval officer, endeavoured to build on his predecessor's slender naval-orientated edifice. He continued Cumming's bias towards gathering information on Soviet Russia and thus failed to understand the full implications of the rise of the Nazi Party in Germany. Sinclair established his best officers in the capital cities ringing Russia as Passport Control personnel, which turned out to be unsatisfactory. Overworked and underpaid, these people's visa duties came first, their intelligence gathering a poor second. Moreover, they failed to set up any local intelligence networks in the countries in which they were working.

The number of men trained to run Stations were few. As a result, the replacement Head of an important city section such as The Hague had been trained in India's North-West Frontier, and John Hooper, a man who had twice defected, was reinstated. Sinclair himself appears to have been dissatisfied with the way SIS was progressing and to have allowed a parallel network to grow up under Dansey. Despite the existence of two tiers of intelligence gathering, the quality, quantity and value of the information collected at the end of the 1930s was poor: Whitehall was extremely sceptical. As a result, when excellent decrypted material from ULTRA was first shown to military and political leaders under the code-name BONIFACE, they ignored it because they had learned to doubt SIS.

Nevertheless, Sinclair had expanded and increased the range of SIS; he had recognized the great importance of the Government Code and Cipher School and had made sure that it came under his command. He had also seen the value of having a burgeoning communications network and, as the possibility of war loomed closer, he had set up new sections to cover subversion and counter-espionage, Sections D and V, which were to prove of inestimable value. Sinclair died at the time of the Venlo incident.

The inner Cabinet, which had responsibility for selecting Sinclair's successor, had little alternative but to confirm Menzies in the post. He had been standing in for his Chief for the previous twelve months and was fully aware of the organization's strengths, and its weaknesses. It cannot be said that Menzies ever displayed a great flair for his work although, taking his handicaps into account, it is remarkable that there were not more catastrophes. At the time SIS had no agents of its own left in Germany, and precious few elsewhere. Its overseas Stations were in chaos and the Abwehr had acquired valuable information concerning SIS's order of battle.

Menzies's performance during his first months in office was entirely governed by circumstance. His links with the Belgian, Dutch, Polish and Norwegian governments in exile were fairly straightforward and he operated from a position of relative strength. The exiled intelligence services possessed no assets except the potential to command loyal, but as yet unformed, resistance groups. With no networks of his own, the Chief was obliged to trade with them, offering equipment and training facilities in exchange for information. The key to the 'intelligence contracts' was Menzies's tight control of communications. However, this useful lever became a liability with the Dutch. By the end of the war relations with the Poles, Dutch and Norwegians had reached a low ebb. The Poles believed themselves to have been betrayed to the Soviets, the Norwegians were angry about lack of consultation, and the Dutch suspected that the loss of their agents was not merely incompetence.

As for relations with the French, SIS never expected an easy ride. The division of two country sections was not the result of some sophisticated policy. It was governed by necessity. Initially de Gaulle's controversial intelligence agencies had no official standing in Whitehall. SIS could not treat them on a par with the recognized governments in exile and had little choice but to operate two separate country sections. It was both practical and expedient.

Perhaps Menzies's greatest attribute was his aloofness. He was not prepared to engage in internecine struggles himself and preferred to leave such conflicts to others. On the few occasions he was required to protect SIS's interests, he invariably compromised. He failed to prevent the development of SOE, but managed to retain control over its communications. He failed to silence Whitehall's criticism of SIS's advice and had the 'commissars' imposed on him. Were these examples of his political adroitness or of his inability to argue and win his case? Judging by the fundamental weakness of his inheritance, one must be generous and conclude that Menzies successfully concealed the truth about Broadway's parlous position. One is tempted to speculate that if Bletchley had not come 'on stream' so fortuitously in 1940, neither Menzies nor his organization could have survived. There can be little doubt that the organization's reputation was saved by the advent of ISOS and Cowgill's determination to protect the source. The fact that it has taken more than forty years before anyone has been in a position to publicly discuss ISOS is a measure of the security that has surrounded it.

Menzies's reluctance to get closely involved with his opposite numbers in the Allied intelligence community gave him a remarkable, elevated quality. Day-to-day relations with the exiled Deuxième Bureaux were left to his liaison officers. Only rarely did individual officers of his own or Allied Organizations ever get granted audiences. He was surrounded by a complicated system of barriers. OSS had to fight its battles with Dansey and Marshall-Cornwall; the Security Service had to deal with Vivian. Few people could fathom the confusing chain of command and the ambiguous titles of 'Vice-Chief', 'Deputy Chief', 'Deputy Director' and 'Assistant Chief'. Menzies seems to have used them deliberately, partly to ensure the loyalty of his principal lieutenants, but mainly to ensure that he remained the final decision-maker. The internal structure of the top level of 21 Queen Anne's Gate was further complicated by the small, privileged number of officers who could claim direct access. They were an assorted group, all characterized by their unique roles. David Boyle, for example, who was based in London, was responsible for the covert plundering of the diplomatic bags of neutral embassies and the analysis of the information obtained from them. He was authorized to see the Chief at any time, and he did so whenever he discovered a particularly interesting snippet of information. Another who exercised this power, by cable, was Charles Dundas in the Middle East. Although he ranked as a mere Head of Station, his pre-war experience in the region enabled him to communicate directly with Menzies, by-passing the regular SIS channels. The net result was that the Chief was sometimes able to do what Churchill enjoyed most: silencing his critics and advisers alike by imparting some juicy morsel of intelligence. Thus by the end of the war both his reputation and that of his organization was at an all-time high. Thanks to Philby and his like, it did not endure.

Appendix

DER BRITISCHE NACHRICHTENDIENST

A summary prepared by the Reich Security Agency early in 1940, in preparation for the German invasion of Britain and discovered after the war by Allied intelligence officers amongst Nazi records.

The Foreign Office, the War Office, the Admiralty, the Secretary of State for Air, the Secretary of State for the Colonies, the Board of Trade and the Board for Overseas Trade all have their own sources of information and their own Intelligence Departments and Divisions. As central authorities they utilize their subordinate offices which include the diplomatic missions and consular services. Even if their interests are in their own subject it can be assumed that any other information would be channelled into the appropriate departments.

Before other sources are dealt with the account given by Stevens and Best of their services shall be set down. It still remains to be seen whether they obeyed premeditated orders, whether they are speaking the truth, whether they have invented anything or whether they have left anything out of their account. It is certain that some of their evidence has been proved to be correct; however, it must not be forgotten that they are only small wheels, or in the previously mentioned allegory – 'freemasons of a minor order'.

Stevens is known to have run the Passport Control Office in The Hague. Still a serving officer, he came into contact with the Secret Service in India and Persia. A linguist, he took over the position which was officially part of the General Consulate and therefore the Embassy, although geographically it was separate. Its official description only covered a small part of its actual activities. Stevens and his staff were mainly concerned with the acquisition of military intelligence from and regarding Germany. They also accepted any other information which came their way. They were, according to Stevens, 'interested in simply everything'. He claims that they were on their own, and that staffing of the PCOs abroad remained as vague to the head of the office as the organization and methods used by the SIS. Stevens reported either to his boss, Admiral Hugh Paged [sic] Sinclair, or to the Admiral's headquarters house in London Broadway Buildings near St James's Park Station. According to Stevens, the Admiral had retired from active service when appointed head of the Secret Service, and he was known as 'CSS'.

His deputy was Colonel Stuart Menzies, a Scotsman, who succeeded his boss on the latter's death on 4th November 1939. His ADCs were Captain Howard RN, Captain Russell and Hatton Hall.

Stevens seems to believe that Sinclair alone was responsible to the Cabinet for the Foreign Office.

Sinclair was reputed to have his offices on the fourth floor of the same building which housed the Chancellery and Registry. On the occasions when Stevens visited the building he noticed that departments had been moved around within the building, but the second and fourth floor contained offices of private firms who had nothing to do with the Service.

On the first floor were the offices of the London PCO, which overlooked Queen Anne's Gate the road running parallel to the Broadway. The following departments were Admiral Sinclair's responsibility:

1. Administration Section
2. Military Section
3. Naval Section
4. Air Section
5. Communications/Telecommunications Section
6. Political Section
7. Chiffre Section
8. Financial Section
9. Press Section
10. Industrial Section

Departmental Duties:

1. Administrative Section
Head of Department: Captain Howard RN; under him, Commanders Slocum and Bowlbey [sic] RN.

Duties: Vetting of personnel, officers as well as civilians employees and the agents as identified by PCOs, which the department accepts or rejects. The organization of the whole service lies with Section One. It distributes the incoming intelligence.

Location: Fifth floor of the Broadway building.

2. Military Section
Head of Department: Major Hatton Hall. No other officers.

Duties: All intelligence as it is received is forwarded to him if it concerns the army.

Stevens gives the following example: 'I inform the department of an impending attack by the Germans. Department One passes the information to Department Two where the intelligence is compared with information received from PCOs. Taking its own stand the department then transmits the information to the War Office, probably the Intelligence Branch.'

Location: Fifth floor.

3. Naval Section
Head of Department: Captain Russell. No other officers.

Duties: As in Department Two, but adapted to naval problems. Information is passed to the Admiralty, Naval Intelligence Division.

Location: Sixth floor.

4. *Air Section*

Head of Department: Wing-Commander(?) Winter-Bottom [sic]. Assisted by two officers, Adams and ?

Duties: As in Departments Two and Three, but adapted to the needs of the RAF. Information is sent to the Air Ministry, Intelligence Section.

Location: Sixth floor.

The Departments Two, Three and Four are mainly for the evaluation of information. But they also give orders, that is express wishes, ask questions etc which are then sent to the PCOs. This is either done on their own initiative or they act as middlemen to the demands of the intelligence departments of the three services.

5. *Communications Section*

Head of Department: Gambier Perry, calls himself Colonel but this seems to be untrue.

Stevens claims to know nothing about the department. It is reputed to have moved to Bletchley.

Duties: Wireless/Radio communications, telephone, pigeon-post etc.

Location: Until recently in the Broadway buildings, floor unknown.

6. *Political Section*

Head of Department: Major Vivien [sic], assisted by Police Officer Mills. (Vivien calls himself Major, but he is also a police officer.)

Duties: Counter-intelligence (see below) in connection with MI5 (see below). The handling of subversive movements, communists, fascists etc. The control of enemies of the state in England.

Stevens and Best do not differentiate between counter-intelligence and espionage. Stevens says 'they overlap so much, there can be no division'. The department keeps in contact with all political organizations for intelligence purposes. Stevens claims that he does not know the title of this sub-section of Department Six. The information by '101 B' (Agent of Hendricks in Antwerp, opponent of Potzsch) was given by Department One to Department Six.

Location: Fifth floor.

7. *Chiffre Section (Cipher and Decipher Section)*

Head of Department: Not known. A retired colonel by the name of Geffreys [sic] works there.

Duties: Code breaking, preparation of own codes and codes for PCOs.

Location: Stevens does not know.

8. *Financial Section*

Head of Department: Commander Sykes.

Duties: Allocation of funds for intelligence work, salaries, PCOs and Central Office.

Location: Fourth floor.

9. *Press Section*

Head of Department: Probably Hennecker-Heaton. No other officers.

Duties: Reading, supervision of insertions, liaison with the press as necessary.

Location: Fourth floor.

10. Industrial Section (Economic information)

Head of Department: Admiral Limpenny, retired.

Duties: Collection of information on the economic situation in foreign countries, how many planes have been manufactured, coal production, supplies of raw materials. Processed information possibly sent to the Board of Trade.

Location unknown.

There was one more office which was situated on the ground floor which, according to Stevens, belonged to the propaganda department. Actually, its true function was that of sabotage, both in the planning and executory stages. The head of department was Colonel Grand, and his assistant Lieutenant Colonel M.R. Chidson (formerly PCO in The Hague). The duties and position of a certain Clively remain obscure. This department is reputed to have been separated from the Service and since June 1939 its offices are no longer in Broadway Buildings. After the outbreak of war several of the above departments are alleged to have been moved to Bletchley. However, the Propaganda and Sabotage Departments are not among these. Apparently Sinclair, although recognizing the need for sabotage, wished to have nothing to do with it. Stevens says of this: To my knowledge the department was still subject to CSS after its separation. It prepared plans and acts of sabotage which were then sent via Sinclair to the appropriate PCOs. It did not carry out these acts of sabotage, it was only the executive organ.

The PCOs are said to have code numbers, Stevens being 33000. The PCOs in all countries are subordinate to the Sinclair Office.

Best was apparently head of the Dutch section of yet another organization known as Z, which was also subject to Sinclair. His office was situated next to the PCO which was already being pointed out by children as the British Intelligence Office. Sinclair had complained that the PCOs in general, and the Dutch office in particular, did not collect enough information. Organization Z was headed by Colonel Claude Dansey, who had been selected by Sinclair. He, in turn, had employed Best whom he had known from World War I. Z kept a small office in Bush House, Aldwych, London WC2. Best's fellow workers were Kenneth Cohan [sic], code name Cowan, Keith Crane and Robert Craig. At the outbreak of war Best's office had been amalgamated with Stevens's PCO. According to Best Z, at least in Holland, was dissolved after his arrest.

Best sent his information by post to Sinclair. As a cover he used the firm Menoline Ltd whose address was 24 Maple Street, London W1. Best was a director of the Dutch firm N.V. Menoline in The Hague. The directors in The Hague included John P. Richards and Pieter Nikolaas van der Willik, a colleague of Best in Z.

On the 19th February 1937 the 'Times' (47 613) printed an article on a speech made by the Minister for the Co-ordination of Defence the previous day in the House of Commons. The speech went as follows:

'Recently a Joint Intelligence Committee has been formed from representatives of the three services. We have formed a committee of industrial intelligence in foreign countries, but it is impossible for me to disclose the nature of any reports we receive! or any information the JIC prepares for the Chiefs of Staff. I can only say that they are an immense and indispensable aid to the planning which continues from day to day.'

It remains undisclosed whether the so-called SIS of Admiral Sinclair was the only one or the main organization of the British Secret Service, or indeed only a branch of it. It is possible that it worked for the JIC or was attached to it in a disguised form. The article makes it clear that in 1937 the three services had their own intelligence services. Both Stevens and Best confirmed that the Admiralty, the Air Force and the Imperial General Staff had intelligence departments or divisions, but as in the First World War they deny that they had independent intelligence services, which included sabotage. One can therefore accept that they are still working in the same manner as in the other branches, especially, according to Stevens, the British–Indian General Staff.

The organization under Admiral Sinclair was not purely military. It had subdivisions for the Army, the Navy and the RAF, but it also worked for the Foreign Office and the Ministry of Economic affairs. The Foreign Office enquired as to the effect of the leaflet campaigns in Germany, and the Ministry of Economic Affairs demanded information relating to Germany's money supply.

According to Stevens the Military Intelligence Service had nothing to do with the SIS. One departmental head of the General Staff is the Director of Military Operations and Intelligence Service. Under him come the Deputy Director of Military Operations (DDMO) and the Deputy Director of Military Intelligence (DDMI). The latter gathers information about countries in which military operations are about to take place; for example, communications systems, etc. This sub-division does not extend to intelligence work by agents. When the placing of officers in Military Intelligence, in Intelligence or at the Intelligence Branch is discussed it is meant to be in the service of DDMI. For all other branches or military activities the expression Military Intelligence is not used.

Best is of a different opinion to Stevens. Unlike Stevens he is not a professional soldier. But he is superior to him as far as experience in the intelligence service is concerned, and as a result his attitude is more penetrating; these qualities he combines with considerable character defects and a complete lack of scruples. He is not a British officer like Stevens. He is a civilian who loves to live well and be a successful business man. He may therefore see things in a clearer light in spite of a pretended lack of significance, or he may say more than Stevens. He has stated that the Foreign Office, the Admiralty, and other departments have their own espionage centres and exchange information. Navy, Army and Air attachés give their reports into the departments I5 of their General Staff headquarters. For the army in the field that department is called Ib, it being an active branch of the Intelligence service, espionage. NI, MI and AI are those departments which process the information which is then transmitted to the headquarters of the Navy, Army and RAF respectively. Special mention must be made to the department of Military Intelligence of the Imperial General Staff, MI5, which concerns itself with counter-intelligence and takes an ambiguous position. (The duties of the departments MI1-4 are not known, MI3 is concerned with Germany.)

In this context one has to discuss once more what the British mean by counter-espionage. Stevens and Best both speak of counter-espionage, and called it either counter-espionage or counter intelligence, but they refused to differentiate between the two. They considered any differentiations as illogical. Best defined it thus:

'Counter-espionage includes all security and police action, which are taken to prevent events that may become the source of national or political danger.'

During the First World War the counter-espionage was, according to Best, the department MI5 in the War Office. It worked closely with Scotland Yard. Detectives from Scotland Yard would come to the Department IB at General HQ in France, with the same brief. Both were then combined into a larger organization with a large staff of intelligence officers and civil servants.

Index